American Casebook Series
Hornbook Series and Basic Legal Texts
Nutshell Series

of

WEST PUBLISHING COMPANY

P.O. Box 64526
St. Paul, Minnesota 55164–0526

ACCOUNTING

Faris' Accounting and Law in a Nutshell, 377 pages, 1984 (Text)

Fiflis, Kripke and Foster's Teaching Materials on Accounting for Business Lawyers, 3rd Ed., 838 pages, 1984 (Casebook)

Siegel and Siegel's Accounting and Financial Disclosure: A Guide to Basic Concepts, 259 pages, 1983 (Text)

ADMINISTRATIVE LAW

Davis' Cases, Text and Problems on Administrative Law, 6th Ed., 683 pages, 1977 (Casebook)

Davis' Basic Text on Administrative Law, 3rd Ed., 617 pages, 1972 (Text)

Gellhorn and Boyer's Administrative Law and Process in a Nutshell, 2nd Ed., 445 pages, 1981 (Text)

Mashaw and Merrill's Cases and Materials on Administrative Law–The American Public Law System, 2nd Ed., 976 pages, 1985 (Casebook)

Robinson, Gellhorn and Bruff's The Administrative Process, 3rd Ed., 978 pages, 1986 (Casebook)

ADMIRALTY

Healy and Sharpe's Cases and Materials on Admiralty, 2nd Ed., 876 pages, 1986 (Casebook)

Maraist's Admiralty in a Nutshell, 390 pages, 1983 (Text)

Sohn and Gustafson's Law of the Sea in a Nutshell, 264 pages, 1984 (Text)

AGENCY—PARTNERSHIP

Fessler's Alternatives to Incorporation for Persons in Quest of Profit, 2nd Ed., 326 pages, 1986 (Casebook)

AGENCY—PARTNERSHIP—Cont'd

Henn's Cases and Materials on Agency, Partnership and Other Unincorporated Business Enterprises, 2nd Ed., 733 pages, 1985 (Casebook)

Reuschlein and Gregory's Hornbook on the Law of Agency and Partnership, 625 pages, 1979, with 1981 pocket part (Text)

Seavey, Reuschlein and Hall's Cases on Agency and Partnership, 599 pages, 1962 (Casebook)

Selected Corporation and Partnership Statutes and Forms, 555 pages, 1985

Steffen and Kerr's Cases and Materials on Agency-Partnership, 4th Ed., 859 pages, 1980 (Casebook)

Steffen's Agency-Partnership in a Nutshell, 364 pages, 1977 (Text)

AGRICULTURAL LAW

Meyer, Pedersen, Thorson and Davidson's Agricultural Law: Cases and Materials, 931 pages, 1985 (Casebook)

ALTERNATIVE DISPUTE RESOLUTION

Kanowitz' Cases and Materials on Alternative Dispute Resolution, 1024 pages, 1986 (Casebook)

Teple and Moberly's Arbitration and Conflict Resolution, (The Labor Law Group), 614 pages, 1979 (Casebook)

AMERICAN INDIAN LAW

Canby's American Indian Law in a Nutshell, 288 pages, 1981 (Text)

Getches and Wilkinson's Cases on Federal Indian Law, 2nd Ed., 880 pages, 1986 (Casebook)

List current as of October, 1986

LAW SCHOOL PUBLICATIONS—Continued

ANTITRUST LAW

Gellhorn's Antitrust Law and Economics in a Nutshell, 3rd Ed., about 470 pages, 1986 (Text)

Gifford and Raskind's Cases and Materials on Antitrust, 694 pages, 1983 with 1985 Supplement (Casebook)

Hovenkamp's Hornbook on Economics and Federal Antitrust Law, Student Ed., 414 pages, 1985 (Text)

Oppenheim, Weston and McCarthy's Cases and Comments on Federal Antitrust Laws, 4th Ed., 1168 pages, 1981 with 1985 Supplement (Casebook)

Posner and Easterbrook's Cases and Economic Notes on Antitrust, 2nd Ed., 1077 pages, 1981, with 1984–85 Supplement (Casebook)

Sullivan's Hornbook of the Law of Antitrust, 886 pages, 1977 (Text)

See also Regulated Industries, Trade Regulation

ART LAW

DuBoff's Art Law in a Nutshell, 335 pages, 1984 (Text)

BANKING LAW

Lovett's Banking and Financial Institutions in a Nutshell, 409 pages, 1984 (Text)

Symons and White's Teaching Materials on Banking Law, 2nd Ed., 993 pages, 1984 (Casebook)

BUSINESS PLANNING

Painter's Problems and Materials in Business Planning, 2nd Ed., 1008 pages, 1984 (Casebook)

Selected Securities and Business Planning Statutes, Rules and Forms, 470 pages, 1985

CIVIL PROCEDURE

Casad's Res Judicata in a Nutshell, 310 pages, 1976 (text)

Cound, Friedenthal, Miller and Sexton's Cases and Materials on Civil Procedure, 4th Ed., 1202 pages, 1985 with 1985 Supplement (Casebook)

Ehrenzweig, Louisell and Hazard's Jurisdiction in a Nutshell, 4th Ed., 232 pages, 1980 (Text)

Federal Rules of Civil-Appellate Procedure—West Law School Edition, 607 pages, 1986

Friedenthal, Kane and Miller's Hornbook on Civil Procedure, 876 pages, 1985 (Text)

Kane's Civil Procedure in a Nutshell, 2nd Ed., 306 pages, 1986 (Text)

Koffler and Reppy's Hornbook on Common Law Pleading, 663 pages, 1969 (Text)

Marcus and Sherman's Complex Litigation–Cases and Materials on Advanced Civil Procedure, 846 pages, 1985 (Casebook)

CIVIL PROCEDURE—Cont'd

Park's Computer-Aided Exercises on Civil Procedure, 2nd Ed., 167 pages, 1983 (Coursebook)

Siegel's Hornbook on New York Practice, 1011 pages, 1978 with 1985 Pocket Part (Text)

See also Federal Jurisdiction and Procedure

CIVIL RIGHTS

Abernathy's Cases and Materials on Civil Rights, 660 pages, 1980 (Casebook)

Cohen's Cases on the Law of Deprivation of Liberty: A Study in Social Control, 755 pages, 1980 (Casebook)

Lockhart, Kamisar, Choper and Shiffrin's Cases on Constitutional Rights and Liberties, 6th Ed., 1266 pages, 1986 with 1986 Supplement (Casebook)—reprint from Lockhart, et al. Cases on Constitutional Law, 6th Ed., 1986

Vieira's Civil Rights in a Nutshell, 279 pages, 1978 (Text)

COMMERCIAL LAW

Bailey's Secured Transactions in a Nutshell, 2nd Ed., 391 pages, 1981 (Text)

Epstein and Martin's Basic Uniform Commercial Code Teaching Materials, 2nd Ed., 667 pages, 1983 (Casebook)

Henson's Hornbook on Secured Transactions Under the U.C.C., 2nd Ed., 504 pages, 1979 with 1979 P.P. (Text)

Murray's Commercial Law, Problems and Materials, 366 pages, 1975 (Coursebook)

Nickles, Matheson and Dolan's Materials for Understanding Credit and Payment Systems, about 1,000 pages, 1987 (Casebook)

Nordstrom and Clovis' Problems and Materials on Commercial Paper, 458 pages, 1972 (Casebook)

Nordstrom, Murray and Clovis' Problems and Materials on Sales, 515 pages, 1982 (Casebook)

Nordstrom, Murray and Clovis' Problems and Materials on Secured Transactions, about 500 pages, 1987 (Casebook)

Selected Commercial Statutes, 1389 pages, 1985

Speidel, Summers and White's Teaching Materials on Commercial and Consumer Law, 3rd Ed., 1490 pages, 1981 (Casebook)

Stockton's Sales in a Nutshell, 2nd Ed., 370 pages, 1981 (Text)

Stone's Uniform Commercial Code in a Nutshell, 2nd Ed., 516 pages, 1984 (Text)

Uniform Commercial Code, Official Text with Comments, 994 pages, 1978

UCC Article 9, Reprint from 1962 Code, 128 pages, 1976

UCC Article 9, 1972 Amendments, 304 pages, 1978

COMMERCIAL LAW—Cont'd

Weber and Speidel's Commercial Paper in a Nutshell, 3rd Ed., 404 pages, 1982 (Text)

White and Summers' Hornbook on the Uniform Commercial Code, 2nd Ed., 1250 pages, 1980 (Text)

COMMUNITY PROPERTY

Mennell's Community Property in a Nutshell, 447 pages 1982 (Text)

Verrall and Bird's Cases and Materials on California Community Property, 4th Ed., 549 pages, 1983 (Casebook)

COMPARATIVE LAW

Barton, Gibbs, Li and Merryman's Law in Radically Different Cultures, 960 pages, 1983 (Casebook)

Glendon, Gordon and Osakive's Comparative Legal Traditions: Text, Materials and Cases on the Civil Law, Common Law, and Socialist Law Traditions, 1091 pages, 1985 (Casebook)

Glendon, Gordon, and Osakwe's Comparative Legal Traditions in a Nutshell, 402 pages, 1982 (Text)

Langbein's Comparative Criminal Procedure: Germany, 172 pages, 1977 (Casebook)

COMPUTERS AND LAW

Maggs and Sprowl's Computer Applications in the Law, about 300 pages, 1987 (Coursebook)

Mason's An Introduction to the Use of Computers in Law, 223 pages, 1984 (Text)

CONFLICT OF LAWS

Cramton, Currie and Kay's Cases-Comments-Questions on Conflict of Laws, 3rd Ed., 1026 pages, 1981 (Casebook)

Scoles and Hay's Hornbook on Conflict of Laws, Student Ed., 1085 pages, 1982 with 1986 P.P. (Text)

Scoles and Weintraub's Cases and Materials on Conflict of Laws, 2nd Ed., 966 pages, 1972, with 1978 Supplement (Casebook)

Siegel's Conflicts in a Nutshell, 469 pages, 1982 (Text)

CONSTITUTIONAL LAW

Barron and Dienes' Constitutional Law in a Nutshell, 389 pages, 1986 (Text)

Engdahl's Constitutional Power in a Nutshell: Federal and State, 411 pages, 1974 (Text)

Lockhart, Kamisar, Choper and Shiffrin's Cases-Comments-Questions on Constitutional Law, 6th Ed., 1601 pages, 1986 with 1986 Supplement (Casebook)

CONSTITUTIONAL LAW—Cont'd

Lockhart, Kamisar, Choper and Shiffrin's Cases-Comments-Questions on the American Constitution, 6th Ed., 1260 pages, 1986 with 1986 Supplement (Casebook)—abridgment of Lockhart, et al. Cases on Constitutional Law, 6th Ed., 1986

Manning's The Law of Church-State Relations in a Nutshell, 305 pages, 1981 (Text)

Miller's Presidential Power in a Nutshell, 328 pages, 1977 (Text)

Nowak, Rotunda and Young's Hornbook on Constitutional Law, 3rd Ed., Student Ed., 1191 pages, 1986 (Text)

Rotunda's Modern Constitutional Law: Cases and Notes, 2nd Ed., 1004 pages, 1985, with 1986 Supplement (Casebook)

Williams' Constitutional Analysis in a Nutshell, 388 pages, 1979 (Text)

See also Civil Rights

CONSUMER LAW

Epstein and Nickles' Consumer Law in a Nutshell, 2nd Ed., 418 pages, 1981 (Text)

McCall's Consumer Protection, Cases, Notes and Materials, 594 pages, 1977, with 1977 Statutory Supplement (Casebook)

Selected Commercial Statutes, 1389 pages, 1985

Spanogle and Rohner's Cases and Materials on Consumer Law, 693 pages, 1979, with 1982 Supplement (Casebook)

See also Commercial Law

CONTRACTS

Calamari & Perillo's Cases and Problems on Contracts, 1061 pages, 1978 (Casebook)

Calamari and Perillo's Hornbook on Contracts, 3rd Ed., about 900 pages, 1987 (Text)

Corbin's Text on Contracts, One Volume Student Edition, 1224 pages, 1952 (Text)

Fessler and Loiseaux's Cases and Materials on Contracts, 837 pages, 1982 (Casebook)

Friedman's Contract Remedies in a Nutshell, 323 pages, 1981 (Text)

Fuller and Eisenberg's Cases on Basic Contract Law, 4th Ed., 1203 pages, 1981 (Casebook)

Hamilton, Rau and Weintraub's Cases and Materials on Contracts, 830 pages, 1984 (Casebook)

Jackson and Bollinger's Cases on Contract Law in Modern Society, 2nd Ed., 1329 pages, 1980 (Casebook)

Keyes' Government Contracts in a Nutshell, 423 pages, 1979 (Text)

Schaber and Rohwer's Contracts in a Nutshell, 2nd Ed., 425 pages, 1984 (Text)

CONTRACTS—Cont'd

Summers and Hillman's Contract and Related Obligation: Theory, Doctrine and Practice, about 1060 pages, 1987 (Casebook)

COPYRIGHT

See Patent and Copyright Law

CORPORATIONS

Hamilton's Cases on Corporations—Including Partnerships and Limited Partnerships, 3rd Ed., 1213 pages, 1986 with 1986 Statutory Supplement (Casebook)

Hamilton's Law of Corporations in a Nutshell, 2nd Ed., about 465 pages, 1987 (Text)

Henn's Teaching Materials on Corporations, 2nd Ed., 1204 pages, 1986 (Casebook)

Henn and Alexander's Hornbook on Corporations, 3rd Ed., Student Ed., 1371 pages, 1983 with 1986 P.P. (Text)

Jennings and Buxbaum's Cases and Materials on Corporations, 5th Ed., 1180 pages, 1979 (Casebook)

Selected Corporation and Partnership Statutes, Regulations and Forms, 555 pages, 1985

Solomon, Stevenson and Schwartz' Materials and Problems on Corporations: Law and Policy, 1172 pages, 1982 with 1986 Supplement (Casebook)

CORPORATE FINANCE

Hamilton's Cases and Materials on Corporate Finance, 895 pages, 1984 with 1986 Supplement (Casebook)

CORRECTIONS

Krantz's Cases and Materials on the Law of Corrections and Prisoners' Rights, 3rd Ed., 855 pages, 1986 (Casebook)

Krantz's Law of Corrections and Prisoners' Rights in a Nutshell, 2nd Ed., 386 pages, 1983 (Text)

Popper's Post-Conviction Remedies in a Nutshell, 360 pages, 1978 (Text)

Robbins' Cases and Materials on Post Conviction Remedies, 506 pages, 1982 (Casebook)

CREDITOR'S RIGHTS

Bankruptcy Code, Rules and Forms, Law School and C.L.E. Ed., 838 pages, 1986

Epstein's Debtor-Creditor Law in a Nutshell, 3rd Ed., 383 pages, 1986 (Text)

Epstein and Landers' Debtors and Creditors: Cases and Materials, 2nd Ed., 689 pages, 1982 (Casebook)

LoPucki's Player's Manual for the Debtor-Creditor Game, 123 pages, 1985 (Coursebook)

CREDITOR'S RIGHTS—Cont'd

Riesenfeld's Cases and Materials on Creditors' Remedies and Debtors' Protection, 4th Ed., about 870 pages, 1987 (Casebook)

White's Bankruptcy and Creditor's Rights: Cases and Materials, 812 pages, 1985 (Casebook)

CRIMINAL LAW AND CRIMINAL PROCEDURE

Abrams', Federal Criminal Law and its Enforcement, 882 pages, 1986 (Casebook)

Carlson's Adjudication of Criminal Justice, Problems and References, 130 pages, 1986 (Casebook)

Dix and Sharlot's Cases and Materials on Criminal Law, 2nd Ed., 771 pages, 1979 (Casebook)

Federal Rules of Criminal Procedure—West Law School Edition, 463 pages, 1986

Grano's Problems in Criminal Procedure, 2nd Ed., 176 pages, 1981 (Problem book)

Israel and LaFave's Criminal Procedure in a Nutshell, 3rd Ed., 438 pages, 1980 (Text)

Johnson's Cases, Materials and Text on Criminal Law, 3rd Ed., 783 pages, 1985 (Casebook)

Kamisar, LaFave and Israel's Cases, Comments and Questions on Modern Criminal Procedure, 6th Ed., 1558 pages, 1986 with 1986 Supplement (Casebook)

Kamisar, LaFave and Israel's Cases, Comments and Questions on Basic Criminal Procedure, 6th Ed., 860 pages, 1986 with 1986 Supplement (Casebook)—reprint from Kamisar, et al. Modern Criminal Procedure, 6th ed., 1986

LaFave's Modern Criminal Law: Cases, Comments and Questions, 789 pages, 1978 (Casebook)

LaFave and Israel's Hornbook on Criminal Procedure, Student Ed., 1142 pages, 1985 with 1986 P.P. (Text)

LaFave and Scott's Hornbook on Criminal Law, 2nd Ed., Student Ed., 918 pages, 1986 (Text)

Langbein's Comparative Criminal Procedure: Germany, 172 pages, 1977 (Casebook)

Loewy's Criminal Law in a Nutshell, 302 pages, 1975 (Text)

Saltzburg's American Criminal Procedure, Cases and Commentary, 2nd Ed., 1193 pages, 1985 with 1986 Supplement (Casebook)

Uviller's The Processes of Criminal Justice: Investigation and Adjudication, 2nd Ed., 1384 pages, 1979 with 1979 Statutory Supplement and 1986 Update (Casebook)

CRIMINAL LAW AND CRIMINAL PROCEDURE—Cont'd

Uviller's The Processes of Criminal Justice Adjudication, 2nd Ed., 730 pages, 1979. Soft-cover reprint from Uviller's The Processes of Criminal Justice: Investigation and Adjudication, 2nd Ed (Casebook)

Uviller's The Processes of Criminal Justice: Investigation, 2nd Ed., 655 pages, 1979. Soft-cover reprint from Uviller's The Processes of Criminal Justice: Investigation and Adjudication, 2nd Ed. (Casebook)

Vorenberg's Cases on Criminal Law and Procedure, 2nd Ed., 1088 pages, 1981 with 1985 Supplement (Casebook)

See also Corrections, Juvenile Justice

DECEDENTS ESTATES

See Trusts and Estates

DOMESTIC RELATIONS

Clark's Cases and Problems on Domestic Relations, 3rd Ed., 1153 pages, 1980 (Casebook)

Clark's Hornbook on Domestic Relations, 754 pages, 1968 (Text)

Krause's Cases and Materials on Family Law, 2nd Ed., 1221 pages, 1983 with 1986 Supplement (Casebook)

Krause's Family Law in a Nutshell, 2nd Ed., 444 pages, 1986 (Text)

Krauskopf's Cases on Property Division at Marriage Dissolution, 250 pages, 1984 (Casebook)

ECONOMICS, LAW AND

Goetz' Cases and Materials on Law and Economics, 547 pages, 1984 (Casebook)

See also Antitrust, Regulated Industries

EDUCATION LAW

Alexander and Alexander's The Law of Schools, Students and Teachers in a Nutshell, 409 pages, 1984 (Text)

Morris' The Constitution and American Education, 2nd Ed., 992 pages, 1980 (Casebook)

EMPLOYMENT DISCRIMINATION

Jones, Murphy and Belton's Cases on Discrimination in Employment, about 1120 pages, 1987 (Casebook)

Player's Cases and Materials on Employment Discrimination Law, 2nd Ed., 782 pages, 1984 (Casebook)

Player's Federal Law of Employment Discrimination in a Nutshell, 2nd Ed., 402 pages, 1981 (Text)

See also Women and the Law

ENERGY AND NATURAL RESOURCES LAW

Laitos' Cases and Materials on Natural Resources Law, 938 pages, 1985 (Casebook)

Rodgers' Cases and Materials on Energy and Natural Resources Law, 2nd Ed., 877 pages, 1983 (Casebook)

Selected Environmental Law Statutes, 965 pages, 1986

Tomain's Energy Law in a Nutshell, 338 pages, 1981 (Text)

See also Environmental Law, Oil and Gas, Water Law

ENVIRONMENTAL LAW

Bonine and McGarity's Cases and Materials on the Law of Environment and Pollution, 1076 pages, 1984 (Casebook)

Findley and Farber's Cases and Materials on Environmental Law, 2nd Ed., 813 pages, 1985 (Casebook)

Findley and Farber's Environmental Law in a Nutshell, 343 pages, 1983 (Text)

Rodgers' Hornbook on Environmental Law, 956 pages, 1977 with 1984 pocket part (Text)

Selected Environmental Law Statutes, 965 pages, 1986

See also Energy Law, Natural Resources Law, Water Law

EQUITY

See Remedies

ESTATES

See Trusts and Estates

ESTATE PLANNING

Kurtz' Cases, Materials and Problems on Family Estate Planning, 853 pages, 1983 (Casebook)

Lynn's Introduction to Estate Planning, in a Nutshell, 3rd Ed., 370 pages, 1983 (Text)

See also Taxation

EVIDENCE

Broun and Meisenholder's Problems in Evidence, 2nd Ed., 304 pages, 1981 (Problem book)

Cleary and Strong's Cases, Materials and Problems on Evidence, 3rd Ed., 1143 pages, 1981 (Casebook)

Federal Rules of Evidence for United States Courts and Magistrates, 337 pages, 1984

Graham's Federal Rules of Evidence in a Nutshell, 2nd Ed., about 450 pages, 1987 (Text)

Kimball's Programmed Materials on Problems in Evidence, 380 pages, 1978 (Problem book)

EVIDENCE—Cont'd

Lempert and Saltzburg's A Modern Approach to Evidence: Text, Problems, Transcripts and Cases, 2nd Ed., 1232 pages, 1983 (Casebook)

Lilly's Introduction to the Law of Evidence, 490 pages, 1978 (Text)

McCormick, Sutton and Wellborn's Cases and Materials on Evidence, 6th Ed., about 1060 pages, 1987 (Casebook)

McCormick's Hornbook on Evidence, 3rd Ed., Student Ed., 1156 pages, 1984 (Text)

Rothstein's Evidence, State and Federal Rules in a Nutshell, 2nd Ed., 514 pages, 1981 (Text)

Saltzburg's Evidence Supplement: Rules, Statutes, Commentary, 245 pages, 1980 (Casebook Supplement)

FEDERAL JURISDICTION AND PROCEDURE

Currie's Cases and Materials on Federal Courts, 3rd Ed., 1042 pages, 1982 with 1985 Supplement (Casebook)

Currie's Federal Jurisdiction in a Nutshell, 2nd Ed., 258 pages, 1981 (Text)

Federal Rules of Civil-Appellate Procedure—West Law School Edition, 607 pages, 1986

Forrester and Moye's Cases and Materials on Federal Jurisdiction and Procedure, 3rd Ed., 917 pages, 1977 with 1985 Supplement (Casebook)

Redish's Cases, Comments and Questions on Federal Courts, 878 pages, 1983 with 1986 Supplement (Casebook)

Vetri and Merrill's Federal Courts, Problems and Materials, 2nd Ed., 232 pages, 1984 (Problem Book)

Wright's Hornbook on Federal Courts, 4th Ed., Student Ed., 870 pages, 1983 (Text)

FUTURE INTERESTS

See Trusts and Estates

IMMIGRATION LAW

Aleinikoff and Martin's Immigration Process and Policy, 1042 pages, 1985 (Casebook)

Weissbrodt's Immigration Law and Procedure in a Nutshell, 345 pages, 1984 (Text)

INDIAN LAW

See American Indian Law

INSURANCE

Dobbyn's Insurance Law in a Nutshell, 281 pages, 1981 (Text)

Keeton's Cases on Basic Insurance Law, 2nd Ed., 1086 pages, 1977

Keeton's Basic Text on Insurance Law, 712 pages, 1971 (Text)

INSURANCE—Cont'd

Keeton's Case Supplement to Keeton's Basic Text on Insurance Law, 334 pages, 1978 (Casebook)

York and Whelan's Cases, Materials and Problems on Insurance Law, 715 pages, 1982, with 1985 Supplement (Casebook)

INTERNATIONAL LAW

Buergenthal and Maier's Public International Law in a Nutshell, 262 pages, 1985 (Text)

Folsom, Gordon and Spanogle's International Business Transactions – a Problem-Oriented Coursebook, 1160 pages, 1986 (Casebook)

Henkin, Pugh, Schachter and Smit's Cases and Materials on International Law, 2nd Ed., about 1500 pages, 1987 with Documents Supplement (Casebook)

Jackson and Davey's Legal Problems of International Economic Relations, 2nd Ed., 1269 pages, 1986, with Documents Supplement (Casebook)

Kirgis' International Organizations in Their Legal Setting, 1016 pages, 1977, with 1981 Supplement (Casebook)

Weston, Falk and D'Amato's International Law and World Order—A Problem Oriented Coursebook, 1195 pages, 1980, with Documents Supplement (Casebook)

Wilson's International Business Transactions in a Nutshell, 2nd Ed., 476 pages, 1984 (Text)

INTERVIEWING AND COUNSELING

Binder and Price's Interviewing and Counseling, 232 pages, 1977 (Text)

Shaffer's Interviewing and Counseling in a Nutshell, 353 pages, 1976 (Text)

INTRODUCTION TO LAW STUDY

Dobbyn's So You Want to go to Law School, Revised First Edition, 206 pages, 1976 (Text)

Hegland's Introduction to the Study and Practice of Law in a Nutshell, 418 pages, 1983 (Text)

Kinyon's Introduction to Law Study and Law Examinations in a Nutshell, 389 pages, 1971 (Text)

See also Legal Method and Legal System

JUDICIAL ADMINISTRATION

Nelson's Cases and Materials on Judicial Administration and the Administration of Justice, 1032 pages, 1974 (Casebook)

JURISPRUDENCE

Christie's Text and Readings on Jurisprudence—The Philosophy of Law, 1056 pages, 1973 (Casebook)

LAW SCHOOL PUBLICATIONS—Continued

JUVENILE JUSTICE

Fox's Cases and Materials on Modern Juvenile Justice, 2nd Ed., 960 pages, 1981 (Casebook)

Fox's Juvenile Courts in a Nutshell, 3rd Ed., 291 pages, 1984 (Text)

LABOR LAW

Atleson, Rabin, Schatzki, Sherman and Silverstein's Collective Bargaining in Private Employment, 2nd Ed., (The Labor Law Group), 856 pages, 1984 (Casebook)

Gorman's Basic Text on Labor Law—Unionization and Collective Bargaining, 914 pages, 1976 (Text)

Grodin, Wollett and Alleyne's Collective Bargaining in Public Employment, 3rd Ed., (the Labor Law Group), 430 pages, 1979 (Casebook)

Leslie's Labor Law in a Nutshell, 2nd Ed., 397 pages, 1986 (Text)

Nolan's Labor Arbitration Law and Practice in a Nutshell, 358 pages, 1979 (Text)

Oberer, Hanslowe, Andersen and Heinsz' Cases and Materials on Labor Law—Collective Bargaining in a Free Society, 3rd Ed., 1163 pages, 1986 with Statutory Supplement (Casebook)

See also Employment Discrimination, Social Legislation

LAND FINANCE

See Real Estate Transactions

LAND USE

Callies and Freilich's Cases and Materials on Land Use, 1233 pages, 1986 (Casebook)

Hagman's Cases on Public Planning and Control of Urban and Land Development, 2nd Ed., 1301 pages, 1980 (Casebook)

Hagman and Juergensmeyer's Hornbook on Urban Planning and Land Development Control Law, 2nd Ed., Student Edition, 680 pages, 1986 (Text)

Wright and Gitelman's Cases and Materials on Land Use, 3rd Ed., 1300 pages, 1982, with 1987 Supplement (Casebook)

Wright and Wright's Land Use in a Nutshell, 2nd Ed., 356 pages, 1985 (Text)

LEGAL HISTORY

Presser and Zainaldin's Cases on Law and American History, 855 pages, 1980 (Casebook)

See also Legal Method and Legal System

LEGAL METHOD AND LEGAL SYSTEM

Aldisert's Readings, Materials and Cases in the Judicial Process, 948 pages, 1976 (Casebook)

Berch and Berch's Introduction to Legal Method and Process, 550 pages, 1985 (Casebook)

LEGAL METHOD AND LEGAL SYSTEM—Cont'd

Bodenheimer, Oakley and Love's Readings and Cases on an Introduction to the Anglo-American Legal System, 161 pages, 1980 (Casebook)

Davies and Lawry's Institutions and Methods of the Law—Introductory Teaching Materials, 547 pages, 1982 (Casebook)

Dvorkin, Himmelstein and Lesnick's Becoming a Lawyer: A Humanistic Perspective on Legal Education and Professionalism, 211 pages, 1981 (Text)

Greenberg's Judicial Process and Social Change, 666 pages, 1977 (Casebook)

Kelso and Kelso's Studying Law: An Introduction, 587 pages, 1984 (Coursebook)

Kempin's Historical Introduction to Anglo-American Law in a Nutshell, 2nd Ed., 280 pages, 1973 (Text)

Kimball's Historical Introduction to the Legal System, 610 pages, 1966 (Casebook)

Murphy's Cases and Materials on Introduction to Law—Legal Process and Procedure, 772 pages, 1977 (Casebook)

Reynolds' Judicial Process in a Nutshell, 292 pages, 1980 (Text)

See also Legal Research and Writing

LEGAL PROFESSION

Aronson, Devine and Fisch's Problems, Cases and Materials on Professional Responsibility, 745 pages, 1985 (Casebook)

Aronson and Weckstein's Professional Responsibility in a Nutshell, 399 pages, 1980 (Text)

Mellinkoff's The Conscience of a Lawyer, 304 pages, 1973 (Text)

Mellinkoff's Lawyers and the System of Justice, 983 pages, 1976 (Casebook)

Pirsig and Kirwin's Cases and Materials on Professional Responsibility, 4th Ed., 603 pages, 1984 (Casebook)

Schwartz and Wydick's Problems in Legal Ethics, 285 pages, 1983 (Casebook)

Selected Statutes, Rules and Standards on the Legal Profession, 276 pages, Revised 1984

Smith's Preventing Legal Malpractice, 142 pages, 1981 (Text)

Wolfram's Hornbook on Modern Legal Ethics, Student Edition, 1120 pages, 1986 (Text)

LEGAL RESEARCH AND WRITING

Cohen's Legal Research in a Nutshell, 4th Ed., 450 pages, 1985 (Text)

Cohen and Berring's How to Find the Law, 8th Ed., 790 pages, 1983. Problem book by Foster, Johnson and Kelly available (Casebook)

Cohen and Berring's Finding the Law, 8th Ed., Abridged Ed., 556 pages, 1984 (Casebook)

LAW SCHOOL PUBLICATIONS—Continued

LEGAL RESEARCH AND WRITING—Cont'd

Dickerson's Materials on Legal Drafting, 425 pages, 1981 (Casebook)

Felsenfeld and Siegel's Writing Contracts in Plain English, 290 pages, 1981 (Text)

Gopen's Writing From a Legal Perspective, 225 pages, 1981 (Text)

Mellinkoff's Legal Writing—Sense and Nonsense, 242 pages, 1982 (Text)

Ray and Ramsfield's Legal Writing: Getting It Right and Getting It Written, about 400 pages, 1987 (Text)

Rombauer's Legal Problem Solving—Analysis, Research and Writing, 4th Ed., 424 pages, 1983 (Coursebook)

Squires and Rombauer's Legal Writing in a Nutshell, 294 pages, 1982 (Text)

Statsky's Legal Research and Writing, 3rd Ed., 257 pages, 1986 (Coursebook)

Statsky and Wernet's Case Analysis and Fundamentals of Legal Writing, 2nd Ed., 441 pages, 1984 (Text)

Teply's Programmed Materials on Legal Research and Citation, 2nd Ed., 358 pages, 1986. Student Library Exercises available (Coursebook)

Weihofen's Legal Writing Style, 2nd Ed., 332 pages, 1980 (Text)

LEGISLATION

Davies' Legislative Law and Process in a Nutshell, 2nd Ed., 346 pages, 1986 (Text)

Nutting and Dickerson's Cases and Materials on Legislation, 5th Ed., 744 pages, 1978 (Casebook)

Statsky's Legislative Analysis and Drafting, 2nd Ed., 217 pages, 1984 (Text)

LOCAL GOVERNMENT

McCarthy's Local Government Law in a Nutshell, 2nd Ed., 404 pages, 1983 (Text)

Reynolds' Hornbook on Local Government Law, 860 pages, 1982 (Text)

Valente's Cases and Materials on Local Government Law, 3rd Ed., about 980 pages, 1987 (Casebook)

MASS COMMUNICATION LAW

Gillmor and Barron's Cases and Comment on Mass Communication Law, 4th Ed., 1076 pages, 1984 (Casebook)

Ginsburg's Regulation of Broadcasting: Law and Policy Towards Radio, Television and Cable Communications, 741 pages, 1979, with 1983 Supplement (Casebook)

Zuckman and Gayne's Mass Communications Law in a Nutshell, 2nd Ed., 473 pages, 1983 (Text)

MEDICINE, LAW AND

King's The Law of Medical Malpractice in a Nutshell, 2nd Ed., 342 pages, 1986 (Text)

MEDICINE, LAW AND—Cont'd

Shapiro and Spece's Problems, Cases and Materials on Bioethics and Law, 892 pages, 1981 (Casebook)

Sharpe, Fiscina and Head's Cases on Law and Medicine, 882 pages, 1978 (Casebook)

MILITARY LAW

Shanor and Terrell's Military Law in a Nutshell, 378 pages, 1980 (Text)

MORTGAGES

See Real Estate Transactions

NATURAL RESOURCES LAW

See Energy and Natural Resources Law

NEGOTIATION

Edwards and White's Problems, Readings and Materials on the Lawyer as a Negotiator, 484 pages, 1977 (Casebook)

Peck's Cases and Materials on Negotiation, 2nd Ed., (The Labor Law Group), 280 pages, 1980 (Casebook)

Williams' Legal Negotiation and Settlement, 207 pages, 1983 (Coursebook)

OFFICE PRACTICE

Hegland's Trial and Practice Skills in a Nutshell, 346 pages, 1978 (Text)

Strong and Clark's Law Office Management, 424 pages, 1974 (Casebook)

See also Computers and Law, Interviewing and Counseling, Negotiation

OIL AND GAS

Hemingway's Hornbook on Oil and Gas, 2nd Ed., Student Ed., 543 pages, 1983 with 1986 P.P. (Text)

Kuntz, Lowe, Anderson and Smith's Cases and Materials on Oil and Gas Law, 857 pages, 1986, with Forms Manual (Casebook)

Lowe's Oil and Gas Law in a Nutshell, 443 pages, 1983 (Text)

See also Energy and Natural Resources Law

PARTNERSHIP

See Agency—Partnership

PATENT AND COPYRIGHT LAW

Choate and Francis' Cases and Materials on Patent Law, 2nd Ed., 1110 pages, 1981 (Casebook)

Miller and Davis' Intellectual Property—Patents, Trademarks and Copyright in a Nutshell, 428 pages, 1983 (Text)

Nimmer's Cases on Copyright and Other Aspects of Entertainment Litigation, 3rd Ed., 1025 pages, 1985 (Casebook)

PRODUCTS LIABILITY

Noel and Phillips' Cases on Products Liability, 2nd Ed., 821 pages, 1982 (Casebook)

LAW SCHOOL PUBLICATIONS—Continued

PRODUCTS LIABILITY—Cont'd

Noel and Phillips' Products Liability in a Nutshell, 2nd Ed., 341 pages, 1981 (Text)

PROPERTY

Bernhardt's Real Property in a Nutshell, 2nd Ed., 448 pages, 1981 (Text)

Boyer's Survey of the Law of Property, 766 pages, 1981 (Text)

Browder, Cunningham and Smith's Cases on Basic Property Law, 4th Ed., 1431 pages, 1984 (Casebook)

Bruce, Ely and Bostick's Cases and Materials on Modern Property Law, 1004 pages, 1984 (Casebook)

Burke's Personal Property in a Nutshell, 322 pages, 1983 (Text)

Cunningham, Stoebuck and Whitman's Hornbook on the Law of Property, Student Ed., 916 pages, 1984, with 1987 P.P (Text)

Donahue, Kauper and Martin's Cases on Property, 2nd Ed., 1362 pages, 1983 (Casebook)

Hill's Landlord and Tenant Law in a Nutshell, 2nd Ed., 311 pages, 1986 (Text)

Kurtz and Hovenkamp's Cases and Materials on American Property Law, about 1300 pages, 1987 (Casebook)

Moynihan's Introduction to Real Property, 254 pages, 1962 (Text)

Uniform Land Transactions Act, Uniform Simplification of Land Transfers Act, Uniform Condominium Act, 1977 Official Text with Comments, 462 pages, 1978

See also Real Estate Transactions, Land Use

PSYCHIATRY, LAW AND

Reisner's Law and the Mental Health System, Civil and Criminal Aspects, 696 pages, 1985 (Casebooks)

REAL ESTATE TRANSACTIONS

Bruce's Real Estate Finance in a Nutshell, 2nd Ed., 262 pages, 1985 (Text)

Maxwell, Riesenfeld, Hetland and Warren's Cases on California Security Transactions in Land, 3rd Ed., 728 pages, 1984 (Casebook)

Nelson and Whitman's Cases on Real Estate Transfer, Finance and Development, 2nd Ed., 1114 pages, 1981, with 1986 Supplement (Casebook)

Nelson and Whitman's Hornbook on Real Estate Finance Law, 2nd Ed., Student Ed., 941 pages, 1985 (Text)

Osborne's Cases and Materials on Secured Transactions, 559 pages, 1967 (Casebook)

REGULATED INDUSTRIES

Gellhorn and Pierce's Regulated Industries in a Nutshell, 2nd Ed., about 400 pages, 1987 (Text)

REGULATED INDUSTRIES—Cont'd

Morgan, Harrison and Verkuil's Cases and Materials on Economic Regulation of Business, 2nd Ed., 666 pages, 1985 (Casebook)

See also Mass Communication Law, Banking Law

REMEDIES

Dobbs' Hornbook on Remedies, 1067 pages, 1973 (Text)

Dobbs' Problems in Remedies, 137 pages, 1974 (Problem book)

Dobbyn's Injunctions in a Nutshell, 264 pages, 1974 (Text)

Friedman's Contract Remedies in a Nutshell, 323 pages, 1981 (Text)

Leavell, Love and Nelson's Cases and Materials on Equitable Remedies and Restitution, 4th Ed., 1111 pages, 1986 (Casebook)

McCormick's Hornbook on Damages, 811 pages, 1935 (Text)

O'Connell's Remedies in a Nutshell, 2nd Ed., 320 pages, 1985 (Text)

York, Bauman and Rendleman's Cases and Materials on Remedies, 4th Ed., 1029 pages, 1985 (Casebook)

REVIEW MATERIALS

Ballantine's Problems

Black Letter Series

Smith's Review Series

West's Review Covering Multistate Subjects

SECURITIES REGULATION

Hazen's Hornbook on The Law of Securities Regulation, Student Ed., 739 pages, 1985, with 1987 P.P. (Text)

Ratner's Securities Regulation: Materials for a Basic Course, 3rd Ed., 1000 pages, 1986 (Casebook)

Ratner's Securities Regulation in a Nutshell, 2nd Ed., 322 pages, 1982 (Text)

Selected Securities and Business Planning Statutes, Rules and Forms, 470 pages, 1985

SOCIAL LEGISLATION

Hood and Hardy's Workers' Compensation and Employee Protection Laws in a Nutshell, 274 pages, 1984 (Text)

LaFrance's Welfare Law: Structure and Entitlement in a Nutshell, 455 pages, 1979 (Text)

Malone, Plant and Little's Cases on Workers' Compensation and Employment Rights, 2nd Ed., 951 pages, 1980 (Casebook)

SPORTS LAW

Schubert, Smith and Trentadue's Sports Law, 395 pages, 1986 (Text)

LAW SCHOOL PUBLICATIONS—Continued

TAXATION

Dodge's Cases and Materials on Federal Income Taxation, 820 pages, 1985 (Casebook)

Dodge's Federal Taxation of Estates, Trusts and Gifts: Principles and Planning, 771 pages, 1981 with 1982 Supplement (Casebook)

Garbis and Struntz' Cases and Materials on Tax Procedure and Tax Fraud, 829 pages, 1982 with 1984 Supplement (Casebook)

Gelfand and Salsich's State and Local Taxation and Finance in a Nutshell, 309 pages, 1986 (Text)

Gunn's Cases and Materials on Federal Income Taxation of Individuals, 785 pages, 1981 with 1985 Supplement (Casebook)

Hellerstein and Hellerstein's Cases on State and Local Taxation, 4th Ed., 1041 pages, 1978 with 1982 Supplement (Casebook)

Kahn and Gann's Corporate Taxation and Taxation of Partnerships and Partners, 2nd Ed., 1204 pages, 1985 (Casebook)

Kragen and McNulty's Cases and Materials on Federal Income Taxation: Individuals, Corporations, Partnerships, 4th Ed., 1287 pages, 1985 (Casebook)

McNulty's Federal Estate and Gift Taxation in a Nutshell, 3rd Ed., 509 pages, 1983 (Text)

McNulty's Federal Income Taxation of Individuals in a Nutshell, 3rd Ed., 487 pages, 1983 (Text)

Posin's Hornbook on Federal Income Taxation of Individuals, Student Ed., 491 pages, 1983 with 1985 pocket part (Text)

Selected Federal Taxation Statutes and Regulations, 1429 pages, 1986

Solomon and Hesch's Cases on Federal Income Taxation of Individuals, about 800 pages, 1987 (Casebook)

Sobeloff and Weidenbruch's Federal Income Taxation of Corporations and Stockholders in a Nutshell, 362 pages, 1981 (Text)

TORTS

Christie's Cases and Materials on the Law of Torts, 1264 pages, 1983 (Casebook)

Dobbs' Torts and Compensation—Personal Accountability and Social Responsibility for Injury, 955 pages, 1985 (Casebook)

Green, Pedrick, Rahl, Thode, Hawkins, Smith, and Treece's Advanced Torts: Injuries to Business, Political and Family Interests, 2nd Ed., 544 pages, 1977 (Casebook)

Keeton, Keeton, Sargentich and Steiner's Cases and Materials on Torts, and Accident Law, 1360 pages, 1983 (Casebook)

Kionka's Torts in a Nutshell: Injuries to Persons and Property, 434 pages, 1977 (Text)

TORTS—Cont'd

Malone's Torts in a Nutshell: Injuries to Family, Social and Trade Relations, 358 pages, 1979 (Text)

Prosser and Keeton's Hornbook on Torts, 5th Ed., Student Ed., 1286 pages, 1984 (Text)

See also Products Liability

TRADE REGULATION

McManis' Unfair Trade Practices in a Nutshell, 444 pages, 1982 (Text)

Oppenheim, Weston, Maggs and Schechter's Cases and Materials on Unfair Trade Practices and Consumer Protection, 4th Ed., 1038 pages, 1983 with 1986 Supplement (Casebook)

See also Antitrust, Regulated Industries

TRIAL AND APPELLATE ADVOCACY

Appellate Advocacy, Handbook of, 2nd Ed., 182 pages, 1986 (Text)

Bergman's Trial Advocacy in a Nutshell, 402 pages, 1979 (Text)

Binder and Bergman's Fact Investigation: From Hypothesis to Proof, 354 pages, 1984 (Coursebook)

Goldberg's The First Trial (Where Do I Sit?, What Do I Say?) in a Nutshell, 396 pages, 1982 (Text)

Haydock, Herr and Stempel's, Fundamentals of Pre-Trial Litigation, 768 pages, 1985 (Casebook)

Hegland's Trial and Practice Skills in a Nutshell, 346 pages, 1978 (Text)

Hornstein's Appellate Advocacy in a Nutshell, 325 pages, 1984 (Text)

Jeans' Handbook on Trial Advocacy, Student Ed., 473 pages, 1975 (Text)

Martineau's Cases and Materials on Appellate Practice and Procedure, about 550 pages, 1987 (Casebook)

McElhaney's Effective Litigation, 457 pages, 1974 (Casebook)

Nolan's Cases and Materials on Trial Practice, 518 pages, 1981 (Casebook)

Parnell and Shellhaas' Cases, Exercises and Problems for Trial Advocacy, 171 pages, 1982 (Coursebook)

Sonsteng, Haydock and Boyd's The Trialbook: A Total System for Preparation and Presentation of a Case, Student Ed., 404 pages, 1984 (Coursebook)

TRUSTS AND ESTATES

Atkinson's Hornbook on Wills, 2nd Ed., 975 pages, 1953 (Text)

Averill's Uniform Probate Code in a Nutshell, 425 pages, 1978 (Text)

Bogert's Hornbook on Trusts, 6th Ed., Student Ed., about 800 pages, 1987 (Text)

Clark, Lusky and Murphy's Cases and Materials on Gratuitous Transfers, 3rd Ed., 970 pages, 1985 (Casebook)

TRUSTS AND ESTATES—Cont'd

Gulliver's Cases and Materials on Future Interests, 624 pages, 1959 (Casebook)

Gulliver's Introduction to the Law of Future Interests, 87 pages, 1959 (Casebook)—reprint from Gulliver's Cases and Materials on Future Interests, 1959

McGovern's Cases and Materials on Wills, Trusts and Future Interests: An Introduction to Estate Planning, 750 pages, 1983 (Casebook)

Mennell's Wills and Trusts in a Nutshell, 392 pages, 1979 (Text)

Simes' Hornbook on Future Interests, 2nd Ed., 355 pages, 1966 (Text)

Turano and Radigan's Hornbook on New York Estate Administration, 676 pages, 1986 (Text)

Uniform Probate Code, 5th Ed., Official Text With Comments, 384 pages, 1977

Waggoner's Future Interests in a Nutshell, 361 pages, 1981 (Text)

Waterbury's Materials on Trusts and Estates, 1039 pages, 1986 (Casebook)

WATER LAW

Getches' Water Law in a Nutshell, 439 pages, 1984 (Text)

WATER LAW—Cont'd

Sax and Abram's Cases and Materials on Legal Control of Water Resources in the United States, 941 pages, 1986 (Casebook)

Trelease and Gould's Cases and Materials on Water Law, 4th Ed., 816 pages, 1986 (Casebook)

See also Energy and Natural Resources Law, Environmental Law

WILLS

See Trusts and Estates

WOMEN AND THE LAW

Kay's Text, Cases and Materials on Sex-Based Discrimination, 2nd Ed., 1045 pages, 1981, with 1986 Supplement (Casebook)

Thomas' Sex Discrimination in a Nutshell, 399 pages, 1982 (Text)

See also Employment Discrimination

WORKERS' COMPENSATION

See Social Legislation

COMPUTER APPLICATIONS IN THE LAW

By

Peter B. Maggs
Professor of Law
University of Illinois at Urbana-Champaign

and

James A. Sprowl
Associate Professor of Law,
Illinois Institute of Technology, Chicago-Kent College of Law

with a chapter on Computers in Law Office Management

By

Richard L. Robbins
Director
Legal Technology Advisory Council
American Bar Association

WEST PUBLISHING CO.
ST. PAUL, MINN., 1987

50 West Kellogg Boulevard
P.O. Box 64526
St. Paul, Minnesota 55164–0526

Printed in the United States of America

Maggs, Peter B.
Computer applications in the law.

(American casebook series)
Includes index.
1. Law offices—United States—Automation.
2. Information storage and retrieval systems—Law—United States. 3. Legal research—United States—Data processing. I. Sprowl, James A. (James Alexander), 1941– . II. Robbins, Richard L. III. Title. IV. Series.
KF320.A9M25 1986 340'.028'5536 86–24734

ISBN 0–314–25907–4

Maggs & Sprowl, Computer Applications In Law

Preface

This book is meant to provide law students and lawyers with the minimum knowledge about computers that they will need to work efficiently in tomorrow's automated law practice. It assumes no prior knowledge of computers and makes no attempt to teach the kind of skills (e.g., programming in BASIC or PASCAL) usually taught in college computer courses. Because of the rapid pace of change of computer technology, the book concentrates on basic principles rather than attempting to survey currently available hardware and software.

Legal education in the United States is based upon the idea that students should participate actively in learning rather than sit passively through lectures. To learn about computers, one needs to use computers. Therefore, software is supplied with this book to give students practical experience with the types of computer applications that they will encounter in law offices. The inside back cover of the book contains a "floppy disk" slot into which programs and creations may be inserted.

The diskette accompanying this book contains software designed to run on IBM Personal Computers and compatible computers obtained from other manufacturers. Full explanations for its use are given in this book, its appendices, and in a file named "read.me" that is present on the diskette. Before using the diskette, you should print out the file "read.me". The file "read.me" contains last-minute information about the software. To print this file, place the diskette in drive A: and type:

```
copy read.me prn:
```

Then strike the <Enter> key.

The authors wish to thank particularly those who have helped them with this book, including the editorial staff of West Publishing Company, Ms. Ruth Manint, secretary at the University of Illinois, Ms. Sheila Wall, law student at the University of Illinois, Mr. Robert Price, a former law student at Chicago Kent, and Professor Gerald Bennett, law professor at the University of Florida. The authors also wish to thank the students who have used the book and the software over the past year. Thanks are also due to the American Bar Association and its "Law Office Of The Future" project for permitting a "Junior" version of the ABA's new LawLink menuing and communications program to be included as the LawComm menuing and communications program that is supplied with this book. And we acknowledge the assistance of those at West Publishing Company and Mead Data Central who were kind enough to review the manuscript for accuracy and to make suggestions for its improvement.

PETER B. MAGGS
JAMES A. SPROWL

Trademarks and Service Marks

Listed below are trademarks and service marks that appear in this book along with the names of the companies that own them.

6502—Mostek, Inc.

6800, 6809, 68000, 68010, 68020—Motorola Corp.

8080, 8086, 8088, 80186, 80188, 80286, 80386—Intel, Inc.

ABA/net—American Bar Association

ABF—American Bar Foundation

ADA—U.S. Department of Defense

ALR—Lawyer's Cooperative Publishing Co.

APL—IBM Corp.

Apple II—Apple Computer Corp.

ASCII—American National Standards Institute (ANSI)

AT—Hayes Microcomputer Products, Inc.

AUTOCITE—Lawyer's Cooperative Publishing Co.

CAPS—West Publishing Co. & Brigham Young University

CMS—IBM Corp.

Crosstalk—Microstuf, Inc.

d Base III—Ashton Tate, Inc.

Dialcom—Dialcom, Inc. (British Telecom)

Dialog—Dialog Information Services, Inc.—Lockheed, Inc.

Displaywriter—IBM Corp.

EGA (enhanced graphics adapter)—IBM Corp.

ELSS—Commerce Clearing House, Inc.

Electronic Legislative Search System—Commerce Clearing House, Inc.

Ethernet—Xerox Corp.

Filing Assistant—IBM Corp.

Framework—Ashton Tate, Inc.

GW-BASIC—Microsoft, Inc.

Hercules—Hercules Computer Technology, Inc.

IBM 3101 Terminal—IBM Corp.

IBM 3101 Terminal Emulator Program—IBM Corp.

IBM 3270 Terminal—IBM Corp.

IBM PC—IBM Corp.

IBM PC–AT—IBM Corp.

IBM Personal Computer—IBM Corp.

Inmagic—Inmagic, Inc.

INSTACITE—West Publishing Co.

JURIS—U.S. Dept. of Justice

Kermit—Columbia University

Kurzweil—Kurzweil, Inc.

Law:Forum—Advertel Communications, Inc.

LawLink—American Bar Association

Law Search—Direct Aid, Inc.

LC and LawComm—West Pub. Co.

Legal Resources Index—Information Access Corp. (Ziff Davis Co.)

LEXIS—Mead Data Central, Inc.

LEXPAT—Mead Data Central, Inc.

Lotus 1–2–3—Lotus Development Corp.

LP and LawProcess—West Pub. Co.

LS and LawSpread—West Pub. Co.

LW and LawWord—West Pub. Co.

Macintosh—Apple Computer Corp.

MCI Mail—MCI, Inc.

MS–DOS—Microsoft, Inc.

NEXIS—Mead Data Central, Inc.

OCLC—Ohio College Library Center

PC–DOS—IBM Corp.

PC–WRITE—Quicksoft, Inc.

PFS:File—Software Publishing Co.

PFS:Report—Software Publishing Co.

PHINET—Prentice-Hall, Inc.

PROKEY—Rosesoft, Inc.

QL—QL Systems, LTD (Canada)

R–Base 5000—Microrim, Inc.

RLIN—Remote Library Information Network

RT–PC—IBM Corp.

Selectric—IBM Corp.

Smartcom—Hayes Microcomputer Products, Inc.

Smartmodem—Hayes Microcomputer Products, Inc.

STAIRS—IBM Corp.

System V—AT&T

TELENET—U.S. Sprint (GT&E)

Teletype—Teletype Corp.

Token ring—IBM Corp.

True BASIC—Addison-Wesley, Inc.

Turbo Editor Toolbox—Borland International, Inc.

Turbo Lightning—Borland International, Inc.

Turbo Pascal—Borland International, Inc.

TYMNET—McDonnell Douglas, Inc.

UBIQ—Mead Data Central, Inc.

UNIX—AT&T

VAX—Digital Equipment Corp.

VERALEX—Vera Corp. (Lawyer's Cooperative Publishing Co. & Mead Data Central, Inc.)

Visicalc—Lotus Development Corp.

VM—IBM Corp.

VMS—Digital Equipment Corp.

VT-100—Digital Equipment Corp.

WALT—West Publishing Co.

WESTLAW—West Publishing Co.

WESTMATE—West Publishing Co.

WESTNET—West Publishing Co.

WILSONLINE—H. W. Wilson Co.

Windows—Microsoft, Inc.

Word—Microsoft, Inc.

Word Perfect—SSI Software

Wordstar—Micropro, Inc.

XENIX—Microsoft, Inc.

ZYIndex—ZYLab, Inc.

Summary of Contents

*

Table of Contents

Appendices

*

COMPUTER APPLICATIONS IN THE LAW

*

Chapter 1

A SOCIOLOGICAL INTRODUCTION TO THE USE OF COMPUTERS IN THE PRACTICE OF LAW

§ 1–1. WHAT IS A COMPUTER?

Computers are perceived by most of us to be utilitarian machines constructed from electronic components, whose functions we do not understand, but assume are analogous to the functions of gears, cams, shafts, and pistons in conventional machines such as automobiles. We believe that each part of a computer is shaped in a utilitarian way to reflect the application of a scientific principle to the solution of a practical problem. The hardware and software components of a computer thus appear to be pure products of science and logic—their names, shapes, and functions as scientifically pure and invariant through time as the laws of physics that govern all real processes. There appears to be nothing at all "subjective" about computers.

This perception is false. Attorneys in particular must not permit themselves to be deceived by the shining technological image the designers of modern computers choose to give them. Computers may not be as fanciful as Picasso sculptures, but they are definitely works of art created by men that have whatever outward appearance their creators wish them to have. The inner structure of a modern computer resembles the structure of a coral reef—it is the fossil relic of the many teams of men and women who built it, layer by layer. Only the outermost layer is visible in the final product. Just as each new roof hides from view the older roofs that lie below it, so each new layer of a computer hides beneath it the man-machine interface of the layer below and presents to the world a new man-machine interface that is more "friendly," more "intelligent," and more "specialized" than the interface it hides from view. Layer by layer, an inner structure constructed from the most primitive of electronic building blocks is transformed into a machine that seems to understand the language of a particular "user" and that performs useful tasks for that user.

The stratified nature of modern computers, and the number and thickness of the individual layers that form their structure, reflect the limited ability of the human mind to cope with complexity. No one individual possesses sufficient expertise and has sufficient time to construct a modern computer in its entirety. Groups of individuals having divergent backgrounds and talents must participate in a joint design effort, with each group contributing one layer to the final product. The specific nature of each layer, and therefore the task that is assigned to each group, is defined by accident and history as much as by logic and science. When viewed from a sociological perspective, viewed as if the group that designed each layer were personally performing the functions carried out by the layer they designed, a computer resembles a large corporation far more than it resembles an automobile. The "user" of the computer sits in the president's chair and gives brief, succinct orders to the top layer of management. Each succinct order is expanded into more and more highly detailed orders by the layers of management below until ultimately thousands of workers the "user" president never sees, who may speak an entirely different language than the "user" president, perform the tens of thousands of orders that enable them collectively to carry out the succinct orders issued by the "user" president. The individuals who design the multiple layers are not actually present in the final machine, but the layers, and the language interfaces between the layers, are there as fossil relics of the design process, of the history of computer science, and of the sociological breakdown of computer technologists into stratified groups of specialists.

How can a single machine be constructed by so many different groups of people? The problem of designing a computer is similar to that of running the Allied armies during World War II in Europe. Each army has its own culture and language, yet all must cooperate if the war is to be fought successfully. To the extent that two armies must cooperate, both must agree on what signals each will use when communicating with the other. A standard code book is agreed upon, printed up, and distributed to the communications officers in both armies. Ultimately, a whole series of such code books define the ways in which all of the armies communicate. One can imagine that the codes are updated frequently to reflect changed circumstances and increased sophistication in the war effort. Each army also has its own internal organizational and communicative needs that are recorded and implemented in the unique language of that particular army which the other armies may not be able to understand. To understand all that is going on, a historian must study the culture and language of every army and then study both the internal and external communications that regulated the war effort. No such historian exists for the computer industry, and that is why it is impossible to find any one book that can satisfactorily answer the question, "What is a computer?"

One would not think the language barriers that isolate the groups designing computers are as impenetrable as those that isolated the

European armies from each other. Do not all the designers of IBM and Apple computers speak English? They do, but each group over time develops its own special subset of English to describe and solve the radically new problems that it confronts in its own specialized area. New languages evolve quickly when a group is faced with new problems, and new cultures evolve just as quickly. One needs only to pick up any technical article on computers to see just how unintelligible the new language of technology can be even to those supposedly "skilled in the art." The languages of the logic chip designers, hardware designers, microcode programmers, high-level language designers, and programmers differ as much from each other as these languages each differ from ordinary English. The modern digital computer is thus a European war effort that was won because the groups learned to communicate just well enough to get the job done.

All of this is highly pertinent to you as attorneys. The legal problems relating to computers flow directly from the complex interactions that take place between these groups. Frequently each group works for a different organization. Each group contributes to the end result, and each group wishes to receive fair compensation for their contribution to the final product, no matter how deeply buried their contribution may be. Legal problems can arise when one group feels that it is not receiving just compensation for its contribution to the final product. Legal problems can also arise when a computer fails to function because a group either fails to perform or is prevented from performing by the failure of some other group to perform—each group may blame the other for the problem. These types of legal problems have become an important part of patent, copyright, trade secret, and contract law.

Legal problems can also arise out of misunderstandings. Misunderstandings concerning what support one group is going to provide for another group can arise when the group technicians do not participate in contract negotiations. Misunderstandings concerning what some lower level of a computer can accomplish frequently make it impossible for two higher-level groups to perform their contracts, as when a computer vendor's sales force promises performance that the computer's lower levels cannot achieve. The bones of many well-intentioned but unsuccessful efforts to design and market computer systems reveal how difficult it is to achieve the proper balance between all of these groups. Attorneys must draft computer sales and purchase contracts with these things in mind—a contract to purchase a computer system is a contract that binds together far more groups of people than there are signatures on the contract.

Because computers have permeated many aspects of modern business, attorneys find themselves called upon frequently to give advice on computer procurement and use. It is not necessary for you to become an electrical engineer or a computer scientist before you will be qualified to give such advice. The legal problems usually flow from the complex interrelationships between the groups that cooperate in designing and marketing the computer, and not from the computer's technical details. To understand the source of the legal problems, you must understand the layered structure of the machine and how each layer is associated with a specific group of designers. It also helps to understand enough of the vocabulary or "technical jargon" of each layer so that you understand in broad overview what each group is contributing to the whole.

Since such an overview will also assist you in using computers effectively in your practice, this chapter begins at the very beginning and explains how modern digital computers are constructed. The following paragraphs cover all aspects of computer hardware and software from the innermost layer of electronic gates to the outermost layer of user-customizeable programming.

§ 1–2. DIGITAL INFORMATION

"Information" is a pattern that has meaning. The "pattern," which represents the information, is distinct from the "medium" within which it is embedded. The same pattern may be spoken, recorded on magnetic tape, written on paper, or recorded in the settings of transistor gates within a computer. An information pattern may be conveyed through time and space, and it may be transferred from one medium to another.

"Noise" is a meaningless, random pattern. The second law of thermodynamics states that the universe becomes more and more random, and less organized, with the passage of time. Accordingly, as time passes information picks up more and more noise, and ultimately, all information will be lost.

Examples of the destruction of information are readily found. The "best evidence" rule, for example, decrees that the "original" must be brought into court if its authenticity is in question. This rule is premised upon the fact that copies, whether made photographically, magnetically, xerographically, or otherwise invariably fail to pick up some of the information that was contained in the original. For example, a photographic print does not reveal all the details of the negative; a magnetic tape copy of a magnetic tape recording of music does not have the quality of the original; and even the reproduction of a recording through a loudspeaker distorts the original to the extent that 5% to 10% of the information on the recording is lost.

"Digital information" is information that is represented by letters and numbers. When making a measurement, some information is always lost when one reads the ruler and marks down 33¾ inches—the original item may have been longer or shorter than this amount. But having reduced the measurement to digital form, one can recopy it hundreds of times, telephone it across the country and back, photocopy it five times and still not lose the fact that the length is 33¾ inches.

Digital information appears to defy the second law of thermodynamics because it is highly redundant—there is more information on the sheet of paper, or in our voice, than the receiver needs. Much of the redundancy can be lost without any loss of information. Digital information is also "reformed" periodically. Each time one retypes, redraws, or re-speaks the information, one restores any redundant information that may have been lost previously.

"Digital computers" are machines constructed from transistor gates that can accept, store, transfer, and reproduce all types of digital information rapidly and accurately. Transistor switches are actually little amplifiers that can transform weak currents into strong currents. Every time digital information flows through a transistor gate, the information is fully "reformed" to its original state of redundancy. Accordingly, digital information within a computer can and frequently does flow through thousands of transistor gates with no loss of accuracy.

From an evidentiary point of view, once information has entered a computer, it is fully digitized, and a copy (even a thousandth copy) is identical to the original entry. So the "best evidence rule" should not be applicable to copies produced by a computer. But since computer-stored data is always fully digitized, it lacks the "nondigital" additional information that courts frequently rely upon when examining a check or a contract to see if it is authentic. The shape of the signature, the safety paper, the background marks—all of these safeguards are lost when information is fed into a digital computer. And most importantly, when digital information is altered, no telltale trace of the alteration is left behind. So alterations cannot be detected. Accordingly, digitized computer data cannot be permitted to fall into the hands of parties who might be motivated to alter the data. Checks, on the other hand, may be freely circulated, since their authenticity is guarded by the "nondigital" information that is inherent in checks. But if computer-stored digital information is not kept out of the hands of those who might wish to falsify it, then there can be no guarantee of its authenticity. If you ever need assistance in this area, a new breed of accountant who specializes in auditing computer systems has emerged who can teach you what types of safeguards are essential to achieve any desired degree of security of computerized information.

§ 1-3. STREET LIGHTS AND TRANSISTOR GATES

Deep down beneath all the layers of software and hardware, deep within all the integrated-circuit logic chip packages, lie the "atoms" from which all digital computers are constructed—the transistors, which are called "gates." It is difficult to describe these transistor gates, since they contain no moving parts that are readily visualizable. They are best described by analogy to something more ordinary and familiar—something that actually could be used to construct a digital computer—street lights.

Think back to the last time that you were driving down a major street shortly after sunset and saw the street lights winking on, one by one. Many modern street lights contain an "electronic eye" on their upper surface that looks up into the sky and signals the street light to turn on when the sky becomes sufficiently dark at twilight or during a storm. At dawn or after the storm passes, the same "electronic eye" senses the brightness of the sky and signals the street light to turn off again.

Visualize, if you will, a street light constructed from a light pole from which extends, outwardly and upwardly, a four foot long arm bearing a light that faces down toward the street. An "electronic eye" is mounted on the tip of the pole, away from and slightly below the light, facing the sky. Such a street light is analogous to the transistor gates that constitute the basic building blocks of all computers.

It is a dark night, and one such street light is standing by itself. No light reaches the "electronic eye" from the dark sky, so the street light turns on and illuminates the ground. Then a little child climbs up the light pole and illuminates the "electronic eye" with a flashlight. This flashlight tricks the "electronic eye" into thinking it is daytime, and the "electronic eye" turns off the street light. By flashing the flashlight on and off, the child can force the street light to blink off and on. When the flashlight is off, the street light is on, and vice versa.

Transistor gates work in precisely the same way, except they respond to and generate electrical currents rather than light. If an electrical current flows into a transistor gate, then no current flows out of the gate. If you halt the flow of current into a transistor gate, the gate immediately starts generating an output current. And just as the street lamp can respond to a small change in the incoming light by producing a large change in the light it generates, a transistor gate can respond to a small change in its input current by turning a large output current on or off.

§ 1–4. SIGNAL PATHS

Next, pretend that there are 99 street lights spaced four feet apart. Each street light is turned sideways so that its light shines directly into the "electronic eye" of the adjacent street light. It is still a dark night, so the "electronic eye" on the first street light receives no light, and accordingly the first street light turns on. The first street light shines directly down on the "electronic eye" on the top of the second street light, and this illumination causes the second street light to turn off. The second street light leaves the "electronic eye" of the third street light in darkness, so the third street light turns on. The light from the third street light causes the fourth street light to turn off, and the absence of light from the fourth street light causes the fifth street light to turn on, and so on. As you can see, street lights 1, 3, 5, . . . 99 are turned on, and street lights 2, 4, 6, . . . 98 are turned off. When our child climbs up the pole of the first street light and blinks the flash light at the first street light's "electronic eye," the child causes all 99 street lamps to blink on and off in synchronism with the flashlight's blinks (to the great annoyance of the man attempting to read the *New York Times* while standing under street light number 99).

By blinking the flashlight, the child can send a Morse code message to the man with the newspaper. In this same manner, a message could be sent through thousands of street lights.

Transistor gates in computers use electrical current, rather than light, to send information over wires from one transistor gate to the next, but in all other respects transistor gates convey electrical signals through a digital computer in precisely the same way that the street lights convey the child's morse code signals to the man with the newspaper. Sometimes "Morse code"-like signals are actually used in computers, as when two computers communicate with each other directly over a single wire. But more commonly, eight or more parallel communication paths are established within a computer, and this is analogous to eight rows of 99 street lights with eight children cooperating to send a single message. Eight flashlights can be turned on and off to create 256 unique patterns, so any one of 256 "messages" may be sent over the eight paths at a given moment. In a computer, these messages might each correspond to a letter or number produced when the operator strikes a key on a keyboard that is coupled to the computer by eight signal wires.

§ 1-5. MEMORY—BITS AND BYTES

Next, visualize two street lights standing four feet apart, facing one another, so that the light of each shines upon the "electronic eye" of the other. It is still a dark night. Assume that a first street light is on, so the light from the first street light strikes the "electronic eye" of the second street light, turning the second street light off. Since the second light is off, no light strikes the "electronic eye" of the first street light. So the first street light remains on and holds the second street light off.

The child climbs up the pole of the first street light and shines a very brief pulse of light upon the first light's "electronic eye." In response to this pulse, the first street light turns off (thinking the sun has come up) and leaves the "electronic eye" of the second street light in darkness. The second street light then turns on (thinking it is night time) and illuminates the "electronic eye" of the first street light, locking the first street light off even after the child extinguishes the flashlight. So the momentary pulse of light from the child's flashlight causes the first street light to turn out and stay out and causes the second street light to turn on and stay on. The pulse of light has caused the two street lights to reverse their "on" and "off" states.

If the child were now to climb the pole of the second street light and shine a pulse of light on the second street light's "electronic eye," the two street lights would revert to their original state with the first light on and the second light off and remain there.

We have created a "memory"—a pair of street lights that "remember" which "electronic eye" was illuminated most recently.

In a digital computer, a "memory" is formed by interconnecting the current inputs and outputs of two transistor gates one of which then generates current and the other of which does not generate current. Even the smallest of modern digital computers contains over half a million of these transistor gate pairs (or their equivalent) interconnected electrically to form half a million memory cells each capable of "remembering" the same amount of information that can be stored in the on-off state of an ordinary light switch—indeed, a transistor gate can be used as a light switch. The electrical current that flows from one of the two transistors forming a memory cell can be passed through a lamp, and then the "on" or "off" state of the lamp indicates the "off" or "on" state of the memory.

Claude Shannon, the "father" of information theory, defined the amount of information that can be stored in such an elemental memory cell to be one "bit" of information, where "bit" is a contraction of "binary digit." One "bit" of information is enough information to tell Paul Revere whether the British are coming by land or by sea—enough to tell the defendant whether he or she is guilty. One "bit" of information may be stored in the flip of a coin, in the bolt on a door, or in a memory cell formed from two street lights or two transistor gates. As you can readily see, the concept of "memory" and "bits" has nothing whatever to do with electronics.

Eight memory cells, formed from eight pairs of street lights or eight children's flashlights or eight pairs of transistor gates, can store eight "bits" of information or one "byte" of information. A "byte" is the amount of information that can be stored in the on-off states of eight light switches. If the Old North Church had had room in its tower for eight lanterns, and if Paul Revere had associated a different route of the British with each possible pattern of "on" and "off" lanterns, he could have learned by glancing at the church tower which of 256 different possible routes the British were about to take. Accordingly, "one byte" of memory can store any of 256 different messages—sufficient messages to assign one to each possible keystroke (including shifted keys) that can be made upon a computer's keyboard, for example, or all the possible characters one might want to print out or display. So a "keystroke" or a printable character may be "stored" in a "one byte" memory that contains eight "bits," or one "byte," of information. Some early computers dealt with data in 6-bit units. However this let them represent only 64 different combinations of keystrokes or display characters, too few for applications such as word processing. Having nine bits would mean having proportionally more memory but also proportionally more expense, for the dubious advantage of being able to represent 512 rather than 256 different characters. Therefore when IBM brought out its highly successfuly 360 series that set the industry standard for computers in the 1960s, it choose 8-bit bytes. Eight-bit bytes were also chosen for similar reasons by all the leading microprocessor manufacturers.

If a computer dealer tells you that a computer contains "512K bytes" of memory, that means it can store approximately 512,000 bytes of information, or 512,000 keystrokes. Assuming 2,000 keystrokes to a typical 8½ by 11 inch double-spaced page, the computer could theoretically hold 256 pages of text in its memory. This figure is approximate because the "K" does not mean "times 1000" in this context; it actually means "times 1024." For technical reasons that relate to the way in which virtually all computers assign addresses to their byte-sized memory cells, the true size of a computer's memory is always a multiple of 1024. So the dealer's 512K memory actually contains 512 times 1024 or 524,288 bytes of memory. But you will not be far off if you assume that "K" means "times 1000" and if you then divide by 2000 to get the equivalent number of manuscript pages that a computer's memory can hold. A 512K byte memory contains 512 times 1024 times 8, or 4,194,304, individual one-bit memory cells each formed from one or two transistor gates or their equivalent. So it takes over 8 million street lights to build a modern personal computer.

"Data" is another term for information. In casual conversation, computer scientists use "data" and "information" interchangeably and use both in the singular. For example, a computer scientist might say "The data is transferred into the memory," or "The information is transferred into the memory." Unfortunately, the word "data" is derived from Latin and is plural in Latin. The singular form "datum" also exists in English but is almost never used by computer scientists. A few English scholars, who have assumed roles as editors of certain rather prominent technical journals, have insisted that "data" must be treated as a plural noun. Accordingly, the above sentence is incorrect and should read: "The data are transferred into the memory," even though this offends the ear—no one speaks this way in normal conversation.

§ 1–6. THE SIGNIFICANCE OF MEMORY—PROGRAMMABLE SIGNAL PATHS

To understand the significance of "memory," pretend that a pair of street lights arranged to form a memory pair is positioned adjacent the row of 99 street lights which, you will recall, the child is using to send morse code messages to the man with the newspaper. The pair is positioned so that the first street light in the pair shines directly down on the "electronic eye" of street light number 20 in the row of 99 street lights. If the first street light in the pair is off and the second is on, then the street light pair has no effect upon the 99 street lights, and the child's Morse code signals get through to the man with the newspaper. But if the first street light in the pair is on and the second is off, then the light from the first street light in the pair illuminates continuously the "electronic eye" in street light number 20 and keeps street light number 20 turned off no matter what the child does with the flashlight. Hence, the child's Morse code message is blocked from reaching the man with the newspaper. In practical effect, the "memory" pair of street lights can "connect" or "disconnect" the morse code signal path between the child and the man with the newspaper.

Speaking now more generally of computers, the state of each individual memory cell within a computer determines whether a specific signal path exists or does not exist. A digital computer is thus a machine that is not fully "wired" until its memory cells are adjusted. By setting the states of a computer's memory cells, you "wire" up a new machine by creating new signal paths between the logic gates. Digital computers are thus "generic" unwired machines that may be converted into a wide variety of "species" machines by proper adjustment of the states of the computer's memory cells through "programming."

§ 1–7. DIGITAL CLOCKS

Returning once again to the street lamps, pretend now that three street lamps are arranged triangularly, four feet away from each other, and rotated so that each shines upon the "electronic eye" of the next one counterclockwise about the triangle. We leave it as a mental exercise for the reader to verify that the street lamps will continuously flicker on and off forever. One lamp is always altering its state, and when it does so, it forces the next lamp to alter its state, and so on round and round the triangle. A series of three transistor logic gates interconnected into a triangle behaves in an analogous manner. We have constructed a digital clock—an important component of any digital computer. By feeding light pulses away from the three street lights or by feeding electrical current pulses away from the three logic gates, and by "counting" those pulses using memory cells, we can measure the passage of time and cause different things to happen at different times. We can thus produce the time sequences of events that govern the operations of a digital computer.

§ 1–8. DIGITAL LOGIC SYSTEMS—THE EQUIVALENCE OF HARDWARE AND SOFTWARE

The above discussion has illustrated how transistor gates (or street lights, if you prefer) may be used to construct signal paths, memories, signal path controls, and pulse-generating clocks. These are the fundamental building blocks of all digital computers. An entire computer can be built from such gates—nothing more is needed. In Symbolic Logic, it is provable that all possible logical expressions can be constructed from AND, OR, NOT, and IF . . . THEN used in combination to form sentences. It can also be proved that a more fundamental logical operator, called the STROKE function, can be used in combination with itself to form sentences equivalent to AND, OR, NOT, and IF . . . THEN. It should not surprise you to learn that the STROKE function is the logician's version of the street lamp. Accordingly, we can rely upon the proofs worked out by the logicians to support the following statement: Any digital computer may be constructed entirely from street lights. Such a computer may be slow and rather large, but in theory you can duplicate the performance of any digital computer if you have enough memories, signal paths, signal path controls, and clocks. Nothing more is needed.

Nothing more is needed—you do not need software or programs. A hospital information system exists, for example, that keeps track of who is in what bed and of patient charges. At night it collects the charges for each patient, sums them, and prints them out. It then goes back and adds up how many inventory items have been drawn out, and does this for each item that has been sold to patients. It has many other features, but it does not contain any computer programs or "software," as computer programs are commonly called. If you wish to modify a report generated by this hospital information system, you have to go in with a soldering iron and rewire the transistor gates!

Transistor gates comprise the "hardware" portion of a computer—the part you can assemble with a soldering iron. Since any digital computer can be built entirely from "hardware" without the need for anything else, where does "software" come into the picture?

"Software" is pure information—millions of "bits" of information. In its most primitive form, "software" is the set of information that describes the millions of information paths that must be established to create a specific machine out of "general purpose" hardware. The key to combining software with hardware to form a distinct machine is the millions of memory cells. Remember that each individual memory cell can either establish a signal path or break a signal path through the computer. Each memory cell is a potential signal path. For each such memory cell, there is a "bit" of information in the software that determines whether that particular memory cell is to make or break its corresponding signal path. When software is "loaded" into a digital computer, each information "bit" in the software is used to set the state of one memory cell within the hardware, and in that manner a "special purpose" machine is established. By simply loading in different software at different times, one can change a digital computer from a word processor to a financial analyzer to an information storage and retrieval system—entirely different machines constructed from the same hardware that is "programmed" with different software. So software interacts with memory cells to convert a completely general-purpose digital logic system into many different special-purpose machines.

Incidentally, the terms "software" and "computer program" are interchangeable. "Software" can include a part of a program, or a single program, or many programs. The parts of a program are also "programs," and many programs are sometimes combined to form a single large "program." The terms "subroutine," "procedure," and "function" are always used to refer to parts of a program. These three terms are not completely interchangeable, but for our present purposes we need not concern ourselves with their different shades of meaning.

The choice of whether to design a given machine entirely from hardware or from some combination of hardware and software is one that engineers confront daily. Hardware-only systems tend to run much faster than hardware-software systems, but hardware-only systems are far more difficult to construct and to maintain. Systems that are predominantly software are easy to modify but may be slow. And, of course, hardware systems are patentable while software systems are copyrightable—or does the law place form above substance when it seems to say that hardware cannot be copyrighted and software cannot be patented? Perhaps laws that permit the way in which an engineer expresses his or her novel ideas to affect the type of proprietary protection afforded those ideas are irrational laws that should be changed. The "hardware/software" dividing line within computers, in particular, is as variable as the length of women's skirts or the width of men's neckties. Should hard legal distinctions be built upon such shifting sands?

§ 1–9. HIGH LEVEL SOFTWARE: FUNCTIONAL INFORMATION THAT MUST BE CONVERTED INTO STRUCTURAL INFORMATION

The computer programs that constitute the bulk of software do not specify precisely how each memory cell must be adjusted, for the programmers who write these programs do not know enough about the computer's hardware to know how the individual memory cells must be set. The real magic in computer programming lies in the absence of any such structural information in the programs that are written out by humans. Computer programs written out in high-level programming languages such as FORTRAN, BASIC, COBOL, C, and Pascal describe "function," not "structure"—they tell the computer what it is to do, and not how to do it.

Computer programmers are modern-day Aladdins speaking to their magic lamps. Aladdin says, "get me 100 pounds of diamonds, a castle with five turrets, and a beautiful queen." If Aladdin is able to express himself clearly, and if Aladdin and the Genie understand each other, the Genie then knows what "functions" Aladdin wants performed. The Genie must convert the "functional" information spoken by Aladdin into "structural" information describing machines (a carbon-squeezing diamond press, a castle building machine, and a wife snatcher) that can carry out these functions. Next, the Genie creates these machines, and the machines attempt to carry out Aladdin's wishes.

But what if the Genie does not speak Arabic? Then Aladdin, who is an Arabian, gets nothing, since he cannot speak Swahili. But a little Swahili girl can sit down with the Genie and provide the Genie with a Swahili/Arabic dictionary, teaching the Genie to translate Aladdin's

Arabic expressions into Swahili which the Genie does "understand" in some sense of the word. Of course, the wishes may suffer somewhat in the translation process, but now Aladdin can communicate with the Genie.

Digital computers are set up in much the same way. Primitive languages understood only by computer "gurus" actually control most computers, but computer programmers write out their instructions in high-level, English-like languages. These languages are not directly "understandable" to the computer but must be translated, by successive steps, into more and more primitive languages that become more and more functional, and ultimately into the "structural" language that must be loaded directly into the computer's memories to create a special purpose machine custom-designed to carry out the programmer's wishes. Modern digital computers are constructed like onions, with layer upon layer of hardware and software gradually converting an extremely primitive core machine into smarter and smarter machines that come closer and closer to speaking the normal English language of the "user." The layers are each designed by a different team to translate a higher-level language into a more primitive and more structural lower-level language that the next layer down can "understand," or more accurately, can translate into an even more primitive language.

Ultimately, the functional, English-like verbs and commands of the end user and of the programmer are transformed, through successive translations, into a description of how each memory cell must be set to achieve a structure that can carry out the desired function. When the memory cells are set accordingly, a special-purpose machine emerges as if by magic that can carry out the desired function.

"Programmable digital computers" are thus machines constructed from gates and low-level software that can accept high-level, functional instruction information; that can convert this functional instruction information into a new set of information that describes the structure of a machine capable of carrying out the desired functions; and that can then create the machine thus described by feeding the individual "bits" of this structural information into individual memory cells to establish a pattern of signal paths interconnecting the gates.

§ 1–10. THE LAYERS THAT COMPRISE A MODERN DIGITAL COMPUTER

The innermost parts of all digital computers are the transistor gates. Specialists who work for the large logic chip manufacturing companies assemble these gates into large arrays of gates that are called logic chips. These logic chips have names that describe their functions: Memories, latches, and registers store information; gates either pass signals or block their flow; and arithmetic units, constructed entirely from logic gates, can accept numbers represented by electrical signals and generate their sums, differences, products, and quotients, presenting the results as another set of electrical signals. If the transistor gates are thought of as nouns and verbs, these logic chip designers can be visualized as writing out sentences in the language of the transistor gates, with each such sentence becoming a noun or verb in the language of the "hardware" designers who assemble these chips into circuits.

The "hardware designers" are typically electrical engineers. They assemble the logic chip nouns and verbs into "hardware" sentences that create the nouns and verbs of the first true "programming" language: the "microinstruction language." Briefly described, the hardware designers install memory units and arithmetic units on printed circuit cards and connect these elements to "busses" by means of gates. "Busses" are simply sets of wires that run about the computer and connect through gates to all of the computer's various memory elements. By opening and closing the gates, information may be transferred over the buss wires from any memory element to any other memory element. These transfers take place in response to pulses from the computer's master clock. Accordingly, each time the computer's master clock generates a pulse, an information transfer occurs, and the particular transfer that takes place is determined by which gates are open and which are closed.

The signal wires controlling all of the gates are brought back and connected to a small set of memory cells called the "microinstruction" register. After each master clock pulse, a new "microinstruction" is retrieved from memory and is placed into this "microinstruction" register, and the information "bits" in the "microinstruction" are converted into gate control signals that determine which gates are open and which are closed when the next pulse of the master clock occurs. A series of microinstructions can cause the computer to perform an "add" operation; another series of microinstructions can cause it to perform a "subtract" operation; and so on for each operation the computer is capable of performing—fetch, store, test, and all the rest.

The hardware designer thus assembles the logic chip nouns and verbs into hardware sentences that actually define the microinstruction language of the computer—the most primitive of true programming languages, and one most computer programmers never see.

The "microcoders" may know nothing about transistor gates and very little about hardware. They write out the sequences of microinstructions that perform addition, subtraction, fetch, store, and all the other primitive functions of the computer. Each such "microinstruction sentence" is placed into a memory, and the address of the first instruction in each such sentence is stored in a "lookup" memory such that, for example, given the computer's higher-level "ADD" operation, the computer can quickly locate the series of microinstructions that perform the ADD function. The microcoders thus write out sentences in the microcode language that define the nouns and verbs of the true "machine language" or native tongue of the computer.

Most computer programmers consider the "machine language" of a computer to be its lowest-level language. Many programmers are unaware of the more primitive microcode language, and programmers frequently know little or nothing about hardware and logic chips that lie even deeper within the computer's structure. Sociologically, everything from the "machine language" level on down to the transistor gate level falls within the general province of the electrical engineers, while everything from the machine language level on up to the user falls within the domain of the computer scientists. This historical dividing line originated as the "hand-to-desk-calculator" interface in the desk calculators that were displaced by the first computer ever constructed, which was designed to compute range tables for artillery towards the end of World War II. In that first computer, the functions carried out by the fingers on a desk calculator (fetch, store, add, etc.) were implemented entirely in vacuum-tube hardware, while the sequences of adds, fetches, etc. were represented by wires plugged into wiring panels. The wiring panels quickly gave way to "machine languages" in which one or two bytes of information stored in a memory, rather than a wire jumper, indicated whether an add, a store, or a fetch was to be performed next. The "machine language" of most computers is not at all English-like, but it is still today the language that the "guru programmers" use when they program computers for maximum speed and efficiency.

The original "hardware/software" line corresponded to the hand-to-desk-calculator interface. Originally, the adds, subtracts, fetches, and stores were all done with discrete hardware logic units, and these were large, complex logic gate units each of which had to perform multiple steps over an extended period of time. By replacing much of this specialized hardware with stored microcode sequences that causes extremely simple hardware to perform precise sequences of information transfers over time, modern system designers have converted about 90% of what used to be "hardware" into stored microcode software. The small amount of true hardware that remains performs arithmetic and moves data about over wire "busses."

The principle difference between a desktop microcomputer and the largest mainframe computer is how many wires their respective busses contain, and therefore how much information they can move about at one time. Mainframes and desktop microcomputers also differ in how many separate operations they can perform simultaneously in hardware. These two distinctions between mainframe computers and microcomputers will blur to the vanishing point over the next few years as microcomputers become far more complex and powerful. Then you will have to judge the power of a computer by the number and size of its accessories, and not by the speed of its central processing unit.

Very few programmers learn to program in machine language any more. When they do program in machine language, they use words such as "ADD" and "PUSH" which are then machine-translated (by programs called "assemblers") into the true machine language of any given computer. If troubles arise, they use "disassemblers" to translate the machine language back into an English-like form. The only two groups of programmers who still frequently program in machine or assembly language are the "systems programmers" and the "compiler designers."

The "systems programmers" are the gurus that write the "operating systems" without which no computer can be used. The "operating system" is a set of instructions that guides the computer in communicating with the outside world—the keyboards, displays, printers, and external information storage devices such as floppy and fixed disks and tapes. One portion of the operating system, called the "shell," actually forms a shell over the rest of the computer system, protecting the "user" from its complexity. When a user first turns on a computer, the user converses with the "shell." Shells vary in their user-friendliness, with some, such as that found on the Apple Macintosh, being quite friendly and presenting easy-to-use "help" menus to the user. Others, such as the PC–DOS operating system presently found on the IBM PC and the MS–DOS operating system found on IBM–PC twins, require the user to memorize a series of commands and do not provide "help" menus. UNIX is the name of an operating system developed at Bell Laboratories that is coming into widespread use on "multi-user" computers. UNIX is also not very friendly. However, some "unfriendly" systems may give users greater speed and more control, like the 5-speed stick shift in a sports car.

Another portion of the operating system provides services to the programs controlling the computer, giving the programs access to the keyboard, the display, and the floppy and fixed disks. Many programs provide their own "shell" to the user, typically duplicating most of the services provided by the operating system's shell.

The system programmers who design the operating system for a computer assemble the computer's machine language instructions into sentences that define the verbs of the two operating system languages—the "user" language of the shell, and the "programmer" language provided to support the needs of programmers.

The "compiler designers" are specialized programmers who write programs that can translate English-like computer languages, such as FORTRAN, BASIC, COBOL, C, and Pascal, into machine language. These English-like programming languages permit instructions to be written out in what appear to be English-like, hybrid languages that are derived from a mixture of algebra and symbolic logic. For example:

```
ASK "What is the value of x?";
ACCEPT x;
IF x IS GREATER THAN y AND x IS LESS THAN z THEN
   LET w EQUAL x +200;
```

```
    ELSE
        LET w EQUAL x  — 200;
    PRINT w;
```

This very simple program asks the user the question "What is the value of x?" (This question appears upon the viewing screen.) Whatever the user types as an answer is accepted as the value of x by the "ACCEPT x;" step. Next, the value of w is computed to be x plus 200 if x is greater than y and less than z; but if x falls outside this range, then w is computed to be x minus 200. Finally, the value of w is printed on the computer's printer. End of program.

It is clearly far easier to write out instructions for the computer in a language such as this one than to write out instructions in the native machine language of the computer The "compiler" program translates each line of such an English-like program into many machine language instructions. This translation process can take considerable time. The LP program provided with this book, for example, is translated automatically from the high-level language Pascal into the Intel 8088 microprocessor machine language, the native language of the IBM Personal Computer, in about 20 minutes. But the resulting machine-language program is quite fast and efficient. Turbo Pascal (Borland International) is an inexpensive, excellent, fast compiler program that includes a program editor which is compatible with LawWord, the word processor supplied with this book.

Instead of using a "compiler" program to translate a high-level language program into "machine language," some modern systems (most notably those implementing the language "BASIC") provide special machine-language programs on the computer that "read" the high-level language programs directly and then carry out the instructions which they contain. These machine-language programs are called "interpreters." A program "interpreted" in this manner runs more slowly than does the same program "compiled" into native machine language form, but interpreted programs are easier to write and to correct. Microsoft's interpreted BASIC program "BASICA" or "GW–BASIC" which comes with IBM–PC-compatible computers, is a very easy language to learn and use, and it is quite powerful. "True BASIC" (Addison-Wesley) by John Kemeny and Tom Kurtz is a more up-to-date Basic language that provides a better bridge into other modern programming languages for those wishing to learn programming on their home computer. Professor John Kemeny is the originator of the language BASIC.

The systems programmers and the compiler writers provide the nouns and verbs that are used by the "ordinary programmers" to design systems. "Ordinary programmers" are the supposedly arrogant ones that do not bathe and that work from three in the afternoon until four in the morning. These ordinary programmers used to design the final "user interface," and that is why computers traditionally are reputed to be so user-unfriendly. But the trend is towards firing most of these individuals, moving the truly skilled and productive ones into the software houses that design "application packages" such as spreadsheet programs, data base programs, communications programs, and word processing programs. These programs are so flexible that they may be "tailored" to the specific needs of the ultimate end users.

Accordingly, there is now emerging an entirely new profession: the "system tailoring" programmers. Typically quite skilled in the end application for which the computer will be used, these individuals "tailor" more generic programs to the needs of a specific end user or organization. In the practice of law, they can create spreadsheets that can be used for tax planning or for projecting law office income, or they can create data bases especially customized to store the litigation records of a particular lawsuit. There is a need for thousands of such individuals in the legal profession today. In this book, we shall teach you how to set up your own automated client interviewing and document assembling systems, data base systems, spreadsheet systems, and communication systems by "tailoring" general-purpose programs to perform specific tasks.

The final "programmer" is the end user. The "user" actually "programs" the computer every time he or she issues a command. Each user-issued "command" is first translated, by the "system tailoring" programmer, into a command sentence in the language of the generic application program. Each of these commands is then further translated, by the "ordinary programmer," into a high-level programming language sequence (written in COBOL, FORTRAN, or Pascal, for instance) that is translated by the systems programmers and the compiler designers into lengthly native machine-language command sequences. Each machine language command in these sequences is then further broken down or translated into a microcode instruction sequence, and each microcode instruction actuates the hardware logic gates to assemble the computer's transistor gates into signal paths that carry out a single data transfer during a single master clock cycle of the computer. So the single command issued by the user is literally translated, through several steps of translation, into thousands of individual data transfer operations within the computer. The dependance of the "user" upon the skill of the many professionals who designed the numerous layers below becomes quite apparent when the computer is viewed from this perspective.

A computer is like a tree. At the roots lie the transistor gates that support the entire tree. In theory, any system could be designed from these gates without any programming, and ultimately all hardware and software is reducible to a complex interconnection of these gates. That is the sense in which the gates support the whole tree.

Moving further up the tree, one finds the hardware level, where everything the computer can do is defined in terms of hardwired logic chips; the microcode level, where microcode sequences define all the operations the computer can perform; the machine-language level, where all of the computer's possible operations are defined in the computer's native tongue; and finally the operating system and high-level programming language level, where all the operations the computer can carry out are defined in the syntax of an English-like language. Each of these levels supports the entire tree above itself. Note that all the upper portions of the tree are supported by the high-level programming-language level. Everything the computer can do must be expressable at this level, either directly or with the help of lower-level operating system support. So the tree rests entirely upon this level just as much as it does upon the transistor gate level at the roots and the machine-language level near the base.

Above the high-level programming language level, the tree begins to branch out widely into the various disciplines. "Tailoring" types of programming are carried out at these levels, but the languages used tend to be specific to the various professional domains. Here we have left the domain of the computer scientist and entered the domain of the business man, engineer, social scientist, librarian, attorney, doctor, and "video game freak," just to name a few. System design at these high levels requires intimate knowledge of the target professional user's problems, needs, and vocabulary. For example, you will find nothing specific about designing business payroll systems in a computer science department library; for that knowledge, you must visit the business school library. An engineering system may perform the same computations as a statistician's system, but the languages used by the two professionals are so different that neither could use a system designed for the other without considerable retraining. More and more "profession-specific" systems are emerging as time passes. You can see why it is absurd to talk of a "computer expert" without specifying in precisely what part of the tree you expect the expert's expertise to reside. There is no such thing as a computer expert who knows his or her way around the entire tree.

"Computer literacy" is defined by the public schools to mean being able to "program" some computer in a language such as BASIC. We disagree with the premise that "programming" and "computer literacy" are synonymous. Learning how to program is analogous to learning how to lay bricks. A master mason knows everything there is to know about bricklaying and is a highly respected craftsman—but could he design a cathedral? Almost certainly not, since he has insufficient training in engineering and architecture. Likewise, mastering a computer programming language such as BASIC and then calling yourself "computer-literate" is analogous to studying the rings in a slice of a tall tree and then claiming that you know all there is to know about trees. Programming is merely a means to an "end" which the programmers may not be able to understand. The "end" lies in the user languages that are found in the upper portions of the tree. "Computer literacy" means speaking the "user" languages that must be mastered by all the members of your profession.

§ 1-11. COMPUTER LITERACY FOR LAWYERS

Just as it is an impossible task to learn to read and write all the languages of the world, so it is impossible to learn all the specialized "languages" that are used for communication between people and computers. The problem of learning foreign languages is not merely one of learning grammar and vocabulary. Each language incorporates the history and customs of the people that speak it. Just as fluent communication in Japanese requires deep knowledge of Japanese tradition, so use, for instance, of a computer-aided drafting system, requires knowledge of engineering design principles. In this book we shall deal with systems designed for use by lawyers, systems that assume the kind of background that lawyers have or should have. For instance, use of a document drafting system assumes a great deal of knowledge of what the final appearance of a formal written document should be—something you suffered through years of high school English and wrote dozens of term papers to learn. In addition, it requires a much smaller amount of knowledge about how computers can assist in drafting documents. Use of a spreadsheet system to calculate taxes assumes knowledge of tax law and of the basic principles of accounting and the rules of arithmetic. It also requires learning a few things about how spreadsheets work—an infinitely easier task than learning grade school arithmetic or mastering the Internal Revenue Code. Use of a legal database system requires extensive knowledge of how information is organized in cases, statutes, and administrative regulations, plus a little knowledge of how computers maintain data bases. The chapters that follow will assume you have had a college education and a basic introduction to the law, and will attempt to impart whatever additional knowledge is necessary for you to communicate efficiently with the types of computer systems used in law firms. Our goal is to familiarize you with many ways in which digital computers are revolutionizing our profession now and will be changing it in the next decade. Our hope is to make you a leader in the ongoing automation of our profession.

§ 1-12. PROBLEMS

1. Assume that you are representing the purchaser of a computer system. In the contract, how are you going to define when "acceptance" takes place so as to protect your client's interests in case the system proves to be inoperative?

2. At trial, the other side is attempting to introduce, under the "business records" exception to the "hearsay" evidence rule, a computer printout purporting to show that your client owes them money. How do you attack its credibility?

Chapter 2

LEGAL WRITING—DRAFTING—DOCUMENT MANAGING

§ 2–1. INTRODUCTION

Humans may communicate by gestures, speech, or writing. Why have lawyers relied to a large extent on written communication? Consider, as an example, the history of formalities for conveying title to land. Early means of conveyancing such as oral grants and livery of seisin by symbolic transfer of a twig did not provide sufficient evidence that a transaction had taken place and were unsuited for complex transactions. Hundreds of years ago we adopted a system in which interests in land were transferred by formal written instruments, copies of which were retained in public record offices. On the other hand, in some situations, oral presentation, accompanied by appropriate gestures, is clearly better than written presentation, or a necessary supplement to it. This is why we have oral summations by counsel to juries and oral argument in appellate cases. Can computers help lawyers to achieve the advantages of written presentation in a more efficient manner? Can computer approaches provide a substitute for some types of presentation of information for which non-written communication is now the custom?

To determine the appropriate role for computers in the preparation of written documents, we must first consider in detail the purposes for having these documents in writing. Generally, as compared to oral presentation, writing is better suited to the making of revisions in the process of composition. Writing once had three other advantages over oral presentation. It was better suited for creation of a permanent record, it could easily be consulted by different persons at different places at different times, and long written documents could easily be accessed at any point. Now, however, these advantages have largely been lost because of the development of videotapes and videodisks.

§ 2-2. FUNDAMENTAL WRITING AND REVISION FUNCTIONS

In a traditional law office both the lawyer and the secretary have important roles in the writing and revision process. The computer plays some parts of these roles, and alters and shifts responsibility for the remaining parts of the roles. Consider the basic functions involved in writing and revision of a document: outlining; recording text; copying, moving, and deleting text; formating; proofreading; and indexing.

(a) Outlining

Computers cannot create the outline for a brief that has not yet been written. However computers can aid a lawyer substantially in the organization and presentation of material. Outlining software such as Word (Microsoft) and Framework (Ashton-Tate) facilitates the use of a "top-down" style of writing. The user can create a basic outline form and then fill in sub-outlines, sub-sub-outlines, and actual text, while having the ability to move easily with a couple of keypresses from one level to another. The computer plays the role of clerical assistant and of disciplinarian (like the high school English teacher who requires students to turn in an outline before starting a term paper). The writer still has great flexibility to change the outline and to move various size pieces of text with their accompanying outline headings from place to place. The computer also can take charge of the chores of keeping section and subsection number and letter designators straight, renumbering automatically as changes are made. Ideally, the outline ultimately becomes fleshed out into the final written product.

(b) Recording Text

Some process must be used to convert thoughts in the lawyer's mind into words that can be processed by the secretary or read by others. In the non-computerized law office, one of three modes is usually used to make a record of these thoughts: dictation to a dictating machine (or to a secretary), writing in longhand (traditionally in pencil on a yellow legal pad), or typing a rough draft on a typewriter (a favorite practice of younger lawyers).

The introduction of the computer substantially changes the costs and benefits of the various modes of introducing information. At the present stage of technology, dictated or handwritten information must be typed by a secretary into a computer before it can be processed. At least two companies, Kurzweil and IBM, are engaged in serious research on the development of a word processor that would take input by dictation. It seems unlikely that a commercial product will be marketed in the foreseeable future that can read lawyers' handwritten drafts. Text neatly typed by a lawyer can be read directly into a word processor by an optical character reader costing under $5000. Thus for the present the lawyer has the following choices of ways of getting thoughts into a word processor:

(1) Dictating and having a secretary transcribe;

(2) Handwriting and having a secretary transcribe;

(3) Typing and having a secretary retype;

(4) Typing neatly and having the typewritten pages read in by an optical character reader;

(5) Typing directly into the word processor.

Because many young lawyers find that typing into a word processor is faster and easier than any of the first four alternatives, we may expect an increasing demand by lawyers for the possibility to type directly into their own word processing work stations.

(c) Copying, Moving, and Deleting Text

A third function is that of copying, moving, and deleting text. Here the standard approach involves scissors, paste, and the office copying machine. Usually the lawyer does the scissoring and pasting and the secretary does the copying. Often this involves a break in the lawyer's train of thought, due to the wait for the secretary to use a central copying facility. Another source of delay is obtaining the necessary law books from the law library so that relevant passages may be copied into legal documents. The computer offers a much faster solution to these problems. Text in a word processor can easily be moved or copied. Quotations from cases and statutes in a data retrieval system such as WESTLAW or LEXIS can be saved during a search and then incorporated into a word processing document. Warning: text in a word processor can also easily be deleted. Be sure your office has a formal procedure for making backup copies.

(d) Formating Text

The formating of text in a non-computerized law office involves both the lawyer and the secretary. The lawyer usually indicates headings for sections of text and paragraphs and indented quotations. The secretary usually decides where lines will end, where to hyphenate, where pages will end, how wide to make the lines, and how far to indent. The choice of headings for text and the breakdown of text into paragraphs requires the judgment of a human who knows the subject matter of the text; the computer cannot replace the lawyer in this judgment.

The details of text formating usually handled by the secretary can be highly automated by a word processor. The word processor will automatically calculate when a word would run over the end of a line and will thus determine when to end a line. Automatic hyphenation is also possible, though most of the present generation of word processors offer only semi-automated hyphenation. Choosing page breaks can also be done in an automated or computer-assisted manner. Line width and tabs can be set and altered easily with computer assistance.

A secretary typing on an ordinary typewriter will be alerted by a bell when it is time to make a decision involving the end of a line. (On a typewriter, a bell rings automatically when typing is about ten spaces before the right margin.) At this point the decision the secretary must make depends upon what was just typed. If the secretary is in the middle of a word, the word must be completed, erased, or hyphenated. If the secretary has just typed a space or a punctuation symbol, the secretary must decide whether to start a new word or to press the "RETURN" key to start a new line. If the secretary decides to hyphenate, and is not sure where to hyphenate, the word must be looked up in a dictionary.

All these operations can be done better and quicker by a computer. If hyphenation is not desired, it is a simple matter for the computer to wait until a word is typed that extends beyond the end of the line and then to move that word to begin the next line. All decent word processors perform this operation automatically. The result is an effective increase of about 10% in typing speed. If the lawyer types text directly into the word processor, this operation will have been performed by the time the secretary receives the text.

Hyphenation is more complicated. The basic rule in English is that a word may be hyphenated at the end of a syllable, but that unaesthetic hyphenation should be avoided. (Aesthetics preclude hyphenating "electricity" after the initial "e" or just before the final "y", even though these constitute separate syllables in the spoken word. The hyphenation of "figurine" presents problems of aesthetic semantics.) Computers have difficulty both with syllabification and aesthetics. A computerized hyphenation system usually involves a set of formal rules for hyphenation and a table showing hyphenation for all commonly-used words whose hyphenation is an exception to the rules. When a word is to be hyphenated, the computer looks up the word in the table of exceptions, and if it does not find it there, hyphenates it according to the rules. This type of system requires a considerable amount of computer memory, and in the past has mainly been used on expensive typesetting systems rather than office word processors. With the dramatic decline in the cost of computer memory, fully automatic hyphenation is becoming available on ordinary word processors. However, most word processors today do not offer automatic hyphenation, but rather the inferior alternative of semiautomatic hyphenation. With semiautomatic hyphenation, the computer goes line by line through the text. If a word extends over the end of the line, a letter in the word is highlighted. It is then the responsibility of the secretary to use "arrow keys" to move the highlight to the place at which the word should be hyphenated and then to press a special key to indicate that the hyphenation place has been selected. If the secretary is not sure about hyphenation, the word will have to be looked up by hand in a dictionary. This process is time-consuming. If for some reason, a decision is made to print a document with wider or narrower margins, or to move the hyphenated document to another document, the whole tedious process must be performed over again. The moral: if you can get automatic hyphenation, you will save a lot of secretarial time.

Hyphenation is further complicated by "hard hyphens" and "soft hyphens." Consider the words "half-moon" and "halfway." "Halfway" is only hyphenated at the end of a line. When hyphenated in this manner, it is said to have a "soft hyphen." "Half-moon" is always hyphenated; in word-processing terminology, it is said to have a "hard hyphen." If it becomes necessary to reformat text to reestablish compact paragraphs and pages after additions and deletions have been made, the word processor must be able to distinguish "hard" hyphens from "soft" hyphens, since only "hard" hyphens should survive the reformating process. Usually this is done by having the secretary use different keys for entering "hard" and "soft" hyphens, and by using different codes for storing them internally in the computer.

In a non-automated law office, the problem of where to end a page is decided by the secretary typing a document. In an automated office, the ending point for pages may be decided automatically by the computer or semiautomatically by the computer in cooperation with the secretary. Obviously there is a physical limit to the number of lines that can fit on a page. However it would not do to merely end pages exactly at this physical limit. In word-processing jargon, the problem is called "widows and orphans." If ending page 9 at the last possible line will leave only one line on page 10, that line will become an "orphan" and page 10 will be unaesthetic. Nor would one want to put a major heading at the bottom of one page and start the text corresponding to the heading at the top of the next page, leaving the heading as a "widow" on the preceding page.

Fully automatic page break systems exist both in unsophisticated and sophisticated forms. The unsophisticated automatic page break systems merely print the maximum possible number of lines on each page. This approach may be adequate for rough drafts, but is clearly unacceptable for finished products. The more sophisticated form checks for "widows and orphans" and takes appropriate corrective action.

Semiautomatic page break systems assist the user in applying aesthetic judgment to determining page break locations. They take the user to the approximate bottom of each page, and then let the user adjust the bottom for the best appearance. These are more time consuming than fully automatic page break systems, but they guarantee an output that is as good as the artistic ability of the user.

Whatever the page break system used, it will have to be rerun if any text is added to or subtracted from the document or if the margins of the document are changed. Any of these actions will affect where the page breaks fall, and lead to bizarre printouts if page breaks are not readjusted. Even correcting spelling errors may require repagination, since a new spelling that lengthens a word may cause a line to lap over the permissible page length.

(e) Proofreading

In a non-automated law office a secretary is responsible for checking spelling. The secretary should check in a dictionary whenever a word is encountered whose spelling is in doubt. Final copy should be carefully proofread to be sure that words have not been misspelled due to typing errors. The problem is that a secretary may not recognize a doubtful spelling, or may overlook a typing error while proofreading. Even the most competent secretary will waste a lot of time looking in dictionaries and proofreading for typing errors. For these reasons, most word processing programs incorporate spelling checkers. Spelling checkers typically include a dictionary of correctly spelled words. Generally, the larger the dictionary the better. Some word processors offer a supplemental dictionary of legal terms. In addition, the user often is allowed to provide a supplemental list of frequently used words not in the spelling checker's dictionary. A good spelling checker is far faster than a human proofreader and will catch many errors that humans miss. However, it will not catch typing errors that result in changing one word into another word in the dictionary. If a secretary accidentally types "too" as "two," the spelling checker will not catch the mistake. Perhaps someday in the future programs endowed with artificial intelligence will be able to catch such errors.

Every spelling checker must provide for interaction with a human. The human must provide correct spellings for misspelled words and must overrule the spelling checker when a correctly spelled word (for instance a proper name) is rejected because it is not in the dictionary. Systems for interaction with the spelling checker vary. Some are much more convenient than others. The least convenient system is one in which the document is analyzed by the spelling checker and the user is presented with a list of doubtful words to either correct or accept. The problem is that out of context it is often impossible to know what word was meant by a particular misspelling. Thus, for instance, "goed" could be a misspelling for "good" or for "goad" or for "hoed." Better spelling checkers either alert the typist with a beep as soon as a doubtful word is typed or present the words for correction in context. A useful strategy with spelling checkers that present words out of context is to add an exotic combination of letters (such as "qq") to the end of each unrecognizable misspelled word. Then the document can be reentered and automatic computer search facilities can be used to find all words containing "qq." At this point, these words can be corrected in context.

Even if it is clear what word was meant to be typed, the secretary may have to resort to a dictionary to find the correct spelling. The better spelling checkers will display on the screen the closest words in spelling from their dictionaries, so as to speed up this task.

Programs are beginning to appear that purport to check for grammatical errors, stylistic infelicities, and readability levels. With the growth of application of artificial intelligence techniques in the next few years, one may expect to see more such software becoming available. Because of the complexity of grammatical analysis by computer, it will be some time until a really useful program for correcting grammatical errors are available. (The authors know of no program commercially sold for office use that would detect and fix the error in the previous sentence.) Stylistic analysis is easier, because a number of aspects of bad style can be defined with enough specificity to be incorporated into a computer program. These include frequent use of cliches, excessive use of the passive voice, and excessive repetition of the same word. It may be dangerous to use a general purpose style program on legal texts, since there are differences between literary and legal style. In a legal document, the same word should always be used for the same concept, no matter how many times the concept is mentioned in the document. The same is not true in a poem. Various readability tests have been devised depending upon objective tests such as use of vocabulary not on an approved list of simple words, upon percentage of long words in a text, or upon length of sentences. These readability tests are important for lawyers because legislation in a number of states requires documents, such as homeowner's insurance policies, that affect the rights of the general public to meet certain readability criteria. Because the readability tests depend upon objective factors, the tests have proved easy to convert into computer programs.

(f) Indexing

Computers can create or assist in creation of indexes to documents. If the lawyer will be satisfied with an index that is in effect a concordance or a list of words used in their context, the indexing can be fully automatic. On the other hand, if the lawyer wants a concept-based index, the computer can only serve as an aid for alphabetizing and formating references to various concepts, while the information as to which concepts are considered on which pages of the text must be supplied by a human indexer.

§ 2-3. OUTPUT FORM AND QUALITY

Before the invention of the typewriter, at a time when labor was cheap, legal documents were beautifully lettered by scriveners—consider, for instance, the appearance of the Declaration of Independence. The economy of typing and improved legibility of typed text rapidly led to the substitution of typed for handwritten output, despite some loss of elegance. Gradually over the years the quality of typing improved, reaching its peak with the IBM Selectric series, which became the standard for law offices. Because the excellent quality available from

IBM Selectric and equivalent electric typewriters did not cost significantly more than poorer quality from other typewriters, the others were forced out of the law office market.

Computers are bringing both long term and short term changes in output quality. In the long run, the issue of output quality is being transferred from the producer to the user of documents, as more and more documents are created and stored as electronic data, and only displayed or printed out by the user as they need to be read. Thus while at present a law firm must provide documents of sufficient quality to be legally acceptable to government agencies where they are filed and to be aesthetically pleasing to clients, in the future government officials and clients will have to decide the quality of display and printout they desire when viewing electronic mail sent to them by law firms. While this trend toward shifting responsibility seems inevitable, the actual technology used is changing rapidly.

At present word processing terminology recognizes five grades of quality for printed output: draft, correspondence, near-letter, letter, and typeset quality. Draft quality is the cheapest and fastest to print, but the worst looking. Correspondence quality is adequate for internal memoranda within an organization and for documents filed for purely formal purposes and not seen by clients. Letter quality is slower and more expensive to print, but better looking. It is the minimum quality that a law firm would dare to present to a client. Typeset quality is required for briefs submitted to some courts and certain government agency filings. If it were not for the factors of cost and time, everyone would want to use letter or typeset quality for all purposes. New technological developments, such as the laser printer and the high-density dot matrix printer, are bringing word processing close to the day when letter and even typeset quality are so close in speed and price to correspondence and draft quality that these inferior modes will be forced out of the law office. The wider availability of typeset quality will create new choices for the lawyer and the secretary, who will have to select from a large variety of typefaces and sizes for the document.

There are three main differences between letter-quality and typeset text. Typeset text is almost always "justified" (with the right margins lined up). Letter quality may have "ragged" right edges. Typeset text is "proportionally spaced" (with more space for wide letters like "w" than for narrow letters like "i"), while letter quality may have equal spaces for all letters. Typeset text uses a variety of type sizes and styles. Headings may be in large boldface, for instance, text in normal type, citations in italics, and footnote numbers in small raised type.

At present, office word processing is in a state of transition between letter and typeset quality. The driving force for letter quality has been the desire to achieve the familiar output quality of the IBM Selectric typewriter. An exotic factor behind the move towards typeset quality is the demand of the Japanese market for screens with sufficient resolution to display and printers with sufficient resolution to print the intricate characters used in the Japanese language.

Systems providing full typeset quality at present are quite expensive, and are only owned by large law firms that have to do a lot of filing of typeset documents. This situation is changing rapidly, however, with the appearance of cheap, high-resolution laser printers. While the first generation of laser printers has fallen short of true typeset quality, a new generation should soon arrive at reasonable prices with this quality. A second requirement for word processing systems to produce typeset quality output is a display screen with high enough resolution and accompanying software, so that the user can preview what will be printed. Such displays and software are still expensive, but their cost, too, is falling.

§ 2-4. SEARCH CAPABILITIES

A great advantage of having text in a computer is that the computer can search for particular words or phrases. The search capability can be useful in retrieving a particular part of a document and also in finding and replacing a particular word or phrase throughout a document. Unfortunately, no word processor at present has the powerful search capabilities of a system like WESTLAW. As will be explained elsewhere, separate software packages are available that have a very powerful logical search capability. This software only allows finding and copying text—it does not allow editing text. However, because the typical word processing document is much shorter than, say, the file of all United States Supreme Court cases, the weaker search powers of the word processor are usually quite adequate.

The details of finding (or finding and replacing) text are explained in the respective word processor manuals. There are dangers in the "find" and the "find and replace" commands that are not always clearly indicated in the manuals. Potential problems involve both finding too much and finding too little. In the short documents used for word processing, if you are just searching for passages that contain particular words, finding too much is usually not serious. In the huge files used on legal retrieval systems, on the other hand, a poorly-drawn search request can retrieve thousands of unwanted passages. Finding too much is dangerous in word processing, however, when using the automatic "search and replace" command. This command replaces all instances of one string of text with another throughout the document. The danger is that unwanted replacements will occur. If, for instance, the computer is commanded to change all instances of "lease" to "sale", it will also change "please" to "psale". Careful use of special commands designed to allow distinguishing between searches for words and for parts of words will often solve these problems. Another defense is a spelling check done after the final search and replace alterations. Such a check would reveal "psale" as a misspelled word. The safest, though slowest course, is to use the command that makes the computer stop and check just before making each replacement to be sure that the user wants to make the change. If the user can remain alert through this process, all danger of making unwanted changes can be avoided. A related danger is failing to find every instance of what one is seeking. A search for "purchaser" may fail to find "Purchaser" at the start of a sentence unless the computer is instructed to treat capital and lower case letters as equivalent. A search for "purchaser" will also fail to find "purchased" and "purchasing", unless the computer is specially instructed to search for "purchas" followed by any two or three characters. However, the user should bear in mind that the broader the search command used, the greater the risk of finding (or finding and replacing) in unintended ways.

§ 2–5. THE TEXT WINDOW

A serious drawback of handling documents by computer is the limited quantity of text that can be viewed at any one time. If a document is typed on paper the number of pages that can be in view at any one time is limited only by the size of the lawyer's desk. When a lawyer is hard at work on a project, it is not unusual to find various documents spread out and books open on the lawyer's desk. The present generation of computer screens shows only 24 or 25 lines of 80 characters each. A few word processors have screens that can show 60 or 70 lines of text, allowing display of a full typewritten page. The ultimate answer is a much larger display or an array of smaller displays. Meanwhile the user of word processing must learn a variety of techniques to cope with the gross inadequacy of the display.

From ancient papyri to modern microfilms, documents have been kept on scrolls. A similar technique is used by word processors. Imagine a 30-page long typed contract, with the bottom of page 1 taped to the top of page 2, the bottom of page two taped to the top of page 3, and so forth. Then imagine winding the top and bottom of the resulting scroll around rollers and spreading the rollers only far enough apart so that 24 lines of the document could be seen at once. (Only 12 lines if the document is double-spaced.) This is the way most word processors work. Most have commands corresponding to rotating the rollers—go up a line, go down a line, go up a screenfull of text, go down a screenfull of text, go up a page, go down a page. All have search commands that allow the user to move automatically to a page containing specific text. Some allow marking particular points on the text, so that the user can return to them. Even with all these commands, finding particular parts of a text in a word processor is a frustrating process compared to consulting a paper typed copy of the same document. The process can be even more frustrating if the word processor is one that is slow to move from point to point in the text. Word processors that can display an "outline" of a document which may be "opened up" to present an editable view of the underlying text will simplify the task of creating and revising such a document.

§ 2-6. CONVERSION OF DOCUMENTS PRODUCED BY ONE WORD PROCESSOR FOR USE ON ANOTHER

There is not yet any standard format for documents produced by word processor. Rather each brand of word processor places different special characters in stored documents to indicate start of paragraph, underline, indentations, spacing, and dozens of other characteristics of the document. Increasingly often it is necessary to load a document written on one word processing system onto another. This may occur, for instance, when a law firm changes brands of word processors, if two law firms with different word processors are cooperating on a case, or if a single law firm has different brands of computers in its offices or in use by its attorneys at home. In the long run the solution may be the creation of a standard format for interchange of information. This could be done either by agreement among word processor companies or by the usual method of standardization in the computer industry—everyone copying what IBM does. (An IBM standard for interchange does exist.) Then each word processor could offer an updated version that would have the capability of producing files in the standard format as well as whatever format it used for its own internal purposes. However, until this ideal situation is reached, lawyers must make do with a number of less-than-perfect approaches. There are a number of companies which for a fee will convert files from almost any word processor to almost any other. Their services are particularly appropriate if a law firm is changing over to a new brand of word processor or standardizing on a single brand and thus has a large number of files to convert. Software that will do a good conversion job between leading brands of word processors is included with some word processors and is also available from independent companies. The standard format method, the use of a conversion service, or the use of conversion software, will allow the preservation of all, or almost all of the paragraphing, indenting, underlining, tabbing, and other detailed format data.

If none of these methods is available, the lawyer must rely on a method that will lose much of the formating data. There are at least three such inferior methods. Most word processors have an option that allows creation and reading of plain text files (often called ASCII text files—see the Chapter 5 below for an explanation of the mysteries of ASCII). Such files lack special formating characters and will require considerable hand editing once they are read into another brand of word processor. Another possibility is transfer of a file over a communications line. Many word processing systems have provisions for such transfer (See Chapter 5 for details of communications procedures). However, once again, the special formating characters will be lost, so that the text as received will require hand editing for transfers between different brands of word processors. Finally, it is possible to print out a typed copy of the text to be transferred and then read it back in through an optical character reader connected to another computer. This method involves the fewest compatibility problems, since almost all word processors can print in standard fonts such as Prestige Elite, and almost all optical character readers can recognize these standard fonts. However, it usually produces the worst results in terms of the quality of the text read in and the time taken to read it.

§ 2-7. WORD PROCESSOR SPEED

Word processors vary surprisingly in the speed with which they perform various operations. Speed depends upon the skill with which the word processor is written, the hardware on which the word processor is used, and the way in which the software uses the hardware. For example, a review of word processors for the IBM Personal Computer reported that one word processor took 11 minutes for a simple reformating task that another accomplished in 15 seconds. Phil Wiswell, "Word Processing: The Last Word," *PC Magazine,* Aug. 20, 1985, p. 110. The slowest aspect of operation of most word processors is retrieving information from and storing it on a floppy disk. There are a number of methods of avoiding access to a floppy disk. The first is to buy a system with a hard disk. Hard disks generally have much faster access time than floppy disks. This is particularly true of systems with high-capacity centralized hard disks. Even faster are systems that store all information in "RAM" (the internal semiconductor memory of the computer), and write it out to disk only occasionally for protection in case of power failure and for storage after the session is over. A dramatic improvement in performance may be obtained by configuring a personal computer system with a large amount of RAM. Some word processor software is smart enough to detect the presence of additional RAM and to use it to increase processing efficiency. Other software must be fooled into thinking that the extra RAM is really a large floppy disk. Software for this purpose is supplied with many personal computers that have large quantities of RAM.

§ 2-8. THE KEYBOARD

One of the most common mistakes in choosing word processing hardware is to fail to appreciate the importance of a good keyboard. There are a wide variety of features to bear in mind in evaluating a keyboard. These include the feel of the keys, the layout of the keys, the number of keys, and how the keycaps are labeled. Most typists prefer a keyboard that gives a solid "click" feeling when keys are pressed, as opposed to one that feels "mushy." Unfortunately, it is expensive to make keyboards that have a solid feeling and maintain that feeling even with heavy usage. Therefore quite a few computer and word processor manufacturers have tried to cut corners by using less than a top quality keyboard. The best test is for a good secretary to type for 10 minutes on a well-used machine of a particular brand. The keys should be laid out so they can be reached easily. While the keyboard of the original IBM Personal Computer had an excellent "feel", the key layout, particularly the location of the SHIFT keys, was felt to be inconvenient by many. Competition forced IBM to offer an improved keyboard configuration.

The next question to consider is the number of keys. Up to some fairly high limit, more is better. The problem is remembering what all the extra keys do. Various approaches are used by hardware and software manufacturers to aid with the memory problem. Easiest to use are keyboards where each key is labeled with the name of its function, *e.g.* "search," "move," "copy." Unfortunately, because different programs have different functions, standardization is not possible. Thus the use of such keyboards is generally limited to dedicated word processors, though a few special word processing keyboards are available for general purpose personal computers. A compromise approach is found in the widely-used IBM Personal Computer keyboard. At the far left are 10 "function" keys labeled F1 through F10. (This location is somewhat inconvenient. Other IBM models and keyboards by other manufacturers often put these "function" keys at the top of the keyboard, where they can be reached without completely removing a hand from the "home" position.) The problem with the function keys is that their labels are not meaningful, so that the user is burdened with trying to remember 10 different uses for these keys for each program. There are several solutions to this problem. One is to use the bottom line of the video screen for a reminder of what the function keys do. The second is to place a paper, cardboard, or plastic template around the keys with notes as to what they do. The third is to have a set of stickers that go on the fronts of the keys and say what they do. The template or sticker solution works well for an individual program. It is a nuisance if you have to change programs. (The template is easy to remove and easy to lose; the stickers are usually destroyed by attempts to remove them.)

§ 2-9. PROBLEMS

1. Learn how to use all the important features of a word processor. Write your next moot court brief or term paper on a word processor.

2. How does this word processor deal with the problems of outlining, spelling, page breaks, *etc.*, mentioned in this chapter?

3. Transfer text written on one word processor to another word processor.

Chapter 3

COMPUTERS IN LEGAL RESEARCH

§ 3-1. INTRODUCTION: DATA BASES AND DATA DELIVERY SYSTEMS

When computers in legal research are mentioned, the first thing that comes to most lawyers' minds is the use of WESTLAW, LEXIS, and similar systems for research in court opinions. However, this chapter will take a much broader view of computers in legal research, and will approach the topic from a functional point of view, looking at both systems outside a law firm, such as WESTLAW and LEXIS, and systems inside a firm, such as personal research notecard and evidence management (or "litigation support") data bases.

For the purposes of this chapter, the following definitions will be used. A "data base" is a collection of information that is useful to an attorney. Examples include the collected decisions of the Supreme Court of the United States; all documents recorded with the Alpine County, California, Recorder of Deeds; all depositions taken in the case of Jones v. Smith; selected articles on partnership taxation; and an index to legal periodical literature. A "data delivery system" is a computer that contains a data base and optionally is attached to a network that provides users with access to the data base. Examples are WESTLAW and LEXIS, which provide access to data bases of court decisions, federal legislation, and law review articles; DIALOG, which provides access to collections of hundreds of data bases including trademarks and patent abstracts; the Georgia Legislative Information System which provides access to bill status information; and a law firm's computer system which provides access to depositions. The delivery system may be public—happy to provide access to anyone who pays the fees, or it may be private—for the exclusive use of a particular government agency or law firm.

A data delivery system includes a "data base" and "data base access software," and may also include "data base creation software." "Data base access software" makes it possible for the data base user to interact with the delivery system. Thus, for instance, the ways in which a user interacts with WESTLAW and with DIALOG are quite different, because their respective access software uses quite different sets of user commands, even though in some instances they may contain the same data. "Data base creation software" is used to turn raw data into a useful data base. It performs such tasks as facilitating data entry, adding indexing terms to data, and creating files, indices, concordances, and directories to aid the computer in speedily processing future access requests.

§ 3-2. DATA DELIVERY SYSTEMS

Data delivery systems store data bases and data base access software and provide a means for user interaction with the data bases. Many variations are possible both in the hardware and software used to perform these functions and in the legal arrangements that must be established between users and delivery system owners.

Every data delivery system requires some form of storage for data, some means of transmitting the stored data to the user, and some way for the user to interact with the system. As an example, consider the WESTLAW data delivery system. Data is stored at a single location, at West's headquarters in St. Paul, Minnesota. A variety of transmission media are used. These include direct wires to terminals for West staff members, leased long distance data lines, ordinary dial up telephone lines, the Telenet and Tymnet public data networks, and the Westnet private data network. User interaction with the data delivery system may be initiated from a computer terminal or from a personal computer running a special WESTLAW access program. A very different example would be a data base of depositions for litigation support, maintained on the mass storage system of a law firm's own computer and accessible only through that computer's keyboard and display. The complex hardware structure of the WESTLAW system illustrates how commercial pressures have forced WESTLAW and other public data delivery systems to accommodate a variety of terminal systems and user hardware and software configurations to expand the number of potential customers who can physically gain access to the data base.

(a) Single Location vs. Multiple Location Data Base Storage

One important variation in data base systems involves where data is stored. Storage at a single location has major advantages in terms of simplifying the maintenance of the data base, protecting confidential information in the data base, and facilitating differential charging for data base use. Storage at multiple locations, for instance at users' sites, has the advantages of reducing communications costs and eliminating communications delays. Today, data meant for a single user—an individual law firm's deposition file in a particular case, or a bill status information for a particular legislative body—is usually stored on a computer at the place where it is to be used. In some cases it is stored on a remote computer because the organization that owns the remote computer has better data base creation and access software. Data bases meant for many users, for instance the data bases in WESTLAW and LEXIS, are typically stored at a central location, with access provided by communications lines extending to the users' workstations.

In the past the physical size of a data base has been a major limitation on storage of multiple copies at different locations. The high cost of storage media has made it necessary to spread the storage costs among many users. No law firm would want to match the millions of dollars the major legal data retrieval systems have spent on computer storage equipment. To date, these storage expenses have far exceeded the costs, both in money and in reduced performance, of forcing the users to access the data base from remote workstations over communications lines. However, recent technological developments, such as inexpensive optical storage disks having huge storage capacities, are greatly increasing the size of data bases for which local storage is a reasonable option. (Chapter 7 of this book—§ 7–2(e)—contains a detailed discussion of the increases in capacity and decreases in prices of computer storage that may be expected in the next few years.) At the same time, other technological advances, such as much faster, error-free methods of communicating (See Chapter 5 § 5–6(c)) are reducing some of the disadvantages of remote storage. At present, the speed (or rather the slowness) of communications with a remote computer is such that it takes about 10 seconds to receive a screenful of text. This slow speed is particularly annoying to lawyers, who at present cannot browse on a screen nearly as fast as they can browse through a book. New technologies will increase the speed of transfer of information to the point where a screenful of data can be transferred in one second, with a consequent increase in user satisfaction and reduction in telephone bills.

While the falling cost of storage capacity and the slowness of remote communications are already making local storage at the user's site the best choice for single-user data bases, the problem is much more complex with multiple-user data bases. The managers of such data bases must consider the effects of any decision to move to local storage upon both their ability to maintain their data base and their ability to use a profitable pricing scheme. In areas such as law where there is competition between data base delivery systems, users expect very rapid updating of data bases. For instance, they would be quite annoyed if a Supreme Court decision handed down on Monday was not available in a data base by Friday, and would naturally prefer a system that made the decision available by Tuesday. Such rapid updating is difficult but possible with a centralized data base. It would be more difficult to achieve if there were numerous remote copies of the data base. One could imagine a mixed system, with older materials stored locally and current materials stored centrally. Alternatively, one could imagine an automated update system, with nightly transmission of updating information to remote computers. The complexities of such systems could well outweigh any advantages of local storage. But imagine your office computer being updated through a TV channel broadcast of the latest cases at 3:00 a.m. Such a system could easily broadcast five cases per second to 30,000 attorneys simultaneously in a city such as Chicago.

Effective recovery of costs may be more difficult with local storage. Delivery systems with centralized data bases generally have a basic charge for time connected to the system, plus an additional charge for time connected to particular data bases, a charge which may vary from data base to data base. Usually charges are lower during off peak hours (to even out the load on the system) and often charges are lower for educational institutions (to "sell" the system to students who will be future professional users). With local storage, it will be much harder to control who is using a data system and when, and thus will be much harder to maintain a system of differentiated charges for data system use.

(b) Minimizing Communications Costs

Once a data delivery system has made the decision to serve many users from a single location, it needs to consider how communications costs can be minimized for such users. The normal method for such cost minimization is the use of a national computer data network, either one created by the data delivery system itself, or a public "packet switching" network such as Telenet or Tymnet.

(c) Specific Data Delivery Systems

There are a large number of public data delivery systems of interest to lawyers. The reader is undoubtedly familiar with WESTLAW, VERALEX and LEXIS, systems that deliver data from data bases of cases, statutes, regulations, law review articles, and other legal materials. But there are also many additional data delivery systems available to lawyers. These include large systems that distribute numerous data bases such as DIALOG, BRS, NEXIS, and SDC. They also include large numbers of systems delivering a single data base each, such as state legislative information systems, and specialized systems in areas such as patent law.

Competition between WESTLAW and LEXIS as delivery systems has had contradictory effects. On the one hand, it has led each to introduce new features not available in the other. On the other hand, it has pushed each to match features of the other as quickly as possible. The original WESTLAW allowed access only to headnotes and offered a weak collection of user search commands. Competition forced it to add full text and some LEXIS-compatible search commands. WESTLAW now provides more search features than LEXIS ("within sentence," "within paragraph," and "locate" searches, for example) but still lacks some LEXIS features (the "KWIC" and "modify" features, for example). Competition has led both systems to become compatible with a large variety of user workstations. Competition is also evident in the way in which each system has been striving to increase the number of data bases and the time periods covered by these data bases. Indeed, both systems are developing so quickly under the influence of competition that readers should contact WESTLAW and LEXIS directly for current information (WESTLAW: 800-328-9833; LEXIS: 800-227-4908).

After WESTLAW and LEXIS, the next most important systems for lawyers are probably DIALOG and NEXIS. DIALOG is a system for providing access to what are mainly bibliographic and informational rather than full text data bases. Unlike WESTLAW and LEXIS, which have created most of the data bases they sell (though not all—consider, for instance Shepard's Citations), DIALOG markets access to data bases created by other organizations. As a result DIALOG has a bewildering variety of data bases, including numerous data bases relating to the patents, trademarks, labor law, and a wide variety of scientific and technical subjects. These scientific and technical data bases are useful not only to patent attorneys attempting to learn the state of the art in a particular field but also to lawyers handling products liability and medical malpractice cases where scientific knowledge plays a large role. Of particular interest on DIALOG is the *Legal Resource Index*, a data base that lists all recent legal periodical articles. (This data base has migrated to WESTLAW and LEXIS.) Other data systems of particular interest to attorneys include: PHINET, a system for delivery of Prentice Hall's on-line tax data base; WILSONLINE, H.W. Wilson's system for providing access to the "Index to Legal Periodicals" data base; RLIN and OCLC, which are library card catalog union list data systems; VERALEX, a case, citation, and ALR service of Lawyer's Cooperative Publishing Co. (the "autocite" data base on VERALEX is also available on LEXIS, and a similar data base, INSTACITE, is available on WESTLAW); and QL, a data system with data bases containing abstracts of Canadian cases offered by QL Systems, LTD.

(d) Data Delivery System Access Hardware and Software

The most important aspect of hardware for accessing a data delivery system is the keyboard, since it is by typing on the keyboard that the user interacts with the system. Undoubtedly the easiest kind of keyboard to learn to use is a keyboard specifically designed for use with a particular data delivery system. Such a keyboard will have custom-made keys, each with words indicating particular system functions, such as "NEXT CASE" or "CITE". Thus the user is spared the task of memorizing what each key does. However, a relatively high price is paid for having such a special keyboard, since in order to obtain the keyboard it may be necessary to lease a special terminal that is only fully compatible with one of several services. Even if a firm is willing to pay for multiple special purpose terminals, there are substantial costs in finding the physical desk space for multiple terminals and in living with the fact that when one special-purpose terminal is broken, no other terminal can be used as a substitute. The need for a user to learn to interact with numerous different pieces of physical hardware may outweigh any advantage provided by the fact that each hardware item has a customized keyboard. Luckily, competitive pressures have forced all systems to become compatible with a fairly wide variety of equipment. An IBM–PC-compatible computer can, with appropriate software, be made compatible with all or almost all data delivery systems of interest to lawyers. The keyboard problem can be solved to some extent by the use of templates that go over parts of the keyboard or stickers that go on the keys. (Such templates and stickers are supplied by a number of data delivery companies.) Another solution, one becoming increasingly necessary as the number of data banks proliferates, is hiring a data access specialist who knows how the keys work for the different systems to assist lawyers searching for information. Our favored solution is to build a "help" mechanism right into the computer that displays, at the touch of the F1 "Help" key, a complete explanation of which key performs which function.

Communication with data delivery systems should be at the highest speed technically possible. (See Appendix A–3(a) for discussion of communications speeds.) Slow speeds are frustrating and time-wasting for lawyers who may need to search through many screens of data to find a needed reference. They are also expensive, since the data delivery systems and data bases are usually sold by minutes of "connect time."

An important feature of personal computers used as terminals to access external data bases is the ability to store retrieved data temporarily on local disk storage for later examination and printing, after the expensive connection with the data delivery system has been terminated. Most "terminal emulation" programs for personal computers offer this feature, though a few data delivery systems try to discourage or prevent this practice of "timeshifting."

§ 3-3. DATA BASE CREATION SOFTWARE

The major data base delivery systems have highly sophisticated proprietary software that runs on the mainframe computers that these systems use to create and maintain their data bases. Lawyers need not be concerned in detail with how these systems work, though they should be able to do a critical evaluation of the end product. If, for instance, a data base contains large numbers of obviously misspelled words, the data base creation system has not incorporated adequate error-checking operations. If new statutes, court decisions, or other data take too long to appear in the system, slow data base creation software and/or inefficient management is at fault.

Many of the major data base delivery systems and a number of smaller companies offer data base creation services for law firms, particularly "litigation support" systems for evidence management in conjunction with large lawsuits. However, an alternative that should seriously be considered by law firms is that of creating their own evidence management data bases, with the aid of commercially-available data base creation software. Then the evidence management techniques developed for large lawsuits may be applied to any size lawsuits.

There are two primary approaches to data base creation: (1) the use of index terms and (2) full text indexing. If index terms are to be used alone or in conjunction with full text indexing, a consultant experienced in data base creation will be needed, particularly if the data bases involved are large.

Data base creation software performs a number of functions. It allows the user to specify the structure of each data "record" in a data file. (A "record" is a case, a note, or some other meaningful unit of information.) It allows the user to design the screens that are displayed to the secretary who enters the data into the computer, or if the data is extracted from existing computer files, to define what data is to be selected from the file and how the data should be arranged. Once the data is entered, the data base creation software automatically creates indexes so that the data may later be retrieved in a speedy manner. This software also must provide easy methods for correcting or updating existing records and for adding new records to the file. It must ensure that as records are changed, the corresponding index entries are also changed. It should provide for the maximum possible amount of automatic error-checking when data is entered, and it should have provisions to ensure that the same data does not have to be entered more than once.

Every law firm of any size is likely to maintain a number of data bases of its own on computer. These will include client conflict files, time and billing files, docketing systems, research notecard systems, brief and memo banks, and litigation support files. Each of these files will need a substantial amount of data to be entered, presumably by the law firm's clerical or paralegal staff. It is important that the data be entered accurately and that clerical staff time used for data entry be minimized. With the possible exception of notecard systems and litigation support files, it is unlikely that a lawyer will be involved in the design of a data entry system for any of these data base applications. However, it is very important that the lawyer be aware of the considerations that are involved in design of a good data entry system. Otherwise, the lawyer may pay forever for excessive clerical time, or, worse, be sued for malpractice because of the results of errors in entering data into client conflict or docketing files.

Good data entry design minimizes the number of keystrokes a secretary must make to enter or correct data. At the same time it provides an effective means to check all data entries for error. If a client changes his or her address, it should not be necessary to type in or change any other part of the client data file. If he changes his telephone number, but not the area code, it should not be necessary to type in a new area code. Some data should be rejected by the computer—for instance, words where there should be numbers, as for a lawyer's billing rate. Others should be questioned by a computer. If a telephone number is typed in with a form other than "654–3210" it should be questioned. However, the number may belong to a client who is in a small backwoods town or a foreign country with a different numbering system, or to someone who has a number left over from the days when numbers started with letters, e.g. PEnnsylvania 6–5000. In such cases, the computer should question the data entry clerk, but should go ahead and accept the information if the clerk persists. In some cases, only a supervisor should be allowed to enter data outside certain bounds. It is said that in a certain Wall Street law firm, where there was great pressure upon associates to put in a maximum number of billable hours, an associate worked all night in New York drafting some documents, continued work on a plane the next morning to San Francisco where the documents were to be signed, and went straight from the airport to a meeting that lasted until midnight when the papers were finally signed. The associate then billed for 27 hours for the day, since he had put in not only a 24-hour day, but also the three extra hours he gained from the difference in time zones. Presumably, if entries for over 24 billable hours of actual time spent a day are allowed, a supervisor should be required to approve such entries.

Not only should the data entry system provide levels of rejecting or questioning doubtful data, it should provide an easy way to set such levels and to check to determine what levels are set.

There are three main types of data entry formats. These are menu selection, fill in blanks, and entry by field codes. Menu selection is the most foolproof, the easiest to use, but unsuitable for many purposes and often slow in terms of amount of information transferred per minute of secretarial time. Filling in blanks allows faster information transfer, requires little training, and works for all types of information transfer. Entry by field codes is fastest, but hardest to learn.

A typical menu selection screen might look like the following:

```
Is client:

(a) A man

(b) A woman

(c) A corporate entity

Type a, b, or c.
```

This menu approach is very easy for untrained users. However it does not work at all unless the number of possible categories is limited.

A typical data entry screen might appear as follows:

```
Client information:

Name:

Company:

Street Address:

City:
```

```
State:
Zip Code:
```

In this case, there is no way to predict and list in advance the possible names, companies, or street addresses. A list of 50 states would be too long for easy menu handling. The number of zip codes is far greater than could be put on a screen menu. Instead the program should allow the user the freedom to move from question to question, typing in the information for each question.

A good data entry system of this type will have the following characteristics. First, it should be easy to make corrections, both on the same line and on previous lines. For instance, if after typing the name of the state, one realizes that there is a spelling error in the name of the client, it should be easy to go back and check the name of the client. Second, the user should be given a chance to double check all the data before it is entered into permanent computer records. This can be done, for instance, by asking the user "Is everything OK?" and then proceeding only if the user answers "YES". Third, flexibility should be offered to take account of possible variations in data encountered in real life. For instance, one line may not be enough for the street address if there is also a building address. Fourth, wherever possible the data should be checked for accuracy. For instance ZIP codes should be checked to see that they are in standard format and state names should be verified. Zip codes and state names can be cross-checked for consistency. And fifth, if the same data is likely to be repeated on successive screens, it should appear automatically as a "default" entry if no other entry is supplied.

§ 3–4. PUBLIC DATA BASES

Public data bases of interest to lawyers fall into a number of general categories. The first is the entire contents of an ideal law library: cases, statutes, regulations, law reviews, treatises, bibliographies, and various government documents. The second is material of legal importance that generally has been available in the past only by access to government agency files or has been available but unindexed and thus practically inaccessible, for instance status of legislation in state legislatures or Securities and Exchange Commission no action letters. The third is the contents of various public record systems: patents, trademark registrations, recorded deeds, etc. With surprising speed all of these types of data bases are becoming available through computerized data delivery systems.

The two leading legal data delivery systems are moving ever closer to the creation of complete data bases of published case law materials. Nearly all new published judicial opinions are being put into both systems and both are gradually adding the older cases to their collections. This competition is now extending also to other types of material usually found in good law libraries, such as law review articles and treatises. Already it is true that these data bases constitute much larger bodies of material than most law firms have in their libraries. Within the next decade, these and other data banks should approach full coverage of the materials found in the legal research libraries of most law schools and large law firms.

One policy of the developers of these systems has in the past severely hampered their use as substitutes for ordinary law libraries. This is their failure to make the page numbers of the published versions of the opinions available in their data banks. In a recent case, it was held that West Publishing Company has copyright protection for a number of features of its National Reporter System. Mead Data Central [MDC], which owns LEXIS, had announced that it planned to insert the page numbers from West's National Reporter System into LEXIS. West brought a copyright infringement action and was granted a preliminary injunction by the District Court. West Publishing Co. v. Mead Data Cent., Inc., 616 F.Supp. 1571 (D.Minn.1985). On appeal, the Eighth Circuit affirmed, stating, "We do not agree with MDC that WEST'S claim here is simply one for copyright in its page numbers. Instead, we concur in the District Court's conclusion that WEST'S arrangement is a copyrightable aspect of its compilation of cases, that the pagination of WEST'S volumes reflects and expresses WEST'S arrangement, and that MDC's intended use of WEST'S page numbers infringes WEST'S copyright in the arrangement." 799 F.2d 1219 (8th Cir. 1986). Unless this decision is overturned in further proceedings, Mead will have to limit itself to providing page numbers for official reports such as the United States Reports and for reports on which the copyright has expired—cases before 1910. The copyrighted page numbers are the page numbers which lawyers must cite in their briefs to comply with court rules and customs. It seems likely that West will respond by providing page numbers for those reports whose page numbers are in the public domain. However, West has not announced any overall policy decision on page numbers. Another approach would require action by the courts and thus would require overcoming the conservatism, inertia, and fragmentation of court administration. This approach would be for courts to begin numbering paragraphs and to permit attorneys to cite paragraph numbers without page numbers in their briefs. If such official paragraph numbers became widely used, competitive pressures could be expected to force the legal data systems to make paragraph numbers available in their data bases. If the existing data systems failed to do so, new entrants could be expected to appear that would do so. This is particularly so since the cost of entry into the legal data base market will fall drastically with the introduction of optical disk storage. Any company is free, for instance, to put the United States Supreme Court reports onto optical disks and to sell them through regular book distribution channels without the heavy sales overhead of the centralized legal data distribution systems. But proprietary editorial additions, such as West's indexing, summaries, and headnotes and comparable additions to some of Mead's collections, will remain protected by copyright.

Data bases, however, are going beyond merely replacing the law library. They are making available types of materials that even good law libraries have typically not been able to provide, like status of bills in state legislatures and access to opinions of state attorneys general throughout the country. Thus, for instance, the Electronic Legislative Search System (ELSS) of Commerce Clearing House provides coverage of bills before state legislatures and Congress. While this service is not cheap, it may be much cheaper to lobby before legislation is passed than to try to alleviate the consequences of legislation for one's client after the legislation is passed. Few law libraries have been able to afford all the published opinions of state attorneys general; now these are becoming available on the major legal data delivery systems. These systems also provide a quality of access to materials such as the opinions of the state attorneys general that has never been available before.

Public registry information is becoming increasingly computerized in such areas as patents, trademarks, and land records. For reasons of both history and law, the form of computerization is different in each of these areas.

Under patent law, both United States and foreign patents describing an invention may be a bar to a new patent application describing the same or a similar invention. Therefore, whether preparing a patent application or alleging that another's patent is invalid, it is important for the patent attorney to have access to United States and foreign patents in point. In the past, nearly all patent searching has been done by professional patent search firms at the library of the United States Patent and Trademark Office in Alexandria, Virginia. Partially this was because of the expertise of the full-time search specialists employed by these firms, but primarily it was because the law firms did not have adequate patent library facilities. Today, the full text of United States patents for recent years and abstracts of foreign patents in certain fields are available in data banks, the former in LEXPAT, the latter in a number of databases distributed through DIALOG. Various indexes to technical literature are available on DIALOG and other data base access systems. These provide valuable information to a patent attorney, since in many instances, a patent application will be rejected or a patent will be invalid if there has been a previous description of the invention in a printed publication. The availability of these data bases is likely to lead patent attorneys to supplement, and perhaps in some cases to replace, search service results with their own efforts. The search services typically provide reports of inventions that bear a superficial resemblance to the invention they are searching, but they are not able to provide the combination of legal and technical judgment that is the essence of the craft of the patent attorney.

Trademark searches also involve consulting a combination of public record data and ordinary publications. While most countries require registration for trademark protection, in the United States common law protection is available without registration. Federal and state trademark registration is optional. Federal registration offers substantial extra protection; state registration provides little or no benefit. A complete trademark search must include the Federal registry, the state registries, and lists of unregistered marks. Traditional trademark protection was limited to a particular class of goods. However, statutes and court decisions now often extend the protection of a trademark well beyond the class of goods upon which the trademark has been used. This broader scope of protection means that a correspondingly broader search must be made. A simple manual trademark search is often useful for preliminary screening, but it would be malpractice to use negative results of a manual search as the basis for advising a client that it could safely use a particular mark. A typical trademark search may involve three steps. First, the lawyer may look in the *Trademark Register of the United States,* an unofficial publication that lists all federally registered trademarks. If the lawyer finds there the trademark the client proposes to use, the search is over—a different trademark will have to be chosen. If the lawyer decides to skip the manual search step, or if the manual search shows no similar trademark, the next step will be to use the various trademark data bases on DIALOG. This file contains a huge collection of both registered and unregistered trademarks. Once a trademark passes this preliminary screening, the lawyer may have one of the professional search firms that keeps a comprehensive private trademark data bank do an exhaustive search. The future will undoubtedly see the creation of a worldwide trademark data bank containing at least the contents of the trademark registries of the economically most important countries.

Land title searches are another area where computers are of great importance. Here the technology has developed somewhat differently. For patents and trademarks, public computer data bases are available that can be consulted by anyone for an appropriate fee. In the land title area, computerized data bases have been created by title insurance and abstract companies. These data bases are kept as proprietary information by the respective companies and are not available for use by the general public, except as it chooses to buy these companies' title services.

There is a serious flaw in present patent, trademark, and land title data bases. They lack graphical information, and so do not contain patent drawings, trademark symbols, and land-use maps. Future systems should overcome this shortcoming.

§ 3–5. LAW OFFICE DATA BASES

All law offices maintain extensive files relating to clients and to matters they are handling. Today, many of these files can be managed more efficiently by computer. As costs of computer file management continue to fall and costs of manual file maintenance and of storage space continue to rise, law firms will be forced to move toward the virtual elimination of paper files. Computer-based files offer the advantages of low storage cost, easy backup, and flexible easy access. The preferred method for computer-based file storage in the near future will be Write Once Read Many Times (WORM) optical disk storage. (Details of the vast capacity of optical disk storage today and the even greater capacities to be available soon are given in Section 7–2(e).)

The problem comes in getting access to the information stored on the optical disk. As a practical matter, some sort of data base creation software must be used to prepare indexes to the document, and these indexes must be stored on the optical disk. Depending upon the type of data base creation system used, up to one-half of the space on the disk will be needed for the index files. Whether a document is in text or image format, usually it will be necessary to add formal indexing information to it as part of the data base creation process. A business letter, for instance, should have indexing information added that indicates what matter it deals with (e.g. Mrs. Smith's will), by whom it was sent, to whom it was sent, and when it was sent. (This information is probably explicit or implicit in the body of the letter, but it will not be easily or reliably available for retrieval unless it is formally made part of the record in the data base system for the document.) Additional formal indexing on the subject matter of the document is useful for text documents (a letter may be about the cardboard carton antitrust case but may never specifically mention cardboard cartons or "antitrust.") If a document is in text format, indexes may be constructed on all important words used in the document to allow retrieval in a manner similar to that used in WESTLAW and LEXIS. If the document is in image format, such retrieval will not be possible unless the image is first converted to text by optical character recognition software. At present, such software exists in two forms. The first form recognizes only typewriter fonts commonly used in business and legal correspondence (such as Courier and Prestige). The second recognizes all types of fonts and can be used for copying from books and for copying from documents not typed in a common font. The first type of software is often included in the price of optical scanning devices or is available for a relatively small extra charge. The second type of software is available at present only with the very expensive (over $30,000) Kurzweil scanner sold by Xerox. Even with a good scanner and good software, initial operator intervention may be needed to "train" the scanner to recognize particular typefaces and continuing operator assistance may be required to correct characters that cause problems for the scanner (for instance because of a "blob" on the paper). Thus when optical character recognition software is used, input costs are substantially higher than for either image input or direct transfer of computer files. No software is commercially available for recognizing handwritten characters. Documents with drawings, for instance subdivision plats, by their nature must be stored as images.

Economic considerations suggest that care be taken not to "over-index" documents. Adding index terms by hand to each document is an expensive process. Optical character recognition to allow full-text indexing also may be expensive. If a particular group of documents are archival—for instance concerning a case that has been settled and is never likely to come up again—minimal indexing, such as attaching the name or other designation to the file for each document, may be sufficient. On the other hand if there are a large number of depositions from a case in active litigation, professional database consultants or a data base creation firm may be needed to provide adequate indexing to allow lawyers working on the case the retrieval capabilities that they need.

§ 3-6. CREATING AND ACCESSING DATA BASES

(a) The Need for Uniformity

The concepts underlying virtually all data base systems of interest to attorneys are simple. No matter what a data base contains—time and billing information, client information, litigation support evidence information, or cases and statutes—the data base always contains multiple "records"—a time record for each block of attorney time, a client record for each client, a litigation record for each exhibit, or an individual case or statute which constitutes a record in a computer-assisted legal research system such as WESTLAW or LEXIS. And each of these records is broken up into "fields": in an attorney time record—date, client name, attorney initials, task description, and hours worked fields; in a client information record—name, address, and telephone number fields; in a litigation record—exhibit number, date, sender, receiver, issue, and description fields, in a case record on WESTLAW or LEXIS—case title, citation, court, date, judge's name, opinion, and dissent fields. Data bases differ dramatically from one another in size, and internally they may be structured very differently depending upon their size and the nature of the information which they contain (financial data, short text items, or long text items, for example). But when it comes to retrieving the information, all data bases work in basically the same way.

To retrieve information, you specify what it is that you want to see in what field, and optionally you require the information be sorted and some of the information to be summed. "Find all the time records for the client "ABC Co." This is a request to retrieve all time records that contain "ABC Co." in the "client name" field. "What is the telephone number of client ABC Co.?" This is a request to display the contents of the "telephone number" field of a client information record that contains "ABC Co." in its client name field. "Get a list of the exhibits that mention 'Jones' and that relate to the 'estoppel' issue. Arrange them in date order." This is a request to retrieve from the litigation support data base all the records that contain "Jones" in the "sender" or "receiver" fields and "estoppel" in the issue field, and to sort the records found in numeric order with reference to the "date" field before printing them out. "Find all the cases decided by Judge Decker that relate to 'estoppel.'" This is a request to search for cases (remember: a case is a "record" in WESTLAW or LEXIS) that contain "Decker" in the Judge's name field and "estop . . ." in either the opinion or the dissent field. While you have not specified sorting, WESTLAW and LEXIS by default automatically sort the opinions in inverse chronological order by the contents of the date field, with higher-court cases shifted to the front.

WESTLAW and LEXIS are "user friendly" and highly flexible—they impose very few limits upon the searcher. They are deficient in not permitting you more "sorting" options and in their lack of sophisticated mathematical and report generating capabilities. But when it comes to searching through textual data, WESTLAW and LEXIS are "state of the art." Many of the better text searching features of WESTLAW and LEXIS are only just beginning to appear in microcomputer data base programs. So any attorney or law student who has mastered WESTLAW and LEXIS will have little difficulty using any other microcomputer data base tool once they master the sorting, math, and report generating facilities of those tools which WESTLAW and LEXIS lack.

But when you attempt to use some other data base system—even a system like DIALOG that works in much the same way as WESTLAW and LEXIS—you will find them difficult to use at first. Why? Because there are no standards. Every system has a different command structure to accomplish the same ends as every other system. When you move from WESTLAW or LEXIS to DIALOG, WILSONLINE, or PHINET, you have to retrain yourself in how to search. And microcomputer data base programs also have their own search languages that must be mastered.

Originally, the WESTLAW and LEXIS search languages differed from each other. But several years ago, West decided to adapt their system so that many of the basic LEXIS search commands would work on the WESTLAW system. West made this change in spite of the fact that in some respects the original WESTLAW syntax was better than that of LEXIS. A "compromise" between the two syntaxes, preserving the best features of each, would have been preferable, but strong competition between the two companies has made it impossible for them to cooperate on such matters. Be that as it may, at least we now have a standard syntax for the most basic search functions that works on both WESTLAW and LEXIS. Other data base providers, most notably DIALOG, have refused so far to adopt this "standard" search syntax for legal applications. The DIALOG syntax strongly resembles that used in most computer programming languages. As a result, most attorneys do not use DIALOG, and some of its formerly exclusive data bases are starting to appear on WESTLAW and LEXIS—most notably the *Legal Resources Index* which allows author, title, and subject matter searches of all recent legal periodical literature. Other data bases will also move from DIALOG to WESTLAW or LEXIS if DIALOG does not join the other two. The *Index To Legal Periodicals,* which may be searched using Wilson's WILSONLINE service, also has its own unique search language, and we expect this service will also fail to attract lawyers as subscribers. Prentice-Hall recently announced its PHINET service which supports yet another search syntax, and Prentice Hall will face similar problems of user resistance. Perhaps eventually, the computer scientists who design these systems will learn that search languages are truly languages, like French and German, that are not readily mastered nor remembered. It is inadvisable to create an entirely new language with every new system.

We thus have our own tower of Babel, with many data base delivery systems each forcing us to learn their unique search language. Attorneys do not have the time to learn multiple search languages. Economics ultimately will force everyone to adopt a common search language, and the commercial success of LEXIS in this field may well force others to follow West's lead in supporting some of the LEXIS language constructs. But the "game" is by no means over. With optical disk data bases appearing soon, IBM or some other major party may come up with an optical disk "search engine" that becomes so widely used for such general applications as searching through encyclopedias and dictionaries that whatever "search syntax" that search engine supports will ultimately replace even the WESTLAW/LEXIS search language. But at the moment, the WESTLAW/LEXIS search language is probably more widely used than any other.

One microcomputer software company, ZyLAB, Inc. (Chicago, Illinois) has already brought out a microcomputer program that works in much the same manner as WESTLAW and LEXIS. This program can search a hard disk full of information for words, phrases, and numbers in precisely the same way that WESTLAW and LEXIS search through cases and statutes for words, phrases, or numbers. ZyINDEX cannot sort the records found into some order other than that in which the information appears upon the disk, and on this ground the program has been faulted by practitioners considering its use for litigation support. But its support of the WESTLAW/LEXIS search language makes it simple for attorneys to master. A ZyLAB representative has informed one of the authors that ZyLAB is hard at work adapting ZyINDEX to work with optical disks having thousands of times the capacity of ordinary microcomputer floppy disks.

Other microcomputer data base programs do not support the WESTLAW/LEXIS search syntax. Since any given law office only has one or two such data base systems, the staff simply masters the systems that they have, and they need not concern themselves about the incompatibility of the others. Still, it would be preferable for attorneys to have personal data bases for client record and research note maintenance and litigation support that work like WESTLAW and LEXIS so that use of the personal system will reinforce an attorney's training for WESTLAW and LEXIS.

The consumption of computer products by the legal profession, large as it is, represents only a small fraction of the total consumption of such products by businesses generally, and the vast majority of data base product consumers use the data bases in inventory, mailing list, and financial applications. The providers of data base software are much more concerned that their products be suitable for use in such applications than for use in searching through large textual data bases. So these products generally may never adopt the WESTLAW/LEXIS syntax in which we all are trained. We may have to develop our own specialized data base tools for our personal use.

(b) Using Data Bases—Selecting, Sorting, and Summing

The key to understanding data bases is understanding three concepts that are as fundamental to data base access as addition, subtraction, multiplication, and division are to arithmetic.

Imagine that we have created a data base about the law students in your school. Each record contains information about one student, with fields assigned to such things as the student's name, year of graduation, college, and so on. One way to represent this data base would be to list all the information for each student on a single line in a lengthy report that devotes one line to each student:

Soc.Sec. #	Name	Yr	Adv	College	St	City	Spec.	Gd.Pt.
245236752	Smith, Jim	88	JJR	Michigan	IL	Chicago	Pat	3.42
366789413	Kline, Don	87	CKL	Illinois	IL	Wheaton	Tax	2.76
256784532	Jones, Jan	87	JJR	Oberlin	CO	Denver	Lab	3.26
344540983	Mack, Ed	88	RPG	Stanford	WA	Seattle	Env	3.00

Imagine that all 800 students in the law school have their names and information recorded in this data base. What kind of reports can we extract from this information? By using the techniques of selecting, sorting, and summing in various combinations, we can extract a surprisingly large number of reports from this one simple data base. For example:

By sorting this information into order by name, we can produce a printed directory that lists every student in alphabetical order.

Now sort the list by city, without disturbing its "alphabetical-by-student-name" organization of the data in the case of students who live in the same city. We now have a listing of all the students broken down alphabetically first by city and for students from the same city broken down alphabetically by student name. Sort this list once more by state, without disturbing the ordering of students from the same state, and we obtain an alphabetic "state-by-state" directory of students, with the students in each state sorted alphabetically by city, and with students from the same city sorted alphabetically by name.

Next, sort the above list by class year. You now have a "state by state" and "city by city" directory of all the students in each class.

Next, go back to the original "sorted by name" report and sort it again by specialty. You now have a list of students ordered alphabetically by specialty for all three classes, with the names within each specialty listed alphabetically. Sorting this report by class year would give a breakdown of each class by specialty, if such a report were desired.

Now go back to the original data base, and sort by social security number. Assuming social security numbers are used on bluebooks to identify the students, you now have a list ordered numerically by social security number that the administration can use to look up which name goes with which social security number.

Next, start with the alphabetic list, and sort it by college name to give an alphabetic list of colleges and the names of the students who attended each college.

We have generated six unique, useful reports using nothing except selective sorts on different keys in different orders. Before performing these sorts, we could have "selected" certain data items. Then our reports would have been more focused. For example, we could have "selected" all the students whose gradepoint was above 3.50 and then generated some of the above reports with respect to the "honors" students so selected. Or we could have selected all the students who were assigned to one "advisor" and generated the above reports for use by that advisor.

In legal applications, we do not do much "summing," but generally summing is the key to generating financial reports. For example, in the above report that listed the names of the students organized by state and within each state by city, we could have "summed" the gradepoints within each city and within each state, divided the result by the number of students in each city and state, and printed the result as the "grade point average" for each city and state. The key to automating this operation is printing the sum whenever the value of the city or state field changes. Thus, we have two gradepoint sums that we are maintaining: one for the city, and one for the state. We keep summing, and counting the number of student records, until the value in the city or state field changes (as when we move from one city or state group of students to the next). When the city or state field value changes, we print the grade average for the city or state and set the running sum as well as the count of records back to zero.

As you can see, searching, sorting, and summing done in a variety of combinations can be used to generate almost any report a data base is capable of generating. Then a "printing program" rearranges the fields to form a neatly-printed report, frequently suppressing some or all of the fields in a record. Thus, the final "gradepoint by state" report does not need to include the student names—only the city and state names and the grade averages. Likewise, the "student alphabetical and city/state report" probably should not display each student's advisor and gradepoint average. So after selecting, sorting, and summing, you run the report through a "report generator" that assembles the pages of the final report.

West Publishing Company is probably one of the most sophisticated users of a data base system in the country. When West publishes a case, West editors write a series of "headnotes" for the case. You may not have realized it, but each headnote is actually a "record" that is entered into West's publication generating data base system. The fields of each West headnote are the following:

West Topic Heading:

West Key Number:

Headnote Text:

Statute Citation:

Full Case Name:

Case Citation:

Court:

Date:

Terms Defined:

West then generates the following "reports" from this data base:

Sort all the headnotes by topic heading and key number, and select those falling into a single 10-year interval, and you have the West *General Digest.*

Now sort them again by topic heading and key number, and select out all the Federal cases, and you have the West *Federal Digest.*

Next do the same for Illinois cases, and you have an *Illinois Digest.* Do the same for other states and regions of the country, and you get other state and regional digests.

Now select all headnotes containing cites to the United States Code. Sort them by code chapter and section cited. Merge in the actual text of the code, add some editorial explanations, and you have the *United States Code Annotated.*

Now sort all the headnotes by the "terms defined" and you have West's *Words and Phrases,* which contains references to all cases that define legal terms of art.

As you can see, many of the West publications are simply reports generated from West's headnote data base, with added editorial input. And since all the West headnotes are in WESTLAW, you may use WESTLAW as your own personal database system for generating customized headnote reports (unfortunately, your "sorting and summing" options are limited with WESTLAW). You can, for example, locate all the cases whose headnotes are assigned to a particular topic heading and key number and contain the cite of a particular statute. You may do the same with LEXIS data bases that contain similar indexing.

The above two examples illustrate the diversity of data bases that can be designed. Case note and litigation data bases can be customized quite easily to meet the specialized needs of any particular litigation by adding special fields that permit you to build additional reports.

(c) Designing Data Base Systems

The above examples illustrate how easy it is to generate lots of useful reports from a relatively simple data base. You will frequently want to design a customized data base to meet a particular need. The process of designing a data base is simple, although it can be time consuming: You start by deciding what reports you wish to have it generate, and then you work backwards from the reports to the structure of a data base that can generate those reports. Then you design a method of entering the pertinent data into the data base.

For litigation support, you begin by studying the nature of the evidence that is available. What type of exhibits do you have? What issues are likely to arise? Is the case likely to take a sudden turn that could raise issues you may not be able to anticipate at the outset? Make a list of the possible issues and see if you can come up with a coding scheme that is not too complicated for use in categorizing the exhibits. Assign a meaningful abbreviation to each issue. Note that a single exhibit may be relevant to a number of different issues, so you want to have sufficient room in your data base to encode a single exhibit under several issues. Next, examine the exhibits and see what type of information characterizes each one. You probably have an internal numbering scheme, and those admitted into evidence will be assigned court exhibit numbers. With letters, you may wish to encode the names of the sender, receiver, and possibly the names of those mentioned. The date is usually significant. With other types of exhibits, such as blueprints, you may want to come up with a way of describing the exhibit succinctly. Every case is different, so do not feel you have to use the same identifying indicia in every lawsuit.

Next, think of what kind of reports you are going to want to generate. What kind of searches are you likely to formulate? Try formulating some sample searches. And to the extent that you need printed reports, write out sample reports. Next, work backwards from the above information to the definitions of records and fields in your data base. Usually, each record will correspond to an exhibit, but with some large exhibits, you may want to break up the exhibit into parts each of which corresponds to a record. You may, for example, assign a record to each question and answer sequence in a deposition. So each record will include an exhibit number field, a court exhibit field, and a variable number of other fields in accordance with your specific needs. For documents, typically you will include a sender field, a recipient field, a subject field, one or more issue fields, and a "comment" field where you can describe the document in free text. This latter field should be searchable in a WESTLAW/LEXIS manner in case a new issue should arise. If telephone bills form some of the exhibits, you may wish to have a field for the originating number and another for the numbers called. If contracts are involved, you may wish to assign fields to the details of what was purchased and for how much—it all depends upon the nature of the suit.

Finally, you must enter the information. In the case of most exhibits, you will have someone type the information concerning each exhibit into a questionnaire displayed upon the face of the computer's screen. But in the case of transcripts, depositions, and other exhibits that you can arrange to receive in machine-readable form, you may just wish to dump the entire exhibit into ZyIndex or some other WESTLAW/LEXIS-like data base system that permits you to search freely for words and phrases.

Having defined the data base, you next must work with the report generator to define the reports that you wish to have generated. Some of these reports will simply be sorted printouts of the data base itself, or you may wish to provide a variety of indices of the data base that are cross-referenced to a single printout of the entire report. You will need indices of the evidentiary materials sorted by your exhibit number, by the court's exhibit numbers, by date, by issue, and by the name of a party, witness, or other individual. Other reports will be "on demand" reports that cause individual records to be displayed upon the screen. You want to be able to search through the data base in a WESTLAW/LEXIS-like manner at any time for any combination of words, phrases, and numbers. And if 500 documents satisfy your search criterion, you want to be able to sort the results of your search into some meaningful order before you print it out so that you do not have to search through the entire report to find one record.

We have yet to find the "optimal" litigation support system for use by practicing attorneys. PFS:File and PFS:Report (by Software Publishing; also sold by IBM under the "Filing Assistant" label) are easy to use and are coming into widespread use as "interim" products until the "optimal" product comes along. More powerful general-purpose data base programs, such as D–Base III (Ashton-Tate) and R:Base 5000 (Microrim, Inc.), are considerably more complicated to use, but are also much more powerful—enabling you to pull data from several data bases into a single report, for example. A program called Cornerstone provides much of the power of D–Base III and R:Base 5000 without requiring the programming expertise needed for full use of those systems. When designing a docketing system, these programs can automatically compute the due dates and deadlines for different types of court filings and administrative actions and generate "tickler" reports for each attorney of what is due today, this week, this month, and so on. Inmagic (Inmagic, Inc.) gives you the flexibility to design your own records and fields and works quite well with large textual data bases.

(d) Formulating Search Requests

Every data base system requires you to formulate a "search request" that then guides the computer in locating and retrieving the proper set of records. The "search request" specifies which fields are to contain what pattern of words, phrases, or numbers. The nature of a search request varies depending upon the nature of the records that are searched and, in particular, the nature of the fields that are searched.

There are two different types of fields: "Text" fields, which may be of any length and which normally contain arbitrary patterns of words and phrases; and "code" fields, which are small and which normally contain only one word or number selected from a limited list of permissible values.

Text Fields

Attorneys and law students are most familiar with "text" fields, since their training in the use of WESTLAW and LEXIS teaches them how to search through "judicial opinion" fields within "case" records looking for patterns of words, phrases, and numbers that relate to the issue or subject under research. To search a textual field, one first selects "terms" (words, phrases, and/or numbers) that are relevant to the problem being researched and that also appear within the fields of the data base that are to be searched. Ideally, one performs a separate search for each such "term" and its synonyms, conjoining them with OR and enclosing phrases in quotation marks:

```
trailer OR "mini van" OR camper OR "station
wagon"
```

On some systems (WESTLAW), the ORs may not be needed or may be optional; on other systems (LEXIS), the quotation marks may be optional; with yet other systems, quotation marks may be required around all words and phrases. Data base systems such as WESTLAW and LEXIS automatically capture records containing plural forms of the words specified if the plural forms are "well-behaved." If the plurals are irregular, or if a data base system does not automatically provide plural forms (and most do not), typically there will be some way to specify the root of a word and to indicate that any suffix is acceptable, e.g., "estop!" Here, the "!" is a "universal suffix" that signals your desire to see any record which contains a field that contains a word beginning with "estop–". WESTLAW and LEXIS both use the "!" in this manner as a "universal suffix" symbol. Other systems use the asterisk or some other symbol, and a few systems imply a "universal suffix" in all cases—without the use of a special symbol.

Unfortunately, a search for only one word and its synonyms frequently captures far too many records to be useful. You are probably all too familiar with having WESTLAW or LEXIS come back and inform you that your search has captured over 2,000 cases—far more than you have time to browse through, particularly since only one out of ten appears to be relevant to your needs. To limit the scope of your search, you must ask the computer to search for two or more words and their synonyms, rather than just one word. Suppose you have a case involving a car that ran into a motorized bicycle. You might try the following search on WESTLAW or LEXIS:

```
car OR automobile AND bicycle OR motorcycle
```

Here you are commanding the computer to search for every record whose fields contain at least one occurrence of "car" or "automobile" (or both) and also at least one occurrence of "bicycle" or "motorcycle" (or both). Of the two thousand records that contain at least one occurrence of "car" or "automobile," you will only see the fifty that also contain at least one occurrence of "bicycle" or "motorcycle," for example.

By using AND in this manner, you avoid the necessity of browsing through so many records, but you also miss seeing some records that you might have wished to see had the computer drawn them to your attention. The computer searches for words—not legal concepts.

Suppose, for example, that the above search is applied to a data base that contains 20,000 records, 2,000 of which contain the term "car" or the term "automobile"; and 2,000 of which contain the term "bicycle" or "motorcycle." Only fifty contain at least one from the "car-automobile" pair and at least one from the "bicycle-motorcycle" pair. But not all the records that contain these terms are "relevant".

If a random 50% of the relevant records contain "car" and an unrelated random 50% of them contain "automobile," then a search for either "automobile" or "car" by itself would miss 50% of those you wished to see. But a search for "car OR automobile" will miss only 25% (0.5 times 0.5 = 0.25) of the relevant records. Likewise, if a random 50% of the relevant records contain "bicycle" and an unrelated random 50% of the records contain "motorcycle," then a search for "bicycle OR motorcycle" will also miss only 25% of the relevant records. So if you search for "car OR automobile," you will see 75% of the documents you would have selected had you browsed through them all.

When you combine these two searches with "AND," unfortunately, you capture only 56% of the relevant records (0.75 times 0.75). And if you use a second "AND" to add a third term to the search, assuming this third term used in a search by itself would also capture 75% of the relevant records, then the number of relevant records captured drops to 42% (0.56 times 0.75). Adding a third AND and a fourth word to the search (again assuming this word would capture 75% of the relevant records) drops the percentage of relevant records captured to about 32% (0.42 times 0.75). So by grouping words together with AND in this manner, you greatly reduce the amount of time that you must spend browsing through irrelevant records, but you also reduce the number of "relevant" records that you can capture. Computer scientists would say that in an effort to increase the "precision" of your search (avoiding the capture of irrelevant records) you suffered a serious loss in "recall" (the ability to capture all the records that you were looking for). In the case of a caselaw data base, this loss means that you found only some of the cases and must now "round out" your search by using citation searching (e.g.: Shepard's), indexed searching (by topic), repeated searches with different formulations, or other comparable approaches to capture in other ways the cases that you missed in your effort to reduce the time you had to spend browsing through irrelevant cases. But if you are intimately familiar with the cases in the "library" or "data base" that you are searching, and if you are certain the words you supply do appear in all the relevant cases, then you need not fear a reduction in "recall" when you add an extra AND to your searches. In the case of your own personal data base, you probably know what words you placed into the records to represent a given concept; hence adding an extra AND onto a search of your own personal data base may not reduce recall in the way it does when you are uncertain about whether a given word appears in all the relevant records. In the case of a litigation support data base, the "recall reduction" caused by adding ANDs will vary depending upon your knowledge of the data base and the words and phrases you and others used in its construction.

To exclude records that contain a certain term, you normally use the NOT operator. For example, on WESTLAW or LEXIS:

```
interfer! W/4 contract! AND "punitive damages"
AND NOT "Taft-Hartley"
```

This search captures all cases that mention interference with a contractual relationship ("interfer-" within 4 words of "contract-") and punitive damages but excludes all labor law cases, which presumably refer to the Taft-Hartley Act at some point. Note that the term "Taft-Hartley" is one that is almost never encountered in anything but labor cases, so its use here does not reduce the "recall" of this search.

Virtually all data bases that support the use of "text" fields permit one to formulate word and phrase searches similar to the above using "operators" such as AND, OR, and NOT. Some data base systems permit you to use AND, OR, and NOT in formulating your search requests. Other systems use symbols instead of words—"&" or "*" for AND, "+" or "U" for OR, and "%" or "–" for NOT. This should cause you no difficulty. Some systems may provide additional operators, such as the "within so many words" operator "W/–" illustrated above.

Where things get confusing is in the area of "operator precedence." In mathematics, an expression such as:

8 + 6 / 2 =

is ambiguous. If the addition operation is performed ahead of the division operation, then 8 plus 6 divided by 2 is 7. If the division operation is performed first, then 6 divided by 2 plus 8 is 11. Without knowing which "operator"—"+" or "/"—has the higher "precedence," one cannot determine which answer is the correct one. You should have learned in high school that negation, which has the highest precedence, is always performed first; multiplication and division, which have a higher precedence than addition and subtraction, are performed next in order from left to right; and addition and subtraction are performed last, again in order from left to right (an informal survey indicates that half of all law students do not remember this rule from first year High School algebra). In accordance with this rule, the above expression requires you to perform the division operation before performing the addition operation. Accordingly, the correct answer is 11. If the addition is to be performed first, you must use parenthesis to so indicate:

$(8 + 6)/2 = 7$

Here, the parenthesis force one to perform the addition operation ahead of the division operation, and the result is 7.

In formulating search requests for submission to computerized data base systems, one faces a similar problem with operator precedence. Consider the following search:

```
trust! OR agen! OR bail! AND commingl!
```

You do not even think about operator precedence when you ask WESTLAW or LEXIS to perform this search, but operator precedence plays a very important part in its execution. Just as the multiplication operator takes precedence over the addition operator, in the above WESTLAW or LEXIS search request the OR operator takes precedence over the AND operator. Accordingly, both WESTLAW and LEXIS began processing the above search by forming a combined list of all occurrences of the OR-conjoined words "trust!," "agen!," and "bail!." After having formed this combined list, the computer then turns its attention upon the AND operator and strikes from this combined list all occurrences of the words "trust!," "agen!," and "bail!" which appear in cases that do not also contain the word "commingl!" Simultaneously, the computer strikes from a list of all occurrences of the word "commingl!" those occurrences of "commingl!" which appear in cases that do not also contain one of the words "trust!," "agen!," or "bail!." By combining the two resulting lists, the computer forms the final "hit" list of the words that are to be highlighted.

This assignment of OR to a higher precedence level than AND is unique to WESTLAW and LEXIS. WESTLAW and LEXIS are also unique in assigning a lower precedence to NOT than they do to AND and OR. Logicians consider ANDing to be analogous to multiplication, ORing to be analogous to addition, and NOTing to be analogous to negation, and they have adopted by analogy the operator precedence scheme that is used by mathematicians. Logicians have thus assigned the highest precedence to NOT, the next highest precedence to AND, and the lowest precedence to OR. In the mid 1960's, computer scientists adopted the logician's convention in the design of the computer programming language FORTRAN IV, and virtually all computer programming languages and data base search languages formulated since then have also followed the logicians in assigning the highest precedence to NOT, the next highest precedence to AND, and the lowest precedence to OR. So do not be surprised when you discover that your litigation support and personal note card data base systems follow the logician's precedence scheme rather than that of WESTLAW and LEXIS. For example, the above search would have to be reformulated with parenthesis around the ". . . OR . . . OR . . . " expression before it could be submitted to Lockheed's DIALOG system:

```
S (trust? OR agent? OR bail?) AND commingl?
```

The parentheses force the DIALOG system to process the OR part of the expression first, as WESTLAW and LEXIS do without any parenthesis. If you omit the parenthesis from this DIALOG search, then it behaves the same as the following WESTLAW or LEXIS search:

```
trust! OR agent! OR (bail! AND comingl!)
```

This search captures all the cases that contain any occurrences of "trust–" or "agent–" without regard to whether the cases contain "commingl–." In addition, it captures all the cases that contain both "commingl–" and "bail–." Clearly, this result is not what the searcher intended, so virtually all DIALOG searches must be formulated with parenthesis around the OR expressions. Jerry Rubin, Ed Gottsman, and the others who designed the LEXIS search language did not wish for attorneys to have to use parentheses in virtually every search request, so they departed from the computer scientist/logician/mathematician convention and assigned a higher precedence to OR than to AND. Hugh Lawford, who designed the original WESTLAW system, did likewise.

Initially, LEXIS assigned the highest precedence to NOT, just as the logicians did by analogy to negation in mathematics. Then after several years of field testing, NOT was reassigned to the lowest precedence where it remains today. This is probably not an ideal choice—it would be preferable to assign AND NOT to the same precedence level as AND in both WESTLAW and in LEXIS (a WESTLAW convention recently dropped in favor of full compatibility with the LEXIS precedence scheme). Then the following problem could not arise:

```
interfer! W/4 contract! AND "punitive damages"
AND NOT "Taft-Hartley"
```

This search finds all the cases that contain the phrase "interference with a contractual relationship" and also the phrase "punitive damages," but it excludes all the cases that contain a reference to the "Taft-Hartley Act." Now reformulate this search in the following manner:

```
interfer! W/4 contract! AND NOT "Taft-Hartley"
AND "punitive damages"
```

This search looks as if it will produce the same result as the previous search, and it would produce the same result if AND and AND NOT were assigned to the same precedence level, as they probably should be. But AND is assigned a higher precedence than AND NOT. So what happens? (Hint: draw parenthesis around the ". . . AND . . ." clause and see if that helps you to visualize what happens).

Note that a precedence is assigned to every operator, including the "W/4" word proximity operator. Its precedence is greater than that of AND but less than that of OR.

In WESTLAW and LEXIS, a text field search is assumed to be directed to all fields unless the search is enclosed within parentheses and preceded by the name of the field towards which the search is directed. In other systems, you are more typically asked first to supply a field name and then to supply a search formulation for that field. A menu of field names may appear upon the screen, and you will be invited to move from field name to field name using the TAB key, typing in search request formulations opposite whatever field names you wish to search. With both WESTLAW and LEXIS, the commands F (WESTLAW) and .SE (LEXIS) enable you to see the field (or segment) names used in the data base that you are searching.

Code Fields

Code fields are fields that do not contain variable-length, free-form text. A code field may contain a date, a name, an address, or some kind of indexing term. In WESTLAW and LEXIS, the DATE and CITE fields are coded fields. Many inexpensive data bases provide nothing but code fields.

Instead of directing a free-form text search towards a coded field, formulated with AND and OR and AND NOT, you normally specify what term, number or date, or range of terms, numbers, or dates the coded field is to contain. You frequently use the comparative operators EQUALS, DOES NOT EQUAL, GREATER THAN, LESS THAN, GREATER THAN OR EQUAL TO, and LESS THAN OR EQUAL TO and their symbolic equivalents (=, < >, >, <, > =, < =) to specify the acceptable values, or the range of acceptable values, that are permitted. With some data base systems, you may also use the mathematical operators (+, −, * for multiply, and / for divide) and parentheses in search expressions. While beyond the scope of this discussion, many data bases are primarily designed to store financial data in code fields and contain many options for reporting the data out in a variety of ways.

Code fields in research and litigation support data bases play an important role in focusing one's searching by helping you to screen out irrelevant material that you would otherwise have to browse through. For example, you should have an "outline" of the material in your research data base, and the provisions of the outline should be numbered sequentially. Then your outline numbers may be stored in "index" code fields. Free-form text descriptions of each case should be stored in separate text fields. By directing your search to a "range" of these outline numbers, you may focus your search on as broad, or as narrow, a range of the topics in your outline as you wish. The "greater than" and "less than" operators permit you to define the range of topics precisely in a way that you cannot do as well on WESTLAW using the West key numbers, since you cannot at present define a range of key numbers on WESTLAW using comparative operators (government lawyers can do this on the Department of Justice's JURIS system).

By assigning names, street addresses, city names, state names, zip codes, telephone numbers, and other data to specific coded fields in a data base, you can set up a client data file that can be used as an on-line set of index cards, as a mailing list, and as a way to generate reports about your clients. A major portion of a legal time record, accounting, and billing system is just such a data base, and frequently such systems are constructed on top of a general-purpose data base system.

(e) Terminals, Personal Computers Programmed to Emulate Terminals, and Beyond Terminals

How does one select equipment to use in accessing WESTLAW, LEXIS, and other remote data bases? The situation is quite confused at present, and it is likely to remain so for some time to come.

The concept of having hundreds of individuals gain simultaneous access to a single large computer originated in the late 1960s and early 1970s. At first, printing Teletype machines were used to talk to the central computers, but they were far too slow. They were gradually replaced by television-and-keyboard assemblies called "terminals." These early terminals were not personal computers. Functionally, they worked in much the same way as did the old Teletype machines. The screen behaved as if it were a piece of paper flowing up from a printing typewriter—the text flowed onto the screen at the bottom and flowed up the screen where it remained in view, unmodifiable, until it scrolled off the top and disappeared forever. When you typed, each character that you typed appeared upon the screen at the bottom and simultaneously flowed out of the terminal to the central computer. Since every keystroke caused a character to flow toward the central computer, these terminals were called "character mode" terminals. When you struck the carriage return key after typing a line on one of these terminals, the "carriage return character" would flow to and "wake up" the central computer, compelling it to respond in some way. Over the years, these "dumb" or "Teletype" terminals, as they have come to be called, have come into very widespread use. Since many people have them, and since they all work in precisely the same manner, they have become the standard terminal for virtually all central computer and data base access in spite of their inferior quality. Today, the DIALOG system and many other centralized data base systems are still designed to be accessed only from these primitive terminals. As a direct consequence, the DIALOG system is not particularly "user friendly" for attorneys.

The designers of the LEXIS system began using dumb Teletype terminals in their earliest experiments, but the shortcomings of these terminals, and the difficulty that attorneys had using them, quickly became apparent. In a move that was way ahead of its time, the designers of the LEXIS system decided that they needed to provide attorneys with a much "smarter" terminal—one designed to permit the central computer to write at any point on the screen, and one that also worked somewhat like a modern "word processor," permitting the attorney to move a "cursor" about with arrow keys, correcting anything visible on the screen. When one types a character on the face of a LEXIS terminal, the character appears upon the screen but is not sent back to the central computer—the attorney is cut off from the central computer until the attorney hits a special "TRANSMIT" key and thereby causes all the information on the screen from the upper-left corner down to the blinking cursor to be transmitted to the central computer as a "block". The LEXIS terminal is thus a "block mode" terminal that transmits information to the central computer in large blocks—it is not a "character mode" terminal that transmits each keystroke individually. The LEXIS terminals look a bit primitive when judged by today's standards, but when first introduced, they were absolutely "state of the art" and represented a true breakthrough in user-friendliness.

The early WESTLAW system was originally developed as the "QuicLaw" Canadian law retrieval system by IBM Canada in a joint venture with Queens University in Kingston, Ontario, under the guidance of law professor Hugh Lawford. Not surprisingly, it utilized standard IBM mainframe terminals. These were "block mode" terminals like the LEXIS terminal, only more sophisticated. Instead of responding to a "transmit" keystroke by sending to the central computer all the information on the screen from the upper-left corner down to the cursor, these IBM terminals responded by sending all the information appearing in certain "user-accessable" areas of the screen. This fundamental difference between WESTLAW and LEXIS terminals has persisted to the present day and can cause confusion when an attorney moves from one to the other. A LEXIS user is frequently surprised when information to the right of (or below) the cursor is sent off to WESTLAW—LEXIS simply ignores such information. WESTLAW, on the other hand, typically reads the top few lines of the display without regard to the cursor placement.

These first WESTLAW terminals were wonderfully fast—faster than most present-day WESTLAW and LEXIS terminals—but required a dedicated, leased telephone line too expensive for many individual subscribers. This service is still available, and because it utilizes standard IBM networking protocols, it provides a way in which large law firms, law schools, and government agencies can provide WESTLAW service to hundreds of terminals using IBM mainframe computer networking techniques. Brigham Young University's law school has pioneered this technology, which is excellent for high-speed browsing.

West soon thereafter introduced a second class of service that utilized Hazeltine "block mode" terminals which could access WESTLAW over ordinary telephone lines. The Hazeltine terminal required users to type their responses at the bottom of the screen, rather than at the top. The Hazeltine terminals were not widely used. West introduced a third class of service that utilized an IBM terminal (the "3101") which again permitted the users to type their responses at the top of the screen. West's latest terminal (the "WALT" terminal) essentially duplicates the IBM (3101) terminal screens but also provides the user with special function keys, a built-in automatic dialing system, and a few other nice features, including the ability to access data bases other than WESTLAW. For technical reasons, West provides a distinct fourth class of service for the "WALT" terminal. Like the custom LEXIS terminal, the WALT terminal provides special function keys. Recently, West released "WESTMATE" terminal emulation software for the IBM PC. The "WESTMATE" software, like the "WALT" terminal, permits the user to type responses at the top of the screen and also permits incoming text to be stored on floppy or hard disks.

Word processing and computer vendors soon began asking both WESTLAW and LEXIS to approve their equipment for use in accessing the two data bases. LEXIS initially declined to certify any third-party equipment and insisted that its proprietary terminals be used. West began a certification program for such equipment, instructing most such vendors to "program" their word processors or computers to emulate the Hazeltine "type your response at the bottom" terminal. Accordingly, much of the WESTLAW personal computer software in the field requires the user to type responses at the bottom of the screen, unlike West's WALT terminal and "WESTMATE" software which requires the user to type responses at the top of the screen.

West has also introduced a fifth class of service that supports "character mode, dumb Teletype" terminals. This "dumb terminal" service is not as user-friendly as the other WESTLAW services such as that provided by the "WALT" terminals and "WESTMATE" software. If you have a regular WESTLAW "WALT" terminal, the central computer can send a multi-line search request to your screen; you may edit the search request and then send it back to WESTLAW by striking the <Enter> key. This permits you to revise and resubmit a multi-line search request without retyping it. With the WESTLAW "dumb Teletype" service, the central computer can send a "multi-line" search request to your screen, but you cannot edit it and send it back; you must type it in all over again. And you can only send one line to WESTLAW at a time. If your search is more than one line long, it is more difficult to enter. When using this service, you may edit your search by sending editing commands to the central computer, but first you must master a special editing command language which is not required when you are using "WALT" terminals or "WESTMATE" software. So this "dumb Teletype" WESTLAW service is lower in quality than the remaining classes of WESTLAW service. However, the existence of this "dumb Teletype" service, which works with almost any communications software, has enabled many vendors that do not provide a high quality WESTLAW service to advertise "WESTLAW" as a feature. Caveat emptor! This service may be satisfactory when you are using your child's Apple II computer at home, but it is not what you want in your office if you have an alternative.

Since WESTLAW supports five incompatible classes of service, the WESTLAW staff has to determine which class your combination of computer and software requires and then adjust your account accordingly. If you have an IBM Personal Computer, you can use Direct Aid's "Law Search" program which emulates a Hazeltine terminal and requires you to type your responses at the bottom of the screen; you can use an IBM 3101 terminal emulator program which requires you to type your responses at the top of the screen; you can use West's new "WESTMATE" WALT terminal emulation software; or, if you do not mind a reduction in the quality of your service, you can use Hayes's "Smartcom" program or Microstuf's "Crosstalk" program both of which can access West's "dumb Teletype" service. You can even use IBM's 3270 program and card to access WESTLAW's original service—the faster "leased telephone line" service. Each requires a different class of service.

LEXIS also now gives you several options which vary in quality. LEXIS has abandoned its policy of requiring every subscriber to have a custom LEXIS terminal. LEXIS can now be accessed from the same IBM 3101 terminals that one may use to access WESTLAW, although they work in different ways. With the IBM 3101 terminal, for example, one sends a search to LEXIS by depressing the "send message" key; with WESTLAW, one depresses the main <Enter> key.

At the request of professional librarians seeking to access the NEXIS New York Times materials from standard terminals, LEXIS also now offers "character mode" terminal support. One may now access LEXIS with almost any terminal or communications program. The LEXIS "character mode" service works best with an emulation of Digital Equipment Corporation's "VT100" terminal, a "smart character mode" terminal that permits LEXIS to move the cursor about and preserve the "look and feel" of LEXIS. Even though this is a "character mode" service, it does permit LEXIS to "write" a search request upon the screen in such a manner that you may edit it and send it back to LEXIS. This service is therefore a "high quality" service, suitable for use in your office. It is also an acceptable "home" service which you may access using many inexpensive home computers. With LEXIS, the user selects a class of service by typing a terminal identification code such as ".VT100 <Enter>" or ".IBM3101 <Enter>".

The character-mode WESTLAW and LEXIS services, as well as the IBM PC programs provided by both vendors, do have one important use: they facilitate the "downloading" of copies of recent cases onto floppy disks. Many attorneys access both WESTLAW and LEXIS using Microstuf's "Crosstalk" program which can emulate a VT-100 terminal and which can be programmed to "download" a full case automatically from either WESTLAW or LEXIS without a human having to sit by the computer striking a key for each screen captured. In our opinion, this "downloading" of single cases by subscribers to the WESTLAW and LEXIS services is not a copyright infringement, since the judicial opinions are not the property of the publishers. The publishers have a copyright interest in their headnotes; but if the law firm subscribes to a publisher's reports anyway, then there is no commercial detriment to the publisher, and the downloading of the publisher's headnotes for temporary retention incidental to copying a case is no more a copyright violation than the reproduction of those same headnotes as an incident of copying the same case xerographically. That is to say, if not done systematically over many cases in a way that arguably reduces the publisher's profits, it probably constitutes "fair use." However, even in cases when downloading is not a copyright violation, it may be a violation of the lawyer's contract with the data base system. Thus, for instance, the standard DIALOG subscriber form provides:

> Under no circumstances may Customer or any party acting by or through Customer copy or transmit data received from the DIALOG service in machine-readable form or, subject to any restrictions published in the current "Database Supplier Terms and Conditions", retain such data in machine-readable form other than temporarily for purposes of making a single human-readable copy thereof, except as may be expressly authorized in advance by the database supplier thereof. etc. etc.

Where does this leave us? First, terminals are now obsolete. Today a personal computer costs no more than a terminal; so rather than purchase a terminal that has only limited uses, you should purchase a personal computer that has many uses. Then you "program" the personal computer to "emulate" whatever terminal is required by the class of service that you select.

Both WESTLAW and LEXIS now offer excellent terminal emulation programs for the IBM Personal Computer that provide full emulations of the LEXIS "UBIQ" terminal and the WESTLAW "WALT" terminal. LEXIS also can provide you with software for the Apple Macintosh, and you may use the "3101 Emulation Program" of QL Inc. (Canada) to access WESTLAW in "block mode" from the Macintosh.

LawComm, the legal communications program supplied with this book may be used to access both WESTLAW and LEXIS, as well as many other remote services, in a uniform manner. For WESTLAW and LEXIS access, this program automatically transforms your personal computer into a replica of an IBM Model 3101 "block mode" terminal. It also automatically distinguishes WESTLAW from LEXIS and sets up its special function keys accordingly to perform "page forward," "page backward," "case forward," "case backward" and other special functions. After you contact WESTLAW or LEXIS, strike the F1 "Help" special function key and you will see a complete list of the assignments of commands to keys as well as lists of other useful commands. Strike F1 again to make this list disappear. Note that to gain the full benefit of the legal communications program, you must arrange for "IBM 3101 terminal" service from WESTLAW. When using the LEXIS personal computer service, you must advise LEXIS that your terminal type is an ".IBM3101" (LawComm does this automatically). When LawComm is not communicating with WESTLAW or LEXIS, it emulates an ANSI standard terminal similar to Digital Equipment Corporation's VT–100 and may be used to access virtually all other services, some of which require or support VT–100 emulation.

The state of the art at present requires you to access WESTLAW, LEXIS, and other remote data bases by having your personal computer emulate a standard terminal. This is not an optimal way to access remote data bases, for terminals are far more limited in their capabilities than are personal computers. We know of one terminal emulation program that reminds its user of this fact every time it is used by flashing on the screen the following notice when it first begins operation:

```
This terminal emulation program has just
transformed your $4,000 super expensive
computer into a cheap $600 terminal.
```

Potentially, there is much more that your personal computer can do to help you with your research than any "terminal" or "terminal emulation" program can do. For example, a new program developed by Direct Aid for use with WESTLAW provides you with an "artificial intelligence" feature that lets you formulate your search requests "off line" and save them before you log onto WESTLAW. This program also automatically adds synonyms to your searches, inserting them wherever appropriate. It also steps you through the process of building a WESTLAW search request and then shows you the resulting search. There is still much more that can be done. For example, all of the "Help" and training mechanisms could be built into your personal computer so that they run much faster. The data base menus could also be stored locally within your personal computer to speed your browsing, and these menus could be updated automatically when you first sign on to WESTLAW or LEXIS. Many additional searching aids, such as an "on-line" thesaurus and dictionary, could be installed on your personal computer so that they are never more than a keystroke away and so that you can never misspell a word when formulating a search request. Also, your PC software could be programmed to capture, organize, and store the information that flows across your screen so that you can browse through it again after you "sign off" of WESTLAW or LEXIS. Integrating WESTLAW and LEXIS access with a note card or full-text-searchable data base system would make a lot of sense if the material on the screen could be arranged to flow right into your personal data base. Additionally, "downloading" could be carried out in the "background" while you are thinking and formulating your next search request.

Even more exotic possibilities also exist. "Optical disk" copies of the printed cases (500 volumes to a disk) could be placed right in your office so that you could have your deskside laser printer print copies of interesting cases without you having to leave your desk. The resolution of these printers is such that the printed copies could be indistinguishable from xerographic copies of the same cases as published. And ultimately, WESTLAW and LEXIS may move right into your deskside computer, searching through optical disk data bases without your having to contact a central computer by telephone. You could then browse through the cases on your screen as rapidly as your finger could push the "PgDn" key on your computer's keyboard. You can clearly look forward to a lot of exciting developments in this field over the next twenty years of your practice.

§ 3-7. PROBLEMS

1. Classify the data delivery systems to which your law school subscribes with respect to the following categories: Data delivery systems; access hardware; access software.

2. What percent of published legal material relating to the law of the state where your law school is located is available in legal data base systems?

3. Your office adds 1,000,000 sheets of 8½" by 11" paper records each year. These records must be stored for 10 years in a filing system that will allow prompt access to them. Can computers help in dealing with this information management problem? What further information do you need? What recommendations would you make based upon some reasonable set of assumptions as to this further information.

4. Go through the data base description book provided by DIALOG and see which data bases may contain data useful to a practicing attorney.

5. Create a simple "note card" file system to store your personal research notes.

6. Create a simple "litigation support" system designed to fit the needs of a case pending in the school's practice clinic.

Chapter 4

COMPUTER PROGRAMMING IN THE PRACTICE OF LAW

§ 4-1. INTRODUCTION

The operations of computers are always controlled by detailed instruction sets, called "computer programs," which were written out by skilled computer programmers. These "computer programs" leave nothing to the imagination—they specify precisely what actions the computer is to take. The term "algorithm" has been adopted and redefined by computer scientists to mean a detailed, step-by-step method of solving a problem. Conventional computer programs are always algorithms—they specify precisely what actions a computer is to take, and in what order. Most computer programs are written out in high-level, English-like languages that contain a strong flavor of the notations used in algebra by mathematicians and in symbolic logic by philosophers. These languages have names such as ADA, APL, BASIC, C, COBOL, FORTRAN, LISP, Modula II, Pascal, and PL/1.

We shall not attempt to teach you how to program using any of these languages in this book—many other texts are available to teach you conventional programming. But if you are interested, we encourage you to learn programming. The Microsoft BASIC language that comes with virtually all microcomputers is actually a very powerful language that you can use to make your computer perform all types of useful tasks. Or if you want more of a challenge and have an IBM personal computer, you can try out Borland's Pascal or Modula II compilers. Excellent Pascal and Modula II systems are also available for the Apple Macintosh.

Instead, we shall teach you how to do some super-high-level programming that will be of immediate use to you in the practice of law. You will recall in Chapter 1 that we described how a new "system tailoring" level of programming is emerging between the conventional "computer programming" level and the end user—a level that did not exist just a few years ago. New languages are evolving at this "system tailoring" level that are actually more powerful, and frequently far more specialized, than conventional programming languages. Several of these emerging languages are so easy to learn and so useful in the practice of law that we have chosen to focus upon them in this chapter. Those wishing to master conventional computer programming techniques will find this chapter to be an excellent introduction to programming in general, since these new languages are rapidly approaching the power and flexibility of conventional programming languages. Many of the rules of syntax introduced here are actually derived from the standard programming languages.

In this chapter, we shall first focus upon the design of automated interviewing and form document assembly systems. Since these systems are still emerging from the research labs, we are providing you with a prototype system that is powerful enough to assist you in assembling wills, trusts, contracts, and other textual legal documents. Next, we shall explain how "spreadsheet" programs can be set up to perform financial computations and to assist an attorney with financial planning and accounting tasks. While not all attorneys use a spreadsheet in their practice, those that do cannot imagine how they ever were able to function without this very powerful tool. We are providing you with a sample spreadsheet program that is able to perform a number of highly complex computations useful to attorneys, such as computing the "present value" of a complex series of future payments made in settlement of tort litigation.

§ 4-2. AUTOMATING CLIENT INTERVIEWING AND FORM LEGAL DOCUMENT ASSEMBLY

Perhaps ten to twenty percent of the practice of law involves the routine drafting of form legal documents for clients in uncontested situations where completeness and accuracy is extremely important. Attorneys are frequently faced with the dilemma of wanting to do a complete and thorough job of drafting such form documents but of not being able to charge the client enough to cover the cost of performing the necessary research. This dilemma is particularly serious for the "general practitioner" who wishes to handle any legal problem that a given client might have but who cannot possibly keep abreast with current developments in all the different fields where a client might need some legal assistance. Such attorneys must either not charge for all the time they put into a task, cut corners on the research, or send the client to a "specialist" who does keep abreast—frequently splitting the fee in some manner by dividing up the work in some way.

The specialist is much better able to keep abreast of the current state of the law, but presently the specialist lacks the necessary programming tools to manage the boilerplate passages that must be marshalled and assembled into the final product. Many specialists have proved to be highly creative in adapting conventional word processing systems and "mail merge" systems to the task of assembling boilerplate passages and client-specific information into form documents. Having developed a form assembly system, specialists frequently then learn that they cannot disseminate their systems to other attorneys, since the systems they create are incompatible with the word processors and computers that are used by others. These and other problems must await the development of full-featured interviewing and document assembly systems with integrated word processing facilities. Several major university research projects are attempting to develop such systems, as we shall explain at a later point.

(a) Introduction to LawProcess

To introduce you to this new technology, we have developed an interviewing and document assembly system called LawProcess, which is a partial implementation of the American Bar Foundation's "ABF Processor." The LawProcess program is designed to work in conjunction with a variety of word processors, including LawWord, the word processor distributed with this book, PC–WRITE, a "freeware" program that you may obtain for free and then pay to register to receive updated versions, and the well-known Wordstar and Word Perfect word processing programs. To use LawProcess, you draft "model" documents using your word processor. You embed into the "model" documents commands (described below) that indicate which passages are optional and at what locations client-specific information is to be inserted. The LawProcess program then asks for the necessary client-specific information and inserts such information at all the appropriate points. LawProcess also asks additional "yes"/"no" questions and determines from the answers provided just which optional clauses are to be included and which are to be deleted. In this manner, LawProcess converts the "model" document, with all of its optional passages and client information insertion points, into a "draft" document that is customized to meet the needs of a particular client. You may then customize the "draft" document further using a word processor to meet specific needs of your client that the model document was not designed to anticipate. LawProcess leaves behind a "client data file" that contains all of the answers to questions that were supplied to the computer during the processing of the model document into the draft document. On another occasion, when you need to prepare some other document for the same client, LawProcess can recover these answers from the client data file, so these same questions will not need to be asked a second time. The client data file can also be corrected using your own word processor, and after such corrections have been made, LawProcess can generate a revised draft without the need for a second interview.

(b) Preparing the "LawProcess" Diskette

LawProcess is contained in a file named "lp.exe" that appears upon the diskette supplied with this book. The LawProcess program asks you questions and uses the answers you provide to guide the conversion of "model" documents into "draft" documents. The "model" documents are stored as files whose file names have the name extension

".mdl" to identify them as models. (File names on IBM compatible personal computers have one or two parts, the name itself and an optional "extension." If an extension is used, it is separated from the name by a period, thus: "name.ext". For example, a model will might have the file name "will.mdl", and a model contract might have the name "contract.mdl".

LawProcess transforms the model documents into client-customized draft documents. The resulting draft documents have the same file name as the model documents but have no name extension. For example, LawProcess "processes" the model will named "will.mdl" into the client-customized draft will named "will", and it "processes" the model trust named "trust.mdl." into the client-customized draft trust named "trust". LawProcess also leaves behind a client data file having whatever name you provide with the extension ".clt" added to mark it as a client data file. If you inform the program that the client is "smith", then LawProcess produces a client data file named "smith.clt" that contains the answers to all questions pertaining to the client Smith.

All of these file names must comply with the computer's rules relating to valid file names: File names must be formed from no more than eight characters selected from the letters A through Z (upper or lower case), the digits 0 through 9, and the following symbols:

! @ # $ % & – _ ´ ` { } ^ ( ) ~

All other printable symbols have special meanings and cannot be used in file names. Upper- and lower-case letters may be used interchangeably.

You must first obtain a copy of LawProcess and several data diskettes (Follow, by analogy, the instructions at the start of Appendix D for obtaining a copy of LawWord).

In many of the command examples presented below, <Enter> means "strike the Enter key." On the IBM personal computer, this is the enlarged key on the right hand side of the keyboard bearing an arrow that starts down and then turns to point left. This key is sometimes called the <Return> key. In the command examples presented below, <Esc> means "strike the key labeled Esc."

(c) Starting the Program

Start your computer (see your instructor for assistance) and insert the LawProcess diskette into drive A.

With the LawProcess diskette in drive A: and your computer in operation, the "A>" prompt should be visible upon the screen. Insert the diskette containing the model documents into drive B:. For now, insert the diskette that came with this book into drive B:, since it contains some very simple model documents that you can use for experimentation. To see what model documents the disk in drive B: contains, type the command:

```
dir b:*.mdl<Enter>
```

This command requests a "directory" listing on your screen of all the files on the drive B: diskette whose file names end with the extension ". . . .mdl" and which are therefore "model" documents which may be "processed" into client-specific draft documents. (If you have a printer, you may print this directory by holding down the <Shift> key on your keyboard and striking the <PrtSc> key.)

To view any of the model documents, use the "type" command. For example, to view the model document called "animal.mdl," type the command:

```
type b:animal.mdl<Enter>
```

and the model having that name will be displayed. The model document "animal.mdl" is a very simple document that assembles into a short story about a child and the child's pet.

To get a printout of a model document, for instance of "animal.mdl", use your LawWord word processor.

To place LawProcess into operation, type the command:

```
lp b:<Enter>
```

This command causes LawProcess to take control of your computer. The "b:" advises LawProcess that the model documents are to be found on drive b: of your computer. If you forget to type the b:, the computer will prompt you as follows:

```
MODELS ARE ON DRIVE:
```

and then wait for you to type:

```
b:<Enter>
```

to advise program where the model documents are stored.

For the remainder of this course, you will use the "lp b:<Enter>" command to start the program (unless your instructor tells you otherwise). But when you enter practice, your model documents may be stored on some other disk drive, or in a directory or subdirectory of a large-capacity, fixed-disk drive. You must learn to type the proper "path" following the "lp" command that will enable your computer to find the model documents. While you will not need to use complex "path" commands in this course, the following complex "path" commands are presented as examples that may be useful to you in your practice when you may have literally hundreds of documents stored within numerous directories and subdirectories of a large-capacity, fixed-disk drive. These examples are presented here for your future reference—do not be concerned if you do not understand them fully right now. (The backward slash is used in these examples to separate directory names from subdirectory names.)

```
lp b:forms<Enter>
```

The models are stored on floppy disk drive B: in a directory named "forms".

```
lp<Enter>
```

The model documents are stored on the "default" disk drive. If your computer's command prompt is "A>", then drive A: is the "default" disk drive, and this means the model documents are stored on the LawProcess diskette.

```
lp models<Enter>
```

The model documents are stored in a directory named "models" on the "default" disk drive.

```
lp models\trusts<Enter>
```

The model documents are stored in the subdirectory "trust" of the directory "models" on the "default" disk drive.

For more information, see your PC–DOS or MS–DOS manual's discussion of disk drives, directories, subdirectories, and "paths." And again, do not be concerned if you do not fully understand these examples.

(d) Operating the Program: Naming the Client and Selecting the Model

After you issue the process command and inform the computer of where the model documents are stored, the following message appears:

```
          AUTOMATIC DOCUMENT ASSEMBLY SYSTEM
         (Copyright 1986 West Publishing Co.)

Please type in the CLIENT file name:
(Type <ctrl>C to EXIT program)
>
```

You must type in a name that will become the name assigned to the client file which the processor is about to produce. The name you type must be a legal file name—no more than eight letters, digits, and the 16 symbols listed above. If you try to type more than eight characters or type an illegal symbol, the computer will "beep" at you and refuse to accept what you type.

At any time, you may quit and exit from the program by holding down the <Ctrl> key and typing "C". Whenever the instructions specify <Ctrl> followed by a letter, the instructions are advising you to strike that letter while holding down the shift key labeled <Ctrl>.

For your first attempt at assembling a draft document, pick the model document "animal.mdl" and assemble it for your client Mary and her pet lamb. Type:

```
MARY<Enter>
```

as your client file name. This will cause all the answers that you supply to be placed in a file name "mary" on the LawProcess diskette. (Note that the file name will appear in uppercase, as shown, even if you type it in lower case.)

The LawProcess program next searches drive A: for an existing client file having the name "mary.clt". Finding none, the program does not know whether you have mistyped the name or whether you wish to create a new client file. So the program asks:

```
Client file "MARY.CLT" does NOT EXIST.
O. K. to create a NEW client file?
(Type <ctrl>C to EXIT program)
(Type Y for YES; N for NO)
>
```

In response, you should type:

```
Y
```

in either upper- or lower-case. You need not type <Enter> after striking the "Y" key. Your answer advises the program that it is O.K. to create a new client file named "mary.clt" on the LawProcess diskette in drive A:

Next, the computer asks you what model document you wish to assemble:

```
What MODEL document do you wish to assemble?
(Type <ctrl>C to EXIT program)
>
```

In response to this question, type:

```
ANIMAL<Enter>
```

to advise the computer that you wish to select the model whose file name is "animal.mdl". Note that you do not need to type the extension ".mdl," since LawProcess adds this extension to the name you type automatically. This makes the program easier for secretaries to use. The computer will not permit you to type an invalid file name—it will "beep" at you if you strike an improper key or try and type more than eight letters or numbers.

The computer next verifies its assignment by displaying the following message:

```
MODEL document = "B:ANIMAL.MDL"
DRAFT document = "ANIMAL"
CLIENT file = "MARY.CLT"
Assembling document "ANIMAL". Please wait...
```

This message verifies that you have instructed the computer to "process" the "model" named "animial.mdl" located on drive B:, thereby generating the client-customized "draft" named ANIMAL for the client whose client data file is named MARY. The final "Please wait . . ." message is typical of messages the program displays whenever it commences a task that may take some time to complete.

(e) Operating the Program: Answering the Questions

The red light on both the disk drives A: and B: will now come on as the computer begins reading the model off of drive B: and assembling the draft and the client data file on drive A:. Soon the program will begin asking you questions. There are two types of questions: Information questions that ask for a client-specific answer, such as the name or address of the client—these answers are inserted directly into the draft document at one or more points; and questions that ask for a "yes" or "no" answer—these guide the computer in selecting or rejecting boilerplate passages. Specific instructions precede each question advising you of your options. The first question reads as follows:

```
INSTRUCTIONS:

Answer the question set forth below.
Type   <esc>       to END your answer;
Type   ?           if you CANNOT answer;
Type   <ctrl>Z     to ERASE your answer;
Type   <ctrl>C     to EXIT program.

VARIABLE: ch nm

   The child's name:

>
```

Read the instructions carefully before you attempt to answer this question. Note in particular that striking the <Enter> key does NOT terminate your answer, but merely inserts a "hard" carriage return into your answer. To terminate your answer and send it into the computer, you must strike the <Esc> key. The reason why you are required to terminate each answer by striking the <Esc> key is because your answer may be many lines or even many paragraphs long. At times, you will want to insert "hard" carriage returns into your answer, as when you are typing in the multi-line address of the recipient of a letter and wish to have the address appear on three separate lines. So the <Enter> key is reserved for use as a "hard carriage return" key for use in your longer answers, and the <Esc> key is the key that you must strike to terminate your answer.

You may backspace and thereby erase and correct anything on the line that you are typing; but if your answer is several lines long, you may not correct the lines that have already scrolled up your screen. You can, however, cause the computer to reject your entire answer, thereby permitting you to start typing it anew, by holding down the <Ctrl> key and striking "Z".

Type your answer just as you would if your were using a word processor. Do not strike the <Enter> key at the end of each line, but instead permit the computer to "word wrap" any word fragments down to the next line automatically. Your word processor may then "reformat" the document freely, breaking the lines wherever necessary to achieve uniform-length lines or justification. Strike the <Enter> key only at points where you really wish to force a line break: for example, in tables, in multi-line addresses, and at the ends of paragraphs.

If you do not know the answer to a question or do not wish to answer for any reason, type "?" as your answer—you need not type

<Esc>. The computer will move on to the next question, and the draft will not be completely processed.

Returning to assembling the model document "animal.mdl" for Mary, you ask the first question: "The child's name:" and the answer to this question is "Mary." So type the answer:

```
Mary<Esc>
```

Note that that first letter of "Mary" is capitalized—you must always type your answer precisely as you wish it to appear in the draft document. If, by accident, you strike <Enter> before striking <Esc>, don't panic—the computer disregards any extra <Enter> keystroke at the very end of an answer. So the answer

```
Mary<Enter><Esc>
```

is equivalent to the above answer, and is accepted as "Mary" and not as "Mary<Enter>."

The message "VARIABLE: ch nm" in the question advises you that the answer you are typing into the computer will be associated with the "variable" whose short name is "ch nm." Ignore this for the moment, since we have not yet discussed variable names.

The interview process continues, with the following questions being asked and answered:

```
    How big is Mary's animal?
```

(Type "big," "little," etc.):

little<Esc>

What kind of little animal did Mary buy?

>lamb<Esc>

```
VARIABLE: an na
    The animal's name:
> Fluffy<Esc>
```

The next two questions are of a different sort. They require a "yes" or "no" answer:

```
INSTRUCTIONS:
Answer Y for YES or N for NO.
Type  ?          if you CANNOT answer;
Type  <ctrl>C    to EXIT program.
VARIABLE: danger
    The animal is dangerous:
        YES OR NO? (Type Y or N)
>
```

The answer to this first "yes"/"no" question determines which of two alternative passages will be selected for inclusion in the draft document—the "dangerous animal" passage, or the "non-dangerous animal" passage. You answer this question by typing a single keystroke—you need not type <Esc> or <Enter>. The instructions indicate that you may type "Y" (or "y") for "yes," "N" (or "n") for "no," or "?" if you do not wish to answer the question. You may also terminate the program by holding down <Ctrl> and striking "C".

Since lambs are not dangerous, you type

```
N
```

without typing <Esc> or <Enter>. You thereby cause the processor to select the "non-dangerous animal" passage for inclusion in the draft document.

The "non-dangerous animal" passage itself contains an optional "gentle animal" passage. Accordingly, the following questions appear next:

```
VARIABLE: your name
   Your name:
>Bob<Esc>
Is Mary's lamb truly gentle, Bob?
      YES OR NO? (Type Y or N)
>
```

If you answer "Y", a "gentle animal" clause is inserted into the "not dangerous animal" passage; if you answer "N", this "gentle animal" clause is omitted entirely—there is no alternative clause. And had you advised the computer in the previous question that yes, the animal is dangerous, you would not have been presented with this question, since the "dangerous animal" passage has no counterpart.

A message now appears upon the screen advising you that the model "animal.mdl" incorporates by reference another model named "color.mdl" which contains language describing the animal's coat and eye color. The message reads as follows:

```
Incorporating model document "COLOR.MDL"
by reference into output document.
```

Then two more questions appear:

```
VARIABLE: coat color
   The color of the animal's coat:
> fluffy white<Esc>
VARIABLE: eye color
   The color of the animal's eyes:
>brown<Esc>
```

And finally, this concluding message appears:

```
DOCUMENT "ANIMAL" COMPLETED.
Do you wish to rename it?
   (Type Y for YES; N for No.)
>N
Draft another document for the same client?
   (Type Y for Yes; N for NO)
> N
A>
```

When the "A>" appears, the draft document is finished. To view the draft document, type:

```
type animal<Enter>
```

The draft will look like this:

```
                Mary's Lamb

   Mary had a little lamb.  Its name was Fluffy.
Lambs make nice pets.  Fluffy is gentle enough
for a baby.

   The lamb has a fluffy white coat.  Its eyes
are brown.
```

You may now revise this draft further with your word processor. Most form legal documents require some manual revision after the automated assembly process is finished. Even if the designer of the automated assembly system could think of all the possibilities, including them all would make the interviews so long that the interviews would take too long. You will need to use your word processor in any event to "reformat" the document so that the lines and pages are all of equal length. With your LawWord word processor, <Ctrl-B> is the "reformat paragraph" command, and <Ctrl-PgDn> and "<Ctrl-End>" are the "adjust page length" commands.

The processor also generates a client file containing the answers to all the questions. To view the client file for Mary, type:

```
type mary.clt<Enter>
```

The client file for the above document looks like this:

```
LET ch nm: the child's name =
<Mary>
LET size: the size of the animal =
<little>
LET type: the type of animal =
<lamb>
LET an nm: the animal's name =
<Fluffy>
LET danger: the animal is dangerous =
<N>
Let your name=
<Bob>
LET gntl: the animal is gentle =
<Y>
LET coat color: the color of the animal's coat =
<fluffy white>
LET eye color: the color of the animal's eyes =
<brown>
```

The client file serves as an "audit trail" of the client interview. It may also be revised using your word processor, and then you can have LawProcess regenerate the draft from the revised client file without any of the questions being asked a second time. And if you prepare other documents for the same client, LawProcess can automatically retrieve values from the client data file and will not need to ask the above questions a second time.

Now you try assembling a draft of "animal" for Sam, who owns a very dangerous pet shark named Jaws, with a black, scaly coat and blood-red eyes. Try assembling a "will" or a "power of attorney" using the sample models supplied with this book.

§ 4-3. DRAFTING DOCUMENTS FOR AUTOMATED ASSEMBLY

LawProcess is designed to work in conjunction with your word processor. To create an automated document drafting system, you begin by using your word processor to create a "model" document. A "model" document is a "generic" document that has not been customized for any particular client. Instead, it contains all of the possible clauses, plus instructions explaining how the document is to be assembled. If you have ever examined an attorney's book of legal forms, you will already be familiar with the concept of a "model" document, for the conventions we are about to teach you were derived from form books used by practicing attorneys. Among others, David Link, presently dean of Notre Dame's law school, was one of the first to suggest the use of bracketed client data descriptors as "spaceholders" for client-specific information in model documents.

The model document drafting language that you are about to learn is a subset of the ABF language developed under the sponsorship of the American Bar Foundation over the past ten years. In addition to the present authors, contributors to the growth of this language include linguist Barbara Sangster; law professors Layman Allen, Gerald Bennett, Michael Heather, Gary Laser, Robert Seibel, and Ronald Staudt; attorney and business professor Charles Saxon; computer scientists Peter Bergsman, Martha Evans, Charles Filstead, Henry Haar, John Pollack, and Greg Suski; and attorneys James Eidelman and Fred Fagg; and numerous law students at Michigan, Northwestern, Newcastle-Upon-Tyne Polytechnic, and IIT Chicago Kent.

(a) Spaceholders for Client Data: Bracketed Descriptions

Square brackets "[. . .]" are inserted into the model document wherever client-specific information is to be inserted. A statement within the brackets indicates what information is to be inserted at each point.

To familiarize yourself with this convention, turn on your word processor and type in the following language which might form the first part of a simple will:

Last Will And Testament Of
[the testator's name]

I, [the testator's name], residing at [the full address of the testator], do hereby declare this to be my last will and testament, revoking all prior wills and codicils.

I give, devise, and bequeath to my [husband or wife, the proper term for the testator's spouse] all of my property, both real and personal, including all of my cash, if [he or she, the pronoun for the spouse] survives me by at least 30 days. Otherwise I give, devise, and bequeath all of my property, both real and personal, including all of my cash, to my children, PER STIRPES.

I appoint my [husband or wife, the proper term for the testator's spouse] executor of my estate if [he or she, the pronoun for the spouse] survives me by more than 30 days. Otherwise I appoint as executor of my estate the oldest of my children or grandchildren who survives me by more than 30 days. My executor shall not have to post security upon any bond that may be required by the court where my estate is probated.

On this [long date], before the undersigned witnesses, I hereby append my signature to this, my last will and testament.

____
[the testator's name]

On this [long date], we did witness [the testator's name] sign the above document and state that it was a last will and testament.

____

____

____

Use your LawWord word processor to create the above model will. Save it on a floppy disk under the name "will.mdl". Insert the floppy disk containing the above will in drive B: of your computer, and insert the LawProcess diskette into drive A:. Type "date<Enter>", and when prompted for the date, to type in the date that you wish to have appear in the will at the locations marked ". . . [long date] . . ." so that you may take full advantage of the automatic date generation feature of the program. At the "A>" prompt, type:.

```
lp b: <Enter>
```

to start the program LawProcess. Next, follow the instructions that are displayed upon the screen. Use "smith" as your client file name and "will" as the name of the model document that you wish to "draft" for Mr. Smith. When you are done and the "A>" prompt reappears, type the commands:

```
type will <Enter>
```

and

```
type smith.clt <Enter>
```

to view the draft will you have prepared for Mr. Smith and to view his client data file. To make further revisions to your will or to print it, read it back into your word processor. You will need to use your word processor in any case to "reformat" the lines so that they are of the right length for printing and to center the title lines. Your word processor may also be used to break up your document into pages and to number the pages.

LawProcess simply scans the text of the model document and writes it out as the text of the draft document. Whenever the program encounters a pair of brackets enclosing a description of an item of client data, the program checks to see if it already has client data that corresponds to the description. If not, then the program displays the description as a question, with its first letter capitalized. Accordingly, the bracketed descriptor ". . . [the testator's name] . . . " is transformed into the question:

```
VARIABLE: the testator's n
   The testator's name
>
```

Normally you answer all of the questions, typing <Esc> at the end of each answer to send it to the computer. The computer writes the descriptor and the answer out to the client data file named "smith" as follows:

```
LET the testator's name =
<Sam W. Spade>
```

and inserts the answer into the will at each point where the same descriptor ". . . [the testator's name] . . . " appears. The computer also retains the answer to each question in its memory, along with the first 16 characters in each descriptor, and accordingly you are only asked each question once, even if the answer is inserted into the draft document many times.

Occasionally, you may need to place brackets into your model documents for reasons other than as markers for client information inserts. For example, you may need to use brackets as parentheses within parentheses or as a mechanism for marking an addition to a quoted passage. To prevent the computer from confusing such brackets with brackets used to enclose client data descriptors, precede each such bracket with a tilde—~. Any character having a special meaning to the computer loses that special meaning when it is preceded by a tilde. But what if you should want to include a tilde in your model document? Simply type two tildes. The first of the two tildes signals to the computer that the special character which follows (the second tilde) is not to have its usual special meaning. Remember: use ~[and ~] when brackets are used to represent brackets to be printed rather than being used to delimit descriptors; and use ~~ to represent a single ~.

The two variables ". . . [short date] . . . " and ". . . [long date] . . . " are predefined by the system so that they do not generate questions. When you first turn on your computer, you are asked the question:

```
Current date is Tue 1-01-1980
Enter new date:
```

You should respond to this question by typing the date that you wish to have inserted into the documents that you are about to have drafted automatically. Usually you will type in today's date, but sometimes you may wish to "post-date" the documents ahead, for example, to the date when they will be signed. For example, you might type in the date:

```
7-20-88<Enter>
```

meaning "July 20, 1988." LawProcess retrieves this date from your computer and computes the following two forms of the date for you automatically:

. . . [short date] . . . becomes . . . July 20, 1988 . . .

. . . [long date] . . . becomes . . . 20th day of July, 1988 . . .

You may insert ". . . [short date] . . . " and ". . . [long date] . . . " into your documents wherever the above two forms of the date, and the date you supplied to the computer when you first turned it on, satisfy your needs.

After your computer is turned on, when the "A>" prompt is present on your screen, you may alter the date stored within your computer, or check to see what date it is, by typing the command:

```
Date<Enter>
```

the computer will then prompt you as follows:

```
Current date is Wed 7-20-1988
Enter new date:
```

If the date is the date you desire, strike <Enter> without typing in a new date, and it will not be altered. If not, then type in the date you desire, as explained above.

(b) Short and Long Names for Variables

When you studied Algebra, you learned that "X" and "Y" in the equation "X + 2Y = 5" are the names of "variables." The descriptors that you insert into the square brackets to reserve room for client-specific data are also the names of "variables." In drafting model documents, we use long, meaningful variables names (like "the testator's name") rather than short, cryptic variable names (like "X") because the computer can then ask long, meaningful questions. But if a document must contain numerous occurrences of a given variable, the typist soon tires of typing out its lengthy name over and over again. In that case, a short, cryptic name can be helpful—but then we do not get a long, meaningful question.

A compromise is therefore needed. LawProcess has been designed to permit you to assign both a short name and a long name to each client data variable, joining the two names together by means of a colon. You may append a short variable name followed by a colon to the front of any long variable name the first time that it occurs in a given document. Thereafter, you may use the short name by itself. The "short name" of the variable is then its true name, and the long name is used to form long, meaningful questions and to improve the readibility of the client data file. For example, we could insert

```
. . . [testname: the testator's name] . . .
```

into the above model will at the first point where the name of the testator is to be inserted. At later points, we would insert

```
. . . [testname] . . .
```

into the will by itself to reserve space for the testator's name. The program PROCESS would then ask the following question:

```
VARIABLE: testname

    The testator's name:

>
```

Now you can understand, for the first time, the true significance of the first line of this question—the line that reads "VARIABLE: testname". This line informs you of the variable's "true" name—its short name. The client data file entry for this variable will contain both the short and long variable names:

```
LET testname: the testator's name =

<Sam W. Spade>
```

And now a word of warning: If you do not provide a short name, the computer automatically forms its own short name from the first sixteen characters in the long name of the variable. If the first sixteen characters of two different variable names are identical, then the computer will think the two variables are identical, even though this is not the case. For example, the following simple will contains two different variables that begin with the same 24 keystrokes:

```
    I, [the name of the testator], do hereby make
this my last will and testament. . . . .

    I give to [the name of the testator's spouse]
. . . .
```

The first sixteen letters of "[the name of the testator]" and "[the name of the testator's spouse]" are the same—"the name of the" in both cases. So the computer asks only the one question:

```
VARIABLE: the name of the
    The name of the testator:
>
```

and plugs the answer received into both spaces. The client file will contain only the following single entry for both variables:

```
LET the name of the testator =
[Sam W. Spade]
```

If you chose not to use "short" names, make sure that all your variables differ within their first sixteen characters. Preferably, you should use short names in conjunction with all of your long names, and then this problem can never arise.

Redrafted with short and long names, the above simple will might read as follows:

```
              Last Will And Testament Of
           [testname: the testator's name]

    I, [testname], residing at [address: the full
address of the testator], do hereby declare this
to be my last will and testament, revoking all
prior wills and codicils.

    I give, devise, and bequeath to my [h. or w.:
husband or wife, the proper term for the
testator's spouse] all of my property, both real
and personal, including all of my cash, if [he or
she: he or she, the pronoun for the spouse]
survives me by at least 30 days. Otherwise I
give, devise, and bequeath all of my property,
both real and personal, including all of my
cash, to my children, PER STIRPES.

    I appoint my [h. or w.] executor of my estate
if [he or she] survives me by more than 30 days.
Otherwise I appoint as executor of my estate the
oldest of my children or grandchildren who
survives me by more than 30 days. My executor
shall not have to post security upon any bond
that may be required by the court where my estate
is probated.

    On this [long date], before the undersigned
witnesses, I hereby append my signature to this,
my last will and testament.

                              ________________________
                              [testname]
```

```
    On this [long date], we did witness
[testname] sign the above document and state
that it was a last will and testament.
```

____

____

____

As an exercise, redraft your simple will so that it uses both short and long names in combination. When you see the questions accompanied by short names that you have selected and view the resulting client files, you will see how much more readable the short names make everything appear.

(c) Optional and Alternative Clauses

Optional clauses are preceded by a bracketed statement which specifies the condition that is to govern their use. The first word within the brackets must be the capitalized word IF. The word IF is then followed by a variable name that states the condition that calls for inclusion of the optional clause. The variable name is followed by the capitalized word INSERT. For example:

```
    [IF cash: a gifts of cash clause is to be
included in the will INSERT] . . .
    [IF p. tx. res: the estate and inheritance
taxes are to be paid out of the estate res
INSERT] . . .
    [IF wv. warr.: a "waiver of implied warranty"
clause is desired INSERT] . . .
```

When the model document is processed, these bracketed inserts give rise to "yes"/"no" questions such as the following:

```
VARIABLE: cash
    A gifts of cash clause is to be included in
the will:
YES OR NO? (Type Y or N)
```

If this question is answered with a "Y" or "y", the optional clause is included in the draft document; if it is answered with an "N" or "n", the optional clause is omitted.

Because optional clauses begin with a bracketed statement that begins with the capitalized word IF, optional clauses are called "IF clauses," and the bracketed statement is called an "IF statement." The end of the "IF clause" must also be marked in some manner. We mark the "end of the IF clause" with a bracketed, capitalized [END IF] statement. Accordingly, a typical "IF clause" in a model document looks like this:

```
. . . .
[IF p. tx. res: the estate and inheritance taxes
are to be paid out of the estate res INSERT]
```

```
    I instruct my executor to pay all
inheritance, estate, and other death taxes that
may be due as the result of my death out of the
estate RES so that the individual legatees and
devisees do not have to pay those taxes out of
their individual gifts.
[END IF]
. . . .
```

When a document containing this "IF clause" is processed, the following question appears:

```
VARIABLE: p. tx. res
        The estate and inheritance taxes are to be
    paid out of the estate res:
    YES OR NO? (Type Y or N)
>
```

If you type "Y" or "y", the bracketed statements disappear and the "IF clause" becomes part of the draft; if you type "N" or "n", then the bracketed statements and the "IF clause" disappear from the draft, and the surrounding passages are pulled together to close up the hole. If you type "?", then the "IF clause" is copied into the draft just as it is, brackets and all.

On occasion, you will want to select between two alternative clauses. Suppose, for example, that your model will is to include two guardianship clauses, one drafted to appoint a single guardian with an alternate and the other drafted to appoint two joint guardians for the minor children. To accomplish the selection, you enclose both clauses within a single "IF clause," separating them by the bracketed, capitalized phrase [OTHERWISE INSERT]. The clause is then called an "IF–OTHERWISE clause" and might appear as follows:

```
. . . .
    [IF jnt. g.: two joint guardians are desired,
rather than a single guardian and an alternate
INSERT]
    I appoint [guard 1: the name of the first
joint guardian] and [guard 2: the name of the
second joint guardian] joint guardians of any of
my children who are still less than eighteen
years old on the date of my death. . . .
[OTHERWISE INSERT]
    I appoint [guard: the name of the guardian]
guardian of any of my children. . . .
[END IF]
. . . .
```

When a model will containing this passage is processed, the following question is generated:

```
VARIABLE: jnt. g.
```

```
    Two joint guardians are desired, rather than
a single guardian and an alternate:

YES OR NO? (Type Y or N)

>
```

If you answer this question "Y" or "y", then the draft will contains the "joint guardian" provision, which would be most appropriate if the joint guardians were a married couple. If you answer "N" or "n", then the draft will contains the "guardian and alternate" clause, which is more appropriate if the guardian is not married.

The real power of the "IF clauses" and the "IF–OTHERWISE clauses" arises from the fact that they may be nested within one another to any desired depth. An "IF clause" may itself be of any length and may contain any number of additional "IF clauses" and "IF–OTHERWISE clauses," and the same may be said of the "IF–OTHERWISE clause." By breaking up your model document into text segments that are enclosed within such clauses and nested within one another, you can achieve automatic assembly of any form legal document, no matter how complex it may be.

As an example of such nesting, the model named "animal.mdl" that served as your first introduction to automatic document assembly is set forth below:

```
    [ch nm: the child's name]'s [^type: the type
of animal]

    [ch nm] had a [size: the size of the animal]
[type: the type of animal]. Its name was [an nm:
the animal's name].

[IF danger: the animal is dangerous INSERT]

    WARNING: [^type]s are very dangerous!

[OTHERWISE INSERT]

    [^type]s make nice pets.

    [IF gntl: the animal is gentle INSERT]

[an nm: the animal's name] is gentle enough for
a baby.

    [END IF]

[END IF]

[color: the paragraph stating the color of the
animal's coat and eyes—incorporated by
reference]
```

The model "animal.mdl" contains an "IF–OTHERWISE clause" that selects between a "dangerous animal" passage and a "nice animal" passage. And the "nice animal" passage itself contains an "IF clause" that encloses an optional "gentle animal" passage.

Note that the "[IF . . . INSERT]", the "[OTHERWISE INSERT]", and the "[END IF]" that form the "IF–OTHERWISE clause" are all fully left-justified so that a straight vertical line could be drawn through their left edges:

```
[IF . . . INSERT] . . . .
. . . . . .
. . . . . .
[OTHERWISE INSERT] . . . .
. . . . . .
   [IF . . . INSERT] . . . .
   . . . . . .
   . . . . . .
   [END IF]
. . . . . .
[END IF]
```

Note also that the "[IF . . . INSERT]" and the "[END IF]" which together form the nested "IF clause" are also carefully aligned with their left edges falling on a straight vertical line, but the line is spaced in from the left margin. If a third "IF clause" were nested within the second "IF clause," the left edges of its "[IF . . . INSERT]" and "[END IF]" elements would also fall on a vertical line, but this time the line would be spaced further in from the left margin. It is important for you to line up the left edges in this manner so that you can keep track of which "[OTHERWISE INSERT]" and which "[END IF]" go with which "[IF . . . INSERT]". Here is another example taken from a model divorce petition which illustrates how important proper alignment of the left edges of these bracketed commands is to the readibility of a model document:

```
          PETITION FOR DISSOLUTION OF MARRIAGE

   Petitioner, [petname: the name of the
petitioner],
[IF pro se: the case is to be handled pro se
INSERT]
PRO SE,
[OTHERWISE INSERT] by [his or her: "his" or
"her," the proper pronoun for the petitioner]
   [IF student: a senior law student is working
on the case INSERT] attorneys, [atty: the name
of the supervising attorney] and [stnt nm: the
name of the senior law student], certified
senior law student,
   [OTHERWISE INSERT] attorney, [atty: the name
of the supervising attorney],
   [END IF] IIT CHICAGO KENT LAW OFFICES,
[END IF] alleges:
. . . .
```

Three and four levels of nesting are not that uncommon in model legal documents.

As an exercise, try adding an optional clause to your model will that requires the executor to pay the death taxes out of the RES of the estate, and try adding alternative guardianship clauses to your model will.

(d) Incorporation of One Model Into Another

The model "animal.mdl" set forth above includes, as its last line, a passage that is incorporated by reference:

```
[color: the paragraph stating the color of the
animal's coat and eyes—incorporated by
reference]
```

This command instructs the program LawProcess to find a model whose name is "color.mdl" and incorporate it into the document "animal.mdl" at this point. The model "color.mdl" contains the following language:

```
   The [type: the type of animal] has a [coat
color: the color of the animal's coat] coat.
Its eyes are [eye color: the color of the
animal's eyes].
```

Incorporation by reference is a very powerful tool. It enables you to take one model "trustee's powers" clause and incorporate it by reference into ten different model wills. A change made in the one model "trustee's powers" clause is automatically incorporated into all ten of the model wills, and you need not revise each model will separately. Any passage that you may wish to include in two or more separate models should be drafted as a "stand-alone" model that can be incorporated by reference into the target models.

Additionally, lengthy models are difficult to work with. It is preferable to draft a complex model as a simple document that incorporates its parts by reference. Then you need never work on more than a page or two of text at a time with your word processor. For example, the following is a model will drafted by Bob Seibel at Cornell:

```
              LAST WILL AND TESTAMENT OF
           [tstr: the name of the testator]

   I, [tstr: the name of the testator], of
[ctyst: the name of the city and state in which
the testator lives], hereby revoke all prior
wills and codicils and make this my Will.


*  [bequests: the article containing bequests of
   personalty]
   [IF csbq: the testator wishes to make specific
   gifts of cash INSERT]
```

```
*  [cash: the article containing cash bequests]
   [END IF]
   [IF spdv: the testator wishes to make a specific
   devise of real estate INSERT]

*  [devise: the article devising real estate]
   [END IF]

*  [residue: the article disposing of the residue]
   IF mi trust: the testator wants a trust for
   beneficiaries under a certain age INSERT]

*  [trust: the article establishing a trust for
   minors]
   [END IF]

*  [execinst: the article containing instructions
   for the executor]
   [IF guard: an article naming a guardian for
   minor children is desired INSERT]

*  [guardian: the article naming a guardian for
   minor children]
   [END IF]

*  [incompet: the article relating to
   incompetents]

*  [execpwrs: the article naming the executors and
   listing his or her powers]

*  [closing: the "in witness" clause and
   signatures]
```

Each bracketed variable marked with an asterisk in the above will incorporates by reference a model document that contains an article of the will.

To achieve incorporation by reference, it is only necessary to arrange for the short name of the variable enclosed within brackets to be identical to the file name of the model that is to be incorporated. For example, the first incorporation by reference in the above will is

```
[bequests: the article containing bequests of
personalty]
```

Normally, the program LawProcess would ask the question "The article containing bequests of personalty:" when it encounters such a bracketed variable. But before asking that question, the program checked the directory of the disk drive that contains the models to see if a model having the name "bequests.mdl" exists. Such a model does exist, so instead of asking a question, the processor incorporates the model "bequests.mdl" into the draft will at the point indicated. If anything goes wrong (for example, if you misspell the name of the model or if it does not exist) then the program asks a question in the usual way, and this warns you that something is amiss with your attempt to incorporate by reference.

Accordingly, if the short name of a variable is identical to the file name of a model, then instead of asking a question, the computer incorporates the model document by reference into the text.

(e) The "LET" Statement—Assigning Values

Frequently you will find that the values of a number of variables all depend upon just a few facts. For example, a trust may contain a variety of personal pronouns for the testator. If the testator is a man, then "he," "him," and "his" are used. If the testator is a woman, then "she," "her," and "her" are used. If there are two trustees, then "they," "them," and "their" are used. And if the trustee is a bank, then the proper choice is "it," "it," and "its." In addition, "s" needs to be added to many verbs to alter their number from "plural" to "singular" if there is only one trustee. So we have at least four different variables all of which can be selected automatically once we know whether the trustee is a man, a woman, a group, or an institution.

The LET statement comes from the popular programming language BASIC, although its use here is greatly simplified. It permits us to assign a value to any variable. For example, to assign the subjective pronoun "he" to the trustee's subjective personal pronoun, one inserts the following into the document:

```
[LET he, she, &c = <he>]
```

and then, at the point where the pronoun is needed, one inserts a bracketed variable:

```
. . . . If [he, she, &c] lives within the state
of Illinois, then [he, she, &c] need not
. . . .
```

The following LET statement assigns "her" to the trustee's objective personal pronoun:

```
[LET him or her = <her>]
```

An "IF–OTHERWISE clause" can then be used to select which LET statement is actually executed by the computer:

```
[IF male: the trustee is a man ]
    [LET he, she, &c = <he>]
    [LET him, her, &c = <him>]
    [LET his, her, &c = <his>]
[OTHERWISE]
    [LET he, she, &c = <she>]
    [LET him, her, &c = <her>]
    [LET his, her, &c = <her>]
[END IF]
```

Here, three variables are computed after only one question is asked.

Note the use of "angle brackets" <. . . .> as quotation marks in these two examples. This usage of angle brackets as quotation marks instead of ". . . ." or '. . . .' makes it possible for the assigned value to contain ordinary quotation marks, as in the following example:

```
[IF warranty: the goods are warranted]
    [LET the warranty phrase =
        <The goods are fully warranted.>]
        . . . .
[OTHERWISE]
    [LET the warranty phrase =
        <The goods are sold "AS IS.">]
        . . . .
[END IF]
```

This use of angle brackets as quotation marks was originated by the G. and C. Merriam Company. In their dictionaries, all examples of usage are enclosed in angle brackets.

The above example uses an "IF–OTHERWISE clause" to select which warranty phrase to use. A slightly more complicated set of "IF-clauses" can solve the problem of the trustee's pronouns plus the "s" for the regular verbs:

```
[IF t inst: the trustee is an institution]
    [LET t he, she, &c = <it> ]
    [LET t him, her, &c = <it> ]
    [LET t his, her, &c = <its> ]
    [LET s or no s = <s> ]
[OTHERWISE]
    [IF two t: there are two or more trustees]
        [LET t he, she, &c = <they> ]
        [LET t him, her, &c = <them> ]
        [LET t his, her, &c = <their> ]
        [LET s or no s = <> ]
```

```
        [OTHERWISE]
            [LET s or no s = <s>]
            [IF t is male: the trustee is to be a man]
                [LET t he, she, &c = <he>]
                [LET t him, her, &c = <him>]
                [LET t his, her, &c = <his>]
            [OTHERWISE]
                [LET t he, she, &c = <she>]
                [LET t him, her, &c = <her>]
                [LET t his, her, &c = <her>]
            [END IF]
        [END IF]
    [END IF]
```

At most, only three questions need to be asked to compute the values of all four of these variables. And if the trustee is a bank, only one question is asked—you can rewrite it so that fewer questions are asked in the case of an individual trustee, if you like. You may have to add some additional LET statements to select between the singular and plural value of any irregular verbs that the trust agreement may contain.

Now consider a will example. Here, there will be personal pronouns for the testator or testatrix and for the spouse, as well as the word "husband" or "wife," whichever is appropriate:

```
    [IF male: the sex of the testator is male]
        [LET t he she = <he>]
        [LET t him her = <him>]
        [LET t his her = <his>]
        [LET s he she = <she>]
        [LET s him her = <her>]
        [LET s his her = <her>]
        [LET husband or wife = <wife>]
    [OTHERWISE]
        [LET t he she = <she>]
        [LET t him her = <her>]
        [LET t his her = <her>]
        [LET s he she = <he>]
        [LET s him her = <him>]
        [LET s his her = <his>]
        [LET husband or wife = <husband>]
    [END IF]
```

Here, we get seven different client values out of one question.

(f) The Capitalization Operator: ^

Personal pronouns cause another problem in automated document drafting. When a personal pronoun comes at the very beginning of a sentence, it needs to have its first letter capitalized; if it falls mid-sentence, its first letter has to be lower-case. In all the above examples, the first letter of the personal pronouns are lower-case. How does one selectively capitalize the first letter of personal pronouns in some cases and not in other cases?

The "up-arrow" (or "caret" or "circumflex"), "^", is located in the "upper-case" position on the "6" key of your computer, if it has a standard IBM keyboard. If an "up-arrow" appears just ahead of a variable name within square brackets, the "up-arrow" signals the computer to capitalize the first letter of the inserted value. For example, consider the following excerpt from a model trust agreement:

```
. . . .

   [^ t he she &c ] may retain any securities
that were part of the trust RES when [ t he she
&c ] accepted the trusteeship, even if

. . . .
```

When assembled for a female individual trustee, the above passage becomes:

```
. . . .

She may retain any securities that were part of
the trust RES when she accepted the trusteeship,
even if

. . . .
```

Because of the "up arrow," the pronoun "She" has its first letter capitalized at the start of the sentence, but not at the "mid sentence" location. The "up arrow" operator makes it unnecessary to have separate variables to represent the capitalized and uncapitalized forms of the same pronoun.

(g) Variables Used as Counters, and the "Advance Counter" Operator: +

Frequently, you will want to number chapters, sections, paragraphs, items in lists, or the headings and subheadings in outlines. Since you will be using "IF–clauses" and "IF–OTHERWISE clauses" to select which chapters, sections, paragraphs, items, and headings are to be included in a given draft, you will not know ahead of time whether a given article of a will is "Article II" or "Article IV." And in addition to ordinary numbers, you may wish to use upper- or lower-case letters or Roman numerals in your numbering.

To assist you with such sequential numbering tasks, any variable may be established as a "counter" as well as a variable. The rules for using a variable as a "counter" are simple:

1. Assign it an initial valid count value using a LET statement; and
2. Insert a plus sign in front of the variable's name within the brackets whenever its count value is to be increased before its next use.

For example, suppose you wish to number the articles in a will with capitalized roman numerals, using the variable "article number" as the counter. At the start of the will, you insert the following LET statement:

```
[LET article number = <I.>]
```

You thereby set the count value to "I." which is the proper number for the first article. Then, at the start of each article in the will, you insert the following standardized header:

```
                ARTICLE [-article number]

        I instruct my executor to pay all of my debts
    and all death taxes and expenses arising out of
    my . . .

                ARTICLE [-article number]

        If . . . .
```

When the draft will is assembled, the articles will be numbered sequentially as follows:

```
                        ARTICLE IV.

        I instruct my executor to pay all of my debts
    and all death taxes and expenses arising out of
    my . . .

                        ARTICLE V.

        If . . . .
```

To make the counters function, you must assign them a proper count value using a LET statement. The acceptable count values are the following:

```
Ordinary numbers:    1  2 3 . . . 200
Upper-case letters:  A  B C . . . Z AA AB . . . CZ
Lower-case letters:  a  b c . . . z aa ab . . . cz
Upper-case roman:    I. II. III. . . . C.
Lower-case roman:    i. ii. iii. . . . c.
All capital words:   FIRST SECOND . . . TWENTIETH
```

The above table gives the proper form for each type of count value as well as the maximum range for each value. A numeric counter can range up to 200. Each of the other types of counters has a range of approximately 100 counts. In the case of letters, the value Z is followed by AA, AB, AC, and so on up to CZ. The maximum count value for the capitalized words is TWENTIETH.

Note carefully that Roman count values must always be followed by a decimal point, whereas number and letter count values may not have a decimal point. This convention is necessary to insure that the computer can distinguish, for example, between the letter "I" and the Roman number one, which is "I." and not just "I" by itself. If you wish to have a decimal point follow a number or letter count value, just place a period immediately to the right of the bracketed counter variable as follows:

```
Section [+section counter].
```

In the final draft, this title becomes:

```
Section 27.
```

When using Roman counters, you have no choice but must accept a decimal point, since it comes with the count value. Accordingly, you need not ever place a decimal point to the right of a bracketed Roman counter, as the above "ARTICLE" example illustrates.

(h) The "Do Not Save Answer" Operator: !

The client data file normally contains all the answers to the questions that the computer asks. These answers are saved in the client data file, along with the names of the corresponding variables, so that the same questions will not have to be asked again when other documents are prepared for the same client. Normally, you will want to have all the client data values saved in this manner.

But on occasion, you will not want to save the answers. For example, as part of a litigation system, you may have form letters addressed to witnesses that you use over and over again, addressing the letters to a different witness each time a letter is prepared. If the name and address of the witness were placed in the client data file the first time such a letter is drafted, then that same witness's name and address will pop automatically into the letter the next time you draft it—but the next time, you will want to send it to a different witness. In such a case, you need to do something to prevent the witness's name and address from entering the client data file.

You can block the value of a variable from entering the client data file by typing an exclamation mark in front of the corresponding variable's name within the brackets. For example, the following might be a witness letter:

```
                                          [short date]
[! w name: the name of the witness]
[! w address: the mailing address of the
witness, with "carriage returns" separating the
lines]
Dear [! w grtg: the salutation for the witness]:
   I represent [c name: the name of the client]
who is
. . . .
```

In this example, the exclamation marks preceding the three variables that relate to the witness's name, address, and salutation prevent this information from entering the client data file. Note that the spaceholder for the name of the client does not contain an exclamation mark, so this value is saved permanently and will not be asked for again.

The exclamation mark prevents any new value from entering the client data file. It does not erase an existing value in the file, however. So if the answer to a question is already present in the data file, no question will be asked, and the old answer will be used automatically. To get rid of such a value, you must edit it out of the client data file using your word processor.

While the answer to a question arising from a variable preceded by an exclamation mark does not go into the client data file, the answer is saved in the computer's memory for the duration of the session with the program LawProcess. This means that the answer may be plugged into multiple slots in multiple documents that are prepared during a single session with the program LawProcess. If you need to draft three or four documents for the same witness all at one time, you may do so without having to enter the witness's name and address more than once. But if you wish to prepare the same documents for another witness, you will have to "exit" from the program LawProcess and restart the program to clear the answers relating to the previous witness from the program's memory.

(i) The Display Command: Displaying Messages

The DISPLAY command permits you to display messages and instructions to the operator of the computer. After displaying a message or set of instructions, the command causes the computer to pause until you "Strike any key to continue . . . . " For example, to instruct the operator that the computer has just determined that the client needs a marital trust, you might place the following message into the model marital trust:

```
[DISPLAY<
   This client needs to have a marital trust
prepared. Accordingly, such a trust will now be
drafted.> ]
```

(j) Logical Analysis: Programming "Law" Into the Computer

The program PROCESS provides one with a subset of a full computer programming language. It cannot perform comparisons, and it cannot evaluate logical and algebraic expressions of the type used in formulating WESTLAW and LEXIS search requests.

Notwithstanding these limitations, through the use of LET statements and a few intermediary variables, you can perform logical computations of arbitrary complexity. With careful design, you can create an automated practice system that can ask multiple questions, draw legal conclusions from the answers provided, and then use those conclusions to control the selection and the drafting of legal documents.

Logicians have proven that any arbitrarily complicated logical proposition can always be expressed as a sentence containing elemental propositions conjoined together by AND, OR, NOT, and IF . . . THEN. So most computer programming languages permit you to write out expressions such as the following:

```
IF    (the sky is blue AND the temperature IS
      LESS THAN 50) OR (the sky is NOT blue AND
      the temperature IS LESS THAN 60) OR it is
      going to rain
THEN  the children should wear their waterproof
      windbreakers when they go out
```

LawProcess does not presently support AND, OR, and NOT, and it cannot perform mathematical comparisons. But you can still implement logical propositions such as the above one. For example:

```
[LET coats: the children should wear coats =
<N> ]
[IF the sky is blue]
   [IF the temperature is below 50]
      [LET coats: the children should wear coats
      = <Y> ]
   [END IF]
[END IF]
[IF the sky is blue]
[OTHERWISE]
   [IF the temperature is below 70]
      [LET coats: the children should wear coats
      = <Y> ]
   [END IF]
[END IF]
[IF it is going to rain]
   [LET coats: the children should wear coats =
   <Y> ]
[END IF]
[IF coats: the children should wear coats]
   [DISPLAY<
      The children should wear their waterproof
   windbreakers when they go outside today.> ]
[OTHERWISE]
   [DISPLAY<
   The children do not need to wear coats
   today.> ]
[END IF]
```

In the above example, the key variable "coats" is initially assigned the value <N> (or "NO') with a LET statement. Next, to perform the equivalent of AND in a logical sentence, two nested "IF-clauses" are used:

The logical expression "A AND B" becomes

```
[IF A]
    [IF B]
        . . . . [more logical steps] . . . .
    [END IF]
[END IF]
```

Next, to perform the equivalent of OR in a logical sentence, two sequential "IF-clauses" are used:

The logical expression "A OR B" becomes

```
[IF A]
    . . . . [more logical steps] . . . .
[END IF]
[IF B]
    . . . . [more logical steps] . . . .
[END IF]
```

And to achieve the equivalent of NOT in a sentence, the OTHERWISE part of an "IF-OTHERWISE-clause" is used:

The logical proposition "NOT A" becomes

```
[IF A]
[OTHERWISE]
    . . . . [more logical steps] . . . .
[END IF]
```

In this manner, we can achieve all the fundamental operations of symbolic logic, and may therefore embed simple legal propositions into our automated systems.

For example, the following logical system determines which documents from a complete set of divorce documents are to be prepared for a given individual:

```
[IF petn: a "Petition for Dissolution of
Marriage" is to be prepared INSERT]
    [certif: the "state of Illinois"
    certificate]
    [rule07: the attorney's affidavit under rule
    7]
    [military: the military form]
    [IF stpfle: the action is to proceed to a
    default judgment by stipulation INSERT]
    [OTHERWISE INSERT]
        [default: the order of default]
```

```
        [IF gone: service is to be by publication
        INSERT]
           [publish: the affidavit for service by
           publication]
        [OTHERWISE INSERT]
           [summons: the summons form]
        [END IF]
  [END IF]
  [IF poor: the client is not able to pay up to
  $100 in court costs INSERT]
     [pauper: the pauper's affidavit]
     [freetr: the free transcript order]
        [IF gone: service is to be by publication
        INSERT]
           [puborder: court order to publish
           notice]
        [END IF]
     [END IF]
  [END IF]
  [IF decr: a decree of dissolution is to be
  prepared INSERT]
     [decree: the decree of dissolution]
  [END IF]
```

This set of "IF clauses" and "IF–OTHERWISE clauses" permits the computer operator to select whether a petition, a decree, or both are to be prepared. If a petition is selected, the petition and several other mandatory documents are incorporated by reference into a single, long draft. Then, if the spouse will not be consenting to entry of a default judgment, an order of default is prepared, and either a summons or an affidavit of publication depending upon whether the spouse's whereabouts are known. If the decree is selected, it, too, is prepared at the same time as the petition.

(k) Repetitive Passages

Many form legal documents contain repetitious passages—repeated, identical passages that differ only in the client information which they contain. For example, a form contract may apply to one state, to three states or to twenty states. While "IF . . . ENDIF" clauses could be used to add multiple copies of a clause, the use of nested "IF . . . ENDIF" clauses quickly becomes cumbersome. We need a simpler way of specifying that a portion of a document is to be repeated a variable number of times.

All such repetitious passages should be preceded by "[REPEAT]" and followed by "[END REPEAT]." At some point within the repetitious passage, a "[WHEN . . . EXIT]" statement must appear that instructs the computer what question to ask repeatedly to determine if enough repetitious passages have been generated. For example, consider the following language taken from a form contract:

```
This contract shall cover the following states:
[LET state counter = <1> ]
[REPEAT]
[+ state counter]. [# stnm: the name of a
state]
[WHEN # done: that is the last state EXIT];
[END REPEAT].
```

This example produces the following interview:

```
VARIABLE #1 stnm
   The name of a state:
> Illinois<Esc>
VARIABLE #1 done
   That is the last state:
   YES OR NO? (Type Y or N)
> N
VARIABLE #2 stnm
   The name of a state:
> Michigan<Esc>
VARIABLE #2 done
   That is the last state:
   YES OR NO? (Type Y or N)
> N
VARIABLE #3 stnm
   The name of a state:
> Minnesota<Esc>
VARIABLE #3 done
   That is the last state:
   YES OR NO? (Type Y or N)
> Y
```

The following document is produced:

```
This contract shall cover the following states:
1. Illinois;
2. Michigan;
3. Minnesota.
```

Note that the semicolon follows the "[WHEN . . . EXIT]" command, and the period follows the "[END REPEAT]" command (why?).

The client file produced by this interview appears as follows:

```
LET #1 stnm: the name of a state = <Illinois>
LET #1 done: that is the last state = <N>
```

```
LET #2 stnm: the name of a state = <Michigan>
LET #2 done: that is the last state = <N>
LET #3 stnm: the name of a state = <Minnesota>
LET #3 done: that is the last state = <Y>
```

Note the number signs "# " in front of the two variable names in this example:

```
. . . [# stnm: the name of a state] . . .
. . . [# done: that is the last state] . . .
```

These number signs indicate that the variable may take on different values in the different copies of the passage that are generated. In the client file, a number "1," "2," . . . is inserted following the number sign to distinguish the values inserted into the different passages from each other and to enable the computer to remember which values go together in the same passage. If the number sign is omitted, then this signals your intention that all of the repetitious passages are to contain the same value for a variable. For example, if the names of the petitioner's children are listed in a divorce petition, and if all the children have the same last name, then in the repetitious clause that sets forth the names of the children you insert the following:

```
. . . [#fnm: the first name of a child] [lnm:
the last name of all the children] . . .
```

to signal that the first name is to be different in each copy of this passage but the last name is to be the same in all the copies.

(l) Replacement Questions

You have finished designing your automated document assembly system, and it works. But the questions are not as meaningful as you would like. What can you do to improve the system's performance?

Do not go back and revise your variables—this takes too much time and does not give you the flexibility that you desire. Instead, you may simply create a "new question" document and instruct the processor to assemble it (in the same way that the processor assembles a will or trust) and display it as a replacement for the default question that the system derives from the name of a variable.

"New question" documents are created using your word processor and are stored as files whose names are identical to the "short" names of the variables to which they correspond. A new question document's file name must have the extension ".qn" or the system will not accept it.

"New question" documents may contain optional and alternative passages, repetitious passages, LET and DISPLAY statements, and any other construct that may appear in your model documents. You can use optional IF passages to include optional explanations for beginners in your questions that experienced users may not need to have displayed. You may also include bracketed variables in your "new question" documents—even variables that have not yet been assigned values and that have their own "new question" documents. In the course of assembling a first "new question" document, the LawProcess program may have to ask questions and may even have to assemble and display some other "new question" document. The "animal.mdl" document provided on your diskette includes several illustrative "new question" documents that illustrate a few of the possibilities.

(m) Your Assignment

The simplest, and perhaps the most practical automated practice systems to build with this program are will assembly systems. So see if you can design such a system, using the materials provided by your state's Continuing Legal Education organization as a source of guidance. This can be done as a group effort, with each member of the group drafting one article. Some one individual should be appointed the "librarian," and this individual should maintain a list of variable names to insure that the same variables are used throughout the system. Prepare a "will" document similar to the one set forth above that incorporates by reference all of the articles and contains the necessary logic to select which ones should be included. And set up counters to number the articles and the powers of the executor or executrix.

§ 4-4. SPREADSHEETS

(a) Introduction

In the first chapter, computer software was discussed as a series of layers, designed to make it easier for people working in a particular area to communicate with a more generalized layer of software developed by another group of people. The first chapter also explained how more specialized higher layers optimized for specific purposes were easier to use than the more generalized lower layers. The spreadsheet is such a specialized higher layer. It is designed to allow easy access to the capabilities of mathematical calculation built into traditional computer languages, without subjecting the would-be user to the torture of taking Computer Science 101, the course introducing the student to a standard programing language, such as Pascal, and notoriously the hardest course on many campuses. The computer science course is difficult because standard computer languages were designed largely for the convenience of the computer rather than for the convenience of the user, and because they lack specialized features for particular groups of users. As a result they are not only hard to learn, but hard to use once learned. Spreadsheet programs provide much easier access to the arithmetic and logical powers of the computer, and also provide many specialized features to solve typical tasks automatically. In turn the spreadsheet programs provide an intermediate layer on top of which are placed special application programs, written in the spreadsheet "language" to perform very specific tasks (e.g., income tax calculation, business forecasting) very easily.

Unlike many innovations in software, whose origins may never be discovered, the origin of the spreadsheet dates to ideas developed by a student while taking classes involving corporate accounting at Harvard Business School. He explained these ideas to a potential business partner over a meal at a restaurant near Harvard Square. The inventor drew a grid on a napkin and explained to his companion that each square in the grid could contain a number or a formula linking its value to the value of other squares. When one number or formula was changed, the others would automatically be changed in accordance with formulas on the spreadsheet. This luncheon led to the creation of Visicalc, the first successful spreadsheet, and made the inventor a millionaire. Unfortunately, the story has a tragic ending. A contract and licensing dispute arose which took up all the energies of the inventor and distributor, while others, particularly Lotus Development Corporation, were developing bigger and better spreadsheets. Visicalc was forced off the market in 1985.

The improvements made by the Visicalc inventor during the course of turning his idea into a commercial product, the further improvements made by his competitors, and advances in personal computer hardware have turned the basic spreadsheet idea into a highly flexible interface between the human and the lower levels of software on which the spreadsheet rests. The original Visicalc supplemented the purely mathematical grid with provisions for labels in ordinary English and provided ways to generate meaningful and good-looking printed reports, thus greatly improving communications with the user and the report recipients. Competitors added a whole series of further refinements that automated many aspects of entering data into the spreadsheet and of preparing the results for printing or further computer processing. The original Visicalc worked on the Apple II personal computer designed in the late 1970s. The limited memory and processing power of this computer did not allow full realization of the potential of the spreadsheet idea, but nevertheless hundreds of thousands of copies of the program were sold. By the mid-1980s, personal computers were available with ten times the memory and ten times the processing speed of the Apple II. These computers allowed spreadsheets to handle larger and more complex problems easily and quickly and easily supported the extra processing overhead involved in a good user interface.

(b) What Is a Spreadsheet?

Each major type of computer program may be thought of as embodying a certain area of human knowledge. The word processor operates from a base of knowledge about typing, spelling, page formating, document formating, grammar, style, and indexing. A spreadsheet operates from a base of knowledge about mathematical operations, financial formulas, statistical methods, the calendar, and logical operations. Unlike a typical word processor, a spreadsheet knows that $2 + 2 = 4$; it knows the present value of winning a state lottery prize of $1,000,000 in 20 equal annual payments; it knows how to calculate a standard deviation; it knows how many days fell between December 7, 1941, and August 9, 1945.

Suppose you are making a projection of your law firm's gross billings for the first six months of next year. If you use pencil and paper (and a pocket calculator), you would end up with something like the following:

January		$ 300,000
February		$ 280,000
March		$ 290,000
April		$ 300,000
May		$ 320,000
June		$ 340,000
	TOTAL	$1,740,000

There are three serious problems with this approach. First, you typed the May figure into the calculator by mistake as $230,000 instead of $320,000; thus your final total is wrong (it should be $1,830,000). Second, if you want to change any figures, you will have to do the addition all over again. Third, the theory behind the lull in receipts in February and the peak in June is not apparent to anyone else looking at the income projection, and you will soon forget it yourself.

The spreadsheet has features to overcome each of these three problems. Because the arithmetic and logical calculations are done automatically by spreadsheet software, no human error is possible in the calculating process. If you change the figures for individual months, the total will be recalculated automatically by the spreadsheet. Receipts for any month may be specified by a formula indicating their relation to other months. The assumptions on which the figures are based will then be available for others to evaluate, and to aid you when you come back to update the report months later. Meanwhile the display on the computer screen or the printed report can keep the classic format of income projections, so the lawyers or accountants using the report will not have to learn any new modes of expression.

(c) The Structure of the Spreadsheet

The Grid

The spreadsheet itself is displayed on the screen as a large grid. Typically columns across the screen are displayed with the initial headings "A . . . B . . . C . . . etc.", while rows have, on the left side, the labels: "1 . . . 2 . . . 3 . . . etc." The lines of the grid intersect to form rectangular cells. These cells are referred to by their letter and number coordinates—the system works the same way as going from an index to a road map to squares on the map. Thus, for instance, the top left cell is called "A1". The strength of the spreadsheet lies in what the cells can contain and how they relate to one another. Each cell may contain any combination of the following:

1. A label (e.g. "RECEIPTS FROM CUSTOMERS");

2. A name (e.g., INCOME). As will be explained below, a name may be attached to a single cell or to a group of cells;

3. A note of explanation (in some systems) (e.g. "RECEIPTS includes all receipts except for cash deposits in our Panamanian Bank.");

4. A numerical value (e.g. 345.23) Some systems also allow logical values (i.e., TRUE and FALSE);

5. A formula expressing a relationship, e.g. (B3 + A2 – A1), meaning that value of the cell with this formula is equal to the value of cell B3 plus that of cell A2 minus that of cell A1;

6. A format to indicate how a value or the result of a formula calculation should be printed. For instance "50000" may be printed as "50000", "50,000", or "$50,000.00" depending upon the format selected by the user.

We will consider each of these in turn.

Labels

Labels provide information to help the viewer remember the relation of various figures on the screen. They also help in the preparation of printed reports by providing essential information for those to whom the reports are directed.

Extremely long labels present a minor technical problem. They may run over the edges of the individual cell on the screen. If the cell or cells to the right of the cell that contains the label is unused, running over the edge is not too bad. Thus most spreadsheets allow the option of running labels over the edge of a cell.

Names for Cells

When the worksheet is originally displayed, each cell has a name implied by the letters at the top of the sheet and the numbers in the left margin (exactly like the index designations for a road map). Thus, for instance receipts could be put in cell A1 and expenses in square A2. Net income then could be expressed as "(A1 – A2)". The better spreadsheets allow a name to be given to a cell or a group of cells. For instance, if cells B1 through B9 contained different types of expenses, this group of cells could be given the name "EXPENSES". Another cell or group of cells could be given the name "RECEIPTS". Then in the cell that was to contain the amount for "income," the meaningful formula "RECEIPTS – EXPENSES" could be used.

Notes About Cell Contents

There are practical limits on the length of cell labels if the object is to produce a concise report with a pleasing appearance. Mathematical formulas used in cells may be difficult or impossible to interpret without help. To aid in these situations, some spreadsheets allow a long note to be attached to an individual cell. This note can be displayed when the cell is accessed or printed as a footnote to a report produced by the spreadsheet.

Values

Many cells will contain numerical values. These may be entered by the user to express known quantities, for instance tax rates or last year's income. Alternatively, they may be the result of calculations under a formula entered by the user.

Formulas

The formula is the key to the operation of the spreadsheet. If a cell has a formula, each time the spreadsheet is updated, the value in the cell is updated to correspond to the formula for the cell. Formulas are written in the same way they are written in most computer programming languages—an adaptation of standard mathematical notation so that everything can be written on one line. (Early computers had trouble with subscripts and superscripts, and even though the current generation of computers can handle them perfectly well, the tradition of programming on one line remains strong.) A typical spreadsheet, such as Lotus 1–2–3 (Registered trademark of Lotus Development Corporation), has a large number of built-in operations. LawSpread, the spreadsheet that accompanies this book, has a subset of the most important functions found in Lotus 1–2–3. This subset will be found in one form or another in almost all spreadsheets. For reasons relating again to the history of the development of mathematical notation and computer languages, these operations are divided into "operators" and "functions".

An operator is placed before or between its operands (the values upon which it operates). For instance in the formula "2 + 2", the plus sign is the operator and the "2's" are the operands. In the expression "–3.4", "–" is the operator and "3.4" is the operand. A function (as used in Lotus and LawSpread) consists of "@" followed by several letters, followed by one or more arguments in parentheses. These are the values upon which it operates. For instance the formula @SQRT(4) will give the square root of 4, i.e., 2. The total number of operators and functions offered by a good spreadsheet is large. Lotus 1–2–3 incorporates close to 20 built-in operators and over 80 built-in functions. In addition, through its Macro facility, it makes it easy for the user to add what effectively become additional functions.

Many of the functions involve arithmetic or other simple calculations and should be usable by anyone with a high school education. Some of the functions, however, deal with areas such as advanced mathematics, finance, and statistics and so may require some special knowledge to use. Of particular interest to the lawyer are the financial functions, not only because important tax and other legal consequences depend upon financial aspects of a transaction, but because a lawyer cannot give good advice to a client without understanding the financial aspects of the client's problem.

Making Formulas Visible

A spreadsheet cell displays its label or numeric value; its formula, if any, is hidden from view. To view the formula within a cell, simply press the four arrow keys until the flashing cursor moves into the cell. Its "formula", if it contains one, will appear in the upper-left corner of your computer screen. Cells that contain labels or numeric constants do not contain formulas. When the cursor moves into such a non-formula cell, the label or numeric constant displayed by the cell appears in the upper-left corner of your computer screen. So normally, except for the one formula that you request the computer to display in the upper-left corner, all the spreadsheet formulas are hidden from your view, and you see only labels and values on the screen.

In many of the example spreadsheets presented below, each cell is enclosed in a box. Each cell box contains two rows: a first "value" row which reveals the cell's label or value; and a second "formula" row which reveals the cell's formula, if it contains one. The reader should understand that the "formula" rows are not actually visible on the computer screen but are included here to let the reader know which cells contain what formulas. In other examples, the spreadsheets are shown exactly as they appear on the screen, with an underline, "_", indicating the position of the cursor, and frequently with a formula visible in the upper-left corner of the example. That formula resides in the cell that contains the "_" mark, which represents the cursor. (See Appendix E for a full explanation of these examples.)

(d) Spreadsheet Operators and Functions

Logical Operators

LawSpread understands the following logical operators:

#AND#, #OR#, #NOT#

These operators work in a manner similar to the same operators on WESTLAW. However, you should be cautious because, as will be explained in detail below, the order in which they are applied by spreadsheets is not the same as on WESTLAW. In logical operations, "0" has the value "FALSE" and "1" has the value "TRUE." Consider the following spreadsheet:

	A B	C D
1	HOMICIDE	1
2	MALICE AFORETHOUGHT	0
3	FIRST DEGREE MURDER	0 (C1 #AND# C2)
4	MANSLAUGHTER	1 (C1)
5	INNOCENT	0 (#NOT# C3) #AND# (#NOT# C4)

This spreadsheet expresses the following grossly oversimplified criminal law rules:

(1) If a person commits homicide with malice aforethought, he is guilty of first degree murder.

(2) If a person commits homicide, he is guilty of manslaughter.

Now suppose we change the value for "MALICE AFORETHOUGHT" to TRUE. We get the following:

	A	B	C	D
1	HOMICIDE		1	
2	MALICE AFORETHOUGHT		1	
3	FIRST DEGREE MURDER		1 (C1 #AND# C2)	
4	MANSLAUGHTER		1 (C1)	
5	INNOCENT		0 (#NOT# C3) #AND# (#NOT# C4)	

Note that the concept of manslaughter as a lesser included offense is correctly reflected by this logic.

Relational Operators

There are the following relational operators:

=, <>, <, >, <=, >=

They have the following meanings:

= (equal to)
<> (not equal to)
< (less than)
> (greater than)
<= (less than or equal to)
>= (greater than or equal to)

Consider the following spreadsheet:

	A	B	C	D
1	ASSETS	1000		
2	DEBTS	998765		
3	BANKRUPT	1 (B1 B2)		

Arithmetic Operators

There are the following arithmetic operators:

+, −, *, /, ^

They have the following meanings:

+ (addition when between operands; positive sign when before an operand)

– (subtraction when between operands; negative sign when before operands)

* (multiplication)

/ (division)

^ (exponentiation)

Their use is illustrated in the following spreadsheet:

	A	B	C	D
1	-1	0	1	2
2	3 (C1 + D1)	1 (D1 – C1)	2 (C1*D1)	0.5 (C1/D1)
3	9 (A2^D1)	?????? (C1/B1)	?????? (A1^D1)	?????? (D1^A1)

Note that the following operations are illegal in LawSpread: division by zero (See B3 above), exponentiation of a negative number (See C3 above), exponentiation to a negative power (See D3 above). Exponentiation to a negative power may be accomplished indirectly with a formula such as:

```
1/(D1^3)
```

Mathematical Functions

LawSpread understands a number of mathematical functions (Lotus 1–2–3 and other commercially sold spreadsheets understand more functions). The authors of this book realize that many law students will not understand what all of these functions are about. If they really understood all of them, they would probably be planning to become engineers or scientists instead of lawyers. The mathematical functions are:

@ABS, @EXP, @LN, @LOG, @SQRT, @SUM

They have the following usages

@ABS(n) is used to give the absolute value of a number. In other words, if the number is positive, it is unchanged; if it is negative, it is made positive. @ABS(3) is 3. @ABS(–3) is 3.

@EXP(n) returns the exponential of a number. For instance, @EXP(3.2) gives the value of $e^{3.2}$. If you do not know that "e" is approximately 2.71828, don't worry—you will never use this function.

@LN(n) returns the natural logarithm (base "e") of a number.

@LOG(n) returns the logarithm (base 10) of a number.

@SQRT(n) returns the square root of a number.

@SUM (vertical range) returns the sum of the values of the cells in a vertical range of cells. A vertical range of cells is designated by an expression like the following "B3 . . B6." See the following spreadsheet for an example:

	A	B	C	D
1	ITEM	NUMBER SOLD	PRICE EACH	RECEIVED
2	WIDGET	5	3	15 (B2*C2)
3	GIDGET	4	8	32 (B3*C3)
4	ZIDGET	2	7	14 (B4*C4)
5	TOTALS	11 @SUM(B2..B4)		61 @SUM(D2..D4)

Business Functions

LawSpread understands a large subset of the business functions found in commercially-sold spreadsheets. This subset is:

@FV, @IRR, @NPV, @PMT, @PV, @RATE, @TERM

They have the following usages:

@FV(payment, interest, term) computes the future value over the number of payment periods represented by "term" at interest rate "interest" of a series of identical payments, each of amount "payment". Suppose, for instance, you plan to invest $1000 per year for the next 30 years in a tax-free IRA paying 9% interest. The value at the end of thirty years may be calculated by @ FV(1000,.09,30) as $136,308. (Note that percentages should be expressed as decimals, for instance "9%" as ".09".)

@IRR(guess, vertical range) calculates the internal rate of return for a series of cash flow payments resulting from an initial investment. The first item in the vertical range should be negative, representing the outflow of funds to the initial investment. The remaining items in the vertical range represent income from the investment. @IRR uses the "Net Present Value" function described below to calculate the present value of these future income receipts assuming the interest rate based upon "guess." If the present value of the income receipts is too high or too low, then the interest rate is adjusted up or down from "guess" until a present value is found that matches the original investment or until the computer program gives up trying. The adjusted interest rate is then displayed as the "internal rate of return" or an error message is displayed if no interest rate can be found to fit the data.

Assume that X lends Y $12,000. Y agrees to pay X $1,200 a year interest for 5 years and then to repay the principal. It is clear that X is getting a 10% rate of return on his money. However suppose the agreement is that Y will pay $1,500 per year for the first two years,

$1,100 a year for the next two years and a year later make a final payment of $14,000. It is by no means obvious what interest rate X is really achieving. It may be important to X to know the true interest rate so that he can compare various possible business deals. It also may be important to the Internal Revenue Service, depending upon the current state of the tax laws, to make sure that anyone who is receiving the economic equivalent of interest is paying taxes on what he receives. The following spreadsheet does the calculation:

```
B8: @IRR(.05,B1..B6)                              VALUE

          A                B              C            D
1 INVESTMENT            -12000
2 Year 1                  1500
3 Year 2                  1500
4 Year 3                  1100
5 Year 4                  1100
6 Year 5                 14000
7
8 RATE OF RETURN         0.119
```

The true interest rate, or "internal rate of return," is 11.9%.

@NPV(interest, vertical range) calculates the net present value of a stream of future payments. Suppose I am to receive payments of 1,200 a year for 5 years and then a payment of $12,000. What is the present value of these payments if the fair interest rate is 10%? The answer is clearly $12,000—we have effectively reversed the internal rate of return calculations. Present value is important in many legal areas where it becomes necessary to value a future stream of payments. Examples would include lost income in personal injury cases and a spouse's rights to pension benefits in divorce cases. While the example above is easy, when payments change over time, calculation of present value becomes much more complex. Suppose, for instance, I receive a payment of $800 the first year, $100 more each following year, and that in the final year I receive $14000.

```
B8: @NPV(.10,B1..B6)                              VALUE

          A                B              C            D
1 Year 1                   800
2 Year 2                   900
3 Year 3                  1000
4 Year 4                  1100
5 Year 5                  1200
6 Year 6                 14000
7
8 PRESENT VALUE          11621
```

@PMT(principal, interest, term) calculates the amount of each equal payment on a loan given the principal, interest rate, and term. Whenever some sort of financing is involved in a transaction, it is necessary to calculate the monthly or annual payments involved. For instance, if one borrows $100,000 on a 20 year 11% fixed interest mortgage, what are the monthly payments? @PMT(100000,.11/12,12*20) provides the answer—$1032 per month. Note how you must divide the interest rate by 12 and multiply the number of years by 12 to find the monthly rather than the annual payment.

@PV(payment, interest rate, term) computes the present value of a series of equal future payments for the period "term," discounted at "interest rate." Suppose your rich uncle promises to give you $10000 a year for the next 10 years, or in the alternative $50,000 in cash at once. Which promise is worth more if you believe you could earn 9.5% interest if you invested the $50,000? To calculate the present value of the stream of payments, use @PV(10000,.095,10). The result is $62,788, so you should accept your uncle's offer of $10,000 a year.

@RATE(future value, present value, term) calculates the interest rate needed over the period "term" for "present value" to grow to "future value." Suppose you are planning for your retirement 30 years from now and hope to invest $20,000 in tax free municipal bonds so that they will grow to $150,000 by the time you retire. What rate of return will you need on the bonds? The formula is @RATE(150000,20000,30) and the result is 6.9%.

@TERM(payment, interest rate, future value) calculates the time it will take a regular payment, at a given interest rate, to appreciate to "future value." Suppose, for instance, that one wishes to know how long it will take to accumulate $300,000 in a tax-sheltered IRA, if one contributes $1,000 each year, and the interest rate is 8.5%. The answer will be given by @TERM(1000,.085,300000). It turns out to be 40 years.

(e) Precedence of Operators and Functions

In junior high school, you learned some simple facts about precedence of operators. For instance you learned that "3 + 4 × 5" is 23, not 35, because multiplication takes precedence over addition. Spreadsheets have large numbers of operators, so you cannot be expected to remember all the rules of precedence. There are two possibilities. One is frequently to consult a chart for the particular spreadsheet giving the precedence of operators. The other is to use parentheses to control the order of evaluation. The second approach requires a little more typing, but it greatly reduces the chance of error by yourself or others who might use your spreadsheet. For instance, if you do not remember the order of precedence of "#AND#" and "#OR#" you can type an expression such as (A1 #AND# (B2 #OR# C3)) to guarantee that the #OR# operation will be done first. The following is the table of precedence for LawSpread. (It is a subset of the table of precedence for Lotus 1–2–3.)

@FUNCTION, IDENTIFIER (A1, B2, etc.), NUMBER (3, etc.)

^ (exponentiation operator)

– (negative sign, as in –2), + (positive sign, as in +3)

*, /

+ (addition, as in 2+2), –(subtraction, as in 3–2)

=,< >,<,>,<=,>=

#NOT#

#AND#, #OR#

Operators higher up in this table are evaluated before operators lower down. Operators on the same line are evaluated as they occur, left to right in the formula. The order of evaluation may be changed by using parentheses.

(f) Updating the Spreadsheet

Each time the spreadsheet is updated, a new value is assigned to each cell with a formula. Thus, by changing the figure for EXPENSES and then updating the spreadsheet, the figure for INCOME will also be changed. The great advantage of the spreadsheet is this capability of updating all the relationships depending upon formulas. Most spreadsheets provide the user with a number of choices for the updating process. A spreadsheet may be updated every time the user changes a value or formula, or it may be updated only on user command. The former method keeps the spreadsheet always current. But if the spreadsheet is large and the computer is small, it may result in an annoying pause or even a substantial wait after each entry. The usual remedy is to set the spreadsheet to update only when the user requests an update. The user may also be able to specify the way in which an update is made. Formulas can be updated left to right a row at a time, or they may be updated top to bottom a column at a time. The direction makes a difference—for instance, it may determine whether taxes are figured on this year's income or last year's income. Another alternative is "natural updating." In this case the formulas are chosen so that there is a logical order for updating and the computer follows that order. Consider the following spreadsheet: (Most spreadsheets only show the formula of the particular cell that is available for change at any given time; the other formulas remain hidden. In the example that follows, these hidden formulas are shown to enable the user to better understand the operations being performed).

	A	B	C	D
1		1986	1987	1988
2	RECEIPTS	200	300 (B3*3)	450 (C3*3)
3	ADVERTISING	100 (B2/2)	150 (C2/2)	225 (D2/2)

Now suppose the figure "200" in cell B2 is changed to 400. If updating is by rows, the spreadsheet will look like this:

1		1986	1987	1988
2	RECEIPTS	400	300 (B3*3)	450 (C3*3)
3	ADVERTISING	200 (B2/2)	150 (C2/2)	225 (D2/2)

If updating is by columns, the spreadsheet will look like this:

	A	B	C	D
1		1986	1987	1988
2	RECEIPTS	400	600 (B3*3)	900 (C3*3)
3	ADVERTISING	200 (B2/2)	300 (C2/2)	450 (D2/2)

Obviously, this particular spreadsheet should be updated by columns, not by rows, since it is designed to reflect the operation of a business where advertising is a percentage of sales and each year's sales are dependent on the previous year's advertising. With some spreadsheets, calculation must be either by rows or by columns and it is the user's responsibility to specify which. Better spreadsheets allow specification of a "natural" order of computation. In this case, in each round, the spreadsheet calculates first the value of those equations that depend upon no other values that have been calculated in this round. Then it calculates equations depending only upon values already calculated in the same round, repeating the process until all equations are calculated. The natural order would also give the correct result for the business example given above. Cell B3 would be calculated first, because it does not depend upon any other variables. Then cell C2 would be calculated because it depends only upon a value already calculated, namely that of B2. The reader may verify that the remaining calculations would take place in the proper order.

The natural method of calculation encounters difficulties in case of a circular calculation. Consider the following spreadsheet:

	A	B
1	RECEIPTS	400
2	ADVERTISING	200 (B1/2)

Now suppose the constant in A1 is changed to the formula (B2 + 300) to show that the amount received depends upon current advertising. We have created a circular spreadsheet. If the computer tries to update it, it will get the following results:

First Update:

	A	B
1	RECEIPTS	500 (B2+300)
2	ADVERTISING	250 (B1/2)

Second Update:

	A	B
1	RECEIPTS	550 (B2+300)
2	ADVERTISING	275 (B1/2)

Third Update:

	A	B
1	RECEIPTS	575 (B2+300)
2	ADVERTISING	287.5 (B1/2)

Fourth Update

	A	B
1	RECEIPTS	587.52 (B2+300)
2	ADVERTISING	293.75 (B1/2)

Each update is moving closer to a set of values that will satisfy both equations, namely:

	A	B
1	RECEIPTS	600 (B2+300)
2	ADVERTISING	300 (B1/2)

Different spreadsheet programs take different approaches when faced with such a circular set of formulas. Some merely flash "CIRCULAR FORMULAS" on the screen and give up. More sophisticated spreadsheets allow the user to specify the number of updates the spreadsheet can try in an attempt to satisfy the equations and the margin of error permitted. Note that some circular formulas can never be solved. If expenses are 110% of income, it will be impossible to find any levels of expense and income that lead to a $1,000,000 a year profit. In such cases, a good spreadsheet will quit after the specified number of iterations and inform the user of its failure.

(g) Spreadsheet Templates

Once formulas have been entered into a spreadsheet to solve a specific problem, they may be generalized to solve many related problems. Sets of ready-to-use spreadsheet entries are called "templates." Templates may be used to solve commonly encountered problems—for instance tax aspects of real estate financing. By including as formulas the way mortgage payments are generally handled by banks and the taxing authorities, one may construct a template useful in many different types of real estate transactions. Templates are really computer programs written in the language of spreadsheets.

(h) Problems

These problems can be done with either the LawSpread spreadsheet that accompanies this book or with a commercially-sold spreadsheet such as Lotus 1-2-3 or Multiplan.

1. Lost Wages

Various approaches to the calculation of lost wages are outlined in the Supreme Court decision in Jones & Laughlin v. Pfeifer, printed below. First read the case. Then develop a spreadsheet that will accept as input information about a disabled worker's predicted future earnings and work life and give as output annual amounts and present values for the various approaches discussed by the court (including those disapproved by the court for use under the Longshoremen's Act, but perhaps applicable under other law). Prepare a presentation using approaches favorable (1) to the worker and (2) to the company. The presentation should be clear and convincing—if you have a commercial spreadsheet, make good use of the print formating and graphics capabilities of the software.

JONES & LAUGHLIN STEEL CORP. v. PFEIFER

Supreme Court of the United States, 1964.
462 U.S. 523, 103 S.Ct. 2541, 76 L.Ed.2d 768.

STEVENS, JUSTICE.

Respondent was injured in the course of his employment as a loading helper on a coal barge. As his employer, petitioner was required to compensate him for his injury under § 4 of the Longshoremen's and Harbor Workers' Compensation Act (the Act). 44 Stat. 1426, 33 U.S.C. § 904. As the owner *pro hac vice* of the barge, petitioner may also be liable for negligence under § 5 of the Act. 86 Stat. 1263, 33 U.S.C. § 905. We granted certiorari to decide whether petitioner may be subject to both forms of liability, and also to consider whether the Court of Appeals correctly upheld the trial court's computation of respondent's damages. * * *

THE DAMAGES ISSUE

The District Court found that respondent was permanently disabled as a result of petitioner's negligence. He therefore was entitled to an award of damages to compensate him for his probable pecuniary loss over the duration of his career, reduced to its present value. It is useful at the outset to review the way in which damages should be measured in a hypothetical inflation-free economy. We shall then consider how price inflation alters the analysis. Finally, we shall decide whether the District Court committed reversible error in this case.

I

In calculating damages, it is assumed that if the injured party had not been disabled, he would have continued to work, and to receive wages at periodic intervals until retirement, disability, or death. An award for impaired earning capacity is intended to compensate the worker for the diminution in that stream of income.[8] The award could in theory take the form of periodic payments, but in this country it has traditionally taken the form of a lump sum, paid at the conclusion of the litigation.[9] The appropriate lump sum cannot be computed without first examining the stream of income it purports to replace.

The lost stream's length cannot be known with certainty; the worker could have been disabled or even killed in a different, non-work-related accident at any time. The probability that he would still be working at a given date is constantly diminishing.[10] Given the complexity of trying to make an exact calculation, litigants frequently follow the relatively simple course of assuming that the worker would have continued to work up until a specific date certain. In this case, for example, both parties agreed that the petitioner would have continued to work until age 65 (12½ more years) if he had not been injured.

8. See generally D. Dobbs, Handbook of the Law of Remedies § 8.1 (1973). It should be noted that in a personal injury action such as this one, damages for impaired earning capacity are awarded to compensate the injured person for his loss. In a wrongful death action, a similar but not identical item of damages is awarded for the manner in which diminished earning capacity harms either the worker's survivors or his estate. See generally S. Speiser, Recovery for Wrongful Death 2d, ch. 3 (1975). Since the problem of incorporating inflation into the award is the same in both types of action, we shall make occasional reference to wrongful death actions in this opinion.

9. But cf. Uniform Periodic Payment of Judgments Act, 14 U.L.A. 1 (1982 Supp.). See generally Elligett, The Periodic Payment of Judgments, 46 Ins.Couns.J. 130 (1979); Kolbach, Variable Periodic Payments of Damages: An Alternative to Lump Sum Awards, 64 Iowa L.J. 138 (1978); Rea, Lump-Sum Versus Periodic Damage Awards, 10 J.Leg. Studies 131 (1981).

10. For examples of calculations that take this diminishing probability into account, and assume that it would fall to zero when the worker reached age 65 see Fitzpatrick. The Personal Economic Loss Occasioned by the Death of Nancy Hollander Feldman: An Introduction to the Standard Valuation Procedure [1977] Economic Expert in Litigation, No. 5, at 25, 44–46 (Defense Research Institute) [hereafter Fitzpatrick]; Hanke, How To Determine Lost Earning Capacity, 27 Practical Lawyer 27, 29–33 (1981).

Each annual installment[11] in the lost stream comprises several elements. The most significant is, of course, the actual wage. In addition, the worker may have enjoyed certain fringe benefits, which should be included in an ideal evaluation of the worker's loss but are frequently excluded for simplicity's sake.[12] On the other hand, the injured worker's lost wages would have been diminished by state and federal income taxes. Since the damages award is tax-free, the relevant stream is ideally of *after-tax* wages and benefits. See *Norfolk & Western R. Co. v. Liepelt,* 444 U.S. 490, 100 S.Ct. 755, 62 L.Ed.2d 689 (1980). Moreover, workers often incur unreimbursed costs, such as transportation to work and uniforms, that the injured worker will not incur. These costs should also be deducted in estimating the lost stream.

In this case the parties appear to have agreed to simplify the litigation, and to presume that in each installment all the elements in the stream would offset each other, except for gross wages. However, in attempting to estimate even such a stylized stream of annual installments of gross wages, a trier of fact faces a complex task. The most obvious and most appropriate place to begin is with the worker's annual wage at the time of injury. Yet the "estimate of loss from lessened earnings capacity in the future need not be based solely upon the wages which the plaintiff was earning at the time of his injury." C. McCormick, Damages § 86 (1935). Even in an inflation-free economy—that is to say one in which the prices of consumer goods remain stable—a worker's wages tend to "inflate." This "real" wage inflation reflects a number of factors, some linked to the specific individual and some linked to broader societal forces.[13]

With the passage of time, an individual worker often becomes more valuable to his employer. His personal work experiences increase his hourly contributions to firm profits. To reflect that heightened value, he will often receive "seniority" or "experience" raises, "merit" raises, or even promotions.[14] Although it may be difficult to prove when, and whether, a particular injured worker might have received such wage increases, see *Feldman v. Allegheny Air Lines,* 524 F.2d 384, 392–393 (CA2 1975) (Friendly, J., concurring *dubitante*), they may be reliably demonstrated for some workers.[15]

11. Obviously, another distorting simplification is being made here. Although workers generally receive their wages in weekly or biweekly installments, virtually all calculations of lost earnings, including the one made in this case, pretend that the stream would have flowed in large spurts, taking the form of annual installments.

12. These might include insurance coverage, pension and retirement plans, profit sharing, and in-kind services. Fitzpatrick 27.

13. As will become apparent, in speaking of "societal" forces we are primarily concerned with those macroeconomic forces that influence wages in the worker's particular industry. The term will be used to encompass all forces that tend to inflate a worker's wage without regard to the worker's individual characteristics.

14. It is also possible that a worker could be expected to change occupations completely. See, *e.g., Stearns Coal & Lumber Co. v. Williams,* 164 Ky. 618, 176 S.W. 15 (1915).

15. See, *e.g.,* Fitzpatrick 33–39; Henderson, Income Over the Life Cycle: Some

Furthermore, the wages of workers as a class may increase over time. See *Grunenthal v. Long Island R. Co.,* 393 U.S. 156, 160, 89 S.Ct. 331, 333–334, 21 L.Ed.2d 309 (1968). Though more efficient interaction among labor, capital, and technology, industrial productivity may increase, and workers' wages may enjoy a share of that growth.[16] Such productivity increase—reflected in real increases in the gross national product per worker-hour—have been a permanent feature of the national economy since the conclusion of World War II.[17] Moreover, through collective bargaining, workers may be able to negotiate increases in their "share" of revenues, at the cost of reducing shareholders' rate of return on their investments.[18] Either of these forces could affect the lost stream of income in an inflation-free economy. In this case, the plaintiff's proffered evidence on predictable wage growth may have reflected the influence of either or both of these two factors.

To summarize, the first stage in calculating an appropriate award for lost earnings involves an estimate of what the lost stream of income would have been. The stream may be approximated as a series of after-tax payments, one in each year of the worker's expected remaining career. In estimating what those payments would have been in an inflation-free economy, the trier of fact may begin with the worker's annual wage at the time of injury. If sufficient proof is offered, the trier of fact may increase that figure to reflect the appropriate influence of individualized factors (such as foreseeable promotions) and societal factors (such as foreseeable productivity growth within the worker's industry).[19]

Of course, even in an inflation-free economy the award of damages to replace the lost stream of income cannot be computed simply by totaling up the sum of the periodic payments. For the damages award is paid in a lump sum at the conclusion of the litigation, and when it—or even a part of it—is invested, it will earn additional money. It has been settled since our decision in *Chesapeake & Ohio R. Co. v. Kelly,* 241 U.S. 485, 36 S.Ct. 630, 60 L.Ed. 1117 (1916) that "in all cases where it is reasonable to suppose that interest may safely be earned upon the amount that is awarded, the ascertained future benefits ought to be discounted in the making up of the award." *Id.,* at 490, 36 S.Ct., at 632.[20]

Problems of Estimation and Measurement, 25 Federation Ins.Couns.Q. 15 (1974).

16. P. Samuelson, Economics 738–756 (1976 ed.) [hereafter Samuelson].

17. See Henderson, The Consideration of Increased Productivity and the Discounting of Future Earnings to Present Value, 20 S.D.L.Rev. 307, 310–320 (1975) [hereafter Henderson].

18. See Samuelson 584–593, 737; Henderson 315, and n. 15.

19. If foreseeable real wage growth is shown, it may produce a steadily increasing series of payments, with the first payment showing the least increase from the wage at the time of injury and the last payment showing the most.

20. Although this rule could be seen as a way of ensuring that the lump-sum award accurately represents the pecuniary injury as of the time of trial, it was explained by reference to the duty to mitigate damages. 241 U.S., at 489–490, 36 S.Ct., at 631–632.

The discount rate should be based on the rate of interest that would be earned on "the best and safest investments." *Id.,* at 491, 36 S.Ct., at 632. Once it is assumed that the injured worker would definitely have worked for a specific term of years, he is entitled to a risk-free stream of future income to replace his lost wages; therefore, the discount rate should not reflect the market's premium for investors who are willing to accept some risk of default. Moreover, since under *Liepelt, supra,* the lost stream of income should be estimated in after-tax terms, the discount rate should also represent the after-tax rate of return to the injured worker.[21]

Thus, although the notion of a damage award representing the present value of a lost stream of earnings in an inflation-free economy rests on some fairly sophisticated economic concepts, the two elements that determine its calculation can be stated fairly easily. They are: (1) the amount that the employee would have earned during each year that he could have been expected to work after the injury; and (2) the appropriate discount rate, reflecting the safest available investment. The trier of fact should apply the discount rate to each of the estimated installments in the lost stream of income, and then add up the discounted installments to determine the total award.[22]

II

Unfortunately for triers of fact, ours is not an inflation-free economy. Inflation has been a permanent fixture in our economy for many decades, and there can be no doubt that it ideally should affect both stages of the calculation described in the previous section. The difficult problem is how it can do so in the practical context of civil litigation under § 5(b) of the Act.

The first stage of the calculation required an estimate of the shape of the lost stream of future income. For many workers, including respondent, a contractual "cost-of-living adjustment" automatically increases wages each year by the percentage change during the previous

21. The arithmetic necessary for discounting can be simplified through the use of a so-called "present value table," such as those found in R. Wixon, Accountants' Handbook, at 29.58–29.59 (1956 ed.), or S. Speiser, Recovery for Wrongful Death 2d § 8:4, at 713–718 (1975). These tables are based on the proposition that if i is the discount rate, then "the present value of $1 due in n periods must be $1/(1 + i)^n$." Wixon, *supra,* at 29.57. In this context, the relevant "periods" are years; accordingly, if "i" is a market interest rate, it should be the effective *annual* yield.

22. At one time it was thought appropriate to distinguish between compensating a plaintiff "for the loss of time from his work which has actually occurred up to the time of trial" and compensating him "for the time which he will lose in the future." C. McCormick, Damages § 86 (1935). This suggested that estimated future earning capacity should be discounted to the date of trial, and a separate calculation should be performed for the estimated loss of earnings between injury and trial. *Id.,* at §§ 86–87. It is both easier and more precise to discount the entire lost stream of earnings back to the date of injury—the moment from which earning capacity was impaired. The plaintiff may then be awarded interest on that discounted sum for the period between injury and judgment, in order to ensure that the award when invested will still be able to replicate the lost stream. See *In re Air Crash Disaster Near Chicago, Illinois, on May 25, 1979,* 644 F.2d 633, 641–646 (CA7 1981); S. Speiser, Recovery for Wrongful Death 2d § 8:6, at 723 (1975).

year in the consumer price index calculated by the Bureau of Labor Statistics. Such a contract provides a basis for taking into account an additional societal factor—price inflation—in estimating the worker's lost future earnings.

The second stage of the calculation requires the selection of an appropriate discount rate. Price inflation—or more precisely, anticipated price inflation—certainly affects market rates of return. If a lender knows that his loan is to be repaid a year later with dollars that are less valuable than those he has advanced, he will charge an interest rate that is high enough both to compensate him for the temporary use of the loan proceeds and also to make up for their shrinkage in value.[23]

At one time many courts incorporated inflation into only one stage of the calculation of the award for lost earnings. See, *e.g., Sleeman v. Chesapeake and Ohio R. Co.,* 414 F.2d 305 (CA6 1969); *Johnson v. Penrod Drilling Co.,* 510 F.2d 234 (CA5 1975) (en banc). In estimating the lost stream of future earnings, they accepted evidence of both individual and societal factors that would tend to lead to wage increases even in an inflation-free economy, but required the plaintiff to prove that those factors were not influenced by predictions of future price inflation. See *Higginbotham v. Mobil Oil Corp.,* 545 F.2d 422, 434–435 (CA5 1977). No increase was allowed for price inflation, on the theory that such predictions were unreliably speculative. See *Sleeman, supra,* at 308; *Penrod, supra,* at 240–241. In discounting the estimated lost stream of future income to present value, however, they applied the market interest rate. See *Blue v. Western R. of Alabama,* 469 F.2d 487, 496–497 (CA5 1972).

23. The effect of price inflation on the discount rate may be less speculative than its effect on the lost stream of future income. The latter effect always requires a prediction of the future, for the existence of a contractual cost-of-living adjustment gives no guidance about how big that adjustment will be in some future year. However, whether the discount rate also turns on predictions of the future depends on how it is assumed that the worker will invest his award.

On the one hand, it might be assumed that at the time of the award the worker will invest in a mixture of safe short-term, medium-term, and long-term bonds, with one scheduled to mature each year of his expected worklife. In that event, by purchasing bonds immediately after judgment, the worker can be ensured whatever future stream of nominal income is predicted. Since all relevant effects of inflation on the market interest rate will have occurred at that time, future changes in the rate of price inflation will have no effect on the stream of income he receives. For recent commentaries on how an appropriate discount rate should be chosen under this assumption, see Jarrell and Pulsinelli, Obtaining the Ideal Discount Rate in Wrongful Death and Injury Litigation, 32 Defense L.J. 191 (1983); Fulmer and Geraghty, The Appropriate Discount Rate to Use in Estimating Financial Loss, 32 Fed.Ins.Couns.Q. 263 (1982). See also *Doca v. Marina Mercante Nicaraguense, S.A.,* 634 F.2d 30, 37, n. 8 (CA2 1980). On the other hand, it might be assumed that the worker will invest exclusively in safe short-term notes, reinvesting them at the new market rate whenever they mature. Future market rates would be quite important to such a worker. Predictions of what they will be would therefore also be relevant to the choice of an appropriate discount rate, in much the same way that they are always relevant to the first stage of the calculation. For a commentary choosing a discount rate on the basis of this assumption, see Sherman, Projection of Economic Loss: Inflation v. Present Value, 14 Creighton L.Rev. 723 (1981) [hereafter Sherman]. We perceive no intrinsic reason to prefer one assumption over the other, but most "offset" analyses seem to adopt the latter. See n. 26, *infra.*

The effect of these holdings was to deny the plaintiff the benefit of the impact of inflation on his future earnings, while giving the defendant the benefit of inflation's impact on the interest rate that is used to discount those earnings to present value. Although the plaintiff in such a situation could invest the proceeds of the litigation at an "inflated" rate of interest, the stream of income that he received provided him with only enough dollars to maintain his existing *nominal* income; it did not provide him with a stream comparable to what his lost wages would have been in an inflationary economy.[24] This inequity was assumed to have been minimal because of the relatively low rates of inflation.

In recent years, of course, inflation rates have not remained low. There is now a consensus among courts that the prior inequity can no longer be tolerated. See, *e.g., United States v. English,* 521 F.2d 63, 75 (CA9 1975) ("While the administrative convenience of ignoring inflation has some appeal when inflation rates are low, to ignore inflation when the rates are high is to ignore economic reality"). There is no consensus at all, however, regarding what form an appropriate response should take. See generally Note, Future Inflation, Prospective Damages and the Circuit Courts, 63 Va.L.Rev. 105 (1977).

Our sister common law nations generally continue to adhere to the position that inflation is too speculative to be considered in estimating the lost stream of future earnings; they have sought to counteract the danger of systematically undercompensating plaintiffs by applying a discount rate that is below the current market rate. Nevertheless, they have each chosen different rates, applying slightly different economic theories. In England, Lord Diplock has suggested that it would be appropriate to allow for future inflation "in a rough and ready way" by discounting at a rate of 4¾%. *Cookson v. Knowles,* [1979] A.C. 565–573. He accepted that rate as roughly equivalent to the rates available "[i]n times of stable currency." See also *Mclett v. McMonagle,* [1970] A.C. 166. The Supreme Court of Canada has recommended discounting at a rate of seven percent, a rate equal to market rates on long-term investments minus a government expert's prediction of the long-term rate of price inflation. *Andrews v. Grand & Toy Alberta Ltd.,* [1978] 2 S.C.R. 229, 83 D.L.R. (3d) 452, 474. And in Australia, the High Court has adopted a 2% rate, on the theory that it represents a good approximation of the long-term "real interest rate." See *Pennant Hills Restaurants Pty. Ltd. v. Barrell Insurances Pty. Ltd.,* 55 A.L.J.R. 258 (1981); *id.,* at 260 (Barwick, C.J.); *id.,* at 262 (Gibbs, J.); *id.,* at 277 (Mason, J.), *id.,* at 280 (Wilson, J.).

24. As Judge Posner has explained it: "But if there is inflation it will affect wages as well as prices. Therefore to give Mrs. O'Shea $2318 today because that is the present value of $7200 10 years hence, computed at a discount rate—12 percent—that consists mainly of an allowance for anticipated inflation, is in fact to give her less than she would have been earning then if she was earning $7200 on the date of the accident, even if the only wage increases she would have received would have been those necessary to keep pace with inflation." *O'Shea v. Riverway Towing Co.,* 677 F.2d 1194, 1199 (CA7 1982).

In this country, some courts have taken the same "real interest rate" approach as Australia. See *Feldman v. Allegheny Airlines,* 524 F.2d 384, 388 (CA2 1975), affirming 382 F.Supp. 1271 (1974) (1.5%); *Doca v. Marina Mercanti Nicaraguense, S.A.,* 634 F.2d 30, 39–40 (CA2 1980) (2%, unless litigants prove otherwise). They have endorsed the economic theory suggesting that market interest rates include two components—an estimate of anticipated inflation, and a desired "real" rate of return on investment—and that the latter component is essentially constant over time.[25] They have concluded that the inflationary increase in the estimated lost stream of future earnings will therefore be perfectly "offset" by all but the "real" component of the market interest rate.[26]

Still other courts have preferred to continue relying on market interest rates. To avoid undercompensation, they have shown at least tentative willingness to permit evidence of what future price inflation will be in estimating the lost stream of future income.

Within the past year, two federal Courts of Appeals have decided to allow litigants a choice of methods. Sitting *en banc,* the Court of Appeals for the Fifth Circuit has overruled its prior decision in *Penrod, supra,* and held it acceptable either to exclude evidence of future price inflation and discount by a "real" interest rate, or to attempt to predict

25. In his dissenting opinion in *Pennant Hills Restaurant Pty. Ltd. v. Barrell Insurances Pty. Ltd.,* 55 A.L.J.R. 258, 266–267 (1981), Justice Stephen explained the real interest rate approach to discounting future earnings, in part, as follows:

> "It rests upon the assumption that interest rates have two principal components: the market's own estimation of likely rates of inflation during the term of a particular fixed interest investment, and a 'real interest' component, being the rate of return which, in the absence of all inflation, a lender will demand and a borrower will be prepared to pay for the use of borrowed funds. It also relies upon the alleged economic fact that this 'real interest' rate, of about two per cent, will always be much the same and that fluctuations in nominal rates of interest are due to the other main component of interest rates, the inflationary expectation."

26. What is meant by the "real interest rate" depends on how one expects the plaintiff to invest the award, see n. 23, *supra.* If one assumes that the injured worker will immediately invest in bonds having a variety of maturity dates, in order to ensure a particular stream of future payments, then the relevant "real interest rate" must be the difference between (1) an average of short-term, medium-term, and long-term market interest rates in a given year and (2) the average rate of price inflation in *subsequent* years (*i.e.,* during the terms of the investments). The only comprehensive analysis of this difference that has been called to our attention is in *Feldman v. Allegheny Airlines, Inc.,* 382 F.Supp. 1271, 1293–1295, 1306–1312 (D.Conn.1974).

It appears more common for "real interest rate" approaches to rest on the assumption that the worker will invest in low-risk short-term securities and will reinvest frequently. *E.g., O'Shea v. Riverway Towing Co.,* 677 F.2d 1194, 1199 (CA7 1982). Under that assumption, the relevant real interest rate is the difference between the short-term market interest rate in a given year and the average rate of price inflation during that same year. Several studies appear to have been done to measure this difference. See Sherman 731–732; Carlson, Short-Term Interest Rates as Predictors of Inflation: A Comment, 67 Amer.Econ.Rev. 469 (1977); Gibson, Interest Rates and Inflationary Expectations: New Evidence, 62 Amer.Econ.Rev. 854 (1972).

However one interprets the "real interest rate," there is a slight distortion introduced by netting out the two effects and discounting by the difference. See Note, 49 U.Chi.L.Rev. 1003, 1017–1018, n. 66 (1982); Note, 63 Virginia L.Rev. 105, 111 (1977).

the effects of future price inflation on future wages and then discount by the market interest rate.[27] *Culver v. Slater Boat Co.,* 688 F.2d 280, 308–310 (CA5 1982) (en banc). A panel of the Court of Appeals for the Seventh Circuit has taken a substantially similar position. *O'Shea v. Riverway Towing Co.,* 677 F.2d 1194, 1200 (CA7 1982).

Finally, some courts have applied a number of techniques that have loosely been termed "total offset" methods. What these methods have in common is that they presume that the ideal discount rate—the after-tax market interest rate on a safe investment—is (to a legally tolerable degree of precision) completely offset by certain elements in the ideal computation of the estimated lost stream of future income. They all assume that the effects of future price inflation on wages are part of what offsets the market interest rate. The methods differ, however, in their assumptions regarding which if any other elements in the first stage of the damages calculation contribute to the offset.

Beaulieu v. Elliott, 434 P.2d 665 (Alaska 1967), is regarded as the seminal "total offset" case. The Supreme Court of Alaska ruled that in calculating an appropriate award for an injured worker's lost wages, no discount was to be applied. It held that the market interest rate was fully offset by two factors: price inflation and real wage inflation. *Id.,* at 671–672. Significantly, the Court did not need to distinguish between the two types of sources of real wage inflation—individual and societal—in order to resolve the case before it.[28] It simply observed:

> "It is a matter of common experience that as one progresses in his chosen occupation or profession he is likely to increase his earnings as the years go by. In nearly any occupation a wage earner can reasonably expect to receive wage increases from time to time. This factor is generally not taken into account when loss of future wages is determined, because there is no definite way of determining at the time of trial what wage increases the plaintiff may expect to receive in the years to come. However, this factor may be taken into account to some extent when considered to be an offsetting factor to the result reached when future earnings are not reduced to present value." *Id.,* at 672.

Thus, the market interest rate was deemed to be offset by price inflation and all other sources of future wage increases.

In *State v. Guinn,* 555 P.2d 530 (Alaska 1976), the *Beaulieu* approach was refined slightly. In that case, the plaintiff had offered evidence of "small, automatic increases in the wage rate keyed to the

27. The Fifth Circuit recommended replacing the estimated stream of actual installments with a stream of installments representing the "average annual income." See 688 F.2d, at 309. As we have noted, a worker does not generally receive the same wage each year. If, as an accurate estimate would normally show, the estimated wages increase steadily, then averaging will raise the estimate for the early years and lower it for the later years. Since the early years are discounted less than the later years, this step will necessarily increase the size of the award, providing plaintiffs with an unjustified windfall. Cf. *Turcotte v. Ford Motor Co.,* 494 F.2d 173, 186, n. 20 (CA1 1974).

28. See *supra,* at 2549–2550.

employee's length of service with the company," *id.,* at 545, and the trial court had included those increases in the estimated lost stream of future income but had not discounted. It held that this type of "certain and predictable" individual raise was not the type of wage increase that offsets the failure to discount to present value. Thus, the market interest rate was deemed to be offset by price inflation, societal sources of wage inflation, and individual sources of wage inflation that are not "certain and predictable." See also *Gowdy v. United States,* 271 F.Supp. 733 (W.D.Mich.1967) (price inflation and societal sources of wage inflation), rev'd on other grounds, 412 F.2d 525 (CA6 1969); *Pierce v. New York Central R. Co.,* 304 F.Supp. 44 (W.D.Mich.1969) (same).

Kaczkowski v. Bolubasz, 491 Pa. 561, 421 A.2d 1027 (1980), took still a third approach. The Pennsylvania Supreme Court followed the approach of the District Court in *Feldman, supra,* and the Court of Appeals for the Fifth Circuit in *Higginbotham v. Mobil Oil Corp.,* 545 F.2d 422 (CA5 1977), in concluding that the plaintiff could introduce all manner of evidence bearing on likely sources—both individual and societal—of future wage growth, except for predictions of price inflation. 491 Pa., at 579–580, 421 A.2d 1027. However, it rejected those courts' conclusion that the resulting estimated lost stream of future income should be discounted by a "real interest rate." Rather, it deemed the market interest rate to be offset by future price inflation. *Id.,* at 580–582, 421 A.2d 1027.

The litigants and the amici in this case urge us to select one of the many rules that have been proposed and establish it for all time as the exclusive method in all federal trials for calculating an award for lost earnings in an inflationary economy. We are not persuaded, however, that such an approach is warranted. Accord, *Cookson v. Knowles, supra,* at 574 (Lord Salmon). For our review of the foregoing cases leads us to draw three conclusions. First, by its very nature the calculation of an award for lost earnings must be a rough approximation. Because the lost stream can never be predicted with complete confidence, any lump sum represents only a "rough and ready" effort to put the plaintiff in the position he would have been in had he not been injured. Second, sustained price inflation can make the award substantially less precise. Inflation's current magnitude and unpredictability create a substantial risk that the damage award will prove to have little relation to the lost wages it purports to replace. Third, the question of lost earnings can arise in many different contexts. In some sectors of the economy, it is far easier to assemble evidence of an individual's most likely career path than in others.

These conclusions all counsel hesitation. Having surveyed the multitude of options available, we will do no more than is necessary to resolve the case before us. We limit our attention to suits under § 5(b) of the Act, noting that Congress has provided generally for an award of damages but has not given specific guidance regarding how they are to be calculated. Within that narrow context, we shall define the general boundaries within which a particular award will be considered legally acceptable.

III

The Court of Appeals correctly noted that respondent's cause of action "is rooted in federal maritime law." *Pope & Talbot, Inc. v. Hawn*, 346 U.S. 406, 409, 74 S.Ct. 202, 204, 98 L.Ed. 143 (1953). See also H.R.Rep. No. 1441, 92d Cong., 2d Sess. The fact that Pennsylvania has adopted the total offset rule for all negligence cases in that forum is therefore not of controlling importance in this case. Moreover, the reasons which may support the adoption of the rule for a State's entire judicial system—for a broad class of cases encompassing a variety of claims affecting a number of different industries and occupations—are not necessarily applicable to the special class of workers covered by this Act.

In calculating an award for a longshoreman's lost earnings caused by the negligence of a vessel, the discount rate should be chosen on the basis of the factors that are used to estimate the lost stream of future earnings. If the trier of fact relies on a specific forecast of the future rate of price inflation, and if the estimated lost stream of future earnings is calculated to include price inflation along with individual factors and other societal factors, then the proper discount rate would be the after-tax market interest rate.[29] But since specific forecasts of future price inflation remain too unreliable to be useful in many cases, it will normally be a costly and ultimately unproductive waste of longshoremen's resources to make such forecasts the centerpiece of litigation under § 5(b). As Judge Newman has warned, "The average accident trial should not be converted into a graduate seminar on economic forecasting." *Doca v. Marina Mercante Nicaraguense, S.A.*, 634 F.2d 30, 39 (CA2 1980). For that reason, both plaintiffs and trial courts should be discouraged from pursuing that approach.

On the other hand, if forecasts of future price inflation are not used, it is necessary to choose an appropriate below-market discount rate. As long as inflation continues, one must ask how much should be "offset" against the market rate. Once again, that amount should be chosen on the basis of the same factors that are used to estimate the lost stream of future earnings. If full account is taken of the individual and societal factors (excepting price inflation) that can be expected to have resulted in wage increases, then all that should be set off against the market interest rate is an estimate of future price inflation. This would result in one of the "real interest rate" approaches described above. Although we find the economic evidence distinctly inconclusive regarding an essential premise of those approaches,[30] we do not believe

29. See n. 23, *supra*.

30. The key premise is that the real interest rate is stable over time. See n. 25, *supra*. It is obviously not perfectly stable, but whether it is even relatively stable is hotly disputed among economists. See the sources cited in *Doca, supra*, at 39, n. 10. In his classic work, Irving Fisher argued that the rate is not stable because changes in expectations of inflation (the factor that a trial court adopting such an approach in a suit under § 5(b) should be reversed if it adopts a rate between one and three percent and explains its choice.

There may be a sound economic argument for even further set-offs. In 1976, Professor Carlson of the Purdue University economics department wrote an article in the American Bar Association Journal contending that in the long run the societal factors excepting price inflation—largely productivity gains—match (or even slightly exceed) the "real interest rate." Carlson, *Economic Analysis v. Courtroom Controversy,* 62 ABAJ 628 (1976). He thus recommended that the estimated lost stream of future wages be calculated without considering either price inflation or societal productivity gains. All that would be considered would be individual seniority and promotion gains. If this were done, he concluded that the entire market interest rate, including both inflation and the real interest rate, would be more than adequately offset.

Although such an approach has the virtue of simplicity and may even be economically precise,[31] we cannot at this time agree with the

influences market interest rates) lag behind changes in inflation itself. I. Fisher, The Theory of Interest 43 (1930). He noted that the "real rate of interest in the United States from March to April, 1917, fell below minus 70 percent!" *Id.,* at 44. Consider also the more recent observations of Justice Stephen of the High Court of Australia:

> "Past Australian economic experience appears to provide little support for the concept of a relatively constant rate of 'real interest.' Year by year a figure for 'real interest' can of course be calculated, simply by subtracting from nominal interest rates the rate of inflation. But these figures are no more than a series of numbers bearing no resemblance to any relatively constant rate of interest which lenders are supposed to demand and borrowers to pay after allowing for estimated inflation. If official statistics for the past twelve calendar years are consulted, the Reserve Bank of Australia's Statistical Bulletins supply interest rates on two-year Australian government bonds (non-rebatable) and the O.E.C.D. Economic Outlook—July 1980, p. 105 and p. 143, supplies annual percentage changes in consumer prices, which gives a measure of inflation. The difference, figure year by year, which should represent the 'real interest' rate, averages out at a negative average rate of interest of –1.46, the widest fluctuations found in particular years being a positive rate of 2.58 per cent and a negative rate of –6.61 per cent. Nothing resembling a relatively constant positive rate of 2 per cent–3 per cent emerges. An equally random series of numbers, showing no steady rate of 'real interest', appears as Table 9.1 in the recent Interim Report of the Campbell Committee of Inquiry (Australian Government Publication Service—1980). For the period of thirty years which that Table covers, from 1950 to 1979, the average 'implicit real interest rate' is a negative rate of –.7 per cent, with 4 per cent as the greatest positive rate in any year and –20.2 per cent as the greatest negative annual rate." *Pennant Hills Restaurants, supra,* at 267.

31. We note that a substantial body of literature suggests that the Carlson rule might even *under* compensate some plaintiffs. See S. Speiser, Recovery for Wrongful Death, Economic Handbook, 36–37 (1970) (average interest rate 1% below average rate of wage growth); Formuzis & O'Donnell, Inflation and the Valuation of Future Economic Losses, 38 Mont.L.Rev. 297, 299 (1977) (interest rate 1.4% below rate of wage growth); Franz, Simplifying Future Lost Earnings, Trial 34 (Aug.1977) (rate of wage growth exceeds interest rate by over 1% on average); Coyne, Present Value of Future Earnings: A Sensible Alternative to Simplistic Methodologies, 49 Ins.Couns.J. 25, 26 (1982) (noting that Carlson's own data suggest that rate of wage growth exceeds interest rate by over 1.6%, and recommending a more individualized approach). See generally Note, 57 St. John's L.Rev. 316, 342–345 (1983). But see Comment, 49 U.Chi.L.Rev. 1003, 1023, and

Court of Appeals for the Third Circuit that its use is mandatory in the federal courts. Naturally, Congress could require it if it chose to do so. And nothing prevents parties interested in keeping litigation costs under control from stipulating to its use before trial.[32] But we are not prepared to impose it on unwilling litigants, for we have not been given sufficient data to judge how closely the national patterns of wage growth are likely to reflect the patterns within any given industry. The legislative branch of the federal government is far better equipped than we are to perform a comprehensive economic analysis and to fashion the proper general rule.

As a result, the judgment below must be set aside. In performing its damages calculation, the trial court applied the theory of *Kaczkowski, supra,* as a mandatory federal rule of decision, even though the petitioner had insisted that if compensation was to be awarded, it "must be reduced to its present worth." J.A. 60. Moreover, this approach seems to have colored the trial court's evaluation of the relevant evidence. At one point, the court noted that respondent had offered a computation of his estimated wages from the date of the accident until his presumed date of retirement, including projected cost-of-living adjustments. It stated, "We do not disagree with these projections, but feel they are inappropriate in view of the holding in *Kaczkowski.* " J.A. 74. Later in its opinion, however, the court declared, "We do not believe that there was sufficient evidence to establish a basis for estimating increased future productivity for the plaintiff, and therefore we will not inject such a factor in this award." J.A. 76.

On remand, the decision on whether to reopen the record should be left to the sound discretion of the trial court. It bears mention that the present record already gives reason to believe a fair award may be more confidently expected in this case than in many. The employment practices in the longshoring industry appear relatively stable and predictable. The parties seem to have had no difficulty in arriving at

n. 87 (1982) (noting "apparent congruence" between government projections of 2% average annual productivity growth and real interest rate, and concluding that total offset is accurate).

It is also interesting that in *O'Shea v. Riverway Towing Co.,* 677 F.2d 1194 (CA7 1982), Judge Posner stated that the real interest rate varies between one and three percent, *id.,* at 1199, and that "it would not be outlandish to assume that even if there were no inflation, Mrs. O'Shea's wages would have risen by three percent a year," *id.,* at 1200. Depending on how much of Judge Posner's estimated wage inflation for Mrs. O'Shea was due to individual factors (excluded from a total offset computation, his comments suggest that a total offset approach in that case could have meant overdiscounting by as much as two percent.

32. If parties agree in advance to use the Carlson method, all that would be needed would be a table of the after-tax values of present salaries and fringe benefits for different positions and levels of seniority ("steps") within an industry. Presumably this would be a matter for stipulation before trial, as well. The trier of fact would be instructed to determine how many years the injured worker would have spent at each step. It would multiply the number of years the worker would spend at each step by the current net value of each step (as shown on the table) and then add up the results. The trier of fact would be spared the need to cope with inflation estimates, productivity trends, and present value tables.

the period of respondent's future work expectancy, or in predicting the character of the work that he would have been performing during that entire period if he had not been injured. Moreover, the record discloses that respondent's wages were determined by a collective bargaining agreement that explicitly provided for "cost of living" increases, J.A. 310, and that recent company history also included a "general" increase and a "job class increment increase." Although the trial court deemed the latter increases irrelevant during its first review because it felt legally compelled to assume they would offset any real interest rate, further study of them on remand will allow the court to determine whether that assumption should be made in this case.

IV

We do not suggest that the trial judge should embark on a search for "delusive exactness." [33] It is perfectly obvious that the most detailed inquiry can at best produce an approximate result.[34] And one cannot ignore the fact that in many instances the award for impaired earning capacity may be overshadowed by a highly impressionistic award for pain and suffering.[35] But we are satisfied that whatever rate the District Court may choose to discount the estimated stream of future earnings, it must make a deliberate choice, rather than assuming that it is bound by a rule of state law.

The judgment of the Court of Appeals is vacated and the case is remanded for further proceedings consistent with this opinion.

It is so ordered.

2. *Personal Injury Damages*

Elaborate on the previous problem by including other types of damage that arguably could be allowed for an accident victim. These might include medical expenses, which have a higher rate of inflation. They might include allowances for income taxes or lost social security benefits. Consult Marilyn Minzer et al., *Damages in Tort Actions,* for further ideas. Make your solution general so that lawyers less skilled in the use of spreadsheets could easily specify the necessary information to be entered for particular accident victims.

3. *Periodic Payment Settlements*

Some states are limiting the amount of lump sum judgments in medical malpractice cases and are requiring periodic payments instead.

33. Judge Friendly perceived the relevance of Justice Holmes' phrase in this context. See *Feldman v. Allegheny Airlines, Inc.,* 524 F.2d, at 392 (Friendly, J., concurring dubitante), quoting *Truax v. Corrigan,* 257 U.S. 312, 342, 42 S.Ct. 124, 133, 66 L.Ed. 254 (1921), (Holmes, J., dissenting).

34. Throughout this opinion we have noted the many rough approximations that are essential under any manageable approach to an award for lost earnings. See *supra,* at 2548–2549, and nn. 11, 25, 26, 30.

35. It has been estimated that awards for pain and suffering account for 72 per cent of damages in personal injury litigation. 6 Am.Jur. Trials § 24 (1967).

Some insurers propose settlements based upon periodic payments. Assume the personal injuries examined in the previous exercises were caused by medical malpractice. As plaintiff's attorney, prepare a spreadsheet that will allow you to evaluate the relative attractiveness to your client of various forms of periodic payment settlement offered by the insurance company. You should evaluate not only the net present value of the payments, but also whether or not they provide a cash flow sufficient to cover your client's predicted expenses for each year.

4. *Air Pollution*

The Environmental Protection Agency regulations (40 C.F.R. Pt. 51 App. A) printed below prescribes a model for calculating air pollution: The Point Model. Prepare a spreadsheet incorporating this model. Assume certain costs for smokestacks that would release emissions in a layer with higher wind speeds and calculate the benefits in terms of reduced emission density.

> POINT MODEL. The ambient air quality concentrations that result from the emissions of a single point source have a large degree of variability depending upon the meteorological conditions. Because of this, the short-term air quality concentrations are of more concern than the long-term. In many cases, the short-term maximum concentrations occur when the plume is trapped in a mixing layer of limited depth. In these cases, the 1-hour ground level concentration from a single point source may be estimated from the following equation:
>
> $$X = Q/\sqrt{2\pi}\sigma_y L_u$$
>
> where:
>
> X = concentration, gm/meter^3.
>
> Q = source emission rate, gm/sec.
>
> σ_y = the standard deviation in the crosswind direction of the plume concentration distribution, meters.
>
> L = height of the mixing layer, meters.
>
> u = wind speed, meters/sec.
>
> The values of the meteorological parameters must be based on the meteorological conditions in the vicinity of the source. Multiplying the estimated maximum 1-hour concentration by 0.25 may be used to estimate a maximum 24-hour concentration. This factor is deemed appropriate for the meteorological conditions to which the above equation applies. The factor implies that the meteorological conditions persist 6 hours of a 24-hour period. During the remaining 18 hours, wind direction and other meteorological parameters are such that the source has no impact upon the location subjected to contamination during the 6-hour period. The estimated maximum 24-hour concentration may be compared to the maximum 24-hour national standards. This procedure may be used in

Priority 1A regions to estimate the existing air quality levels for developing a control strategy.

Under certain source and metereorological conditions, the above equation may not be appropriate; however, other equations are available that may be used. (See Turner, D.B., "Workbook of Atmospheric Dispersion Estimates", Public Health Service Publication No. 999–AP–26. U.S. Department of Health, Education, and Welfare. Public Health Service, Consumer Protection and Environmental Health Service, National Air Pollution Control Administration, Cincinnati, Ohio. Revised 1969.)

5. Legal Logic

Use the spreadsheet's logical operators to express the rules contained in Sec. 2–205 of the Uniform Commercial Code and the related "Definitional Cross References". Include any necessary background rules of contract law not specifically stated in the U.C.C. (E.g.: An offer may be revoked at any time unless consideration has been given to hold it open.)

Chapter 5

COMMUNICATIONS

§ 5–1. INTRODUCTION

Attorneys carry out most of their formal work through written communications. Internally, they craft memoranda summarizing the results of legal research. Externally, they communicate with the client and with counsel for the opposition using letters. Legal relationships are established and later modified through the use of contracts. Communication with the courts is carried out primarily with formal pleadings, motions, orders, and briefs. Without meaning to minimize the importance of oral communication both face-to-face and by telephone, oral communication almost invariably leads to formal written communication summarizing what transpired and establishing the rights and interests of the parties.

As computers begin appearing on the desktops of attorneys nationwide, it becomes possible to bypass paper and to carry out both formal and informal work by "electronic mail," using direct computer-to-computer communication to speed communication and lower the cost of communicating by bypassing secretarial assistance and the postal service.

The savings that can be achieved by using electronic mail rather than letters or telephone calls are quite impressive. Say, for example, that you wish to contact an attorney in another state to arrange a meeting for next week. If you call, the chances are good that you will be forced to play "telephone tag" for some hours, each repeatedly calling when the other is unavailable, and this consumes considerable time on the part of both you and your staff. And when you do get through, the chances are good that you and the attorney in the other state will spend ten to twenty minutes talking about "how your daughter likes law school" and other such important topics. Chances are the call will come back when you are in the middle of a project, and it will take you another ten minutes to get yourself back into the groove again—particularly since you had to pile the telephone-related files on top of the other files on your desk, which was already overflowing.

If you send a letter, it has to be typed, corrected, and mailed—all of which takes several hours before the letter even leaves your office and costs at least $25.00 in time and trouble. Then it takes several days for the letter to reach its destination. And if the other attorney needs to get back to you, there will be another $25.00 charge plus another mail delay; or if time is short, a round of "telephone tag."

With electronic mail, you type out a brief note and then command your computer to send it to the other attorney. The next morning, you turn on your computer and spend only half a minute reading his or her reply. If further communication is necessary, it takes only 30 seconds for you to respond to the other attorney's reply. No telephone tag, no feeling that you have to "socialize," no secretarial time and proofreading time, and no mail delay. And a printed copy of the communication can be placed in the file if a permanent record is needed. If time is of the essence, you can send electronic messages back and forth almost instantaneously, provided both parties agree to keep their electronic mailboxes open continuously.

When drafting briefs and contracts in cooperation with others, you may transmit passages back and forth for study and revision. This "uploading" (sending out) and "downloading" (receiving back) facility of computers can cut the time it takes to consummate a contract from days to hours.

You probably already use a form of electronic mail to communicate with WESTLAW or LEXIS. While most computer-assisted legal research is still carried out using special "custom" terminals, more and more attorneys now use their personal computers for this purpose. The trick is to find a computer program for your personal computer that will make it behave precisely like the custom terminals. Then you may "download" the results of your research onto floppy disks for temporary retention, or you may transfer case language and citations directly from WESTLAW or LEXIS screens into your briefs and memoranda without the necessity of retyping, though, unfortunately, proofreading against the official published report is advisable due to the high number of errors in some legal data bank files.

You may also transform your personal computer into a terminal that connects directly to your office's "time and billing" system, and then type in your time records without ever leaving your desk.

All of the above topics are part of "Communications," the topic of this chapter. While there are numerous applications for electronic communications in the practice of law, the underlying principles for all forms of computer-to-computer communications are the same and are set forth in the paragraphs that follow.

§ 5-2. GENERAL PRINCIPLES AND COMMON PROBLEMS OF COMMUNICATIONS

Communication of data from one computer to another involves sending data stored in the first computer over a telephone or other communications line while receiving it and storing it in the second computer. If all computers always represented information in exactly the same way in storage, and if all telephone lines always worked perfectly without any static, communications would be simple. In the real world, information is represented in a variety of ways within computers, and telephone communications are frequently faulty. The solution to the problem of data representation lies in standardization, so that the different methods of data representation can be reduced to a manageable number; and in coordination, so that the sending and receiving computer use the same system of data representation. There are various solutions to faulty communications. These include use of better telephone lines, sending data redundantly so that errors can be detected or even corrected, and automatic resending of garbled data. Error detection, error correction, and resending of data require a high level of coordination between the software programs on the sending and receiving computers. The sending computer must use exactly the same system for dealing with errors as does the receiving computer, otherwise bad data will be mistaken for good and vice-versa.

(a) Data Representation

The problem of data representation is that of what meaning to attach to each of the 256 possible states of a standard eight-bit byte of memory. You will recall from Chapter 1 that computers store information in memories constructed from pairs of transistor gates which are analogous to pairs of streetlights—one on, and one off. Such elemental memories have two stable states, so they can store the same amount of information as an "ON" —"OFF" light switch. It is helpful to think of such memories as having an "ON" state and an "OFF" state. Logicians prefer to think of them as having a "TRUE" state and a "FALSE" state, and mathematicians like to think of them as having a "1" state and a "0" state. Unfortunately for nonmathematical attorneys, the mathematicians won this debate about how to refer to the states of memory elements.

You should also recall from Chapter 1 that the computer industry has standardized upon the storage of information in eight-bit bytes of memory. Accordingly, given "one byte of memory," one can represent the "ON" or "OFF" state of each of the eight elements by a "1" or a "0". A typical byte thus might be represented as follows:

0 1 1 0 1 1 0 1

The above series of "1"s and "0"s informs us that the first, fourth, and seventh elemental memories are "OFF" or in the "0" state, while the second, third, fifth, sixth, and eighth elemental memories are in the "ON" or "1" state. By analogy to Paul Revere, his assistant has lit only a particular five of the eight lanterns hanging in the church tower.

As we noted in Chapter 1, such a byte of memory can have its elemental components arranged into 256 unique possible patterns. Accordingly, by studying which lamps are lit and which are dark, Paul

Revere can determine which of 256 possible different routes the British will take. To list just a few of the possible patterns:

Pattern 0	0 0 0 0 0 0 0 0
Pattern 1	0 0 0 0 0 0 0 1
Pattern 2	0 0 0 0 0 0 1 0
Pattern 3	0 0 0 0 0 0 1 1
. . .	
Pattern 125	0 1 1 1 1 1 0 1
Pattern 126	0 1 1 1 1 1 1 0
Pattern 127	0 1 1 1 1 1 1 1
Pattern 128	1 0 0 0 0 0 0 0
Pattern 129	1 0 0 0 0 0 0 1
. . .	
Pattern 252	1 1 1 1 1 1 0 0
Pattern 253	1 1 1 1 1 1 0 1
Pattern 254	1 1 1 1 1 1 1 0
Pattern 255	1 1 1 1 1 1 1 1

So every "byte" of memory contains one of 256 possible different messages or patterns. We shall arbitrarily assign the numbers "0" to "255" to these patterns and thereby avoid having to refer to them as "pattern 10110110" or "pattern 01101110" in our discussion. Instead, we shall speak of "pattern 0," "pattern 128," and so on.

(b) The ASCII Standard for Communication

The "meaning" assigned to each of these patterns is totally arbitrary. Paul Revere could assign each pattern to a different possible route that the British might take, or he might use the first four lanterns for that purpose, giving himself 16 possible routes, and preserve the remaining four lanterns for indicating how large the British army appears to be.

Within any given brand of computer, the manufacturer could assign any arbitrary meaning it wished to each of the 256 possible states. However, in fact two standards have emerged and the vast majority of manufacturers use one of these standards or a variation upon it. The first standard is the EBCDIC standard. This standard was established by IBM for its highly successful 360 series of computers in the 1960s and has become an industry standard for mainframe computers. In order to be able to offer 100% IBM-compatability, competing sellers of IBM-type mainframes and peripherals generally follow the EBCDIC standard exactly. The second standard, and the standard more commonly used in computers found in law offices, is the ASCII standard. Because of the need for a standard, the American National Standards Institute (a non-governmental organization), commonly called "ANSI," established a committee some years ago to establish what is now called the "American Standard Code for Information Interchange," or the "ASCII" standard. With the exception of a few of the symbols in the ASCII standard (the curly braces, etc.) that are replaced with accented letters in the codes of some foreign countries, the ASCII code is also an international standard. So messages formulated in the ASCII code that do not contain symbols such as curly braces can be "understood" by computers all over the world. For this reason, almost all manufacturers of personal computers, including IBM, have adopted the ASCII standard on their lines of personal computers. The ASCII standard is also used by IBM for its 3100-series terminals and by many other manufacturers of computer terminals.

The ASCII standard assigns meanings to only the first 128 patterns that a "byte" of information can represent. Unfortunately, this means that there is not room in the ASCII character set for all the symbols that law offices need. In particular, the ASCII character set lacks the paragraph sign (¶), section mark (§), and characters needed by international law firms such as (£, é, ê, è, ô, and ü). It also lacks graphics symbols such as lines, borders, and corners. Computer and word processor manufacturers have deviated from the ASCII standard in different ways to supply these needed characters for lawyers and others who need them. Because there is no standardization in the ways they have deviated, these deviations can cause annoying problems in computer communications, problems that will be outlined below.

"Parity" and Paul Revere's Eight Lanterns

Since the ASCII standard assigns meaning to only the first 127 patterns that a "byte" of information can represent, it requires only seven lanterns hanging in the tower of the Old North Church to transmit a one "byte" ASCII message to Paul Revere. Unfortunately, there is disagreement over what should be done with the eighth lantern. Traditionally, the eighth "lantern" has been used to check the remaining seven lanterns for accuracy. Paul Revere and his agent agree in advance that a valid message must have an "even" number of lanterns lit—if an "odd" number are lit, the message is erroneous. The eighth lantern, which must be adjusted so that an even number are lit, is called the "parity" lantern, and the message transmitted by the eight lanterns is said to have "even parity." But Paul and his agent could just as well agree to adjust the eighth lantern so that a valid message contains an "odd" number of lit lanterns, and then the message is said to have "odd" parity. Or Paul could ignore the eighth lantern entirely and assume the message was correct, as many computers do, in which case Paul's agent might leave it lit all the time (this is called "mark" parity) or leave it unlit all the time (this is called "space" parity) or set it to "even" or "odd" parity or simply not have an eighth lantern (in which case the message is said to contain "seven data bits and no parity bit"). Paul and his agent can agree that if the eighth lantern is out, the remaining seven lanterns form an ASCII message; and if the eighth lantern is lit, then the agent is sending Paul one of 128 "private" messages not in accord with the ANSI standard (the IBM Personal Computer follows this convention internally, using patterns 128 to 255 to represent foreign characters and special graphic symbols). Or a "lit" eighth lantern can indicate the remaining lanterns are signaling a normal ASCII message, while an "unlit" eighth lantern can indicate an ASCII message that is underlined or highlighted (the Apple II computer follows this convention internally).

Unfortunately, all of the above schemes are currently in use and they are all mutually incompatible. And of course, Paul and his agent can abandon the ASCII standard entirely and establish their own system of 256 messages. Furthermore all of the above schemes are totally incompatible with the EBCDIC system often used for communication with IBM-compatible mainframe computers and also used with IBM Displaywriter word processors. This is why Displaywriters have such difficulty "talking" to other personal computers—Displaywriters speak EBCDIC, not ASCII.

Printable Characters in ASCII

In the ASCII code, the printable characters (the letters, numbers, and symbols on the keyboard) are assigned to code patterns "32" through "126." The capital letters "A" through "Z" are assigned to patterns "65" to "90". The lower-case letters "a" to "z" are assigned to patterns "97" to "122," so each lower-case letter is exactly 32 patterns away from the corresponding upper-case letter. Your computer can convert "lower-case" to "upper-case" by simply subtracting "32" from the pattern number, and vice-versa. The numbers "0" to "9" are assigned to patterns "48" to "57," and all the other printable keyboard characters are assigned to the remaining patterns. Striking the space bar generates pattern "32," which, of course, prints a blank space.

The 95 printable ASCII characters include the space, the numbers, the upper- and lower-case letters, and the following symbols:

! " # $ % & ' ( ) * + , – . / : ; < = > ? @ [\ ] ^ _ ` { | } ~

If you plan to send documents to computers and word processors that differ from your own, you can improve your chances of compatibility if you limit yourself to numbers and letters and the above symbols. You are even safer if you avoid symbols not found on a standard typewriter keyboard, such as " ~ ."

Nonprintable Commands in ASCII

Code patterns "1" through "31" are not printable characters—they are commands that call for specific action. The commands of most interest to us correspond to the keys on your keyboard that do not print: "back space" (pattern "8"), "tab" (pattern "9"), "carriage return" (pattern "13"), and "escape" (pattern "27"—to be discussed below). Some computers and terminals have a "line feed" key (pattern "10") which moves the cursor down one line. Patterns "17" and "19," which you can generate by holding the <Ctrl> shift key down and striking the "S" and "Q" keys, control the inflow of information to your computer screen from remote sources: pattern "19" (<Ctrl–S>) says "stop sending;" pattern "17" (<Ctrl–Q>) says "start sending again." You can use "<Ctrl–S>" and "<Ctrl–Q>" to halt and later restart the scrolling of data across your screen when you are communicating with a remote computer. Pattern "7," which you can generate by holding the <Ctrl> shift key down and striking the "G" key, is the "bell" command that can make your computer, terminal, or printer go "Beep!"

The "Control" Shift Key—How it Differs From the "Escape" Command Key

Note that the key labeled <Ctrl> is actually a second "shift" key that causes the letter keys and certain symbol keys to generate the unprintable ASCII commands instead of printable characters. The ASCII standard specifies which command is generated by which letter key, so <Ctrl–S> and <Ctrl–Q> will halt and restart the flow of incoming information, and <Ctrl–G> will ring the bell, on virtually all computers and terminals. And if your computer or terminal has no "line feed" key, <Ctrl–J> will move your cursor down one line. Another useful command is <Ctrl–L>, which generates a "form feed" or "new page" command (pattern "12"). Typing <Ctrl–L> will sometimes erase your viewing screen, and sending a <Ctrl–L> to virtually all printers causes them to roll the paper to the top of the next page.

The <Esc> key on your keyboard is NOT a shift key—it actually generates the ASCII "escape" command (which is explained more fully below). The <Ctrl> key on your keyboard IS a "shift" key. The different ways in which these two keys function is not well understood by most users of computers. When you are instructed to type "<Ctrl–S>," this means, "hold down the <Ctrl> shift key, and strike the S key while you are still holding down the <Ctrl> shift key." When you are instructed to type "<Esc> <S>," this means, "strike the <Esc> key (do NOT hold it down!) and then strike the <S> key after you release the <Esc> key." If you hold the <Esc> key down too long, the key will start "repeating," and you will generate multiple "escape" commands which will probably get you into trouble. If you fail to hold the <Ctrl> key down while you strike the <S> key, then instead of sending a "halt transmission" command to the remote computer, you will simply send the letter "S" to the remote computer, and the information you wished to study will scroll right off your screen.

The History of the "Break" Key

Another key that causes some confusion is the <Break> key, which is not a shift key and which also does not generate an ASCII command—it is a relic of the early Teletype days. The early Teletypes were connected together by a "loop" of wire that sometimes covered many miles and many machines. To transmit, a sending Teletype machine would send current through this loop of wire by hooking the ends of the loop to a battery. The battery current then passed through current sensors in all the other machines. To transmit a character, the sending machine halted the flow of current and then rapidly started and stopped the flow in a way that corresponded to the "1" and "0" pattern of the message or "byte" that was being sent. The other machines responded to these current fluctuations by typing out the transmitted character. But only one machine could transmit at a time.

If one of the machines became unplugged or if the wire broke, the current flow would stop. The sending machine would sense this absence of current flow and would turn on a red "BREAK" light to warn the operator that the loop had been broken and that the message was not getting through.

If some other machine wished to interrupt the sender, the operator of the interrupting machine pushed a "BREAK" button which literally "broke" the current path, stopping the flow of current around the loop momentarily. This caused the "BREAK" light on the sending machine to flash and signaled the operator that someone wished to interrupt the transmission and send a return message.

The "BREAK" key on a computer terminal simulates a "BREAK" in the current loop of the old Teletype machines by holding the outgoing signal line of your computer positive for an extended interval—far longer than would be needed to transmit a character. Special hardware in the receiving computer detects this extended positive signal level and generates a "BREAK" signal within that computer. Special software must detect this signal and "interrupt" whatever program is running to process the "BREAK" request. In modern computers, ordinary ASCII commands can also be arranged to generate such "interrupts," so the "BREAK" function is not really needed any more. But because there is a "BREAK" key on virtually every terminal and computer, program designers cannot resist putting this key to use.

Many computers, including the IBM Personal Computer, respond to the command "<Ctrl–C>" (pattern "3"—the ASCII "end of text" command) as if it were the "BREAK" command by halting whatever program is running. On the IBM PC, "<Ctrl–C>" and "<Ctrl–Break>" generally produce the same result.

On terminals, the <Break> key will always generate a "BREAK" request. On personal computers, you are at the mercy of the programmer who wrote the "terminal emulation" program that you are using. When using the IBM Personal Computer, you may find that programmer assigned the "BREAK" function to the "<Ctrl–Break>" key combination as the designers of the computer intended, but the programmer is just as likely to have assigned the "BREAK" function to some other key, or made it possible for you to assign it to your favorite key, or left it out entirely—you must check your "terminal emulation" program's manual carefully on this point.

When using the LawComm, legal communications program supplied with this book, you generate a "BREAK" request by holding the <Ctrl> shift key down and striking the key labeled <Break>. When using the American Bar Association's electronic mail service ABA/net, this is how you halt the reception of a lengthy electronic letter that you don't wish to read through to the end.

The "Null" and "Delete" Commands—The Impact of Punched Paper Tape on the ASCII Standard

ASCII pattern "0," which corresponds to the data bit pattern "0 0 0 0 0 0 0," is called the "NULL" pattern—it is a message that is ignored by the recipient. ASCII pattern "127," which corresponds to the data bit pattern "1 1 1 1 1 1 1," is assigned the meaning "RUBOUT" or "DELETE" and is also ignored by the recipient. These two patterns, which have the same "non-meaning," have an interesting history. The original way in which data was transmitted over telephone lines was by first having human operators punch the data into paper tape. On the tape, each row of punches represented a single printable letter, number, or symbol. A hole represented a "1," and the absence of a hole represented a "0." Naturally, a stretch of blank tape contained no holes (and therefore no information) and presented the code value "0 0 0 0 0 0 0" to the primitive early transmitters, so the early receivers had to be designed to ignore this code. If the person punching the tape made an error, they backed up the tape and punched out all the holes across that row. The key that punched out all the holes was called the "RUBOUT" key, and the code pattern generated was "1 1 1 1 1 1 1." The early receivers had to be designed to ignore this "RUBOUT" code as well. Paper tape is no longer the medium of choice for data communication, but its primary role in the early days is now immortalized in the ANSI standard by the seemingly redundant presence of two patterns that both mean "ignore me."

With some remote services, most notably those using Digital Equipment Corporation's VAX minicomputers, the "DELETE" pattern is used as a "BACKSPACE". To generate it using LawComm, hold down the <Ctrl> shift key and strike the <Backspace> key.

Generating Commands and Non-ASCII Symbols When Using the IBM PC

Most of the remaining commands assigned to the patterns "1" through "31" by the ASCII standard, while interesting to historians of technology and to some having highly specialized needs, are not relevant to our needs as attorneys who wish to communicate. You may generate them all using your IBM Personal Computer keyboard in one way or another, either by using the <Ctrl> shift key in combination with a letter or symbol key or by depressing and holding down the <Alt> key while typing the pattern number of the desired command on the numeric keypad. You may also generate foreign characters and special non-ASCII symbols that IBM has assigned to the patterns "128" through "255" (not covered by the ASCII standard) by holding down the <Alt> key while typing a pattern number on the numeric keypad.

If you experiment using your word processor, you will discover that IBM has also assigned useful, printable symbols to some of the "command" patterns "1" through "31." The most useful of these for an attorney are pattern "20," which generates a "paragraph" symbol, and pattern "21," which generates a "section" symbol. Try generating these using your word processor. If you have an IBM printer, these special symbols may be printable on your printer. You may send these symbols to other IBM Personal Computers by electronic mail. But because they are not supported by the ASCII standard, you cannot in general expect other printers or computers to recognize these symbols. When using the LawWord word processor, you may generate the section symbols on the screen by typing <Ctrl–P> and <Ctrl–U>, and you may generate the paragraph symbol by typing <Ctrl–P> and <Ctrl–T>. But don't expect to be able to print them without a lot of trouble. An exotic sequence of printer codes may be required, and LawWord must be set for "generic" printing with the ".GE" command. If you are brave, see your printer manual.

The <Ctrl–Z> "End of Text" Command—Beware!

Two other nonprintable ASCII command patterns are important to the users of personal computers. The first is code pattern "26", the

ASCII "substitute" command. Since this code pattern can be generated conveniently by striking "<Ctrl–Z>" and is not otherwise assigned to special use, it has been adopted by the PC/DOS and MS/DOS operating systems as an "end-of-text-file" marker. Most word processors and other text-handling programs stop reading a text file on your diskette when they encounter a "<Ctrl–Z>." Unfortunately, this can cause you serious problems on occasion. Imagine that you are downloading an important contract to your personal computer's disk and that the process takes over an hour. Static on the telephone line occasionally can transform one incoming character into another, and on this occasion it transforms a "Z" character (pattern "90") into a "<Ctrl–Z>" (pattern "26"). Your 42-page contract now contains an "end of text file" marker in the second line on page one.

You are in serious trouble. When you attempt to print the contract, only two lines appear on the paper; and when you attempt to load it into your word processor for review and revision, only two lines appear upon the viewing screen. The remainder of the lengthy contract appears to have vanished, yet your disk directory indicates that it is all there! Before you can load the contract into your word processor or print it out, you will need to use your computer's debugging tool to enter the contract file and replace the <Ctrl–Z> character with something less devastating. (This is a task best left to your 15-year-old "computer freak" or to a "computer guru" at your nearby computer store.) To simplify the making of this type of correction, and to assist you in finding files that become "lost" on a diskette or that are erased in error, every law firm should have on hand a copy of "The Norton Utilities," which is perhaps the best value in software today.

"Escape" Sequences

The second additional ASCII command pattern that is worthy of further study is code pattern 27, the "ESCAPE" command. The designers of the ASCII standard recognized that the thirty predefined control commands in the ASCII code were not nearly enough. Accordingly, they included in the code an "ESCAPE" command which transforms the normally printable character or characters that follow it into additional commands. For example, if you send an "ESCAPE" command (code pattern "27") followed by the capital letter "E" (code pattern "69") to a particular computer terminal, the terminal erases its screen completely. If you send an "ESCAPE" character followed by the capital letter "B" to this same terminal, the terminal moves its cursor down one line. Such multi-character commands that start with the "ESCAPE" command are called "escape sequences."

By sending the proper "escape sequence" to your printer, you can cause your printer to start or stop underlining what it prints, start or stop printing superscripts, start or stop justifying the text on each line, or do any number of other similar things. When you communicate with a mainframe computer, you may be asked to transmit escape sequences to the computer as commands by striking the <Esc> key on your terminal and then typing the additional letters or symbols that comprise the command.

When using a terminal, you can always rely upon the <Esc> key generating an "ESCAPE" command. But when using a personal computer, you will frequently find that the programmer who wrote the program you are using may have reassigned the <Esc> key to some other function—most usually, the <Esc> key lets you "escape" or "exit" from whatever it is that you are doing. Even some "terminal emulation" programs designed to emulate commercial terminals having normally functioning <Esc> keys reassign the key in this manner, to the intense frustration of those attempting to use such programs to communicate with central computers that need to be fed escape sequences. Once again, check your program manual carefully if you have need to generate the "ESCAPE" command. When the LawComm program is running the <Esc> key functions as an "escape from what you are doing" key and does not generate "ESCAPE" command.

The ANSI organization has attempted to standardize some of the more common of these "ESCAPE" control sequences, but with little success so far—very few vendors have adopted the new standards. Most manufacturers of printers and terminals have their own proprietary "ESCAPE" control sequences that no one else supports. But some "de facto" standards are emerging with respect to personal computers due to the success of certain vendors. Accordingly, when selecting printers and terminals, you should give preference to those that can "emulate" the following ("emulate" means "respond in the same way to the same escape sequences"):

Printers: Epson printers; Diablo 630 printer;

Terminals: Digital Equipment Model VT–100;

IBM Model 3101 ("Block" mode for WESTLAW and LEXIS use);

Televideo Model 760

The VT–100 terminal actually does implement a substantial subset of the new ASCII standardized escape sequences, so it is preferable to other terminals for general-purpose use. The LawComm legal communications program supplied with this book emulates a VT–100 but switches to an IBM 3101 emulation automatically wherever you access WESTLAW's or LEXIS's IBM 3101 service.

Now that you are an expert in telecommunications, let's talk about communicating from your office to a remote computer.

§ 5–3. TERMINALS—ACCESSING SHARED AND REMOTE COMPUTERS

Humans communicate with computers by typing upon a "keyboard" and by viewing messages displayed upon a viewing screen or "display."

Most personal computers use "monitors" as their displays. Monitors are television receivers with no "tuner" and no antenna connection. Author Sprowl's monitor for his home personal computer is a 25-inch Zenith color "component TV" that also connects to the family's video cassette recorder. Some home personal computers (most notably the Apple II family) generate a standard (or "composite") single-wire television video signal that can display 40 columns of text upon any conventional television monitor. Other personal computers (including the IBM Personal Computer with a "Color/Graphics" display card) generate what is called an "RGB" signal—separate red, green, and blue signals conveyed by separate wires to a monitor having a special connector—to achieve the higher resolution required for 80-column text display. Some business computers (most notably the IBM Personal Computer with a "Monochrome" display card) generate a non-standard video signal to achieve more horizontal lines of resolution than can be achieved on a standard television display.

"Multiuser" computers are accessed by means of "terminals." A "terminal" is actually a microcomputer with a monitor, a keyboard, and an industry-standard "serial communications port"—a socket designed to connect any terminal to any computer. The cable that connects the serial communications port to the multi-user computer is an industry-standard "RS–232c" cable which can be used to connect any terminal to any computer. IBM, Wang, and a few other large vendors have proprietary ports and cables, but the RS–232c standard is widely used throughout the world.

Up until recently, "terminals" were dedicated pieces of equipment that could be used only as terminals. But virtually any microcomputer having a "serial communications port" can now be programmed to "emulate" virtually any kind of dedicated terminal. Because general purpose microcomputers are able to "download" incoming material onto floppy disks as well as display it on their displays, and because they can emulate different terminals at different times, they are rapidly displacing the dedicated terminals. "Terminal emulation software" that can transform an IBM Personal Computer or an Apple Macintosh into almost any type of terminal is available today for around $100.00. You should avoid purchasing a dedicated terminal if you can program a personal computer to emulate it. Microstuf is the leading vendor of terminal emulation software for the IBM PC and compatibles.

Note that terminals are used to access computers of all types and sizes. The same terminal can be used at one time to access WESTLAW and at another time to access the office time accounting and billing computer. Your deskside personal computer can be used as a word processor at one time, as a WESTLAW or LEXIS terminal at another time, and as an office accounting terminal at yet another time. The computer could be in the same room, several rooms away, or in a different continent. But in all cases, the underlying principles of communication are the same.

If the computer is more than one-hundred feet away, frequently telephone lines are used to connect the computer to the terminal. At both ends of the telephone link, devices called "modems" are used to connect the telephone line to the industry-standard RS–232c cables that lead to the terminal and to the computer. The "modems" simply translate the fluctuating voltages on the wires in the RS–232c cable into fluctuating tones suitable for telephone transmission and then back into fluctuating voltages at the other end of the connection.

(a) Setting the Transmission Parameters

The terminal and the multiuser computer must agree on certain things: How fast is the information to be transmitted? What is to be done with the eighth (parity) data bit? How many "stop" bits (or trailing data bits) are to be added to each character? And because the industry-standard RS–232c cable contains numerous wires, which of those wires are actually to be used? The short answer to all of these questions is: Select "1200 Baud" as your communications speed; set your system up for no parity, eight data bits, one stop bit, and "full duplex" or no echo (or else set it to match the computer's settings); purchase a "Hayes compatible" modem; use LawComm, the legal communications program provided with this book, Microstuf's Crosstalk, Hayes' Smartcom or some other "terminal emulator" program that is able to take full advantage of the modem's auto-dialing capabilities; and set the modem switches as the manual for the "terminal emulator" program indicates.

The long answer to these questions is set forth at length in Appendix A. If you are using a Hayes (or Hayes-compatible) modem and the Smartcom, Crosstalk XVI, or PC–TALK terminal emulation program, Appendix A will illustrate precisely how your emulation program should be set up. LawComm does not normally require any adjustment or setting up and works with most modem switch and jumper settings.

(b) Handshaking Your Way to Your Destination

Now you must dial up your destination and then issue the necessary commands to connect yourself up to your destination. If you communicate with the same destinations frequently, you will find a programmed computer to be far easier to use than a terminal, since the computer can "learn" the necessary command sequences and send the commands out far faster than you could type them out yourself. If you communicate infrequently with a wide variety of destinations, then there is no easy way—the computer is still to be preferred, since it can allow you to copy the incoming data onto floppy diskettes for temporary retention. But even with a personal computer, you must install the necessary commands at least once. One of the hardest parts about communicating is learning exactly what the commands are.

The following steps are essential:

Send "dialing" instructions to the modem;

Optionally, issue the necessary commands to a "packet switching network" to route your call to a remotely located computer;

When the computer answers, enter into a "logon dialog" with the computer, including the initial handshake, the address, the account number, and the password;

Having reached your destination, enter into the "business" handshake to accomplish your primary task;

Complete the "Logoff" handshake.

With many dedicated terminals or with very poor quality "terminal emulation" software, you will have to do all of these handshakes essentially manually. With reasonably good "terminal emulation software," you can automate everything except the "business" handshake, and you can even automate the "business" handshake in routine cases, such as checking your electronic mailbox for mail.

Dialing the Remote Computer

If you have a good modem and a good communications program, the dialing should take place automatically after you have supplied the telephone number of your destination to your communications program. For a complete explanation of automatic dialing and of the possible problems that you may encounter when you connect your computer or terminal to your modem, see Appendix A.

Most "auto-dial" modems contain a speaker that permits you to listen to the progress of your telephone call. After your computer sends the "dial" command to your modem, you will hear the dial tone, the modem-generated dial pulses or tones, the ringing, and finally the high-pitched "squeal" generated by the modem of the remote computer as it answers the telephone. Listen carefully to all of this.

If you hear nothing, then something is wrong with your modem. Is it plugged in and turned on? Is the modem connected to the computer? Has someone borrowed your modem and "reset" its little switches?

If you hear dialing pulses or tones but no dial tone and no "ringing" sounds, check to see if the telephone line is properly connected to the modem. Push in on the telephone line plug where it enters the modem—this is a troublesome point. Hook a standard telephone to the line and see if you can dial manually. If not, then call your friendly telephone repair service.

You may hear the dial tone, the dialing tones and pulses, the ringing signal, and then no one answers; or you hear a "busy" signal; or you hear a recorded message advising you that there is "no such number;" or you hear someone pick up a telephone at the other end and say, "Hello? . . . Hello? . . . Who is it? . . . @#%#&*$#!" and then hang up in anger (typically, this happens at 4:00 in the morning when you are attempting to take advantage of the lower "on line" rates charged at that hour by computer service vendors).

Some make the serious mistake of turning the volume of their speaker all the way down so they do not hear all this helpful information.

You should listen carefully for hiss and static during the "ringing" signal period and after the remote computer answers. Any unusual sound probably means you have a "faulty" telephone connection that will badly "garble" the messages you wish to transmit. Command your computer to hang up and redial—preferably before the remote computer answers and you incur a toll charge on the call.

Ultimately, if all goes well, the remote computer will answer. You will hear high-pitched tones as the two modems conduct their own private handshake and turn on their respective tone generators, and then the speaker will shut itself off.

Accessing a Remote Computer Through a "Packet Switching" Network

If you are dialing up a personal computer in another attorney's office or a "mainframe" computer in your own town or city, then you have no need to use the services of a "packet switching" network. If you are dialing up a remote mainframe or minicomputer in a distant city, you can place a "long distance" call directly to the computer, and you can thereby bypass the use of a "packet switching" network. But such a call is likely to be quite expensive, and you may encounter serious static problems on conventional long-distance telephone lines. Therefore the preferred way to communicate with remote computers at the present time is to have your computer dial up the local number of a "packet switching" service. In addition to being less expensive than direct-dial "long distance telephone" services, these packet switching services are designed to detect and correct all transmission errors that may occur. In the near future, with the introduction of new modems that can transmit information over ordinary long-distance telephone lines in an error-free manner at speeds eight times faster (9600 Baud) than is possible today, the economics may shift in favor of direct-dial long distance communication, particularly for the transmission of documents between offices.

The most commonly-used "packet-switching" vendors are Telenet, Tymnet, and Datapac. These vendors are "long-distance carriers" comparable to AT&T and MCI that can connect your computer or terminal to any one of thousands of remote computers across the country. But they do so in an error-free, economical manner by routing your "packets" or messages over long-distance lines that are also shared by many others at the same time. Like all other computer service vendors, these vendors have breakdowns and are affected by occasional overloads that can slow their transmission rates. You should try to provide yourself with at least two different ways of accessing any given destination. If your transmissions seem to be coming very slowly, try accessing the same central computer via a different packet switching vendor or via an 800 telephone number.

After you dial them up, the packet switching service may start sending you a message immediately, and that message may be at the wrong "Baud" rate (or speed) so that it may appear as "garbage" characters on your screen. Or the packet switching service may do nothing until you send it an initial message. Since the service has to determine your "Baud" rate (or speed of transmission) and your computer's character set (ASCII versus EBCDIC, for example, when conversing with an IBM mainframe system) and what type of terminal you are using by examining the first few keystrokes that you send, you need to send the right initial message or "handshake."

There are no standards governing this initial "handshake," and each packet switching service has its own protocol. Each requires you to send a unique series of keystrokes to initiate communication. You may type these initial keystrokes yourself, but preferably you should instruct your "terminal emulation" program to send the proper sequence of keystrokes for you.

The handshake protocols for Telenet, Tymnet, and Datapac are set forth in Appendix B. You may obtain information on Westnet and Meadnet access from your local WESTLAW and LEXIS marketing representatives. [As of this writing, it looks like your LawComm program will automate all of these handshake protocols—check the "READ.ME" file on your program disk for further details.]

The "Logon Handshake"—Talking to the Remote Computer

Now you have finally reached the remote computer. A new round of handshaking now begins. You may have to "wake up" the remote computer by sending it some special message, or you may have to wait until it has sent you some greeting. Typically, the remote computer will prompt you to submit an account number. You should program your computer to wait for the last character in this prompt message, typically a colon; then wait one-half second more, and then send back your account number followed by <Return>. (On an IBM PC strike the <Enter> key to send <Return>). Next, you will be prompted to supply a password, and you should again wait for the prompt character, then wait a bit longer, and then send back your password followed by "<Return>".

If your destination is a personal computer, then there may be no account number and password handshake, and the computer may be preset to operate at only one speed. But you must make sure that your computer or terminal and the destination computer are set to the same speed, parity, and number of data bits or you may not be able to communicate. This may require some experimentation on your part.

The Business Handshake

You have now finally established communication with a remote service. You may wish to automate one additional handshake to take you into some "program" of the remote computer—for example, into its "electronic mail" service. But most personal computer users are satisfied if their computer carries them up to this point in a fully-automated fashion. If you had to do anything other than select the service on a menu up to this point, then you are not as fully automated as you could be.

At this point, your personal computer has become a "terminal" attached to the remote computer. (See the discussion of terminals which follows.)

The "Logoff" Handshake

The "logoff" handshake is much like the others and may be automated. You must first carefully log off of the remote computer, using whatever command the remote computer requires. The WESTLAW and ABA/net "logoff" command is "OFF<Enter>". The LEXIS "logoff" command is ".SO<Enter>". Other possibilities are "LOGOFF<Enter>", "QUIT<Enter>", and "SIGNOFF<Enter>". It is important to log off properly, or the central computer may continue to bill you for use after you have stopped using the service. It is also possible for someone else dialing in to get into your account, so that you would be billed for their usage, if you do not log off of some poorly designed equipment. So don't simply turn off your terminal or computer and walk away without logging off properly. When using LawComm the legal communications program supplied with this book, the F2 function key will log you off of WESTLAW or LEXIS.

Next, you must command your modem to "hang up" your telephone to stop the charges for telephone services. Ideally, your "terminal emulation" program will hang up the telephone for you in response to some command such as "<Alt–H>" (for "hangup") or "BYE<Enter>," for example (see Appendix A for a discussion of problems relating to the use of the modem's "data terminal ready" signal as a "hangup" signal). Turning off your computer or terminal may not be sufficient if your "modem" is separately powered—the telephone may remain "off-hook." Unplugging the telephone line from the modem is guaranteed to hang up the telephone if all else fails. Law office computers frequently are not programmed to hang up the telephone properly, and this can cause your firm's telephone bill to soar. To insure that your modem does hang up, hook an ordinary telephone to the same line by means of a dual-phone connector and see if you can get a dial tone after the computer has supposedly hung up. LawComm, when used with an internally-mounted Hayes compatible modem, hangs up the telephone whenever you strike the <Esc> key.

§ 5-4. VARIETIES OF TERMINALS USEFUL IN THE PRACTICE OF LAW

The only fully standardized type of terminal is the "dumb" terminal—the lowest common denominator in the world of terminals. A dumb terminal provides no features beyond those found on the early Teletype machines. Because of their "Teletype" parentage, "dumb" terminals are frequently called "TTY" terminals. (Similarly, the lowest common denominator in printers is the "dumb" or "TTY" printer. If your word processor and printer are otherwise incompatible, you can advise your word processor that you have a "TTY" printer, and then both the word processor and the printer will be content—but you will lose italics, superscripts, justification, and many other fancy features.)

Every terminal is at least a "dumb" terminal. What features does such a terminal support? You will recall that the old Teletypes printed on paper which scrolled upwards past the print head and could not be backed up. So when you are using a "dumb" terminal, all the incoming information will scroll up from the bottom of your screen. And once texts scrolls up past the bottom line, it is lost—you cannot move the cursor up to "edit" or "save" it. There is no way to position the cursor in an arbitrary location and write on the display, and there is no way to selectively erase some areas on the display and not others.

Many remote computers will give you far better service if you have a "smart" terminal that permits the remote computer to position the cursor, erase selectively, establish and operate scrollable windows, highlight and underline text, and even select alternate character fonts or squeeze more characters onto each line (132 instead of 80). But you must obtain a "smart" terminal or a program that emulates a "smart" terminal, and sometimes you will need to advise the remote computer of what type of terminal you are using. (Some remote computers assume you have a particular terminal The Prentice Hall PHINET tax service, for example, presumes that you have a Digital Equipment Corporation VT-100).

The most popular "smart" terminal is Digital Equipment Corporation's VT-100 and its progeny. This terminal also happens to implement a substantial subset of the internationally-standardized escape code sequences recently promulgated by the ANSI organization as an extension of the standard ASCII code. So it is a good thing to have around. We have yet to find a VT-100 terminal emulation program for the IBM-PC that does a full VT-100 emulation, including such rarely-used features as the VT-100 optional double-height characters and optional 132-column screen width, but most PC emulations of the VT-100 are satisfactory for the purpose of accessing a remote computer. The most common deficiency of VT-100 emulators is their failure to implement the VT-100's optional "graphics" character set: When the remote computer thinks it is drawing a box around a message on your screen, you see a box made up of lower-case ps and qs. But at least the emulator works properly—this is a cosmetic defect that should not concern you. LawComm is a fairly complete VT–100 emulation, but it does not support the "graphics" character set. With LawComm, keys F7, F8, F9, and F10 correspond to the VT–100's "special function keys".

Another useful emulator for law offices is the IBM "block mode" 3101 terminal. "Block mode" means that what you type goes to the screen and is not transmitted until you strike a "transmit" key. Most terminals and terminal emulator programs, including "dumb" terminals and the VT–100, operate in "character mode," which means that when you strike a key, that character or command is transmitted, and it is echoed back from the remote computer to your screen. When you strike the <Enter> key at the end of the line, the remote computer accepts the information on that line. Using a "dumb" "character mode" terminal, you cannot possibly create or revise a three-line WESTLAW or LEXIS search request and then send it in as a block—you can only send in one line at a time, and this limits what you can do. So a VT–100 (for LEXIS) or a "block mode" terminal is preferable for WESTLAW and LEXIS use. Other than the custom software supplied by the two vendors, your only "block mode" option that will work with both WESTLAW and LEXIS is an emulation of an IBM 3101 "block mode" terminal, or such a terminal itself. LawComm automatically transforms itself into an IBM 3101 "block mode" terminal emulator when you use it to access WESTLAW or LEXIS's 3101 terminal service. (While this emulation is satisfactory for legal research, it is not a full emulation of the 3101 terminal, we should note.)

When communicating with the remote computer, you will send it commands that may be difficult to remember. You can set up your personal computer so that these commands are automatically assigned to its special function keys. You may use a utility program such as "PROKEY" to perform this task, or your terminal emulation program may be able to do this for you. In LawComm, the various WESTLAW and LEXIS commands are automatically assigned to the function keys in a uniform manner such that the same key always performs the same function regardless of which service (WESTLAW or LEXIS) you are using. For example, the "<PgDn>" and "<PgUp>" keys on the IBM PC's numeric keypad are assigned the LEXIS ".NP<Enter>" (next page) and ".PP<Enter>" (previous page) commands when you communicate with LEXIS. These same keys are assigned the WESTLAW "P + 1<Enter>" (next page) and "P – 1 <Enter>" (previous page) commands when you communicate with WESTLAW. The program thus enables, researchers skilled in using one service to use the other service without retraining. To see what commands are assigned to each key, strike the F1 function key.

§ 5–5. ELECTRONIC MAIL AND CONFERENCING

Imagine yourself sitting in your office a few years from now when a client calls up and asks you to arrange a settlement conference for a lawsuit that involves fifteen attorneys located in five different cities. It is important for tax reasons to hold this conference the following week.

Imagine first that you try to arrange this conference by telephone. Fifteen telephone calls are required, ten of them involving bouts of "telephone tag" that last for two days. Each call lasts for 10 to 30 minutes, and many include idle conversations with your colleagues. Two days later, you have spent 6 hours, and you have still only talked to most of the attorneys once. You have discovered that the times you originally proposed did not work out for three of the attorneys, so you now need to contact them all again.

Now imagine that all of the attorneys are subscribers to the American Bar Association's new ABA/net electronic mail service, and that each one arranges for his or her mailbox to be checked at least once a day. You turn on your desk-side computer and select "ABA/net" on the communications menu. One minute later, you type out a succinct electronic letter and send it simultaneously to all 15 attorneys. The next morning, you browse through 15 answers, send a brief second reply, and you are done. Total time: 15 minutes.

Now imagine that you are negotiating a contract between three companies located in different cities. The contract is ten pages long and contains some sensitive passages. If you were to "express mail" it to the clients and their attorneys, they would not receive it until the next day, and they would then have to retype major portions before they returned it to you. Contrast this procedure with "uploading" the contract into the electronic mail service in an "error free" manner and then delivering copies to all the parties so that they receive it in "machine readable" form less than an hour later.

Now imagine a lawsuit that involves two parties whose attorneys are located in different cities, with the courthouse in yet another city. By prior agreement between the parties and the Court, all the noncontested motions are delivered to the parties and to the court by electronic mail, with each party having a day within which to respond to motions filed by the other. The judge, who has a personal computer at home, frequently rules on the motions, or asks for additional information, from home in the evenings. When the parties are involved in "out-of-town" discovery, they can frequently file written arguments by computer and receive a decision from the judge assigned to the case within a few hours, or at least overnight.

Next, imagine that you are a "general practitioner" who practices in a small rural town in South Dakota. You have a probate tax problem come up that involves "income with respect of a decedent." You read the Internal Revenue Code and the applicable regulations, but you can make no sense of it. So you turn on your personal computer and enter into a "computer conferencing" program that involves many other practitioners from all over the country. This conference is entitled "LAW:FORUM," and it is established on a large mainframe computer at Wayne State University in Detroit. The conference organizer is law professor Jennifer Bankier from Dalhousie University in Halifax, Nova Scotia.

This conference, which has been running for several years, has attracted over 500 attorneys, law professors, and law students. A printout of the conference would now be several inches thick. The conference participants have discussed over 400 agenda items ranging from legal topics to parties for conference participants to discussions of important social problems.

After browsing through the new comments that have been added to the agenda items which you have elected to follow, you create a new agenda item entitled "Income With Respect To A Decedent—Nonsense In The Tax Code." Then you describe the provision in the tax code and ask if "anyone out there" can make any sense out of it.

Several days later, you reenter the conference and discover that 20 "responses" have been appended to your new agenda item. The first response is from a graduate law student in Toronto who briefly explains what the statute is all about, and then contrasts it with the corresponding Canadian statute relating to the taxability of dividends declared, but not yet paid, on the date of death. This response is followed by a lively debate over the merits of the law, proposals to change it, and discussions of the impact of the latest tax revisions upon that particular provision. After reading the responses, you send a private electronic letter to the student in Toronto offering to hire him as a consultant to help you with the tax problem.

These are just a few examples of the types of things that are happening to practitioners all over the country as they discover the efficiencies of electronic mail and conferencing. American Bar Association committees that used to meet only once or twice a year can now continue meeting all year long through the medium of electronic conferencing. Law students can now debate legal topics with their colleagues at law schools all over the United States and Canada, and it is even possible to send electronic messages to law students in the United Kingdom.

Electronic communications now makes it possible for groups to meet and discuss issues without having to come together at a common point in time and space. It provides a public, detailed log of all interactions and gives participants time to think about their contributions. Yet it preserves the "personal" contact that is so important to meaningful interaction between individuals. Electronic mail, in addition to greatly speeding the delivery of information, eliminates the delay and expense inherent in dictating letters, having them typed and proofread, and stamping and mailing them—perhaps $25 or more per letter in the average law firm.

§ 5-6. ELECTRONIC DOCUMENT TRANSMISSION

Most electronic mail services are set up so that you type in the letters you wish to send "on line"—that is, each keystroke you type is sent in to a central computer as soon as you type it. While you can "backspace" within a line, once you strike <Enter> the line is gone, and it is difficult to revise it after that. While most such services do have editors, they are difficult to use, at best.

In the case of important documents, you may wish to type them using your word processor "off line" in an editing environment where you can freely change them. Then you may want to "upload" them into ABA/net or MCI/Mail and send them electronically to their destination. You may also send briefs, contracts, and articles by e-mail after creating them with your word processor.

(a) Word Processor Incompatibilities

The ASCII code and industry practice standardize the way in which virtually all personal computers and word processors (with the exception of IBM mainframes and IBM Displaywriters) represent letters, numbers, the following punctuation symbols:

! " # $ % & ' ( ) * + , – . / : ; <= > ? @ [\] ^ _ `

{|} ~ and the following ASCII commands:

<tab> <return> <formfeed>

In order to insure that the documents you wish to transfer are acceptable to any word processor at the other end, you must take steps to insure that the document contains nothing other than the above.

One way to do this is to use a word processor that does not embed special characters into the document text that might be unacceptable to a word processor at the other end. Unfortunately, most word processors do use special embedded commands to control such things as title centering, underlining, and footnote control. These embedded commands are unintelligible to other brands of word processors. But every word processor is designed so that you can write a document out as a "pure ASCII" file as an option. This provision may be an explicit feature of the word processor, or it may be "implicit" in the ability of the word processor to "print" a document into a file on a diskette, rather than sending it to a printer. By advising such a word processor that your printer is a "dumb Teletype" printer, you can cause your word processor to produce an ASCII file that will be acceptable to any other word processor. Unfortunately, this "print file" technique inserts a "hard" line break at the end of each line and may add blank spaces to the start of each line, and these may have to be edited out at the other end.

The LawWord word processor supplied with this book is especially designed to generate pure ASCII files if you avoid using printer features such as underlining and bold. And hopefully every law office will have a copy of this inexpensive program. LawWord is thus the word processor of choice when you know you will be sending documents by electronic mail to other offices. Because LawWord documents are in compliance with the standards for the widely used WordStar word processor, you will find that LawWord documents are acceptable to virtually all modern word processors without modification. We suggest that you use LawWord whenever you need to send documents to another office having a different word processor than your office.

(b) Transmitting Documents Containing Word Processing Commands

If your correspondent has the same word processor that you have, then you may send word processing documents back and forth without first converting them into pure ASCII files. But now you will encounter another serious problem—if you simply try and "upload" a word processing document with all its embedded codes straight into ABA/net, you will discover that the embedded word processing codes cause all types of additional problems. Some of the codes are intercepted by the telecommunications network and do not survive the trip. Other codes, those whose numeric values are above 127, have their eighth "lantern" lit—the "parity" bit lantern. This lantern also does not survive the journey, so these control codes are transformed into printable characters whose numeric values are less than 128. So the word processing document arrives at the end of its journey badly damaged.

To prevent this damage, you can transform your word processing document into a different form before attempting to transmit it via electronic mail. Programs are available that can transform a word processing document, a computer program, or any other kind of computer file of information, into a code in which every character is represented by printable characters that can be sent over an electronic mail service. Typically, the 256 possible codes that can appear in any file are transformed into printable "hexadecimal digit pairs" where each code in the file is represented by two letters or numbers assigned as follows:

Ch. #	Hex Dig.	Ch. #	Hex Dig.	Ch. #	Hex Dig.	Ch. #	Hex Dig.
0	00	8	08	16	10	24	18
1	01	9	09	17	11	25	19
2	02	10	0A	18	12	26	1A
3	03	11	0B	19	13	27	1B
4	04	12	0C	20	14	28	1C
5	05	13	0D	21	15	29	1D
6	06	14	0E	22	16	—	—
7	07	15	0F	23	17	255	FF

This transformation makes the file over twice as long and totally unintelligible, but since the transformed file contains only printable characters, it can be sent over any electronic mail service without any damage. Then the encoding process can be reversed at the destination to reconstruct the original word processing document, program, or data file. The "error free transmission" procedure described in Appendix C uses this technique to make "mailable" electronic letters out of "unmailable" word processing documents and programs.

(c) Error-Free Transmission of Documents

An even better way to transmit documents is to send them in a completely error-free manner to the electronic mail service, store them as "hexadecimal digit pairs" within the service for delivery by "e-mail" to the destination, and then receive them in a completely error-free manner at the other end.

Error-free transmission is impossible using the standard transmission schemes described above, where only the parity bit is provided to give some indication of transmission errors. To give full protection against errors, one must break up a document into packets and generate some form of "check digit" for each packet of information that is transmitted, sending the "check digit" along with each packet. Then the receiver must recompute the "check digit" for each packet of information and compare the computed check digit with the check digit transmitted by the sending station. Then if the two check digits do not match, an error has occurred, so the receiving station orders the packet retransmitted.

The most widely-used scheme for error-free transmission was developed by Ward Christensen. This protocol is now called the "Xmodem" protocol for error-free transmission. In its original (and still widely used) form, the Xmodem protocol breaks up a file of characters into packets and computes a simple checksum digit, as just described. In its later, more sophisticated version, this protocol computes what is called a "cyclic redundancy check character," a special type of check digit developed originally by IBM for use in detecting and correcting errors in data stored on magnetic tape and since widely adapted for use in other error-detecting applications. A detailed explanation of how to use Xmodem (or its successor, Ymodem) to transmit documents over ABA/net can be found in Appendix C. The technique described requires the use of a special communications program which supports the Xmodem protocol, on the computers at both ends of the link. Within the ABA/net electronic mail service, the technique described converts the codes in the word processing document into pairs of hexadecimal digits so that the document can be transmitted within ABA/net as an electronic mail item with no loss of the word processor command codes.

The Xmodem protocol was originally designed to be a way of transmitting computer programs by electronic mail without error. Programs sent by the Xmodem protocol arrive in excellent shape. But word processing documents may be found to contain some "garbage" characters appended to their end. This happens because the Xmodem protocol always sends fixed-sized data packets. If a word processing document cannot be broken up into equal-size packets, then the document is lengthened by the addition of NUL characters (character number "0") to the very end of the document. These may show up in your word processor as strange characters at the end of the document.

Another popular protocol for error-free transmission of documents, particularly around universities, is Kermit, developed at the University of Columbia. A public domain program, Kermit facilitates error-free uploading and downloading to and from university minicomputers and mainframes.

A third "error-free" document transmission protocol has been developed by Microcom. The Microcom protocol is built into an automatic document transmission program sold by IBM called the "Personal Communications Manager." This program, used at both ends, can "wake up" computers to send documents between offices in the middle of the night when the telephone rates are low and the computers are not busy.

Perhaps a better way to achieve error-free transmission between two sites that communicate regularly is to use a special modem that has error correction built into its logic. Perhaps the most impressive of such modems are some new ones that can transmit at up to 9600 bits per second over normal telephone lines, thereby transmitting even a lengthy document in just a few minutes. By the time this book reaches you, there should be several such modems available. One to be marketed by Digital Communications Associates, Inc. (1000 Alderman Drive, Alpharetta, GA 30201—telephone (404) 442–4000) looks particularly promising.

(d) Transmitting Documents Without an Error-Free Protocol

Almost any communications software can "download" an incoming electronic mail document and store it in a file on a diskette. You simply turn on the "capture to disk" facility of your communications software and then command the central computer to start sending you the material. If possible, you should set up your communications software or terminal emulator to use the "XON/XOFF" flow control protocol to prevent the document from coming in too fast. You should be able to "download" incoming documents using a 1200 Baud modem. But if you encounter too many errors, start over using the slower 300 Baud speed of transmission.

"Uploading" is also easy, particularly if your communications software responds properly to the central computer's "XON/XOFF" flow control commands. If "XON/XOFF" flow control is not possible, then adjust your software to pause at the end of each line for a second or two, or have it pause until the next "prompt" character comes in from the central computer. Do not transmit so fast that you overload the input buffer of the central computer.

A complete explanation of how to use the ABA/net "PCMAIL" program to "upload" a whole series of electronic letters in a single operation appears in Appendix C.

Chapter 6

ACCOUNTING FOR TIME, BILLING, AND REPORTING ON TIME, COSTS, AND REVENUES

§ 6–1 INTRODUCTION

Lawyers practice law. They provide advice, negotiate on behalf of clients, and take clients through administrative and court processes. Some lawyers practice alone, but most lawyers band together in partnerships. Partnership linkages are sometimes loose, sometimes tight among the lawyers. Partnerships come in all sizes. But no matter the type of practice—whether it be creating probate plans or tough litigation, whether the lawyer be a sole practitioner or part of a two hundred person firm—one thing is common. Every type of practice must account for time, bill clients for time and costs, post receipts against bills, and provide income and profits. Even the firm practicing wholly on contingent fees needs to know where and how money is being spent and made on the cases.

As a result almost every law firm forces every attorney to keep track of time—for without tracking time few bills can be rendered and no one can really determine what lines of services are or are not profitable. Similarly every travel expense, sheriff's fee, reporter's fee must be tracked so that the client can eventually be billed. Bills must timely issue and the bills must describe the work in a way that encourages the client to pay. Subsequent reminder bills must be sent to recalcitrants. Receipts must be applied to bills and allocated so that the firm knows which attorney generated what income. Management reports are needed to provide the firm with information on who worked for how long on what cases, who generated receipts, and what types of practice were profitable.

A law practice involves not merely the practice of law—it is a small business with many of the needs of other types of small businesses. The lawyer who enters a firm needs to know about the business aspects of the law practice. An associate needs to know how the hours the associate spends end up in reports to the partners since these may serve as part of the partnership evaluation process. A partner who shares in the proceeds from various clients needs to know how that allocation is made. A managing partner, and even a new associate, should know how productive the firm is in a particular area of specialty.

There are countless examples of misdirected firm policies that could be corrected by a sound time accounting system. A firm needs to know if real estate transfers done for a fixed fee cost the firm far less than the fee, or if some contingent fee cases cost far more than has been collected. There are firms where partners with many billable hours mark down the rates and amounts so much that they are being subsidized by other partners. There are associates who pull their weight and others who have far fewer billable hours.

Clearly time and billing is not the only measure of a lawyer's contribution to a firm. One lawyer might do nothing billable but can provide the firm with most of its clients. Another associate might do exquisite work which is eminently saleable but take too long to do it.

The fact that lawyers now compete for business makes financial information even more important. To the extent that the competition is based on cost, or on the ability of the firm to justify the cost in comprehensive bills, sound accounting practices permit the firm to fix the lowest possible cost and better control costs.

§ 6-2. THE LAW FIRM AS A BUSINESS

Every lawyer and every law firm is a business—aiming to earn income for the lawyer. The firm also attempts to satisfy clients and works to keep present clients and gain more clients. But lawyers are also professionals and law is a profession. What this means is that the lawyer is a special type of business person. Billing practices are guided as well by professional conduct rules.

(a) ABA Model Code and ABA Model Rules

According to the Preamble to the ABA Model Rules of Professional Conduct "A lawyer is a representative of clients, an officer of the legal system and a public citizen having special responsibility for the quality of justice." The Model Rules place the lawyer in a special position as a business person. The ABA Model Code of Professional Responsibility, the predecessor of the Model Rules of Professional Conduct, is widely accepted as the basic guide to law practice in a number of states.

The Model Code has a number of points controlling lawyer conduct in billing practices. The lawyer must be aware not only of these rules, but also of the increasing number of court decisions that have opened practice to more competition and have voided some traditional precepts of "legal ethics" that were found to violate Constitutional principles, rights to "freedom of speech" or the competitive principles of the antitrust laws. Even some of the present Code's controls on fees and costs may eventually be found to conflict with these principles.

Model Disciplinary Rule 2–106 (DR 2–106 as amended August, 1980) states: "A lawyer shall not enter into an agreement for, charge, or collect an illegal or clearly excessive fee". Excessive fees are defined as those in excess of a reasonable fee.

Under the Code, what is a "reasonable" fee is determined by examining such factors as:

(1) time and labor required, the novelty and difficulty of the questions involved, and the skill requisite to perform the legal service properly;

(2) the likelihood that the work for the client will preclude other employment;

(3) customary fees;

(4) amount involved and the results obtained;

(5) time limitations imposed by the client;

(6) the nature and the length of the professional relationship with the client;

(7) the experience, reputation and ability of the lawyer . . . performing the services . . . ; and

(8) whether the fee is fixed or contingent. (DR 2–106(B) as amended, August, 1980).

The ABA Model Rules, as amended August 1984, contain substantially the same guidelines but they are stated in a slightly different manner and add an additional requirement: "When the lawyer has not regularly represented the client, the basis or rate of the fee shall be communicated to the client, preferably in writing, before or within a reasonable time after commencing the representation." ABA Model Rules 1.5(b).

It is by no means clear that lawyers' fee arrangements are watched that closely by disciplinary agencies. However, when controversy does arise the time accounting and billing system used by the law firm should be responsive to the Model Code. Even the attorney who bills on a fixed fee may have to keep time records to validate the time and labor required and the other factors described above.

Under the Code, a lawyer may request permission to withdraw from representation before a court or other tribunal if the client does not comply with an agreement as to expenses or fees. (DR 2–110(C) as amended 1980). Of course, there must be a fee agreement and records to support the non-payment of fees if the withdrawal is based upon such a failure. The Model Rules are broader. They permit withdrawal when the "client fails substantially to fulfill an obligation to the lawyer regarding the lawyer's services," or when representation would result "in an unreasonable financial burden on the lawyer" or for other "good cause."

Should state disciplinary commissions scrutinize fee claims more closely, or should a collection suit be needed, then a lawyer might protect the firm by carefully documenting in writing the basis for the fee—listing all eight points of the Model Code and the resolution of those points.

The Code also says a lawyer may not "advance or guarantee financial assistance to his client, except that a lawyer may advance or guarantee the expenses of litigation . . . provided that the client remains ultimately liable." DR 5–103(B). Under this rule the lawyer needs to keep sound records of these advances and needs to ultimately bill the client for costs.

Another part of the Code, Ethical Consideration 2–23, states that "A lawyer should be zealous in his efforts to avoid controversies over fees with clients and should attempt to resolve amicably any differences on the subject. He should not sue a client for a fee unless necessary to prevent fraud or gross imposition by the client." This suggests that sound billing practices which clearly delineate fees due should be adopted and billing done frequently in such detail as to encourage payment.

Funds held by the law firm as retainers, client's funds or trust funds are also governed by the Model Code and the Model Rules. Under DR 9–102 "funds of clients, paid to a lawyer or law firm, other than advances for costs and expenses" must be deposited in a separate identifiable account from those "belonging to the lawyer or law firm". Any portion of the funds "belonging to the lawyer or law firm may be withdrawn when due". The lawyer must "maintain complete records of all funds . . . and render appropriate accounts to his client. . . . " (Model Code, DR 9–102) The Model Rules require the lawyer to "hold property of clients . . . in the lawyer's possession in connection with representation separate from the lawyer's own property. Funds shall be kept in a separate account . . . . Complete records of such account funds . . . shall be kept by the lawyer and . . . preserved for . . . a period of [five years] upon termination of representation." (Model Rules, Rule 1.15(a))

To meet Code and Model Rules standards a time accounting and billing system for a law office needs to be responsive to the following considerations:

(1) There should be a means to show that fees are reasonable and not excessive. Time and labor expended are one basis of a reasonable fee which is not "excessive". This can be shown by a timekeeping and billing system that clearly notes the time and time charges incurred. Even for fixed fees ($500 for a real estate closing) records of time and labor can show the actual amount of work done and validate the fee. A fee can also be justified by proving that it was customary. This could be partially shown by keeping records of fees charged to other clients for substantially the same work. Another possibility would be to maintain records listing which lawyer charged

which rate to a client to relate the fee to the particular experience of a lawyer.

(2) The timekeeping and billing system should communicate the basis for the fee to the client and demonstrate the conformance of billing method to the basis selected. A highly detailed bill clearly illustrates the basis for the fee and can serve as further notice of the original fee agreement as well as conformance with that agreement.

(3) The timekeeping and billing system should maintain records showing non-payment. When a client fails to pay bills or advance costs, and the lawyer wants to withdraw from representation, reports generated from these records are useful to show a court that fees or costs were not properly paid.

(4) A full trust accounting system recording deposits and withdrawals of client's funds must be used by each law firm. Client's funds must be first placed in a separate client's funds account then drawn upon as the firm becomes entitled to them. The status of a client's account must be regularly reported to the client. Records should be kept for a suggested period of five years following termination of representation. The Model Code, but not the Model Rules, exempts advances for costs and expenses from any special requirements.

(b) History of Billing—Two Approaches

When the Disciplinary Rules and Ethical Considerations are satisfied the lawyer is free to deal with clients on financial matters as any business person would. But such an entrepreneurial approach has not always been the norm in law practice. Lawyers of fifty or one hundred years ago often did not use law practice as a principal source of income.

The English barrister is a perfect example of this early evolution. It is said that the barristers (those who argued appeals) disdained the receipt of income for their services. Independently wealthy, they saw law as a public service. Even when money was proferred it might be accepted but not face-to-face. The funds were often placed surreptitiously in a small pocket located in the barrister's robes. Even the pocket was discreetly hidden from the barrister's view at the back of his neck. Today barristers still have weak or nonexistent legal agreements for their fees and, according to the English, will never sue for an unpaid fee.

Until recently many American lawyers were as casual as the barristers of England. Clients paid lawyers because clients did not switch lawyers as they did other tradesmen. Lawyers were skeptical about new clients that came from other lawyers' bailiwicks without adequate explanation. Few clients even quibbled over prices or bills. In some cases the client merely paid what the lawyer asked for and very little detailed information was used to substantiate a bill. In those bygone days money was important to the law firm but not the driving force behind practice. There was generally enough income for everyone. Even the associates were happy with a meager portion of the fees rather than the ransom often extracted today at large firms in larger cities. Billing in these firms was done frequently but probably not regularly. In some firms, even today, bills are sent months after the work has been completed. Some firms still wait for the accountant to discover that cash is low before they mobilize lawyers to fill in and submit time sheets, clerks to sort the time slips, accountants to add up the figures and secretaries to type the bills—a mobilization similar to an invasion of a small country and one which, when done by hand, truly does disrupt the "peacetime" operation of the firm.

To determine the contribution of a partner or an associate to the firm's revenue was rarely a statistical job. Since the bills could rarely be sorted by lawyer or client group, it would be hard for the firm to determine if any lawyer or group of clients were profitable; nor was there any indication of how much billable time was cut out of bills as excessive (written off)—the firm had to rely on bits and pieces of data, hunches really, to determine what and who brought in what kind of income.

The computerization of the large firms' back offices (where accounting and billing took place) began the trend toward more information and more rational decisions that evaluated the income production from lawyers and clients. This computerization began in the late sixties and continues unabated. And soon the concern with funds and income began to trickle down to the medium-sized and smaller firms. Soon lawyers began talk about "realization" (actual payments) per lawyer rather than just who seems to bring in clients or the totals of bills sent out.

Competition for clients, the increase in the number of lawyers and competition among lawyers also helped to change the older methods.

(c) Institutional and Entrepreneurial Law Firms

Two approaches to the business of law practice now coexist. There is the "institutional" approach and the "entrepreneurial" approach. The institutional approach is the older method of practicing law much like the one described above. Firms consider both clients and lawyers bound to the firm. They minister to the client, a small or large business, when the client needs service. No special effort is made to attract clients or to keep clients. Firm lawyers rarely consider moving to other firms. The rate a client is charged is based strictly on the expertise of the firm and has little relationship to the market.

The "entrepreneurial" approach is the more modern approach. Lawyers look at the firm as a small (or large) business. They market their product by deliberately meeting potential clients, speaking, writing articles, and informing clients of law changes. They set rates based on market needs. They look for special niches in which they can provide services more efficiently and more attractively than other firms. These firms not only court new clients but they consciously attempt to keep old clients. They know that the firm's lawyers must be kept happy if they are to stay in the firm and they adjust income and allocation of receipts to keep partners and associates with the firm. They are very concerned with productivity and constantly monitor billable hours, write-offs per lawyer and the profitability of various types of fee arrangements and clients. They plan for the future and project the nature of their work and the demands made upon individual attorneys. They carefully plan the workload and examine allocation of work so that they are efficient.

The old "institutional" law practice based on technical excellence serving a few steady clients is slowly changing to the new "entrepreneurial" model with its "strategic planning" and concerns with marketing, specialization or other means to gain and keep clients. Lawyers today expect to make money from their efforts and to make as much as they can. Other firms may charge less or more and other firms may earn more for their lawyers because they are more efficient. Lawyers may jump from one firm to another if the income is not enough, or there are not enough clients, or the distribution of income is perceived as unfair.

Clients are money conscious as well. Clients may select firms by looking at experience, reputation and rapport; but they also look at prices. Clients may leave firms when they are dissatisfied with the quality of the work; but they also leave when they are unhappy with the price of the work or with the extent of the justification for the cost of work that is done.

As the number of lawyers continues to climb, as the chains of law firms continue to act more efficiently and more entrepreneurial and as the larger firms tend to become more market-oriented all of these changes will increase.

The "entrepreneurial" law practice needs more data than the institutional practice and needs it faster. This is one reason for the computerization of time accounting and billing. Data is needed for speedy and accurate computation of clients' bills, for determining productivity of lawyers, for billing recalcitrants and for many other purposes including the assessment of profitability. It is the time accounting and billing systems and their associated management reports that are called upon to help the law firm.

§ 6-3. WHAT IS A TIME ACCOUNTING AND BILLING SYSTEM?

A time accounting and billing system is a system that allows a firm to collect money due from clients and produces the necessary records and reports needed to collect that money and manage the firm. A computerized law office time accounting and billing system is more sophisticated than a manual system. It generally does the following:

(1) Allows attorneys to record the amount of time spent on a given piece of work completed for a client, noting whether the time is billable or non-billable;

(2) Permits attorneys or other staff to record the costs and disbursements associated with a client or with the office management-costs such as sheriff's fees, copying or postage;

(3) Permits a firm to record payments and apply them to bills;

(4) Permits a firm to list cost or time to be applied to a client's account and to determine if those transactions should in fact be charged to the client;

(5) Permits a firm to select rates or the total fee to be charged to a client based on at least one of these bases:

 __ the transaction itself ($750 for filing a patent application);

 __ the lawyer working on the case ($100 per hour if Kane does the work);

 __ the client or matter itself (this matter is always charged at $125 per hour);

 __ the type of client or matter (corporate, probate, property)

(6) Prints bills or invoices;

(7) Prints management reports on lawyers, work, on clients and matters and on transactions;

(8) May process funds of the client kept by the law firm in anticipation of later use (retainers, trust funds or client's funds), and may permit transfers of those funds to the firm's account when the firm does the work, bills the client or otherwise becomes entitled to the funds;

(9) Automatically does the necessary sorting after data is entered, automatically does necessary arithmetic and balances all related accounts.

Since the totals that appear in a time accounting and billing system are often merely reentered into a firm's books and journals for the year some systems will link directly to a general ledger system. This linkage often notes the areas where expenses were incurred, the allocations of receipts to various lawyers (Senior partner receives ten percent of all receipts), the total receipts and sources and other information useful to firm bookkeeping.

Other linkages may generate checks so that all the outside costs are not only recorded by the system but automatically paid by the system. Some systems also allow the firm to transfer bills to a word processor where they can be edited to more closely meet the peculiar needs of special clients.

A time and billing system is nothing but a system to record time and costs and to eventually issue bills to clients, handle and record the receipts and also produce needed reports so that a firm can be more effectively managed.

§ 6-4. WHY COMPUTERIZED SYSTEMS ARE VALUABLE

Of course much of the above work could be done manually. However, computerized systems have some advantages. Funds can often be more easily collected. Clients can be billed almost immediately after the lawyer has successfully negotiated a contract or defended a suit; when the client is both aware of the firm's effort and grateful for results. Early billing increases the potential for collecting the full amount of the bill.

Computerization also makes bills more accurate. Data needs to be typed in only once for each transaction. Since no manual computations are ever required no manual errors ever creep into the process. Accurate bills encourage payment and speed up the payment process.

Computerized systems often allow bills to be more closely tailored to the needs of clients. Bills can easily be created on a cycle tuned to a client's needs. For example, specific totals, responsive to a client's needs, perhaps listing hours totaled for each lawyer working on the case or subtotals for all costs associated with a deposition can be readily printed.

Some users contend that computerized systems increase the ability of a firm to capture all time and costs—some are lost in a manual system. Areas of profit can be recognized more easily through the management reports that are generated from exactly the same data used to create bills. Almost anyone can examine data or print reports.

There are other benefits as well. Anyone can enter data at any time. When a client calls with a legal question for a lawyer in the firm a desktop terminal in the lawyer's office may permit the lawyer to not only provide advice but also to put that advice in the context of the money the client owes the firm or the extent of business provided by the client to the firm.

§ 6-5. FEES, COLLECTION, PROFITABILITY, AND ALLOCATION

(a) Fees

Any timekeeping and billing system needs to be responsive to clients. Fee arrangements, such as fixed fees, contingent fees, and special hourly rates are negotiated with the client. For some clients particular billing methods will be used to insure that fees are collected. These include advance payments (trust funds), cost-only billing, and highly detailed bills.

There are at least three methods of fee assessment. These include charging by the hour for work done, charging a fixed fee, and charging a percentage (or contingent) fee based on the successful prosecution of a case. Each of these involves certain subcategories. Hourly rates may be fixed—$90 for every lawyer; or they may be variable—$125 for partners, $250 for a partner with a a specialty in the area, $60 for associates. Or the breakout might be based on a different scale—the highest rate each firm member charges ($250 for attorney A, $185 for attorney B, and $85 for attorney C); or the lowest rate (Attorney A, $75; B, $30; and C, $0).

The rate structure is designed partly to satisfy clients and partly for reasons of internal economics. Profits for the partners and salaries for associates are part of those economics.

A firm can earn money on a $24,000 associate (paid $12 per hour for the 2,000 hours per year that is billed) by charging $60 per hour or $96,000. Overhead and training by partners, which may or may not be billed to clients, can hardly account for more than 30 or 40 per cent of the difference in income and cost to the firm. The rest is profit. A good associate is very valuable to a firm even when $40 an hour leaves a $56,000 net before overhead and training.

A client may also be charged a fixed fee—$250 for a real estate closing, $12,000 for a security filing, $250 to file trademark papers. Even for this simple fee structure and for the percentage (or contingent) fee the firm will need to know what they actually spent in time and costs. Suppose trademarks are taking two hours of partner time at $100 per hour plus $300 in drawing and filing fees. If this is consistent, the practice is not profitable if in fact the partner could be selling that time at $100 per hour to another client.

(b) Collection

Collection, too, is part of the client satisfaction process. To insure collection of fees, a firm may ask for a retainer. There are really two types of fees that are called retainers. In the first type the firm receives, say, $1,000 per month to handle most of the legal work of a small business—no further charges accrue except for those laid out in the retainer agreement.

In the second type the client provides funds to the firm before work begins to cover fees and costs. The firm estimates the risk they will take with the client, the rate at which fees and costs will accrue and asks for a fixed amount against those fees and costs. A good example might be $15,000 to negotiate with the Environmental Protection Agency a claim that hazardous waste was illegally disposed of on property of the client. When the fees and costs use up $10,000 of the fund another $10,000 is deposited. All the funds belong to the client, but are kept by the law firm in a trust account (client funds account) and eventually transferred by the law firm to the firm's account when the work is billed. Another type of "trust account" may hold client funds which are escrowed until paid out to others outside the firm (a real property contract deposit, for example).

There are other means to improve collection—the best of course being that just described—having the money in hand before doing the work. But this is not always feasible or necessary. Prompt and complete billing is another method.

According to many lawyers clients are most likely to pay immediately after the services are rendered. They recall the work done, the effort of the attorney and the time spent. If the firm was successful at either gaining funds for the client or an advantageous agreement, they feel as if they should reward the firm for its work. At the other end of the time frame a bill received twelve months later is likely to be heavily discounted by some clients. The client will have forgotten the work, forgotten the benefit, forgotten the skill of the lawyer. Some lawyers suggest a client may feel then that he did not even need the lawyer but could have done the work himself.

Collection can also be improved with some clients by detailed billing. Listing what was done, when and by whom, how many hours were spent and what individual costs were incurred tends to show the client that something substantial was done.

The way in which a bill is written is often important to collecting funds. Some experts suggest that a bill that says on one line of many:

"July 28 RLR Reviewed File—2.6 hours"

is less likely to be paid than one that lists all the work done but is more specific:

"July 28 R. Robbins researched legal issues and relevant cases; drafted response to complaint—2.6 hours".

See Figure 1.

Bills with more specific statements that look like work done with professional skill are more likely to be paid with less reluctance and more enthusiasm.

(c) Profitability

On the whole the law firm must be profitable. Income must at least equal expenses. Profitability can be assured in a number of ways. The firm can assess its basic costs of operation and charge based on these costs. These costs include the minimum costs for staff and the minimums that must be raised to pay associates and provide partners with expected income. It can adjust the basic rates for each lawyer, often called "required" rates, with this figure in mind. Unless, for instance, business can be found that will allow charging a rate high enough to cover the costs involved, it would be unwise to add additional associates.

Only recently have firms begun the kind of cost accounting and checking that determines this basic minimum cost. For the most part this effort involves calculating what are called "fixed" costs as well as hourly costs. "Fixed" costs are those such as basic copier rental, office rental, furniture amortization, and secretarial services not billed to

```
Jefferson Insurance Co.
300 West A
Suite 220
Lincoln          NE   68510                                   07/31/84
                                                               200-030

         General File

        PREVIOUS BALANCE                                      $856.50

                                                 HOURS

07/15/84
      FAJ Office conference with Peter Smith,
          insurance salesman for company.        1.75          130.88

      FAJ Letter to corporate headquarters        .75           56.09
      JP Prepared for conference with client

07/16/84
      SJM Put together a proposal for Mid-State
          Insurance Company.                     3.50          213.14
      JP Office conference with client           1.25           80.13

07/20/84
      FAJ Telephone conference with Sam Reader,  1.25           93.48
          Sally Farrows and John Darrington
                                                 ----          ------
      FOR CURRENT SERVICES RENDERED              8.50          573.72
      SALES TAX                                                 22.95

07/15/84 Phone calls to Mid-State                               25.52
07/18/84 Mileage to Omaha                                       25.00
07/20/84 Filing fee for petition                                35.00
07/23/84 Phone calls to agents                                  25.75
                                                               ------
      TOTAL COSTS                                              111.27

07/10/84 Payment - thank you                                  -300.00
                                                               ------
      TOTAL PAYMENTS                                          -300.00

      FINANCE CHARGE                                             7.95

      BALANCE DUE                                            $1272.39
                                                               ------
```

Figure 1. Detailed Bill. A detailed bill listing the initials of the attorney completing the work, an explanation of each item of work done and a total of the charges for that individual transaction. Note how each day's work appears in a single block without restating the date. Copyright 1986, Software Technology, Inc.

clients. These plus salaries and partner income describe how much needs to be earned by the firm in the year.

Suppose these cost figures total $450,000 for a four lawyer firm—with a breakdown for partners of $100,000 each, and two associates expecting $35,000 each. The balance of expenses are for rent, supplies, postage, employee benefits and secretaries. Somehow $450,000 must be earned by the firm. Each partner is assumed to bill for about 1,200 hours per year. Billing at an average of $120 per hour, the partners bring in $288,000. For the firm to receive $450,000 in billings, the two associates must earn $162,000 per year for the firm (450,000 − 288,000 = 162,000). Billing rates for 1,500 hours annual work by each associate therefore must not be less than $54 per hour (2 x 1,500 x 54 = 162,000). If each associate brings in $81,000 per year and is paid $35,000, a year, each will produce a surplus of $46,000 a year to go toward fixed costs and partners' shares. An effective accounting system can track hours billed, receipts and other data to determine how and whether these goals for profitability and partner income can be achieved.

(d) Allocation

In order to operate profitably and successfully a law firm must assess the contribution of partners and associates to the firm. Clearly some lawyers find clients for the firm, others are legal experts. Some lawyers may merely lend their prestige and name to the firm. But many lawyers are judged on their financial contribution. A computerized law office system allows the firm to determine quickly such items as:

(1) number of billable hours per year for the firm and for each lawyer;

(2) total charges for each lawyer's time;

(3) average hourly rate charged;

(4) profitability of each of a lawyer's clients;

(5) lawyers whose clients actually paid billed amounts;

(6) amounts that had to be written off as markdowns on the bills or uncollectable debts.

§ 6–6. HOW TIME–ACCOUNTING AND BILLING ARE DONE

To some of you reading this text it would be hard to practice law without certain technology. When the author of this chapter was in law school, and this was not during the Civil War either, there were few copying machines. If you wanted to make notes from a case, you copied it out diligently by hand. Later when the author first practiced law he prosecuted a complaint on a contract. A copy of the contract needed to be attached to the complaint when it was filed and served. In order to do this the author's typist had to labor for three days on this eighteen page contract—carefully retyping it with four carbons on the typewriter. Of course each carbon copy had to be corrected by hand. Even the first copy could not be corrected with a "correction ribbon" but had to be "erased". Then the author had to proofread the results and verify the copy's correctness.

Time accounting without a computer is about in the same era in some offices—the "institutional" ones mainly. The common system involves "time strips". There is a sheet on each lawyer's desk. There are about ten rows on each sheet. Each row is called a strip and represents one item of work—listing the client or client number, the matter or matter number, a date, a description of the work ("Meeting with client to discuss strategy") and a column for hours spent. The sheet also lists the attorney's initials. The edges of each strip are perforated.

When the sheet is filled-in the strips are torn apart. A clerk then puts them in piles by client. If a client has more than one matter, then it is filed by matter. The strips are then organized in chronological order. In a large office a conference room table is covered with strips for days (or weeks). Similar strips are made for costs or disbursements on behalf of the client. They, too, are put in chronological order. A secretary is given all these strips and asked to type a listing of work done. The list is then sent to the lawyer in charge of the client, who edits the list, puts a price on the hours spent, and finishes up the bill. A secretary multiplies hours by rates and lists the totals. Sometimes the firm's accounting office does complex calculations where different lawyers charge different rates. Finally a secretary again types—this time a final bill. A copy goes to the lawyer in charge of the client and to the office manager or accounting. All in all each transaction has been entered at least three times.

This manual system has a number of obvious drawbacks. It is prone to error each time data is reentered or manually calculated. It is cumbersome and slow. Some lawyers feel it is inefficient to list small amounts of time (5 minutes, 15 minutes) since the process of writing the bill is so costly. The system also means a great deal of effort by a lot of people in an office. They put off the day of reckoning (reckoning in its actuarial sense) for a long time preferring to earn money rather than collect it. This is why billing is done "yearly" for some clients, why fixed fees are used regardless of profitability, and why clients often complain about late and high bills.

Slips also get lost and misapplied. The system provides no easy means of using the same data to find out about productivity such as hours per month per attorney or funds received per attorney. All data would be reentered again for such reports. Without additional controls the system cannot even detect a failure of an attorney to enter any time at all.

§ 6–7. USE OF COMPUTERS FOR TIME ACCOUNTING AND BILLING

(a) How Computers Help

Computers are data processors. They can take an initial item of data such as a specific transaction "Attorney RLR Met with client ACME to discuss research needs, 2 hours, July 2" and use the data over and over again in various ways. For example, the data may be sorted by attorney to give a listing of all the hours worked by the attorney on that day, or in that month for all clients. It may be sorted by client to give a listing of all the hours worked for a particular client. It may be used to produce a preliminary or final bill. The data may be merged with other data to price the hours spent and to provide additional billing information. The same data may be matched with other data to list the total hours billed for the client that year or even total hours still unbilled. The "meeting with client" might be encoded as MWC and the firm, for whatever reason, might build statistics on how much meeting with clients occurred for all clients. See Figure 2.

Computerization not only allows one entry to provide a great deal of output but it speeds the entry. Special codes can be used for such items as the name of the lawyer (RLR), the name of the client (ACME) and the type of work done (e.g. MWC, above). The user may not even need to enter a billing rate ($100 per hour) since some systems can automatically search the lawyer or client information to find a rate. Or the system may look at the transaction code ("Processed Application for State Trademark" abbreviated as "AST") and disregard all hourly rates using the $175 fixed fee automatically associated with that type of work. Some computer systems can keep track of the hours spent on all trademark cases, multiply by the lawyer's basic rate and determine at the end of the year if the $175 fee is profitable for this type of work.

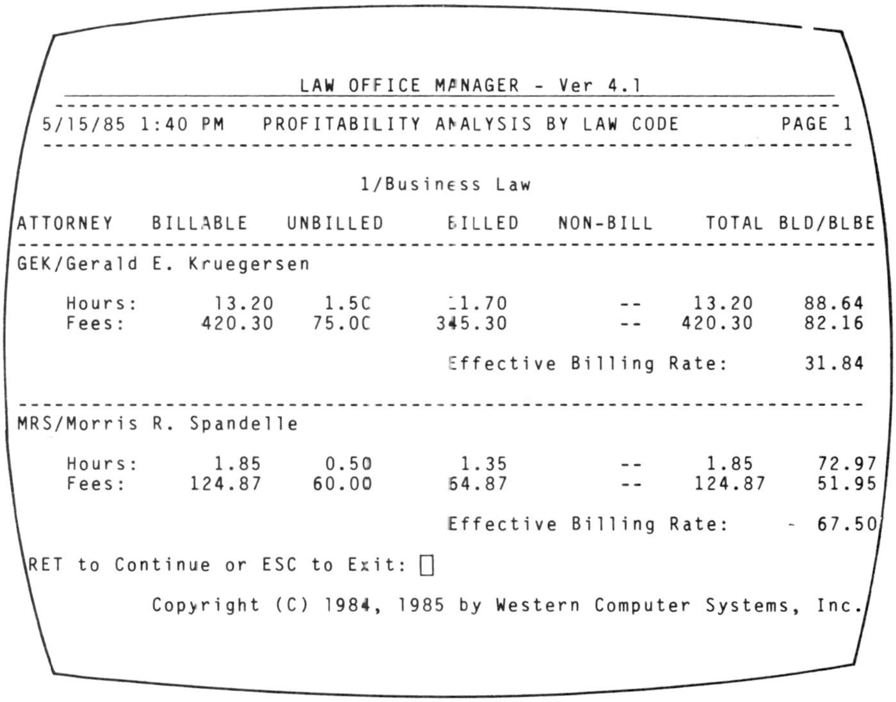

LAW OFFICE MANAGER - Ver 4.1

5/15/85 1:40 PM PROFITABILITY ANALYSIS BY LAW CODE PAGE 1

1/Business Law

ATTORNEY	BILLABLE	UNBILLED	BILLED	NON-BILL	TOTAL	BLD/BLBE
GEK/Gerald E. Kruegersen						
Hours:	13.20	1.50	11.70	--	13.20	88.64
Fees:	420.30	75.00	345.30	--	420.30	82.16
			Effective Billing Rate:			31.84
MRS/Morris R. Spandelle						
Hours:	1.85	0.50	1.35	--	1.85	72.97
Fees:	124.87	60.00	64.87	--	124.87	51.95
			Effective Billing Rate:			67.50

RET to Continue or ESC to Exit: □

Copyright (C) 1984, 1985 by Western Computer Systems, Inc.

Figure 2. Profitability Analysis by Law Code. This report describes the amounts and hours the office will bill for practice in a particular area of law, in this case "Business Law". This is the first screen of the report which shows for each lawyer the hours and amounts of time both billed and unbilled for practice in the business law area.

Entry by computer is also faster and easier. Computers prompt the operator for information and require it before allowing the operator to move on. The details are often immediately verified to see if they are consistent with other data in the computer. Correction speed is also improved. If a lawyer sees a printout of the work done for a client and realizes that there was an error, it can be easily corrected without much retyping. For example if an entry were made for a meeting with a client, when the meeting was actually with the client's witness, the error can usually be changed with a single entry. And all other places where the data are used are automatically changed as well.

Many options are available to match the computerized reports and bills to the needs of a law firm. Of course, manually typing a bill permits the most options. But in firms with many clients, customized, manually generated bills are not often done—they are too costly. So even if bills are hand-typed, a standard form bill is used for everyone except particularly important and demanding clients. The computer allows the firm to select a particular bill format for each client and to have it automatically used each time a bill is prepared. Some clients receive details on every piece of work done—a WESTLAW search, a call to opposing counsel, etc. Others are merely satisfied with a list of hours spent by each attorney and a total.

Computers speed up the billing process. In some cases the final entry for a given matter can be entered at 2 p.m., e.g., RLC (initials of the lawyer) CNK (abbreviation for "Completed negotiation of buy-out contract") for ACME, July 6, 2 hours; and the bill to the client can be issued at 3 p.m. with hundreds of entries from many lawyers with varying rates for each. This rapidly produced bill may also be paid quickly.

(b) The Place Where a Computer Is Used

Until recently both manual and computerized billing took place in the law firm's back office. A back office is the accounting section of a law firm. It is there that all time sheets filled in by attorneys were routed, where reports on work done for a client emerged, and where bills were eventually dispatched. The attorney had little or no direct interaction with the back office. Information was sent, calculations made there and the information was returned in the form of a report of some kind. The attorney made corrections by hand, the report was returned to the back office, corrected and again returned. The widespread use of the on-line computer (one operating at all times) on the lawyer's desk increases the advantages of computerization by another order of magnitude. This computer workstation permits the lawyer to input data directly, to correct data directly, to read and print reports without intervention of the back office.

(c) The Hardware, the Costs, the Printers

There are at least two categories of systems for time accounting and billing. One type of system is called a proprietary system, sold as a single unit of hardware and software. A second group is composed of systems where the software is sold separately and can be matched by the law office with whatever hardware is appropriate. Systems are also distinguished by whether they are single user or multiuser. In a single user system only one user at a time can work with the program. In a multiuser system more than one user can operate the system. For example, the office manager may be creating bills for the month while one attorney, using her office terminal, is looking up details on a particular client and a managing partner is checking the amount of billed time that an associate has built up in the last six months.

Time accounting and billing systems can operate on small microcomputers when the firm size is from one to somewhere around fifteen or thirty attorneys. Fast microcomputers or a minicomputer are needed for larger applications. The important considerations in sizing a computer to a time accounting workload include the number of attorneys and clients and the number of transactions to be held in the system. Another important consideration is the amount of time the system will take to sort through records to generate reports. Faster computers with larger memory allow a firm to do its billing and reports in a few hours rather than in ten or twenty hours.

In 1986 costs for time accounting and billing software ranged from \$99.00 to \$5,000.00 or more for microcomputer systems. Minicomputer and mainframe software systems sold for \$10,000 to over \$100,000. Cost is usually related to two factors. The first is the sophistication of the program: how many reports it has, how complex the calculations are, how easy it is to use. The second factor is the potential market for the system—the fewer buyers of minicomputer and mainframe software must still absorb substantially similar costs of software development.

Printers used with time accounting and billing software are of two kinds—those suitable for professional-looking bills and those suitable for rapidly producing in-house reports. In 1986 the laser printer or other letter quality printer was used for billing by those firms that wanted a typewriter-like output and the laser or dot matrix printer was used for reports and documents used in-house by the firm.

§ 6-8. OVERVIEW OF TIME-ACCOUNTING AND BILLING SYSTEMS

In selecting a time-accounting and billing system, firms consider a number of features of the system, in particular availability of source code, ability of the system to expand with the law firm, convenience of data input, speed and accuracy, presence of audit trails, training and user assistance, suitability of bills and reports generated, and integration with other computer systems used in the firm.

(a) Source Code Availability and Access to Information on the Program

Source code availability is critical to a law firm when the firm's financial future is entirely dependent on the computer. Vendors who manufacture software often go into bankruptcy. Some vendors lose interest in the product and turn all their energies to other products. Some merely go out of business. The users, now "orphans", may need someone for technical assistance, someone to correct bugs in the system, or someone to help them integrate the system with some other software they will be using such as a general ledger or a spreadsheet.

The vendor generally supplies the user with object code—machine readable language which humans can use to run the machine, but cannot correct or change. Correction of a program or adaptation of it to a new situation (for instance income tax law changes that require more detailed documentation of certain charges) can only be done by a skilled computer programmer with access to the program's source code—a version of the program in a computer language understandable by humans, such as COBOL or PASCAL with detailed annotations explaining how the program works. (Once the programmer's changes are made, the computer will automatically translate the revised source code into the machine language needed for actually running the program.) The problem is that most software companies regard source code as proprietary information and strongly prefer to keep it secret.

There are various possible arrangements to ensure that the law firm will have access to the source code if such access becomes necessary. The most straightforward means is for the law firm to buy the source code outright from the software vendor. But the software vendor may absolutely refuse to sell the software or demand a prohibitive price. The reason for the reluctance to sell source code is that it can all too easily be duplicated or reappear in a disguised form in a competitor's hands, with little practical legal recourse on the part of the vendor, due to the high costs of proving software copyright infringement and the chance that the pirate will be judgment-proof.

An alternative to purchase of the source code is called source code escrow. The vendor places the source code, updated to reflect what the law firm bought, with a neutral third party. If the vendor defaults on its obligation to maintain the software, the third party loans or gives the source code to the law firm. Source code escrow has been widely used by many vendors; but there are certain problems. The code actually filed with the escrow may not be the actual code used by the law firm. Even without fraud this is more likely than not since the code is usually being changed constantly as the vendor improves the product. Vendors may also fear the escrow process and may deliberately place an improper source code in escrow. Finally, when bankruptcy occurs, there is considerable concern that the escrowed source code may be attached by the trustee as an asset of the vendor, or the escrow agreement renounced as executory and not beneficial to the vendor. The escrow then is ineffective. A third means is to have the vendor provide information that tells the user the layouts in the software of various data files. If the system fails, or must be linked to another system, these layouts can be used simply to transfer the data to a new and operative system. This means learning a new system but does save reentering all the firm's clients, lawyers, and recent transactions.

(b) Memory Size and Storage Needed to Operate the System and to Expand When the Law Firm Expands

Programs and data take up disk space in a computer. Time accounting and billing systems usually utilize from one to two megabytes of storage for the program. Data will use more space. The data space used will depend upon the size of the firm, the amount of data stored for clients, matters, lawyers, and transactions. Other sources using storage space could include data summarized as reports, codes, and basic firm information. Once a transaction is billed all transactions could be removed shortly thereafter when a reasonable time for corrections has ensued; but some firms may keep data for the entire fiscal year and some forever. For a fifteen person firm, with eight transactions per attorney per day, thirty thousand transactions must be stored for a year. This could utilize from 300,000 to 3,000,000 bytes depending on the amount of data for each transaction and the method of storage. Since a floppy disk can barely hold 300,000 bytes, while a hard disk can hold ten megabytes (just over 10,000,000 bytes) or more, all but the very smallest firms use hard disk storage for their accounting and billing systems. Since a thirty megabyte hard disk costs only a few hundred dollars more than a ten megabyte hard disk, firms usually buy the larger disk initially, for protection against later expansion problems. As the quantity of data on disks becomes larger, it becomes important to have a computer powerful enough so that the data can be handled with reasonable speed.

A second requirement is space in internal computer memory (RAM). A time and billing program is generally subdivided into small program modules. Each of these modules is moved from storage into RAM to carry out the current work requested "such as adding a new client". Simply stated, the RAM must be large enough to hold the largest module needed in the program; or the program must be configured to permit partial loading of the modules—a slower but perfectly adequate process. Because RAM has become extremely cheap and is very easy to add to computers, programs are chosen on their merits, not on the basis of how much RAM they use.

It is much more serious if the software selected places low limits on the number of lawyers, number of clients, or number of transactions. Such software may be barely adequate for a law firm's current needs, but may have to be replaced with a totally different system if the law firm's business expands. Such a changeover is expensive and traumatic.

(c) The Mechanisms Used for Input of Data

Mechanisms used for data input include typing directly on a keyboard into screens produced by the program, typing on copies of the program which produce disks that are merged into the master data file, multiple-user versions of the system which allow simultaneous on-line data input and input typed on word processors or ordinary typewriters which is machine scanned. Another emerging type of input is the use of a desktop or portable input device, resembling a miniature keyboard.

(d) The Speed of the System, Its Accuracy and the Presence of Audit Trails

Speed is important to time and billing systems. Depending on the software and hardware a system may use one day to complete a bill for one client with 75 matters (not uncommon in insurance defense), or two days of full time computer work to complete all the monthly billing for a ten person firm. Speeds are adequate if the time for various functions is suited to a firm's operation. In some systems the slower processes can operate on their own. A computer can be left unattended overnight to sort files and calculate bills. Actual printing of the bills requires only the presence of a relatively unskilled employee to add paper and ribbons or toner to the printer and to deal with paper jams. To reduce the impact of this extensive use other activities may be simultaneously carried out on some systems. New data can often be added while reports are printing.

Data entry can be almost instantaneous or slow. Repetitious entry can be avoided. When an attorney's time sheet is being added there is often no need to add the attorney's name for every new entry. If sheets are entered daily even the date can reappear automatically. Time to change functions (from data addition to report generation) can be rapid (a few seconds) or slow (20 seconds). Reports may take anywhere from ten seconds to hours to print depending on data needed and system speeds.

Accuracy is critical to a time and billing system. The sum of detailed records should total to what the system totals. Accuracy defects are not acceptable in law firm systems.

Audit trails are also important. Without proper controls the firm can erroneously change data or erroneously enter data where it was not desired and never learn about it. When data are entered a hard copy can be made available to insure data were entered properly and to retain data in case of system failure. When changes are made to data, such as a write-off or write-up, hard copy output can report this.

Every input of a receipt can be recorded in hard copy so that all check payments are properly controlled. A sound audit process should prevent a felonious employee from endorsing checks to himself, entering the account as fully paid, making other file changes and successfully defrauding the firm of income.

(e) The Training and Information Methods Employed to Help the User, Including Technical Assistance, Manuals, Training, Education Programs, On-Screen Help and Tutorials

No law office can use a time accounting and billing system without some sort of education. Education can be provided in a number of ways. For the off-the-shelf system purchased in a local computer store, or the $99 special, the only education may be a manual. Systems sold directly by the vendor may be supported by a manual and by technical assistance hot lines. Users of the "hot lines" may or may not incur an extra charge. Other mechanisms include on-screen tutorials—where the user is led through a training program which is embedded in the software. A vendor may also supply "help" commands. When the firm operator is in trouble he calls for help by pressing a designated key. Classes may be provided for new users—with or without additional charge.

In examining all of these alternatives, there are certain clearly desirable features:

(1) Some manuals, the screen-provided information, or technical assistance, may display a knowledgeable understanding of law office operation, an understanding of the expertise and experience of the average user in the law firm, and full knowledge of the computer system itself. Some systems have excellent training which tracks each of the steps used in the system.

(2) Some systems' manuals, help screens, or technical assistance may be available when they are needed (usually in a crisis). Materials may have a usable index, but the index may or may not be related to the problems users might have. (i.e. How do I reverse or unbill a bill that is full of errors?).

(3) Some system's training program may be taught in such a way that the teachers are knowledgeable in computers, law firms, and the system and are good teachers as well.

(f) The Adequacy of the Reports and Bills for the Firm

A very sophisticated system can produce from thirty to fifty types of reports including management reports, work-in-progress reports, lists of lawyers, summaries of other data, and lists of transactions recently added. A more basic system can produce only five or ten reports.

Parameters, such as range of dates, are used to select the data used in a report. A firm may not want a list of unbilled time from day one of the system's operation until today—but only for the last month. A date range permits the selection. Similarly, a range of clients or attorneys can often be printed.

On some systems reports may be run that are limited only to corporate clients or only to divorce cases. In some systems bills may be issued only for clients with balances due over $500 or for balances overdue for thirty days or more. Ranges of selection are often as important as the availability of the selection itself.

(g) The Integration of the System With Other Systems

Sooner or later a law office will want to take the data from a time accounting system and do more with it. In some systems accounts receivable totals can be placed in the general ledger. Costs may be broken down by type and general ledger account. A firm may also be able to word process certain bills for very persnickety clients. Or the firm may be able to place certain types of data into a spreadsheet to do annual summaries and projects. The interfaces with other types of computer software are varied and should become more so in the future.

§ 6–9. ACCESS CONTROL

An important aspect of any time accounting and billing system is a security system. Law firms do not want "anyone" to work with this important financial data. They want no fraudulent changes made and they want to insure that only the skilled operate the system. Small changes can have big impacts. Security systems to carry out these goals come in at least two levels. The first level of security bars entrance to the entire program. A user needs to know a password to gain access to any part of the program whatsoever. The second part of any security system operates internally within the program. It may be linked with the first part in that more than one password is assigned and each user receives a different password to enter the system. This or an additional password then serves to permit entry into certain parts of the system. See Figure 3.

Passwords can be used for at least three purposes within a program:

(1) to bar a user from certain functions such as billing and report generation;

(2) to bar a user from making changes in data but permit examination of data and reports;

(3) to bar a user from access to specialized data such as receipts per lawyer or other information that the firm considers confidential.

Systems may have a number of different codes for each of the functions. For example, a system may provide a list of functions across the top row of a matrix displayed on the screen. The row might list such functions as data entry, data correction, write-offs, billing and report generation. On the left side in a vertical column could be listed each of those in the firm by code. An "X" at the proper intersection of function and lawyer gives that user access to that function. This is an extremely flexible system. Many systems merely group certain functions together as level 1, level 2 up to level 5 or so and require assignment of each user to one of these levels.

```
                    LAW OFFICE MANAGER - Ver 4.1
---------------------------------------------------------------------
                PASSWORD MAINTENANCE - CHANGE MODE
---------------------------------------------------------------------
  1  Password DMS

  2  Client Add (AA)      Yes       15  Management Reports (RM)    Yes
  3  Client Update (AU)   Yes       16  Forms (FM)                 Yes
  4  Case Add (CC)        Yes       17  Post Transactions (PT)     Yes
  5  Case Update (CU)     Yes       18  Update Transactions (UT)   Yes
  6  Cal/Dckt Add (AD)    Yes       19  Client Billing (RB)        Yes
  7  Cal/Dckt Update (UD)Yes        20  Finance Charges (FC)       Yes
  8  Conflict Add (AC)    Yes       21  Tax Calculations (TC)      Yes
  9  Conflict Update (UC)Yes        22  Promis Options (PO)        Yes
 10  Conflict Query (QC) Yes        23  Systems Maintenance (SM)   Yes
 11  Account Query (QA)   Yes       24  Password Maintenance       Yes
 12  Cal/Dckt Query (QD) Yes
 13  Name Query (QN)      Yes
 14  Library Query (QL)   Yes

---------------------------------------------------------------------
Select # to Change, ESC to Exit, or RET to Update Password Record: []
---------------------------------------------------------------------
     Copyright (C) 1984, 1985 by Western Computer Systems, Inc.
```

Figure 3. Password Maintenance. This screen illustrates one form of assigning access to an operator. A password is assigned in the first row and the next 23 rows are used to determine whether or not the person using that password has access to the function listed on the row.

Systems may also limit attempt to enter the initial signon password. Following a number of failures (usually three) the system may shut off and after a significant delay allow more attempts. This slows down computerized attempts at using "random" inputs to try to break into a system.

§ 6-10. ENTERING INFORMATION

(a) Speed and Verification

Systems range from the rapid to the slow in the entry of information. Since the most important consumer of employee time is entry of transaction information, this is the one where speed is most important. Repetition of prior data, described above, is often used to increase entry speed. But other means can also improve speed. The major means to improve speed is the use of codes. Codes in most systems exist for attorney names, clients and matters. Most systems also provide shorthands to describe the work done, for example, "MWC" is the only entry needed to print out "Meeting with client". Sometimes codes for descriptions can be concatenated. This means that an operator can enter a succession of codes to create a longer description. Such systems might allow the following to be entered MWC TDW FDD, which will translate as "Meeting with client to discuss witnesses for depositions and discovery". See Figure 4.

Codes come in all sizes and shapes. Some are assigned by the system—the first client is 00001, the first matter for that client is 01. Some are numeric, some alphabetic, some alphanumeric, such as "001," "RLR," or "R01" for Richard L. Robbins attorney. Sometimes errors are corrected early in the entry process by a program that automatically spells out after entry the full name that correlates with the abbreviation. A valid but inappropriate code may then be corrected. Others

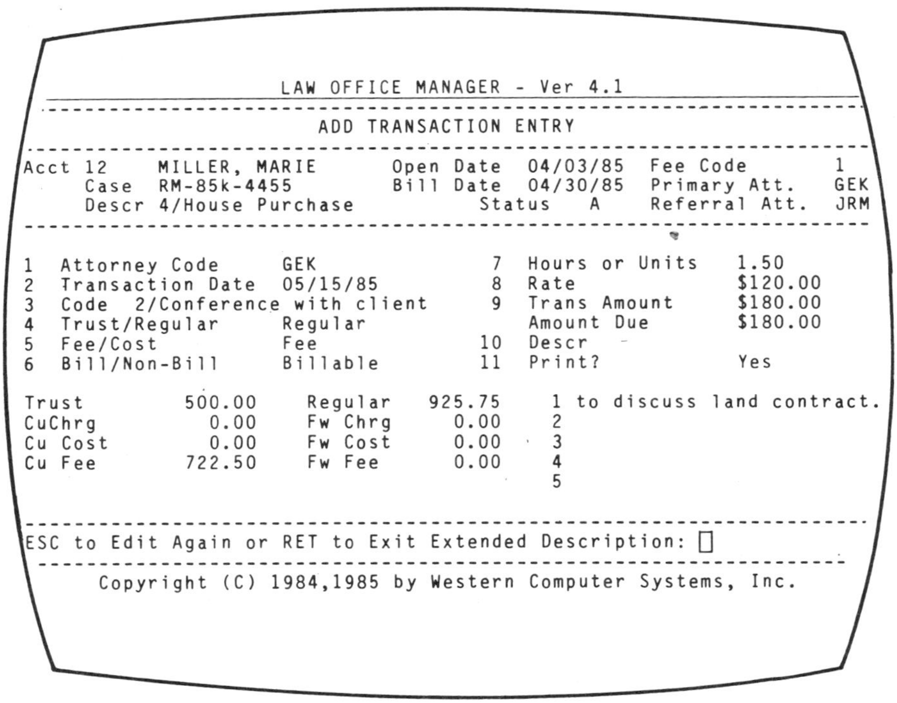

Figure 4. Add Transaction Entry. This screen illustrates one method of adding time transactions. Note how the screen contains additional detailed information about the client at the top. Information is added for lines 1 through 11 and for the client name and matter name. Data at the bottom of the screen describe the state of the client's account with the firm. The five lines at the lower right contain a typed-in description that is added to the coded description, # 2, added at line 3 in the center. The final description will be shown on a bill as "Conference with client to discuss land contract."

may merely reject entries that are invalid when a sort is attempted. These latter systems assume that the operator has not entered a valid but inappropriate code. A few systems provide on-line help by listing all possible codes if the code is unknown, as when client code entry is made. And some allow search for the right code based upon the first few letters of the client's name. In at least one system a checking system operates which requires not only the client and matter code but an additional key which is the first four letters of the client's name or the matter description.

Other codes may also be used to categorize clients, matters or attorneys. Area of practice codes list the type of practice—real estate, probate, or litigation—that a particular matter involves and permits the firm to later print out reports on profitability, productivity and work done in those areas. Type of client such as corporate, non-profit organization, insurance company may also be denoted by code when a client is entered so that similar data can be later extracted.

Speed of entry is not only measured when the data is entered but must include any further steps that must be taken before the data is usable. For example, data may need to be "posted," which means sorted to the appropriate file of lawyer, client or matter. This sorting time needs to be added to the time used for input.

Correction while data is being entered is done in many ways. In some systems the user can move a cursor to the erroneous field, in others the movement is by tabbing from field to field until the erroneous one is found. Some systems require the user to move to the end of the screen, note that the screen is in error and then reenter all the data. Other streamlined systems allow the operator to merely note the number of the field and immediately correct it. Changes made later in the operation after an attorney has reviewed a list of all a client's transactions preparatory to billing are described below. Most systems automatically correct related financial totals when a correction is made but a few require resorting of all data.

(b) Specific Information About Firm, Lawyers, Clients, Matters and Transactions

Firm

Systems often allow the firm to add particular headers to bills or to omit them completely in order to use firm letterhead for bills. In some systems messages may be added to all bills (at holiday times or tax time).

Other important firm information that some systems allow the user to customize include the ageing periods for reports on bills overdue in payment (0–30, 31–60 days or 0–45 days, 46–90 days), the names of various types of lawyers (partner or senior lawyer), the removal of unneeded entry fields in many entry areas (i.e. "Referral source" in the client file), macros that permit consistent printing of reports wanted every month without tedious reentry of ranges of the reports and clients or matters included, and the selection of minimum amounts for billing.

Some more sophisticated systems charge sales taxes, allow the setting of interest rates on overdue amounts and permit the firm to section itself into various divisions or departments for report purposes (the Chicago office, the Denver office, the patent department, etc.).

If, for example, a firm is starting the computer system in the middle of a fiscal year, systems may permit the firm to enter summary data about the firm for the earlier part of the year. This data may include hours billed to date, hours not yet billed to date, non-billable hours to date, amounts and receipts. The more conservative systems permit this to be done only once, upon installation of the system. Repeated use or misuse of this entry system could unbalance bookkeeping records, since no detailed records of transactions would support the charge.

Client and Matter Information

Law practice generally comprises doing work for clients—Acme Chemical, Mrs. John Brown, the Jones Family Trust. But each of these clients also has special work that is done for them. If they involve court action they are often called "cases." If they do not involve court action they are often called "matters" or "files". In this material we will call them "matters" since that is generally the term used most widely in computer systems. A matter is an individual piece of work done for a client. It could be a personal injury defense, a contract negotiation, preparation of a deed or tax advice on investment credits. For each client of a firm there will be one or more matters.

Computer systems handle this matter/client difference in a number of different ways. For some systems there are only matters. In some, clients have specific matters assigned to them. In some systems the computer can produce a bill for the client which separately lists all matters, subtotals work done on each and presents a total bill to the client. In some systems reports can be generated by matter or type of matter as well as by client. See Figure 5.

Client and matter files generally contain some similar data such as the name of the client, address and phone information and other details. Computerized systems often relieve the firm from entering this data more than once. Client or matter data entry may also be the point at which the firm enters three other types of information: the billing cycle, the bill format and the billing rates—though the latter two may often be entered at the time of billing as well.

Billing cycles describe when a bill is sent. Most systems allow a bill on demand (that is, a bill can be sent whenever the firm desires) but billing cycles are the standard way to promote regularity of billing. Systems offer a set of fixed cycles such as quarterly, monthly, semi-annually (many firms do bill this way), with a code for each cycle. The firm picks a code for monthly, such as the letter "A" then puts "A" as

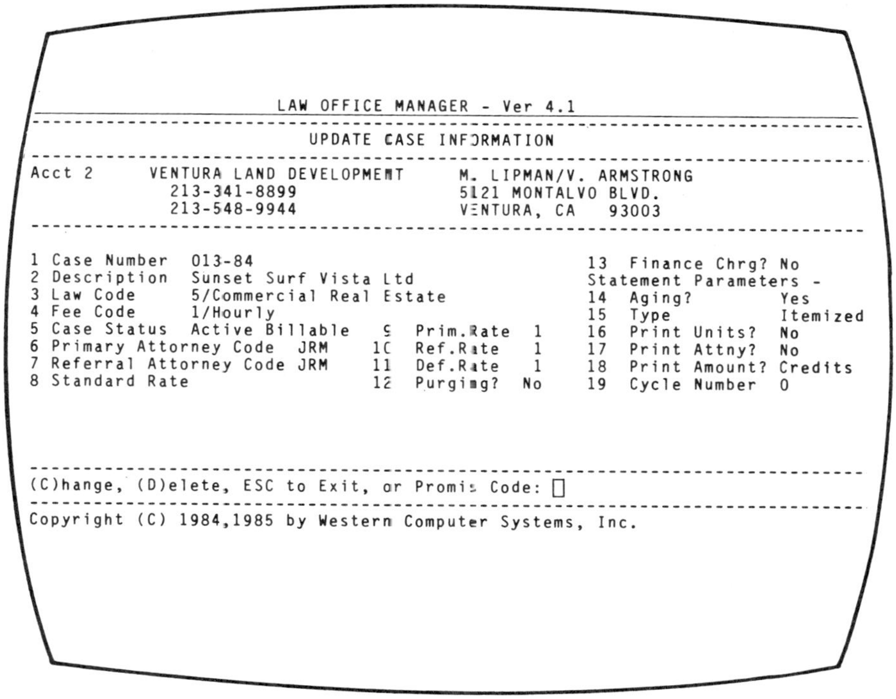

Figure 5. Update Case Information. This report provides information on a matter and permits the user to charge (update) the information. Such information as type of law, the type of fee, the related attorneys, whether a finance charge is assessed and the billing cycle are set using this screen.

the cycle for clients where monthly billing is desired. For the microcomputer systems up to 20 or more choices are often permitted.

Bill format determines what type of bill is sent to a client. Systems often offer some of the following choices and the firm and the client make a decision about which is most appropriate for the work.

They include:

(1) cost billing only (used on a contingent fee case);

(2) retainer billing only (used where a monthly fixed fee is collected);

(3) a full detailed bill listing each time transaction with all details such as the day work was done, the attorney doing the work, a work description, the hours spent, the fee for the work and similar detail on any costs incurred. This is often called an "interim bill" or an invoice;

(4) variations on the above where specific items are omitted;

(5) a bill called a "final bill", often called by other names ("reminder statement" or "accounts receivable" statement) which lists only prior fees and costs due, new fees and cost totaled, payments totaled and balance now due. No details are listed;

(6) various summary bills which list in full paragraphs a summary of the work done. See Figure 6;

(7) the above bills with various subtotals of fees by matter, fees by attorney, costs by type of effort and other information;

(8) additional information on overdue accounts listing amounts overdue by 30, 60 or 90 days or for other periods; and

(9) information on balances from clients' funds or trust accounts that are to be applied to bills, amounts that have been applied to bills and current balances in these accounts.

The client and matter files may also be the point where rates are entered. There are a number of different kinds of rates that are charged by law firms depending on custom, marketing, negotiation with the client, bookkeeping ease and other factors such as how clear the scope of work is.

Jefferson Insurance Co.
300 West A
Suite 220
Lincoln NE 68510

07/31/84
200-030

General File

PREVIOUS BALANCE	$856.50
Charges include office conferences, phone calls and correspondence with client.	

FOR CURRENT SERVICES RENDERED	573.72
SALES TAX	22.95

TOTAL COSTS THRU 7/23/84	111.27
07/10/84 Payment - thank you	-300.00

TOTAL PAYMENTS	-300.00
FINANCE CHARGE	7.95
BALANCE DUE	$1272.39

Figure 6. Summary Bill. A typical bill which summarizes in one sentence all of the work done for a client. This bill is probably printed on firm letterhead. Copyright 1986, Software Technology, Inc.

A client may be charged a fixed fee for something like a real estate closing or creation of a trust. An hourly fee is used for litigation defense and similar matters. For hourly fees there are many variations. A client may be charged the highest rate that is listed under each attorney working on a case, or the lowest rate or something in between. A firm assesses the depth of the client's pocket and the skill needed to perform the work. This requires that each attorney data file contain a rate for three to ten different rate categories. This fee could be called a "lawyer-based fee." In a variation on this the client is told that senior firm members are charged at higher rates than junior members. A client may be charged $150 per hour for senior partners, $125 for other partners, and $70 per hour for associates. This fee could be called a "type of lawyer fee". It is well-related to skill and experience. A client may be charged a fixed rate—of, say, $125 per hour for all attorneys working on the case—a simple bookkeeping method but not always equitable for firm or client. The rate may also be selected whenever a transaction is entered, cumbersome but done if only a few transactions are to be entered or if lawyers always select their own fees.

Some systems also handle contingent fees at this point of entry—calculating a percentage of a recovery.

Other information is also entered in the client and matter files. Each client can be associated with one to three or more lawyers—often called originating, supervising and working lawyer. Depending on the system one of these lawyers may receive reports on the client and edit bills, another might receive allocations of the receipts which are credited toward her contribution to the firm at the end of the year. Still a third lawyer might receive credits on productivity reports for hourly work done.

In some systems where the computer comes on-line in the middle of a fiscal year, this moment is also the point to enter data on the client about hours billed to date, costs billed to date, payments to date, last bill sent date and amount and other financial information. Where entry is not permitted here, and the computer system is to be relied upon for accurate yearly records, a series of single but large transactions may have to be entered to represent information to-date.

Whether or not financial information is added at the point of adding a client or matter, many systems keep financial information in the client or matter files. Sometimes these are rapidly accessible on the screen so that an attorney can see a readout of a client's position with the firm while discussing further work with the client.

Lawyer Information

Lawyers, too, are represented by codes in most systems. Depending on the complexity of the system, either a single hourly rate may be entered to be charged all clients without their own hourly rate or two to ten or more rates may be entered so that the firm can set one of these rates as the rate to be charged to the client—the "Lawyer-Based Fee."

Similar to client and matter data, financial data to-date may or may not be added here to bring the computer system fully in line with the firm's fiscal year.

Transaction Data

Entry of information on transactions—costs, time spent and receipts—is added by codes as was client, matter and lawyer data entry. Entry generally includes date of work (or cost or receipts), code for attorney doing work, client and matter codes, hours spent, and amount. A description of the work done is added using a code or additional description.

Information is often added in batches; the batches are often numbered and the operator's name is appended to the batch. A batch total of hours, or costs or receipts is generated by the system and compared to a hand-generated batch total to insure that all data have been entered. Comparing batch totals is a helpful and sound procedure since loss of eight hours of client time could cause a firm and the attorney to lose $800 or more in billed amounts.

Codes used for abbreviated entry of lawyer, client and matter have already been discussed, as have been the on-screen listing of what the code stands for, to improve accuracy. Verification that a code actually exists is also important at this time and is done by most systems.

In addition to the coded description many systems permit the lawyer to add additional description of at least 60 characters to describe the work done. Some systems allow unlimited description here; and have easy editing of that description. Transactions, on some software, can be entered on other machines simultaneously then merged with the central system making a single user system effectively multi-user but not real time multi-user. See Figure 7.

During transaction entry the final override rate, fee, or cost is often entered. For costs the code itself may set a cost (all real property residential closings $300) and in some systems this can be overridden ($400 for an especially difficult one). Or the rate per hour or total fee can be changed. Usually the change made in transaction entry overrides all others.

Systems usually have a hierarchy of rates extended beyond this override. In some the lawyer's basic rate is the lowest on the scale (The minimum "standard" rate set for each lawyer to insure profitability). It is overridden by "lawyer-based fees" if they are selected, for the client. "Lawyer-based-fees" are overridden by a "type-of-lawyer fee," which in turn is overridden by the fee added at transaction entry.

Some systems go so far as to set ranges of data acceptable in transaction entry such as no hours over 24, no rate over $999 per hour,

```
FEE ENTRY VERIFICATION LIST:     07/15/84       9:41   am    BJB        Page:     1

REF*      CLIENT    TIME  CAT     DATE      H/P  TCODE    RATE     HOURS          AMOUNT
----      ------    ----  ---     ----      ---  -----    ----     ----           ------
   1      102.00     01    1    07/15/83     P       1    50.00    1.50           75.00
      Office conference with client.
   2      102.00     01    1    07/15/83     P       5    50.00    0.50           25.00
      Letter to client's banker.
   3      102.00     01    1    07/20/83     P       3    50.00    0.25           12.50
      Telephone conference with client.
   4      102.00     01    1    07/20/83     P   10007    50.00    0.50           25.00
      Prepared for conference with client.
   5      102.00     01    1    07/21/83     P       1    50.00    1.25           62.50
      Office conference with client concerning mortgage
      payments.

                                                                   ----          ------
                                                  BILLABLE         3.50          175.00
                                              NON-BILLABLE         0.50           25.00
                                                  SUBTOTAL         4.00          200.00

   1      101.00     02    1    07/16/83     P       1    52.00    2.50          130.00
      Office conference with Karen Barrett and all of
      the apartment managers concerning the payment of
      damage deposits collected.
   1      200.03     02    2    07/16/83     P      27    57.00    3.50          213.14
      Put together a proposal for Mid-State Insurance
      Company.
                                                                   ----          ------
                                                  BILLABLE         6.00          343.14


                                                                   ----          ------
                                                  BILLABLE         9.50          518.14
                                              NON-BILLABLE         0.50           25.00
                                               GRAND TOTAL        10.00          543.14


CLIENT CHECKSUM = 72103


REPORT EXPLANATION:

REF *  - reference number identifying the transaction entry
TIME   - timekeeper number

CLIENT CHECKSUM - total of the client numbers (the decimal is not used in
                  the addition, i.e. 10200 + 10200+ 10200 etc.)
```

Figure 7. Fee Entry Verification List. This listing is printed out after fees are entered into the computer enabling the operator to check against the original written entries. Note that each item has a reference number which can be used for retrieval of the item for further correction. The client "checksum" at the bottom left hand corner is the sum of all client numbers added in the session and allows the operator to independently check whether all items on the manually generated timesheets have been entered. Copyright 1986, Software Technology, Inc.

no billed cost over $9,999 and no date more than two years from the present. This might prevent some major errors but, unless the user has the ability to countermand the limits, there is no ability to start the system in the middle of a fiscal year where mass entry of fees, costs or hours can be completed in no other way. Control over date range is important but not widespread. This control eliminates an error of entering 1907 instead of 1987 and forever losing the time entry when lists of client work or bills are printed only for the year 1987.

Receipts are also entered as a transaction. They often can be allocated among matters of the same client, between costs and fees, among specific invoices (a bill for specific amounts) or among attorneys to whom the receipt is to be credited. Systems also have their own internal allocation which needs to be known by the user—such as first applying receipts to costs—the usual method—then to fees or to older invoices then newer.

§ 6–11. EDITING AND ALTERING FEATURES

Very often lawyers find problems with the printouts of what a client owes and want to change transaction information later on. This printout is called a "pre-bill or "work in process" (WIP) report. It generally lists the detailed information about the unbilled transactions for a client or matter. A lawyer reviews this and makes written changes on the WIP.

Following this the transaction must often be changed. Most systems allow a change without deleting the entry and starting over. Hours, rates, amounts, costs, and descriptions can generally be changed and associated records will be changed automatically. In some cases changes can also be made after billing when a client complains. The client is unbilled and then rebilled. This is generally more complex since the books must be rebalanced—"billing" makes some more permanent changes.

Clients, matters and attorneys need to be deleted from a system at various points and most systems allow it. Some do not allow deletion unless no balance due remains—fees and costs must be paid or formally written off. Some do not allow posting any new time to the deleted items; but others assume they will be added again later. This causes some problems in that it may allow the erroneous entry of a deleted client code instead of a current client code. The transaction may never be billed to the proper client or any client at all since the deleted client is not reported or billed.

Write-downs, write-ups, and write-offs are another part of the editing process and some systems, but not all, permit this to be done. A write-down follows from a decision that the fees are too high for the work done. A write-off charges the client nothing. A write-up is a decision that charges are too low. Write-downs and write-offs are often done in a separate module of a program to insure better security control and a clear audit trail.

Write-downs can be carried out in various ways. For example, a $15,000 bill might be written down to $10,000 by proportionally reducing all fees and costs by one third. However, law office bookkeeping practices often suggest that only fees be written down. Some systems allow only fees for particular attorneys to be written down since other attorneys, usually associates, need the credit for the work. Other systems may start eliminating fees from the latest transactions and move backwards in time until a fixed amount has been removed.

§ 6-12. BILLING AND THE BILLING PROCESS

The billing process commences with the entry of transaction data on costs, receipts and time and is completed with the printing of a bill to a client. Billing formats and cycles have already been discussed earlier in this chapter.

In some software systems billing cannot be completed without a number of separate steps. The transaction data must be sorted to the appropriate clients and matters. In other systems this step is automatically done after data is entered. In either case this process involves putting all transactions for client ACME in a special file called "ACME" in date order.

In other systems this type of sorting never needs to be done since the transaction information is kept in a serial file listing all transactions. This file is accessed when a bill or other report has to be constructed from the data. For example, when a prebill or WIP is requested the program would search through the serial list for all time transactions that were unbilled and were charged to client ACME. Once these were retrieved the software would organize them by matter, order them by date, calculate totals and print them out.

A similar search would be done for unbilled time for attorney RLR. The system looks for all time entries with the attorney initials "RLR" then sums up the hours and prints the proper report.

The next step in the billing process is the printing of the prebill or WIP report. See Figure 8.

A WIP report is printed for each client with subcategories for matters. The report lists in detail all time, cost and receipt transactions for the client. It may also list billing history. This may include the date of the last bill and its amount, the last payment and a listing of aged accounts receivable, billing this year to date and other important client information. This information is displayed so that the billing attorney has a full picture of the client's overall relationship to the firm. Based on the record of payments, or the totals billed to date, the billing attorney may want to increase or decrease the current amount due for unbilled services. The WIP, however, is generally used for more mundane purposes. The billing attorney checks the detailed time and cost transactions to insure that they are complete, correct and properly reflect the work done by the firm. At this point the firm may not want to charge $1.80 for copying where time charges are $48,000. Or the time charges may need to be written more artfully to better describe the work done.

DATE: 07/31/84 DETAIL WORK IN PROCESS REPORT PAGE: 1

FROM: 07/01/84 THRU: 07/15/84
PRIMARY TIMEKEEPER: 3 Frederick Johnson
CLIENT: 200.030 Jefferson Insurance Co. PREV BALANCE: 856.50
JEFFERSON General File PHONE: 402-482-1198
CONTACT: Mike Johnson
PRIMARY TIMEKEEPER: 02 FAJ CATEGORY: 002 Insurance Companies
SECONDARY TIMEKEEPER: 05 SPA RATE-CODE: 2 FEE-FMT: 3-4 COST-FMT: Y

DATE	TIMEKEEPER	CATEGORY	TCODE	REF #	RATE	HOURS	AMOUNT	WRITE UP/DOWN
07/15/84	3 FAJ	2	1	0002	70.00	1.75	130.88	8.38
Office conference with Peter Smith, Insurance salesman for company.								
07/15/84	3 FAJ	4	5	0003	70.00	.75	52.50	
Letter to corporate headquarters.								
BILLABLE TOTAL FOR TIMEKEEPER 3						2.50	183.38	
TOTAL WRITE UP								8.38
0/7/15/84	4 JP	2	7	0006	60.00	2.75	176.28	11.28
Prepared for conference with client.								
BILLABLE TOTAL FOR TIMEKEEPER 4						2.75	176.28	
TOTAL WRITE UP								11.28
TOTAL BILLABLE FEES						5.25	339.66	
TOTAL WRITE UP								19.66
07/15/84			20	0001			25.52	
Phone calls to Mid-State								
TOTAL COSTS							25.52	
PAYMENTS/CREDITS								
07/10/84			28	0006			-300.00	
Payment - thank you.								
TOTAL PAYMENTS/CREDITS							-300.00	

******** R E C A P ********

FEES:	359.66	COSTS:	25.52	TOT WIP:	385.18
PREV BAL:	856.50	PYMT/CR:	-300.00	BAL DUE:	556.50 TOTAL: 941.68
CURRENT:	0.00	PAST 30:	556.50	PAST 60:	0.00 PAST 90: 0.00

BILLING CODES: FB:N CS:N AT:N PO:M FC:Y PI:Y ST:Y FF:B SF:M CF:Y **

REPORT EXPLANATION:

CLIENT	- client number follwd by billing frequenty (if other than 'N')
FEE-FMT	- billing format codes for fees and fee subtotaling
COST-FMT	- billing format code for costs
REF #	- reference nunmber identifying the transaction entry
WRITE UP/DOWN	- difference between AMOUNT and (RATE & HOURS)
RECAP FEES	- total billable fees
RECAP COSTS	- total billable costs
RECAP TOT WIP	- total billable fees and costs
RECAP PREV BAL	- client's balance due from last statement
RECAP PYMT/CR	- total payments and credits
RECAP BAL DUE	- client's PREV BAL minus PYMT/CR
RECAP TOTAL	- TOT WIP plus BAL DUE

RECAP CURRENT - amounts owed that are not past due
RECAP PAST DUE - amounts owed that are past due 30, 60 and 90 days
"u" preceding CODE # indicates the transaction has been billed and is ready to be updated.

BILLING CODES:

FB - flat fee Billing	CS - Cover Statement	AT - Archive Transactions
PD - Past Due Message	FC - Finance Charge	PI - Print Initials
ST - Sales Tax	FF - Fee Formate Code	SF - Subtotal Fee Code
CF - Cost Format Code	** - indicates client is "released for billing"	

Figure 8. Detail Work in Process Report. This is a typical work in process report or prebill which describes all the work that is not yet billed for a particular client. The primary timekeeper, often called the billing attorney, uses this document to correct errors and to determine how much should be billed to the client. Note the billing history at the lower part of the report called "Recap". The line labeled billing codes describes in shorthand the method of billing this client. The key at the bottom of the page helps the billing attorney interpret this line. Copyright 1986, Software Technology, Inc.

In one article, entitled "How to Draft Bills Clients Rush to Pay", J. Harris Morgan, a Texas lawyer, provides some guidance for bill drafting. This guidance can be used at various steps of billing from transaction entry to just before the bill is put in an envelope for mailing. Morgan says that:

—Bills should project effort. Lawyers should use action verbs such as "filed, mailed, copied, . . . contacted, secured, determined, concluded, . . . compared, searched, researched, . . . drafted, . . . closed . . . demanded, . . . [and] revised . . ." Abbreviations should never be used in a bill. Block billing formats are recommended. These fill the page with continuous listings of work done without blank lines between activities. The description of the work done should dominate the space on the bill.

—Bills should demonstrate concern for the client. Handwritten notes should be appended to each bill with statements such as "Please pay this amount" or "Thank you for permitting me to represent you in this closing on your home. I know you will enjoy the neighborhood".

—The bill must evidence a high standard of honesty. Every payment, advance or cost should be set out clearly in a bill, deposits of funds into a trust account and transfers from that trust account should be reflected on a bill.

—The bill should reveal basic competence. Projection of competence is done by a clear step-by-step description of all the steps necessary to complete the project. This might include such items in a zoning case as "Examined property and nearby uses with trained assessor and planning expert," "Compared facts in this suit with current law" or "Researched damage determination elements".

—The billing process should be perceived by the client as resulting in a "fair fee". The process should give reliable updated information at frequent intervals on the fee charged so that when estimates of cost given to the client are exceeded the client can be notified early. According to Morgan if "the estimate is corrected by the lawyer at or before the wrong estimate becomes a fact, the ultimate fee will be perceived as fair in the eyes of the client". Regularly printed WIP reports should reveal these problems. [Excerpts Copyright © 1985, Legal Economics, the publication of the Economics of Law Practice Section of the American Bar Association].

When reviewing the WIP, rates and fees are also corrected. The billing attorney examines hourly rates and insures that they are both adequate and reflective of the skill of the attorney. Often in some firms billing rates are not even calculated until work is completed so that the firm can use the rate as a means of adjusting the bill to provide a "fair" or "competitive" bill. The WIP is also the point where bills are written-off, written-down or written-up. In some systems the write-down may be done by eliminating transactions from the bill. In some of these the transactions remain as credits to the lawyer's account and as data in the client account but the amounts are not billed.

Following a WIP report the corrections to transactions and totals are entered and the system is ready to produce a bill. Since production of a bill generally takes all unbilled transactions placed on the bill and turns them to billed, the firm may want to print a bill that is a draft bill that does not make these changes. This will further insure that the corrections are properly entered, that the bill is in the right format, for the right amount and for the right client and matters. The bill is now printed by the firm.

Following billing the firm may find that the bill was in error, either by examination of the bill or from a complaint from a client. Some systems then allow the firm to unbill the client, make appropriate changes to what are now unbilled transactions, then rebill the client. This approach insures that the financial records for a client—amounts due, amounts paid—are always kept in balance.

Systems may also print summary lists of bills sent and amounts due so that a firm can calculate current receivables.

Some software permit the firm to add general messages to bills during the billing process—a useful means to "demonstrate concern for the client."

Transfers from trust accounts (client's funds) are also added in the billing process. Usually the WIP provides the information on trust fund balances and the lawyer requests the appropriate transfer and, if necessary, further billing to replenish the trust account.

The client and matter distinction may also be considered during the billing process. Clients often like to receive bills that summarize what the client owes for all matters but contain detailed information on each matter appended to the summary bill.

Where systems link matters to clients, the system itself may automatically produce this kind of bill. Even though the linkage exists the software may permit the user to disable the overall summary. The disabling feature may be useful where different departments of a large company employ the firm and are interested only in the particular bill for services rendered them. The system may also have a technique to report to house counsel on the total bills rendered each separate entity if this reporting is desired by the company.

Billing processes following transaction entry for a fifteen person firm with 150 active clients might take two to ten hours on a microcomputer system if all clients are billed in the cycle. During that time users may be unable to use the software for other purposes. Some systems do allow time entries during that time, others will bar all other use of the system.

§ 6-13. PRODUCTIVITY AND MANAGEMENT REPORTS

Most software systems for small and medium-sized law offices provide a number of management reports. Usually at least five are provided and systems may provide up to thirty. A unique management report is defined as one with different row or column headings. Many of these reports can be printed for various ranges. Data for the reports could be selected from various time ranges (April, May and June; or the fiscal year to date); or for various lawyers (all partners, all associates); or for various clients (all corporate, all clients in litigation); or for one of any item in the data (all clients, matters and dates for one attorney). Reports may also be limited only to clients or matters that are active or closed. The information may often be ordered or listed in various forms—alphabetically by client or by client code, or by attorney, then client, then matter. See Figure 9.

Reports may sometimes be printed, displayed on the screen or written into a computer file for later use. Screen display is helpful to the lawyer and office manager so that information can quickly be retrieved. Writing to a file is generally faster than printing, and does not require that the printer or associated personnel to tend the printer be available.

There are many types of reports available on time and billing systems. The following description includes only a few of these. They may also appear in different forms from those described.

(a) Lists

Lists of clients, matters, and attorneys are one set of reports. Lists of clients and matters often contain not only the name, address, contact person, phone number and codes but may also contain information on billing rates, billing formats, billing cycles, a description of the client and the type of matter. Sometimes financial information, the same information that appears in the client file or additional information, is summarized here—recent bills, accounts receivable, receipts to date, hours spent on the client's work and other data. This data help an attorney quickly research a client's billing status with the firm to determine if advances or retainers are needed when the client requests additional work, if the client must be encouraged to pay a prior overdue account or if the client's history over the past few years and substantial contribution to the firm's income suggests that these problems be overlooked.

Lists of attorneys may contain the name, the type of attorney (associate or partner), the associated billing rates and other basic information. Financial information on the attorney's work may also be provided—billing year-to-date, hours in the last month, unbilled time, receipts allocated to the attorney and other data.

Other lists include lists of codes used for abbreviated transaction descriptions, codes used for area of practice and type of client and codes used for general ledger accounts.

(b) Management Reports

Systems offer many different management reports. The names change from system to system and some of the reports described here appear as two or three different reports in some time accounting and billing systems. A few of these are listed here.

```
                      LAW OFFICE MANAGER - Ver 4.1
-------------------------------------------------------------------------
6/6/85   11:16 AM         CASE SUMMARY REPORT                      PAGE 1
-------------------------------------------------------------------------

                          Gerald E. Kruegersen

ACCT    CLIENT NAME                    CASE        DESCRIPTION
--------------------------------------------------------------------------

4       HUIZENGA, CARL                 663-82      Syntron Electronics
22      JONES, TOM                     2           Business Law
                                       5678        p/i
18      KELLY, MARILYN                 1           Residential Real Estate
17      KELLY, SUSAN                   1           Business Law
16      LADAR, JEFFREY                 1970        "Promis" suit
13      LAUFFENBERG, DAVE              1           House Purchase
5       LIONELL RAILROAD PARK INC      068-84      Stock Option Plan
11      MILLER, MARIE                  1           BUSINESS MATTERS
                                       2           House Purchase
12      MORRIS, GEORGE                 1           Dissolution
19      RAMSAY, DON                    GEK-0585    House Purchase
                                       GEK-0585-2  Commercial Business
7       STAGECOACH RESTAURANT          091-81      General Corporate
RET to Continue or ESC to Exit: []

       Copyright (C) 1984,1985 by Western Computer Systems, Inc.
```

Figure 9. Case Summary Report. This report shows for the lawyer's name listed at the top the name of each client of that lawyer.

Report by Lawyer or Client on Adjustments, Payments and Write-offs

This type of report provides data on adjustments, payments and write-offs listed by lawyer for all clients and matters, providing information on the actual cash generated by a lawyer or attributed to a client's account allowing the firm to assess the contribution to the firm of the lawyer or the client.

Profitability Report by Area of Practice

This type of report provides data on each area of practice (probate, property, litigation) and the hours spent on the work, the percentage of time which is unbilled, billed and not billable, similar totals for amounts and a total of receipts from the area of practice. A summary report listing all areas of practice and the hours utilized and amounts billed as well as the percentage of total hours and total amounts provides a comparative analysis of each area. Using this report a firm can compare the profitability of various types of practice.

A similar report could contain information based on transaction codes (Meeting with Client, WESTLAW Research, Deposition), or type of client (corporate, individual, public agency). These reports permit the firm to determine the amount of hours spent on various types of activity done for a client, such as research and the contribution to firm income. Data on types of clients can also be analyzed to discover where the firm is more profitable. See Figure 10.

Bill Report

This report lists bills sent in the period selected by the operator permitting the firm to total receivables.

Receipts Report

This report may be organized by client or by attorney and lists receipts received for each attorney's clients or for clients in general. The report enables bookkeeping to reconcile deposits with receipts recorded in the system. It also permits a lawyer to readily determine whether clients have paid. More complex varieties of this report could also list accounts receivable that remain unpaid, write-offs or adjustments made, initial billing before these changes and other data useful to assessing the contribution of a client or a lawyer to firm income. See Figure 11.

History-Type Reports

This type of report compares present monthly, or fiscal year-to-date information on billings, unbilled time, hours and other data with other years or other months so that law office trends can be examined.

Reports on Productivity by Clients and Matters

This type of report can be generated by attorney, with clients and matters listed under each responsible attorney, or it can be merely a listing by client and matter. The object of the report is to provide

LAW OFFICE MANAGER - Ver 4.1

CODE	DESCRIPTION	HOURS	PERCNT	AMOUNT	PERCNT
1	Business Law	17.55	7.71	820.17	1.30
3	Probate	11.70	5.14	--	--
4	Residential Real Estate	12.75	5.60	1555.00	2.46
5	Commercial Real Estate	34.80	15.28	2931.24	4.64
9	Firm Administration	38.50	16.91	1464.89	2.32
10	Plaintiff's Litigation	88.90	39.04	54873.80	86.84
11	Litigation Defense	23.50	10.32	1542.06	2.44
	Total	227.70	100.00	63187.16	100.00

5/15/85 1:41 PM LAW CODE ANALYSIS REPORT PAGE 6

* * * * * * * * * * * * * * * GRAND TOTALS * * * * * * * * * * * *

CODE	DESCRIPTION	HOURS	PERCNT	AMOUNT	PERCNT
1	Business Law	17.55	5.25	820.17	1.29
3	Probate	11.70	3.50	--	--

RET to Continue or ESC to Exit: □

Copyright (C) 1984,1985 by Western Computer Systems, Inc.

Figure 10. Law Code Analysis Report. This report lists the various types of law and their contribution to the hours and income of the firm. The illustration shows at the top a breakout for a single client's work, at the bottom, part of the data on the breakout for the entire firm.

information on individual clients and to describe the financial situation with the firm of the clients of a particular attorney.

Items appearing in this report could include for each client: billed and unbilled hours, fees and costs for the year-to-date, average age of unbilled amounts and unpaid amounts, and the actual billing rate averaged over all working attorneys considering write-downs and write-ups.

Unsubmitted Time Report

This report is used to encourage attorneys to submit time sheets. The report lists, by attorney, for the previous one, two or three months all days for which time has not been entered into the computer.

Report on Projected Client Fees and Costs

In some systems a report compares the estimate provided to the client, or an internal estimate of the total cost of the work, with the amount spent to date. This report permits the firm to keep matters within a budget, to alert attorneys to the need to keep costs and fees

LAW OFFICE MANAGER - Ver 4.1

6/6/85 11:10 AM TIME AND RECEIPTS REPORT

Amy Charles

* * * * * * * * * * * * * SUMMARY TOTALS * * * * * * * * * * * * * * * * * *

	HOURS	CHARGES	COSTS	FEES	TOTAL
Billed	10.00	--	--	229.75	229.75
Non-Billable	--	--	--	--	--
Total	10.00	--	--	229.75	229.75
Payments		--	--	--	--
Adjustments		--	--	--	--
Write Offs		--	--	--	--
Total	--	--	--	--	--

6/6/85 11:10 AM TIME AND RECEIPTS REPORT
RET to Continue or ESC to Exit:

Copyright (C) 1984,1985 by Western Computer Systems, Inc.

Figure 11. Time and Receipts Report. This report lists receipts (rather than just amounts billed) for each lawyer. Amounts billed, actual payment, adjustments to bills and amounts written off are listed.

within control and to alert supervising attorneys that the client needs to be contacted for additional retainer and a revised estimate of the fee.

Attorney Productivity Reports

This type of report describes the work done by each attorney. It could list the billable and nonbillable hours in a given period, the average rate of billing, the receipts for the attorney, the bill amounts for the clients of the attorney and other data that permits the attorney to assess workload and contribution to the firm's income.

Unbilled Hours, Amounts, and Costs Report

This report enables the firm to determine hours that have not yet been billed and to estimate receivables that could arise. It also serves to encourage timely billing of those hours.

Trust Accounting Reports

These reports describe the activity in a client's fund account, noting the title of the account, the various subaccounts within the account and the transactions and balances within each of the accounts.

Some systems warn the operator when any one of the accounts is out of balance and thus is in violation of fiduciary standards.

§ 6–14. TRUST ACCOUNTING

Many time accounting and billing systems also handle the funds of clients which are kept either to be applied later to fees generated or to be transferred to other parties. Time and billing systems are mainly concerned with those funds kept for fees. These trust funds are often called "retainers" or "client funds". Funds which the firm has not yet earned are often requested from clients and kept on their behalf when the firm is either unsure of payment from the client or wants some substantial commitment from the client to the representation. Clients who have already contributed funds to legal work are often more cooperative with a firm than those who are not. Unknown clients or those with poor credit records are often asked for funds in advance to protect the firm. These funds must not be kept in the firm's checking account but must be placed in a separate account. The funds may be placed in a single account with other client funds but strict procedures must be followed to insure that the individual funds are not improperly invaded. Generally, bookkeeping reports must separate the funds from other funds to meet requirements of the Model Code and state bar rules.

Time accounting systems often permit the billing of clients for "retainers" to add initial or additional funds to these accounts and the movement of receipts on those bills to the proper trust account. Systems also permit the transfer of funds out of the trust account into the firm's general account when a bill draws on the account for payment. In some software a bill can automatically be set to reflect payment from the trust account, to show that payment on the bill, to show the remaining account balance and to properly debit the trust account.

Additional reports may instruct the firm's accountant on the change in both the trust account and the firm account. Audit trails are often available to show any changes made in accounts or any transactions.

§ 6–15. MULTI-USER OPERATION

Some software systems operate in multi-user mode. More than one user can simultaneously operate the system from different terminals. Generally this is useful to a law office when bills or reports are being printed by the office manager, time entry is underway by a secretary or lawyer and another lawyer is looking up a client's payment record while discussing new work with the client over the phone.

In multi-user systems not all of the above actions can take place simultaneously. Data entry while a report using that data is being printed is confusing to a computer system and often cannot be carried out. Similarly, examining a client's file while billing is being done has the attorney looking at a changing target—some of the transactions are being changed from unbilled to billed. Systems, therefore, lock users out of certain functions while others are being carried out.

A complete function may be unavailable or a user may merely be barred from entering data that is used by the system. For example, during printout of a bill for "CHENERY" client, another user may not be able to enter unbilled time for "CHENERY" but could enter time for "BIMETALLIC" or "OVERTON PARK".

System speed may also be affected by operation in multi-user mode. While a major sorting of files is going on to generate an attorney productivity report for each attorney, the hardware may be unable to effectively and rapidly receive transaction entries.

§ 6-16. CONCLUSION

A computerized time accounting and billing system is at the heart of the entrepreneurial law office These systems come in many forms, ranging in price from $99.00 to $100,000 or more. They range in sophistication from those that produce a small number of reports and only a few varieties of bills to those that produce many reports, many types of bills, provide extensive audit trails and complete management information.

Some systems are easy to learn yet unsophisticated. Others are both easy to learn and sophisticated but more expensive. Others are hard to learn but very easy to use. For all systems there are variations in the manner in which data is entered and in the speed of entry. Some systems have more control than others on what data is entered and some offer more help to the user when a data entry problem arises.

Security systems to prevent unwanted access vary from those with only a few choices to those with virtually unlimited choices of security levels. Audit mechanisms to protect data and to protect balances are sometimes internal and sometimes external allowing manual checking of totals. The former automatically protect the system and the latter rely on the user to cross check totals.

The billing process may involve many steps from transaction entry to final bills or it can involve only a few. Sorts (or posting) may be required in some systems and not in others. WIP reports generally provide enough information to change the transactions or do write-offs where needed. But the WIP can also provide important additional data on client payments and billings to date which often color the changes made in a current bill. Sometimes bills can be "unbilled" when errors occur. Choices for bill formats are often extensive ranging from details on everything to summary one line bills covering many transactions done for the client. Client billing can be done on demand or in various cycles—sometimes created by the user, sometimes constrained by the system.

Some systems offer many management reports on attorney and client productivity, receipts, unbilled amounts, profitability by area of practice and other factors. Others offer a more limited menu of management information. Screen reports on the state of a client's account are often available and some contain detailed account information.

Trust accounting systems of considerable sophistication can often track client funds, report on them, allocate interest paid on the account, and transfer funds to pay bills. Multiuser systems sometimes offer the appealing potential for two, five or fifty users simultaneously entering time, printing reports, correcting errors and billing client.

The range of time accounting and billing systems is large and growing larger. A lawyer can learn about systems by using a demonstration model of the program, using his or her own set of test data to add transactions and generate reports or by reading manuals and advertising literature. The American Bar Association's Legal Technology Advisory Council system of "approving" and reporting on software can also help. LTAC tests software in a one to sixteen week objective test in its laboratories, publishes forty- to sixty-page reports on each piece of software outlining what the software does and whether it meets the guidelines promulgated by the ABA.

§ 6–17. PROBLEMS

(1) You are a sole practitioner defending an insurance company and often appearing in court. What characteristics would you like to find in a time accounting and billing system that would assist you in billing the insurance company for defending their insureds?

(2) You are worried that your office manager might some day take a client's fee payment of $20,000 or more, endorse the check to himself, credit the client's account but not put the money in the firm's account or a trust account. What would you like to see in a time accounting system or your own manual system to protect the firm from this kind of activity?

(3) You are concerned that your time accounting system may break down some day and force you to do all billing manually from that point on. What printouts would you save from the system on a regular basis to insure that you do this with only one week's loss of data? How would you protect that week's data?

(4) You want to follow what J. Harris Morgan suggests about billing practices. (See Sec. 6–12) What do you ask the software vendor to provide you in order to do that?

(5) Many of your clients are not paying their bills on time. What elements of a time accounting system will be needed to improve the payment of these bills?

(6) How can you use the time accounting system to make your firm more profitable? Data on attorneys? on clients? on types of clients?

Chapter 7

SELECTION OF HARDWARE AND SOFTWARE—WHERE THE TECHNOLOGY IS HEADED

§ 7-1. IBM-PC COMPATIBLE HARDWARE

(a) The IBM-Compatible Computer as an Inexpensive Commodity—Will It Do What the Model T Ford Did for Cars?

Introductory economics courses often present students with the problem of the economic effects of a particular item becoming available free of charge. If beer were distributed free by the government, for instance, one could expect a sharp reduction in sales of wine and whiskey and a sharp increase in the sales of pretzels. The price revolution in computers is having a similar drastic effect on many areas of the economics of law practice. At the time this book is being written, generic IBM-compatible personal computers are being sold for as little as $500, and prices are continuing to fall. This continued sharp reduction in computer costs may be expected to crowd out substitute goods (such as typewriters and filing cabinets) just as free beer would crowd out whiskey. At the same time, it may be expected to greatly increase the demand for complementary goods, such as IBM-compatible software, just as free beer might increase the demand for pretzels.

Economic theory also suggests that prices tend in the long run to fall to the marginal cost of production and distribution. This theory suggests that lawyers may see generally falling prices for software once the initial demand caused by the great growth in the number of computers is overcome. Software requires a substantial capital investment to create. However, once it is created, it costs very little to reproduce and distribute. The growing market for software, caused by the continual increase in the number of law firm computers, will attract new entrants, who can hope to spread their costs over a large number of buyers with a low-price, high-volume approach.

A leading business text, Michael E. Porter, *Competitive Advantage* (New York, 1985), suggests that through product differentiation and "locking in" customers a company can charge considerably more than normal competitive market prices. The key tactical management question for the lawyer is how to avoid being victimized by this type of strategy so that the law firm can take advantage of the continuing cost reductions in hardware and software. The best approach would appear to be to avoid heavy investment in hardware compatible only with other hardware and software from a single manufacturer, but instead to invest in hardware compatible with hardware and software from many competing manufacturers. However, this is easier said than done, because a good law office computer system requires not only hardware and software, but also considerable expertise in "system integration"—putting together a system that works as a system, where the whole is in some sense greater than the sum of the parts. If one deals with a specialized supplier of hardware and software, one may pay more—often three times as much for hardware and software—but hopefully along with the software and hardware will come system integration expertise and consulting.

(b) Standard Hardware Configuration

At the time this book was written, the most generally compatible workstation is an IBM-compatible personal computer with: 640 kilobytes of memory, at least one 360 kilobyte floppy disk, a 10 megabyte or larger hard disk, an IBM-compatible monochrome display, a Hercules-compatible display card, a Hayes compatible 1200 baud modem, a letter quality printer, a draft speed printer, and perhaps a graphics printer. Consider each of these items in turn, why it is now the standard, and how the standard is likely to evolve in the next few years.

First, what is an IBM-compatible personal computer? IBM advertises that only IBM makes a 100% IBM compatible personal computer. The usual definition of IBM-compatibility is, however, functional. To be IBM-compatible, a computer must: (1) run without change all leading software packages for the IBM personal computer, including specifically two programs—Lotus 1–2–3 and Flight Simulator—that interact in complex ways with the hardware and built in firmware (software in read only memory) of the IBM personal computer; and (2) function properly with all major plug-in boards manufactured for the IBM-personal computer. At one time a number of companies made personal computers that were only partially IBM-compatible. However, massive buyer resistance has reduced the number of such companies to a handful of well-financed, die-hard organizations and has reduced their sales to an insignificant fraction of the market. The huge financial losses sustained by companies that declined to be IBM-compatible suggest that as IBM introduces new and improved models, other manufacturers will make these models into a de facto standard, whatever the theoretical advantages of different computer configurations.

Second, 640 kilobytes of memory. Memory costs have fallen rapidly, so that 640 kilobytes of memory now cost no more than the 16 kilobytes supplied with the original version of the IBM personal computer. As memory costs have fallen more and more, users have upgraded the size of their computer memories, and the amount of memory required by typical software programs has expanded steadily. There will probably be at least a brief pause in this expansion at 640 kilobytes, because the design of the IBM computer makes it impossible for programs to use memory beyond the first 640 kilobytes in a standard and efficient manner. A number of efforts are underway to solve this problem; however, a generally-accepted solution will require IBM's blessing, and this benediction has not yet been forthcoming. Once IBM sets a standard for the use of larger amounts of memory, it is likely that the total internal memory of typical IBM-compatible personal computers will expand rapidly.

Third, the 360 kilobyte floppy disk. There are three types of floppy disks used on IBM-compatible computers. These are a 3½" diskette used on some portable computers, a 360 kilobyte floppy disk used on the vast majority of IBM-compatible computers, and a 1.2 megabyte floppy disk used on the IBM PC/AT. The 1.2 megabyte disk drive has the capability of reading, but not of writing compatible 360 kilobyte floppy diskettes. Thus, if a computer is to be able to transfer data by diskette to the outside world, it must have at least one 360 kilobyte floppy disk drive.

Fourth, the 10 megabyte or larger hard disk. At one time, hard disks were an extremely expensive option. However, as prices of hard disk equipment have fallen, they are rapidly turning into standard equipment. Hard disks have numerous advantages. They can handle large files that will not fit on floppy disks. Access to and transfer of data is usually much faster on a hard disk than a floppy disk. Complex operations involving a number of different programs can be performed without swapping diskettes. Hard disks are less subject to accidental physical damage than floppy disks (though good backup procedures are necessary, since huge amounts of data can be lost by damage to a hard disk). Another important reason for having a hard disk is to avoid problems with using "copy-protected" software. Such software, if used on a floppy disk, requires that the original copy of the software be in the disk drive when the system is turned on or even the whole time that the program is in use. However, most such software now provides options to "install" and "uninstall" the program on a hard disk. Once the program is installed on a hard disk, it can be used in the same way as unprotected software is used. In the next few years, we may expect not only to see hard disks as standard equipment, but to see the size of these disks grow substantially. As large hard disks become standard, software will begin to offer features that require huge amounts of storage. For instance, a spelling checker works better, the larger its dictionary. With a floppy disk, there are practical limits on dictionary size—the dictionary must fit on the disk (and perhaps still leave room for other software). With a hard disk, a really huge dictionary can be used that prevents falsely identifying rare words or technical terms as misspellings.

Fifth and sixth, an IBM-compatible monochrome display and a Hercules-compatible monochrome/graphics display card or an IBM Enhanced Graphics Adapter and a compatible color display. IBM originally provided two display options for its computer, a color/graphics display and a monochrome, text-only display. The color/graphics display (also available in black and green or black and amber versions from other companies) has very poor resolution when used to display text and thus is unsuited to the heavily text-oriented work of law offices. The IBM monochrome display provides much higher quality text display and thus is ideally suited to the kind of work done in law offices, but has no provision for graphics or color. Corresponding to the two types of displays, IBM provided two types of display adapter cards that plugged into the computer and provided the appropriate signals to the displays. Users who needed both graphics and high-quality text capability were expected to buy both display cards and both monitors. Many users needed the graphics capability, particularly for creating charts to accompany spreadsheets made with programs such as Lotus 1–2–3. However they rebelled at the cost and desk space involved in having two display cards and two monitors. Hercules Computer Technology, Inc. solved the problem by providing a display adapter card which gave exactly the same excellent text quality as the IBM monochrome adapter card, but also provided good graphics with higher resolution on the IBM monochrome display than IBM's color/graphics display card can provide on the IBM color display. Software makers quickly adapted their products to work with the Hercules card, and other hardware manufacturers quickly started making Hercules-compatible cards. For law office use, with its emphasis on word processing, but with an occasional need for business graphics, the Hercules-compatible display card would seem to be a good choice. For those willing to pay a considerably higher price to get color rather than monochrome graphics, IBM's new EGA (Extended Graphics Adapter) card and high-resolution color display are now available. Leading software companies are rapidly adapting their software to take advantage of the features of the EGA card. This card supports all the features of IBM's color/graphics display card and introduces new, higher-resolution color/graphics display options as well. Be sure to order it with extra memory so that it can achieve its full potential. A number of independent manufacturers offer single cards that implement all of the display standards mentioned in this paragraph, thus eliminating software compatability problems.

Seventh, a 1200 baud Hayes compatible modem. Almost all leading manufacturers of modems for the IBM PC have incorporated the features of the Hayes modem in their modems, and all communications software assumes that a Hayes-compatible modem is present. This modem, with appropriate software, allows communication with the outside world, including major legal data banks and electronic mail systems.

Eighth, printer capability for letter-quality, high-speed draft, and graphics printouts. While at one time it was necessary to buy one printer for letter-quality work and another for high-speed draft printing and graphics, laser printers are now available that provide all three capabilities and are virtually silent, an extremely important feature in an office environment.

§ 7-2. THE CHEAP MEMORY REVOLUTION

There has been a revolution in the cost of computer memory. This revolution has affected all existing types of memory devices and has also introduced revolutionary new types of memory systems. The desktop computer of the mid-1980s supports five or six different types of memory. Each of these and possible future developments will be considered in turn.

(a) RAM

The main internal memory of the computer is called "RAM." The computer can retrieve the contents of any location in RAM extremely rapidly—in less than a millionth of a second. However, when the computer power is turned off, the contents of RAM memory are lost. The same can happen if there is a momentary interruption in the power supply. Ordinary RAM cannot be run economically from batteries, because it requires too much power. There is a more expensive type of RAM that has very low current requirements and thus can be used with batteries to prevent loss of memory. This type of RAM is used in desktop computers to store the time and date which is updated by a battery-powered clock chip even when the computer is turned off. A more important use for low current RAM is in battery-powered portable computers.

The typical desktop personal computer in 1986 has 512 or 640 thousand bytes of RAM, while the typical portable computer has 256 thousand bytes of RAM. Users of large spreadsheets frequently encountered the ominous "MEMORY FULL" message and began demanding more memory. Luckily, the price per byte of RAM fell precipitously in 1985, while the number of bytes on a typical memory chip rose from 64,000 to 256,000 in the course of that year. Numerous companies began offering memory boards to expand the memory of an IBM Personal Computer to 4,000,000 bytes or more, and leading software producers adapted their software to work with these boards. Early in 1986, Apple announced the Macintosh Plus, with 1,000,000 bytes of memory standard, expandible up to 4,000,000 bytes. By 1990, 8,000,000 to 16,000,000 bytes of memory should be commonplace. The capacity of portable computers will lag somewhat behind because of the higher cost of low-power-drain memory. The larger memory capacity will make possible major improvements in software. It will be possible to make extremely large spreadsheets and to keep numerous variations of spreadsheets in memory at the same time. Software designers, freed from memory restrictions, will be able to incorporate many more user-friendly features in their programs. For several reasons, all types of software will run much faster. Access to disk storage will be replaced by much faster access to RAM memory in many programs, since there will be room to have all the data and all parts of the program in RAM. The large size of the memory will allow the substitution of fast look-up tables for slow calculations. For instance a 300,000 word dictionary could be kept in memory and used to check each word as it was typed in. There will be enough memory for multiple function programs that allow easy transfer of data among word processing, spreadsheet, data base, planning, and expert system routines.

(b) ROM

Each computer also has a relatively small amount, perhaps 32 kilobytes, of "ROM." This is memory whose contents are permanently written at the factory. It is used to provide the essential control functions needed by almost all programs that run on the computer. Even though ROM is becoming much cheaper, it is unlikely that the amount of ROM used in a typical computer will increase substantially. The problem is one of software maintenance. If the manufacturer discovers a mistake in software in ROM or wishes to upgrade it to provide new features, it is necessary to have a "recall" under which each computer owner brings in his or her computer to have new ROM chips installed. Thus the tendency is for manufacturers to keep the amount of ROM to a minimum and instead to distribute the necessary operating programs on floppy diskettes. When programs are changed or upgraded, the manufacturer merely needs to distribute new floppy diskettes with the improved programs. But ROM-based programs are becoming popular in "briefcase" portable computers, since no program disks and no battery backup power are required.

(c) Hard Disks

A hard disk provides large scale permanent storage, with moderately fast access time. At present, the typical desktop computer has a 20 megabyte hard disk. As with other types of computer storage devices, hard disk capacities are increasing and prices are falling, so that within a few years, 200 megabyte hard disks may become standard on personal computers. The larger hard disks will provide new possibilities and new problems. The possibilities are for maintaining moderate sized data bases on the hard disk. For instance, the client billing records of a fair sized law firm, or the text of depositions taken in a lawsuit can be stored on such a disk. The problems concern finding a way to "back up" the hard disk to protect data in case of damage to the disk. For a 20 megabyte hard disk, the best backup method is a tape cartridge system that can backup or restore all 20 megabytes in a couple of minutes. It may be that the capacity of the inexpensive tape cartridge backup systems will grow with that of hard disks so that by the time 200 megabyte disks are available, 200 megabyte tape systems will be compact and affordable. Alternatively, some new technology, such as the writeable optical disks discussed below, may replace tape for back-up purposes.

(d) Floppy Disks

Floppy disks are an ideal medium for distributing programs to customers or for exchange of data where time pressure is not important. The standard capacity of floppy disks has gradually grown and is now 360 kilobytes. Higher capacity floppy disk drives, for instance 1.2 megabytes, are available, but have not sold well. The main problem is that for the floppy disk to serve its primary function as a distribution medium, there must be standardization, and it is hard to change the present standard of 360 kilobyte disks.

In the early 1980s floppy disks were widely used, not only as a distribution medium, but as a working storage medium. For this purpose, floppy disks are grossly inferior to hard disks, because floppies have a low storage capacity, slow access time, and exposed magnetic surfaces that are easily damaged. With the fall in price of hard disks, the use of floppy disks for working storage will decline rapidly. Users can be expected to transfer programs and data received on floppy disks to hard disks immediately and thereafter keep the floppy disks only as backup copies.

(e) Optical Disks

The most exciting new storage technology is the optical disk. These disks use the same technology as "compact disks" use to store recorded music. Use of optical disks for computer storage is just beginning but should grow rapidly. Optical disks have the great advantage of low cost and huge storage capacity. One disadvantage is that the life of data on optical disks has not been determined and at present is not guaranteed to be greater than five years. It may be necessary to make backup copies of optical disks every few years on new optical disks to preserve the integrity of data, a procedure unnecessary with other forms of archival storage such as books or microfiche.

There are three types of optical disks: read-only, write-once, and read-write. Read-only optical disks have the highest storage capacity and are the cheapest to produce in large quantities. Production of a read-only disk requires preparation of a "master," a process costing several thousand dollars. Additional disks can be mass-produced by the same methods used for mass-production of compact audio disks. If produced in large quantities, manufacturing costs may be below $10 per disk. Read-only disks currently have storage capacities of 500 megabytes to one gigabyte (one gigabyte equals 1024 megabytes). Larger capacities, up to 5 gigabytes, should be available in the next few years. To give an idea of what this capacity means, consider the question of the practicality of putting the West National Reporter System on a few optical disks. There are now approximately 6000 volumes in the National Reporter System. If we make the assumption that the average volume contains 1000 pages and that the average page contains 4000 characters, there are 4,000,000 characters per volume. If a volume of text were recorded directly as data, it would require 4,000,000 bytes of storage. However, relatively straightforward methods of data compression would allow reduction of the necessary storage to 1/3 of the length of the original text, or 1,333,333 bytes of storage. The entire National Reporter System then would occupy 8 gigabytes (6,000 x 1,333,333 = 8,000,000,000) of storage. On a 5 gigabyte optical disk, 2 gigabytes could be used for text from the National Reporter System, another 2 gigabytes could be used for an indexing system similar to that used in WESTLAW, and the remaining gigabyte could be used for error correcting purposes. Four such disks could hold the whole National Reporter System.

Write-once optical disks have a lower storage capacity than read-only disks, with typical capacities now in the 200 megabyte range, with capacities likely to expand to the 1 gigabyte range in the near future. Data can be written to such disks, but cannot be altered once written. This limitation is actually an asset for archival records such as accounting information or court files, where preservation of data integrity is important. The limitation is no particular problem with respect to local data bases, since these usually are augmented but not altered. It is not a particular problem for uses such as backup of large hard disks, provided that the cost of write-once disks falls to the point where they can be used economically for this purpose without being recycled.

Read-write optical disks can be read from and written to many times. These disks are still experimental but are expected to be available soon in capacities up to 1 gigabyte. Read-write optical disks may be an ideal medium for backing up large hard disk storage units.

§ 7-3. HARDWARE FOR FASTER COMPUTATION

Expanding memory to reduce disk accesses can speed up many types of software. However, some software requires large quantities of actual computation. For instance, updating the information in a large spreadsheet may require many thousands of complex mathematical calculations. There are a number of ways in which greater computational speed can be obtained. Users of existing IBM Personal Computers may speed up their calculations in one of three ways. The first is to use a faster clock speed. (All calculation in a computer occurs in synchronization with the computer clock; if clock speed is increased by 50%, calculation speed will be increased by 50%.) One way to do this in some models of computers is to simply replace the clock crystal with a new, faster crystal. This practice is risky and is strongly discouraged by computer manufacturers. The problem is that the other components in a computer built with a slow clock are not rated to perform properly in synchronization with a faster clock speed. Replacing the clock crystal is like putting a Cadillac engine in a Volkswagen Beatle. The result is tremendous speed along with tremendous risk.

A second way is to buy a higher speed computer. For about $700 one can buy a special high-speed board which essentially is a "computer-on-a-board." The board contains a high-speed clock, a high speed microprocessor chip, and high-speed memory. The original computer functions essentially as a terminal and disk controller for the new high-speed computer board. A safe approach is to buy a new computer with a faster clock speed. The IBM PC/AT, for instance, has a clock speed 70% faster than that of the regular IBM PC. The Compaq 386 has double the speed of the PC/AT. The other components of these faster computers are all rated to work properly at this higher speed. Unfortunately, the price of a faster computer is also substantially higher than that of a slower one.

A third way to increase speed is to add a "mathematics processing chip" to the computer. IBM-compatible personal computers come with one processing unit with relatively weak mathematical power, and with an empty socket for a special high-speed mathematics processing chip. By having a dealer install the mathematics chip, a dramatic improvement in spreadsheet recalculation time can be obtained, if the spreadsheet software is smart enough to sense the presence of the mathematics chip in the computer and to make proper use of it.

By 1990, the average desk top computer will use a number of techniques to give it at least three times the speed of today's fastest computers. It will combine a fast clock with components capable of operating at high speed. It will access thirty-two data bits at a time instead of eight data bits at a time as in the original IBM Personal Computer. It will provide additional microprocessors for specialized operations such as screen display management to take this burden off the main computer. It will process several instructions at the same time in a "production line" manner, executing one while simultaneously fetching the data values for another. And it will provide a local, extremely high speed "cache" memory for values and instructions that are accessed frequently.

§ 7-4. SOFTWARE

The next few years should see major advances in software. These changes will involve both the development of improved software and the standardization of formats for information exchange among software packages.

Expert systems that will give lawyers advice on a variety of topics and assemble form legal documents will emerge as a supplement to and sometimes as an alternative to data base systems such as WESTLAW and LEXIS. The LawProcess program accompanying this book is a simplified example of the more powerful expert systems that you will see emerging in the near future. A more advanced version of the ABF system is under development at Illinois Institute of Technology's Chicago-Kent College of Law under the supervision of author Sprowl. A project at Brigham Young University under Professor Larry Farmer's direction has produced an expert system called CAPS that runs on Digital Equipment Corporation VAX minicomputers. At Stanford, law students under the supervision of Professor Paul Brest are developing law-related expert systems using an IBM mainframe computer and PRISM, an IBM expert-system generation program. And LegalWare, a Toronto-based company, is developing such software for Apple's Macintosh and the IBM PC.

In the past, it was common to hire a programmer to write custom programs to meet the particular needs of a given end user. More and more, the trend is toward doing just the opposite: Not hiring the programmer, but instead purchasing a highly flexible computer program that someone on your staff can tailor to your specific needs. Hence, spreadsheet programs such as Lotus 1–2–3 are displacing more and more custom-programmed financial programs, and database programs such as DBase III and R:Base 5000 are displacing more and more programs that used to be "hard" coded in COBOL or some other conventional language. If you or someone on your staff can "tailor" such a program to fit your immediate needs, you can just as easily "retailor" it later on as your needs change. So think twice before you call in a programmer who is not a lawyer, paralegal, or student law clerk and who therefore has to be trained in the operation of your office before he or she can begin work. You will find that it is frequently more difficult to teach a programmer how your office runs than to teach someone who already knows how your office runs to "tailor" a general purpose program to your specific needs.

§ 7–5. NETWORKING: TYING IT ALL TOGETHER

The term "networking" actually covers four distinct topics each of which requires separate treatment. First, it covers reaching out from your desk-side workstation to the outside world—accessing WESTLAW, LEXIS, electronic mail and conferencing services, and the local courthouse. Other chapters have discussed WESTLAW and LEXIS as data bases and have also covered the technical details of telecommunications and error-free document transfer. There remains for this chapter the subject of how to connect the workstations in your office to the external world.

Secondly, "networking" includes reaching out from your desk-side workstation to your office time accounting and billing system, general ledger system, brief and memo data bank, and any other shared multi-user computer system that your office may provide.

Thirdly, "networking" covers sharing data storage devices and printers. How can an attorney gain access to documents stored within a secretarial workstation? And how can several people share a high speed printer?

And finally, "networking" covers the selection of "hardware" to interconnect all the workstations, printers, data storage units, multiuser computers, and telephones in your office, and perhaps even your office copier, into an integrated "network" that gives every one access to everything in every conceivable way. Should the office telephone system serve as the backbone of the office network? Should networking be accomplished through the single shared central computer having a cable leading to each workstation? Or should the office utilize a "local area network"—a single cable threading its way past every workstation? Or should the office rely upon "standalone" workstations and simply transfer information back and forth on floppy diskettes?

This fourth topic, the selection of network hardware, clearly overlaps the first three topics, namely, the uses to which a network may be put. Accordingly, the discussion of networking that follows is organized as a discussion of the various types of networking hardware that are available. Each section focuses upon a different type of hardware and how it may be used to accomplish the three goals of accessing external computers such as WESTLAW and LEXIS, accessing internal computers, and sharing printing and storage resources.

(a) The First Alternative: No Network At All

Twenty years ago, the most expensive component on any computer was the central processing unit or CPU. Most companies could only afford one CPU, and that one CPU had to be shared by everyone. It accepted data from terminals, processed the data, stored it on tape or on spinning magnetic disks, and routed it to high-speed printers. The IBM Corporation still dominates the world of business computers with gigantic CPUs that are connected by cables to thousands of terminals.

As the cost of CPUs began to fall, minicomputers came into widespread use, manufactured by companies such as Digital Equipment and Data General. These minicomputers enabled companies to establish much smaller networks around larger numbers of smaller computers.

Next we saw the development of distributed computing, with a CPU in every workstation. Wang is the leader in this field. By providing each operator with a CPU and providing shared central storage and printing facilities, Wang was able to achieve many times the processing power of centralized computers and a degree of "user friendliness" that centralized computers simply cannot match. And the Wang system does not slow down as more operators begin using their workstations.

Apple, North Star, and IBM next pioneered the concept of the "personal" computer, where every workstation includes its own CPU, data storage facilities, and a printer. Initially limited in power, these personal computers are now rapidly becoming as powerful as the minicomputers that Digital Equipment and Data General have been selling at much higher prices. By the time you graduate from law school, you will be able to purchase a relatively inexpensive personal computer containing a $100 CPU chip that is as powerful as the mainframe computers were twenty years ago. You will also be able to purchase more than enough storage to hold thousands of documents for less than $500, and you will be able to purchase a laser (or other "nonimpact") printer for less than $1,500 that can print "letter quality" copy at the rate of one page every eight seconds. For less than $5,000 per workstation, you will be able to provide everyone in your office with the equivalent of a vintage 1970 mainframe computer, high-speed printer, and storage unit. Add a "modem card" that connects to a second telephone line, and you gain access to WESTLAW, LEXIS, ABA/net electronic mail, and the office time accounting and billing system.

Since the printer is the most expensive unit, you may wish to share the printer with one or two others. By then, most laser printers will come equipped with several plugs that may be connected to several different computers, or you may use a "switch box" to give several computers access to the one printer.

The above system is the "no network" alternative. Since you need not invest in any "networking" hardware, it is quite economical. At the present time, it is less expensive to provide each computer with a "hard disk" storage unit than it is to "network" multiple computers to a shared "dataserver". And the "no network" alternative is highly redundant.

Redundancy is extremely important. When a "mainframe" computer goes "down", the company goes down with it and stays down until the computer is fixed. The same may be said of minicomputers and of Wang's shared data storage and printing facilities. Service contracts for such computers frequently specify the maximum "downtime" that is permissable before the service team arrives on the scene, and law firms demanding "3 hour service" must pay a high price to insure that they will not be shut down for more than half a day. But if every workstation is self-sufficient, then the office can get by with a much less expensive "carry in" service contract and a spare machine in the library.

Accordingly, you should always strive for redundancy. Even the smallest office should always have at least two of everything—two CPU's and two printers. For example, two attorneys with one secretary can provide the secretary with an IBM PC with a hard disk drive, a "daisy wheel" printer for typing "client" letters and envelopes, and a "laser" printer for printing drafts and court papers. A second IBM PC with a hard disk can be set up for time accounting and billing, WESTLAW and LEXIS access, and attorney use (although the attorneys may each want to have their own computers). Then if either computer or printer breaks down, the other can take over, since both are capable of performing all the essential tasks.

The one undesirable feature of the "no network" networking option is the inability to centralize the "backup" function. It is essential always to have multiple copies of all documents stored off the computer. When an office provides centralized storage, as on many Wang systems, one person can back up all the active documents in the office on a single disk pack or tape, and then the individual secretaries do not need to concern themselves with this task. But, of course, when that centralized storage unit is "down", the documents cannot be accessed at all. So there are tradeoffs both ways.

If you pursue the "no networking" alternative, you must train everyone to back up their work. Each important document should be backed up with two floppy disk copies, one in the client file and the other in a separate safe location in case of fire. The secretarial staff should be trained to update one of these floppy copies every hour or so. Word processors should be arranged to maintain at least two copies of any work in progress so that a momentary power surge or "software glitch" that destroys the current copy does not destroy more than ten or fifteen minutes worth of work. And the entire hard disk on each machine should be backed up onto floppy disks or tape at least once every few days—this should be done by someone other than the secretaries, since they will forget to do it. Then there will be plenty of backup copies in case of a disaster.

Notwithstanding your best efforts and intentions, your staff will not take "backing up" seriously until the first great disaster which may not happen for a year or more. Making backup copies is simply a "bother", somewhat akin to wearing seat belts. Maintaining a copy or two in the client file is probably the most painless procedure possible from the secretary's point of view, and it gives the secretary the option to "purge" from the hard disk documents that have been dormant for some time, since there is always a backup copy or two in the client file. Remember: Floppy disks are cheap in comparison to secretarial time, and they should be used generously for backup purposes.

The solution to the backup problem will probably appear in a few years in the form of effective centralized automated backup systems that access local files on work stations. Such systems, which have long been available for mainframe computers, automatically write each file that has been changed onto a backup tape without interfering with the normal operations of the computer. A few automated backup systems have started to appear for microcomputers, but they are not yet satisfactory, because existing microcomputer hardware is not designed to facilitate such operations. Meanwhile, use lots of floppy disks.

(b) The Telephone System as a Network

We have already discussed using the telephone system as a "network" to reach remote computers such as WESTLAW and LEXIS. By simply using a "modem" to connect your computer's "asynchronous serial port" to a telephone line, you make it possible for your computer to contact computers all over the world.

You may use this same option within your office to permit attorneys and others to gain access to your time keeping, accounting, and billing system. If that system normally supports four terminals, you can simply terminate three of the terminal lines with modems that connect to your private branch exchange (PBX). Then any modem-equipped computer or terminal in your office may "dial up" your time keeping, accounting and billing system in the same way that they access an external electronic mail system.

The more modern PBX telephone systems are actually digital computers themselves. These systems use digital signal transmission techniques to send information from telephones to the central unit. More and more of these systems are now designed so they can transmit computer data over the same pair of wires that are used for voice data—and do so without a conventional modem at a much higher rate of speed than the usual "1200 baud" (or 120 characters per second) rate that is commonly used for modems. If your office obtains such a "voice/digital PBX," you may be able to connect your deskside workstation's "asynchronous serial port" directly to your telephone. You may also hook your office's timekeeping, accounting, and billing system's three input lines to the PBX system without the use of any modem. Now any one in the office may gain access to your central accounting system with a much faster screen writing rate than is possible when modems are used.

Such a system also permits you to share modems. A small number of modems hooked to the PBX system may be shared by many workstations around the office. But with Hayes–compatible modems costing less than $200, this is hardly necessary except for special high-speed modems.

The main disadvantage of such PBX-based networks is their slow speed which limits their usefulness for some purposes. The 9600 baud PBX data transfer rate is quite adequate for browsing through shared data bases but is too slow for transferring programs or large data files to and from a central computer. For instance, it would take over six minutes to transfer the contents of a single 360 thousand byte floppy disk to a central computer at this 9600 baud rate.

(c) Local Area Networks (LANs)

A "local area network" providing high-speed data transfer capability is an ideal way to enable multiple workstations to share printing and storage resources. There are several ways in which such networks can be physically wired and several ways in which data can be sent over the physical connections.

The oldest physical wiring arrangement is the "star network" in which a central network coordinating computer is connected by a separate cable to each user work station. This is the system used in the highly successful Wang OIS system. A newer approach is to have a single cable "daisy chain" from workstation to workstation around the office. "Linear" LANs, such as "ETHERNET," use a single cable that can start at one end of the office and terminate at the other end. These cables must be properly terminated, or signals will reflect back and forth and cause considerable trouble. "Circular" LANs, such as IBM's "token ring" network, require the cable ends to come together to form a circular path about which the data circulates in a manner analogous to a traffic circle. If cost is no object, such systems can be wired up to numerous network outlets so that any number of work stations can be plugged in anywhere in a building and immediately have access to shared printers, storage, and telecommunications resources, just as an electric light can be plugged into any electric outlet and immediately turned on and used.

It is tempting to connect the entire office into such a single gigantic LAN. Resist this temptation. It may be sensible to do so in a small office, but LANs work more efficiently when confined to a small group of individuals who logically would wish to share printers and trade documents stored on a common data server. A group of four attorneys and their assistants might share several printers and a data storage hub, for example.

LANs differ in their speed of transmission and in their ability to handle "overload" periods when everyone is calling for service at the same time. You can also greatly improve the performance of a LAN by equipping each workstation with a "hard" disk and by installing frequently-used programs and data files on the workstation disks. Ideally, the workstations should "download" data sets and programs from the LAN's storage unit into the local workstation and then manipulate the data locally, rather than accessing the data frequently and randomly over the LAN. "Diskless" low-cost, low-maintenance workstations are possible with a LAN, but such workstations must use the LAN for all their disk storage and can slow down the LAN by generating too high a volume of data transfer requests.

LANs vary considerably in the speed at which they can transmit data. The slowest use twisted telephone cables, while faster LANs use coaxial cables (where one wire in the cable surrounds and shields the other). The fastest LANs, and the LANs most resistant to interferance, will use light tubes or optical cables and will transmit information using lasers.

A slow LAN transmits data at the rate of about 800,000 bits per second or 80,000 characters per second. Such a LAN can transmit all the data from a full floppy disk into a central storage unit in about 5 to 10 seconds if no one else is using the LAN. But if ten individuals attempt such a transfer simultaneously, then the same transfer may take 50 to 100 seconds.

A fast LAN can transmit 8 million bits per second or 800,000 characters per second. Such LANs can carry out simultaneous transfers for several individuals quite rapidly. But if ten individuals are attempting to retrieve data from the same storage unit simultaneously, a fast LAN may simply shift the bottleneck from the LAN to the data storage unit. Special purpose data storage units can handle multiple simultaneous access requests from multiple users far better than can an ordinary computer that doubles as a network storage unit. And no secretary will enjoy using a computer that is also busy as a network data hub.

The most commonly used networks today are all patterned after Ethernet, a Xerox network standard. Ethernet-style LANs work best with a light load and can "choke" up when too heavily loaded. "Token passing" networks, such as that recently announced by IBM, are able to handle overload conditions in a systematic manner and should be selected in situations where you expect heavy contention for the storage device. But it is best to plan your system so such bottlenecks are unlikely to occur.

A properly-installed local area network does not affect the operation of a personal computer. The storage server simply appears as one or more additional disk drives that behave as if they were local. And the "PRINT" command in programs work as usual, with the material to be printed simply being routed to the remote printer, rather than to the computer's regular printing port.

In practice, present day LANs suffer from two defects. The first relates to marketing schemes for software. Legal restrictions based upon copyright law or license terms often forbid the use of programs on LANs. Even where there are no legal restrictions, copy-protection schemes adopted to prevent software piracy may have the side effect of making LAN use impractical or impossible. Finally, some programs involving shared data bases require major reengineering to work on a LAN, since levels of security must be provided to prevent attempts at simultaneous modification of individual records and to protect the integrity of data bases from unauthorized modification. (For a single-user computer, security can be provided merely by locking the computer and giving only one person the key.) Companies have been slow to adopt their license terms, copy protection schemes, and software to LANs because the LAN market is still small and it is unclear which LAN system or systems will become the industry standard. When a "LAN-ready" version of a program is available, the seller will generally expect the buyer to sign a "site license" agreement and pay a substantially higher fee than for a single-user version of the same program. Thus for some time to come, even when a computer is physically connected to a LAN, much of the software it uses is likely to be stored locally with the computer in a box of floppy disks or on a hard disk.

The second defect in most LANs today is their inability to handle terminal emulation programs. If you wish to access WESTLAW or LEXIS or the office minicomputer, you may still require a modem or a PBX that supports computer communications. And as the LANs begin to support terminal emulation programs, special versions of the programs will probably be required that may not support all the features to which you have become accustomed. Ultimately, LANs will provide excellent support for terminal emulators and communications, but not for a few more years.

Future PBX systems will use optical LANs to connect to both telephones and computers, and this type of product, sold by such companies as A.T. & T., Rolm, and Northern Telecom, may ultimately dominate the networking field in law offices of all sizes.

(d) Central Computer Networks

Wang, DEC, and IBM all market a variety of minicomputer systems that can serve as a network hub, with individual lines extending out to personal computers programmed to function as terminals. The Wang VS system is the most popular in law firms and law schools at present. Wang and Informatics jointly market a time accounting and billing system that runs on Wang's VS minicomputer. The Wang VS system supports both the "asynchronous" communication system commonly used by personal computers and the "synchronous" communication system used by IBM mainframes. However, these options do not yet provide the terminal emulation features needed for most effective use of legal data bases, features readily available on a stand-alone personal computer with a modem card and a telephone line.

IBM sells the System 36, a "vintage" minicomputer designed primarily to be used by small businesses to manage inventory and accounting functions. Its word processing is probably not adequate for use by legal secretaries. IBM and Manac jointly market a time-keeping, accounting, and billing package that runs on the System 36. Due to the limited user base of these systems in law firms, far less 3rd-party software for law offices is available for the System 36 than is available for stand-alone IBM PCs. The System 36 can operate as a remote printer and data storage device for distributed workstations, but conventional LANs may provide these functions more flexibly and economically. Expect to see the next "generation" of IBM PCs (with the new Intel 80386 central processing unit) completely displacing the System 36 as a shared-user central processing unit in law firms, connecting to individual workstations by means of a LAN and running a much larger variety of 3rd party software in such a manner that different users can be running different programs at the same time.

IBM's mainframe computers are used only in a small number of law offices. The 4300 series of IBM minicomputers are somewhat high priced for law firms right now, but this situation could change. The VM operating system for the 4300 series can run CMS, an IBM operating system, and also UNIX, an A.T. & T. operating system that is coming into widespread use by 3rd party software vendors. Stairs, a WESTLAW-like full text retrieval program, and PROFS, an office automation program, are available from IBM in versions that run under CMS.

Digital Equipment Corporation has not been very successful in penetrating the law office marketplace. Their PDP/11 minicomputer has not worked out well as a centralized word processor because it tends to slow down as additional users start using the system. The newer VAX minicomputer is now attractively priced and can serve as a data storage device and shared printer at the head end of a LAN. The VAX can run UNIX as well as DEC's proprietary VMS operating system. Several law schools now have VAXs—Harvard, Arizona, and Brigham Young. Timekeeping, accounting, and billing software is available for the VAX.

Hewlett-Packard minicomputers have been appearing in a surprising number of law firms recently. At least two different firms market law office administrative software for Hewlett-Packard minicomputers.

§ 7–6. NETWORKING: WHERE IS IT HEADED?

We are right in the middle of a transition from centralized computing, where the high cost of central processing units forces most computing to be performed on centralized units, to localized computing, where most processing will be done locally. Look for this trend to continue. Local workstations will continue to increase in power and decrease in price for at least another five years, at which point every workstation will have the power and storage capacity of a 1970 mainframe computer. Some of these PC-compatible workstations will also emerge as tomorrow's "multi-user" systems for performing accounting and billing functions. LANs will migrate towards the improved "token passing" design recently introduced by IBM and will increasingly take over all communications between computers. PBX systems may also migrate into LAN networks that will include both computers and telephones.

In the meantime: Do not network any more than is necessary; use LANs for printer and storage sharing; and use your PBX system to network your "in-house" multi-user administrative computers to your office workstations and to the outside world. And give the "no network" option at least some consideration.

Appendix A

DETAILS OF COMMUNICATION

§ A–1. BRIEF OVERVIEW

It is unfortunate that the industry has "agreed to disagree" about the standards for communication. If in doubt, you should select the following options: No parity; eight data bits; one stop bit; full duplex; no echo; modem sends the command "ATDT1234567<Enter>" (where "1234567" is the telephone number of the destination) to initiate a call; modem set to generate "carrier detect" signal only when an incoming carrier is present; and modem hangs up the telephone when computer's "data terminal ready" signal terminates.

The computer industry has agreed to disagree on the above items, so when setting up a terminal or computer to communicate, you must at some point set the speed, parity, number of data bits, and number of stop bits. On some terminals, you do this by adjusting switches on the back or bottom of the terminal before it is turned on. With personal computers, this information must be fed into the computer's data transmission hardware by the "terminal emulation" program that you use to transform your "general purpose" computer into a "terminal." And at some point, you must feed this information into the "terminal emulation" software. Virtually all such programs can store this information on a disk, so you need to enter it only once. A few programs now come "preprogrammed" for a number of destinations, unfortunately not the ones attorneys customarily use. But WESTLAW and LEXIS terminal emulation software is available. There is a need for more such programs to relieve us from having to concern ourselves with such details. Hopefully LawComm, the legal communications program provided with this book, will handle most of these details for you.

§ A–2. EXAMPLES

Hayes' Smartcom program should be set up so that its "setup" menu appears as follows:

```
                                PARAMETERS
                        Name of Set: MCI Mail
                                                          Press F2 For Help
                    TRANSMISSION PARAMETERS
                           Duplex: FULL                  KEYBOARD DEFINITIONS
                  Connection Type: Bell 1200             Escape Key: 128 (F1)
            Character Processing: FORMATTED                Help Key: 129 (F2)
              Show Control Codes: NO                    Printer Key: 130 (F3)
                      Page Pause: NO                    Capture Key: 131 (F4)
               Show Status Lines: YES              Macro Prefix Key: 132 (F5)
                    Confidential: NO                      Break Key: 133 (F6)
              Include Line Feeds: YES                  Break Length:  35 (0.01 sec.)
                 Character Delay: 0 (0.001 sec.)        Protect Key: 134 (F7)
                      Line Delay: 0 (0.01 sec.)
                Character Format: 8 DATA + NONE + 1 STOP   PROTOCOL PARAMETERS
                        Emulator: TTY               Receive Time-out: 60 (sec.)
                                                       Send Time-out: 10 (sec.)
                                                 Error-Free Protocol:    HAYES
TELEPHONE PARAMETERS                         Stop/Start— Stop Char: 19 (DC3)
Answer On Ring: 1                                         Start Char: 17 (DC1)
Remote Access: NONE      Password:           Send Lines— EOL Char: 10 (LF)
 Phone Number: 1 (800) 000-0000                          Prompt Char: 32 ('' '')
```

Microstuf's Crosstalk XVI should be adjusted so that its "set up" menu appears as follows:

```
                        CROSSTALK — XVI Status Screen
NAme       MCIMAIL ACCESS                                LOaded   A:MCI.XTK
NUmber  1 (800) 000-0000                                 CApture  Off
        Communications parameters                        Filter settings
SPeed 1200   PArity None   DUplex  Full DEbug    Off   LFauto     Off
DAta  8      STop   1      EMulate None TAbex    Off   BLanxex    Off
POrt  1                    MOde    Call INfilter  On   OUtfilter  On
             Key settings                            SEnd control settings
ATen    Esc      COmmand ETX  (| C)                CWait None
SWitch  Home     BReak END                         LWait None
                        Miscellaneous parameters
DRive    A:                ACcept  Everything         PWord
DPrefix  ATDT              DSuffix |                  TUrnaround Enter
PRinter  Off               UConly  Off                ANswerback Off
                           BLsize  1
```

PC–TALK, the shareware communications program distributed by Headlands Press, Inc., P.O. Box 82, Tiburn, CA 94920, should typically be set up as follows:

```
DIALING DIRECTORY 1 ==          Modem dialing command = ATDT
                           Long distance service +# =
                                                 -# =

  Name
1 -MCI Mail               Phone #  Comm Param Echo Msg Strip Pace
2 -(etc)                  0000000  1200-N-8-1  N    N    N    N
```

§ A–3. DETAILED EXPLANATION OF ALTERNATIVES

Recalling Paul Revere and the Old North Church, remember that each ASCII character is represented by seven lanterns hanging in the church tower. When such a character is transmitted from a terminal to a multi-user computer, the character is sent over a single wire. Returning characters flowing to the terminal are transmitted over a second single wire. Imagine a single aerial wire leading from the Old North Church tower down to the ground, with Paul Revere's assistant hanging the seven lanterns onto the wire by their handles and sliding them down to Paul who is waiting on the ground below. The seven lanterns representing each ASCII character are first expanded into sets of ten lanterns each by the addition of an eighth "parity" lantern that causes the total number of "lit" lanterns in each set of eight to be an even (or an odd) number; by the addition of a ninth, darkened "start bit" lantern at the head end of each set of eight lanterns; and by the addition of a tenth, lit, "stop bit" lantern at the tail end of each set. The ten lanterns representing each character are then slid down the aerial wire at a steady rate of speed (1200 lanterns per second, for example—"1200 Baud" means 1200 lanterns per second or 120 keystrokes per second). The groups of lanterns are launched at irregular intervals, and in between groups Paul's assistant slides lit lanterns down the line continuously to keep it full of lanterns. Only instead of sending lighted and darkened lanterns down the line, we send negative and positive voltages over a first line that leads from a terminal to a multi-user computer and over a second line that leads back from the computer to the terminal. The modems simply translate these fluctuating voltage signals into fluctuating tone signals suitable for telephone transmission.

(a) Speed or Baud Rate

How fast is the information to be transmitted? The speed of transmission is measured in "lanterns per second" or "potential communications channel fluctuations per second" or "baud," with this unit honoring Jean M.E. Baudot who invented the first practical multiple-signal telegraph and the "five-lantern-per-character" Baudot code that is still widely used internationally. The possibilities are as follows:

300 baud:	Slow but reliable—good for noisy telephone lines. Well standardized. Available as an optional speed on most 1200 baud modems.
1200 baud:	The standard today. Acceptable with a good connection. Well standardized. Modems reasonably priced ($200).
2400 baud:	A new standard—far faster. Fairly well standardized. Modems more expensive ($400). Error detection and correction advisable.
Higher speeds:	Possible on leased lines. Coming soon on ordinary telephone lines.

For the time being, 1200 baud is probably the speed of choice for most purposes.

(b) Eighth Data Bit Or Parity Bit

What about the eighth data bit? The sender and receiver must agree on one of the following:

- It is to be ignored by the receiver. So the sender can send whatever he or she wishes. Most central computers ignore the eighth data bit.
- Both parties agree to adopt "even" parity, such that the sum of the "1" data bits is an even number.
- Both parties agree to adopt "odd" parity, such that the sum of the "1" data bits is an odd number.
- An eighth (parity) bit is sent, but it is always "1" or "mark." This is sometimes called "mark parity."
- An eighth (parity) bit is sent, but it is always "0" or "space." This is sometimes called "space parity."
- Eight data bits are sent, and there is no parity. The parties have agreed in advance on what each of the possible 256 messages will mean.
- The eighth bit is not sent at all (this is unusual, but speeds up communications slightly).

"Even parity" is probably the most common choice for the sender; ignoring the parity bit is probably the most common choice for the receiver.

(c) Stop Bit

The number of "stop bits," which are lighted lanterns that are appended to the end of each message, is normally set to "one stop bit."

(d) "Echo" versus "No Echo" or "Full/Half Duplex"

Dumb terminals operate either in "echo" or "no echo" mode. The term "full duplex," which used to mean "two-way communication," now means "no echo;" and "half duplex" now means "echo." This is an area where your terminal and the central computer must agree. If you see double when you type, then turn off your terminal's "echo" feature. If you see nothing when you type but the central computer responds properly to your invisible commands, then turn on your terminal's "echo" feature. The standard today is "no echo," but some services, most notably Lawyers Cooperative's AUTOCITE legal citation checking service, require the "echo" feature in your terminal to be operative.

(e) XON/XOFF

Note that "XOFF," "<Control-S>," and "DC3" are three different names for the ASCII "stop sending!" command; and "XON," "<Control-Q>," and "DC1" are likewise three different names for the ASCII "commence sending!" command. These are the "flow control" commands that you, your terminal, and the central computer can use to start and stop the flow of information from the other end of the communications link. Whatever this feature is called, you should turn it "on." You can stop incoming information from scrolling off your display by holding down the <Control> shift key and striking "S", and you can start the scrolling again by holding down the <Control> shift key and striking "Q".

(f) Wrap at the End of Lines

One other feature of virtually all terminals is the "do/do not wrap at the end of line" feature. When a character is written into the rightmost column on your screen, most terminals move the cursor down one line and all the way to the left. This is called "wrapping." But some mainframe computers do not expect the terminal to do this, and the result is double spacing. To cure this problem, simply turn off the "wrap" feature of your terminal. But then other remote computers, on the assumption that you are wrapping, send you an entire screenful of characters with no "<Enters>" between the lines (LEXIS VT-100 service does this, among others). The result is a single line on your screen, with all the transmitted characters piling up on top of the rightmost character of this one line. In that case, you must turn the "wrap" feature back on.

(g) Connecting the Terminal/Computer to the Modem

An industry-standard set of plugs and cables are used to connect your terminal to your modem. So no problem can arise here. Right?

Wrong. The Electronic Industry Association RS-232c standard does specify what size plug to use and what each wire does, but it does not require everyone to use all of the 25 wires in the plug. For our purposes, we only need wires 1 through 8 and 20, so you can save money by purchasing 9-wire modem cables. But some cables have fewer than 9 wires—beware! Also, there is a possible plug "sex" problem. Gradually, a standard is emerging that the modem should have a "female" socket and the computer or terminal a "male" plug. So a "male" to "female" cable is required. But this is far from a universal standard, and your computer or terminal may have a "female" socket.

Now that you have the proper cable, you must set your terminal or computer and your modem so that they agree on how all those wires are to be used.

Nine wires—two "grounded wires" connecting the chassis of the computer to that of the modem; one for carrying data to the modem; one for carrying data back to the computer; and five more to cause you endless problems, because there are no standards for their use.

"Data Terminal Ready" and "Request to Send" Signals

These signals say, "Modem, I'm ready for some input. Send away." Conversely, absence of these signals mean, "I'm not ready for input, please do not send any." Question: Should the modem ignore the absence of this signal and send the information anyway? Or should the modem "hang up" the telephone when the terminal says it is "not ready?" Does the terminal or computer really generate these signals?

"Clear to Send," "Data Set (or Modem) Ready," and "Carrier Detect" Signals

These signals mean, "Terminal, I'm ready for output. I am connected via the telephone system to the destination, and all systems are 'go.' Send away." Question: Will the terminal or computer refuse to send information to the modem if one or more of these signals are not present? So should you set the modem so these signals are always present? But if you do that, some "terminal emulation" software may refuse to dial because the software thinks the connection is already established.

Here, the problem is that signals are present that enable the computer and modem to act as a closely-integrated unit, with the computer or terminal knowing instantly when the remote computer answers the telephone, and with the computer able to make the modem hang up the telephone at will. But if either the terminal or the modem is not "smart" enough to take advantage of all this integration, then the other partner must be adjusted to also act "dumb."

The answer here is to obtain a quality, auto-dial and auto-answer modem, and use a personal computer with the best "terminal emulation" software that you can find as your terminal. Then adjust the computer and the modem to generate and respond to all the signals. Inexpensive modems and terminals and low-quality software are simply not worth the aggravations that they will cause you, even in the short run.

With personal computers, you can purchase "card modems" that plug into a slot within the computer. These will give way to "modem chips" built into the computer itself over the next few years. Unfortunately, even though you cannot see the five signal leads in these two cases, the "signals" are still present within the card or chip, and you will still have to inform the computer's "emulation program" and the modem's internal logic how these signals are to be handled.

Finally—the speed, parity, and stop bits are set; the modem and the terminal are interacting properly. Are we done? Unfortunately, no. We have just begun to communicate. Now the real problems begin.

(h) Commanding the Modem to Dial

Now your computer or terminal must command the modem to dial up your destination.

Dialing used to be done manually When your computer or terminal was ready, you dialed up the remote computer. When it answered with a "tone" signal, you placed the telephone cradle into the "modem." These "acoustic" modems ran at the slow data rate of 300 baud (or about 30 typewritten characters per second). While still convenient for travelers who must set up shop in hotels having "hard-to-steal" telephones with permanently-installed cables, these acoustic systems are rapidly disappearing.

Most modems today come equipped with standard telephone jacks so they may be plugged directly into the telephone system. Offices having "multi-button" telephones may purchase from Radio Shack an adapter that permits them to connect a modem to such a telephone system. But preferably you should provide your computer with its own dedicated telephone line and number. No matter how carefully designed, telephone lines that pass through your "Private Branch Exchange" system are always more prone to static and interference than are outside lines. Our experience has demonstrated that even Centrex lines are significantly more noisy than dedicated lines. But specially-conditioned "data lines" do not appear to give much benefit.

The simplest of "direct connect" modems still require you to do your own dialing, and then throw a switch on the modem when the remote computer answers. These systems are satisfactory if you communicate only rarely and do not communicate regularly to the same destinations. But much better modems can be obtained today that can dial with either pulses or tones, "hang up" on command, and "auto answer" incoming calls.

We have no formal standard for modem control commands, and for a time every modem manufacturer adopted their own conventions. But this chaotic situation could not have endured for long. The companies offering "terminal emulation" software needed at least a "de facto" standard to guide them in designing their programs. Ultimately, the commands used in the "Smartmodem 1200" (Hayes Microcomputer Products, Inc.) were adopted by virtually all the other modem manufacturers as the industry-wide standard modem control commands.

Briefly summarized, the Hayes commands are short ASCII-character messages that the computer (or the operator, in the case of a terminal) sends to the modem over the same wire that will later be used to send information to the remote computer. These commands instruct the modem to dial a certain telephone number. The modem then takes the telephone "off hook," generates dial tones or pulses, and waits for the remote computer to answer. Once the remote computer answers, the modem opens the communications channel and takes itself almost entirely out of the picture. To "wake up" the modem and to order it to hang up the telephone, the computer must terminate its "Data Terminal Ready" signal. But some computers and terminals are incapable of controlling this signal, so a series of three plus signs "+++" preceded and followed by several seconds of no transmission, can be used to "wake up" the modem which can then be commanded to "hang up" the telephone.

All Hayes commands must begin with the capitalized letters "AT" (for "attention") and end with a carriage return. The most important commands are the following:

1. "Tone" dial the number 312 567 6800: AT DT 312 567 6800<Enter>
2. "Tone" dial the number 9 312 567 6800 with a pause after the initial 9: AT DT 9, 312 567 6800<Enter>
3. "Pulse" dial the number 312 567 6800: AT DP 312 567 6800<Enter>
4. Modem "wake up" command: [1 second of silence] +++[1 second of silence]
5. "Hang up" command (following "+++"): AT H<Enter>
6. Do not answer incoming calls: AT S0=0<Enter>

You may type these commands youself. But most "terminal emulation" programs will permit you to store these commands in a directory on your diskette, with one entry for each different number that you frequently dial. Then you can have your computer display your personal "directory" of destinations as an "on-screen" menu, and you can pick out the one you wish to contact and command the computer to "auto-dial" it for you. You can even use your computer as a substitute for a card file of telephone numbers. but in that case, you type a semicolon ";" at the end of the Hayes' dialing command to keep the modem from interfering with voice communication.

(i) Special Problems With "Block Mode" Terminals

If you frequently use both WESTLAW and LEXIS, you may wish to obtain an "IBM 3101 Terminal Emulation (block mode)" software package for your personal computer so that you can access both services in a uniform manner from the same program, with features like "downloading" working the same way for both services. IBM 3101 Terminal emulaton programs abound, but very few of them can duplicate the special "block mode" performance required for both WESTLAW and LEXIS. LEXIS requires a "transmit message" feature to be included. So far, only IBM's 3101 Terminal Emulation Program comes close to satisfying the needs of both WESTLAW and LEXIS, and it lacks the "transmit message" function at present.

Look for Microstuf and Direct Aid to bring out block mode IBM 3101 emulators that will be suitable for use with both WESTLAW and LEXIS in the near future. LawComm also provides a satisfactory "block mode" 3101 emulation that works acceptably with all aspects of WESTLAW and LEXIS except for some of the WESTLAW tutorials which require a fuller emulation than LawComm provides.

Appendix B

HANDSHAKE PROTOCOLS FOR TELENET, TYMNET, AND DATAPAC

§ B–1. INTRODUCTION

The following handshaking protocols have been tested out and found to be satisfactory for use in reaching "ABA/net," the American Bar Association's electronic mail service. These same protocols may be used to reach other destinations by simply substituting the address of the desired destination for ABA/net's address in the examples. You begin these handshakes after the packet switching service responds to your telephone call. Preferably, you set up your personal computer to automatically perform these handshakes:

§ B–2. ACCESS TO ABA/NET

(a) Telenet Access to ABA/Net

After a one-second delay, send three <Enter> keystrokes to Telenet, spaced one-half second apart. Then wait for Telenet to send you a "@" character. After another half second delay, send Telenet the address of "ABA/net," which is "C 201 444<Enter>."

(b) Tymnet Access to ABA/Net

Tymnet will begin the handshake by sending you a message: "please type your terminal identifier." Unfortunately, this message is sent at 300 Baud, and it will appear as garbage characters on your screen, since you are set for 1200 Baud. Do nothing before this message has finished coming in, which takes seven full seconds. Then send Tymnet the lower-case letter "a" with no <Enter>. Wait to receive a colon ":" prompt back from Tymnet. Wait one-half second more, and then send Tymnet the address of ABA/net, which is "DIALWH;44<Enter>."

(c) Datapac Access to ABA/Net

This is for Canadians. The sequence is somewhat more complicated than the above sequences, since Datapac accesses ABA/net indirectly through Telenet, rather than directly. Wait at least one second, and then transmit to Datapac the message "..<Enter>." Wait for Datapac to send you a colon ":" prompt which will be embedded in the middle of a short message. Wait one-and-one-half seconds more, and then send Datapac a double address that includes the Datapac address of the Telenet tie line plus the Telenet address of ABA/net, as follows: "1 3110 20100444<Enter>."

Appendix C

DOCUMENT TRANSMISSION USING ABA/NET ELECTRONIC MAIL SERVICE[1]

§ C–1. INTRODUCTION

Many attorneys use the American Bar Association's "ABA/net" electronic mail service regularly to send short letters to their colleagues. They call up ABA/net, type in their letter, and type ".SEND<Enter>" to send it on its way. All fine and good if the letter is short and does not need correcting or proofreading. But if the "letter" is a 3-page letter, a contract, or a section of a brief, then one should draft it using a word processor and then arrange for a personal computer to send it to ABA/net. This process is called "uploading," and the process of receiving such a letter, contract, or brief and transferring it from ABA/net onto a floppy diskette is called "downloading."

If a personal computer is equipped with a "modem" or "modem card" that connects it to an outside telephone line, then a computer program can be purchased that can "upload" and "download" electronic mail, transferring it directly between ABA/net and the computer's floppy disks. For "error free" document transfer, and to send and receive word processing documents and computer programs, the sender must obtain a program that supports Ward Christiansen's Xmodem document transfer protocol, and the receiver must have a similar program. The newer, faster Ymodem protocol may also be used at either end.

The two sections that follow explain how one goes about "uploading" the documents one wishes to send and how one goes about "downloading" the documents one wishes to receive. If you wish to transmit word processing documents without stripping out the special codes so they may be further processed on the same brand of word

1. This material was first published by author Sprowl in the Vol. 2, No. 1 issue of the "PC Newsletter" of the American Bar Association's Economic Section's IBM–PC and CP/M User's Group (Winter 1986).

processor by the recipient, if you wish to send a computer program by "e-mail," or if you wish guaranteed "error-free" delivery, then you must procure the Xmodem program and use ABA/net's FT utility which is described in the first section that follows. But if you simply wish to prepare several electronic letters on your computer and then "upload" them into ABA/net, and if error-free transmission is not essential, then you can get by without an Xmodem program by following the instructions contained in the second section of this appendix which explains how to use ABA/net's simpler PCMAIL facility.

§ C–2. FT—SENDING WORD PROCESSING DOCUMENTS AND COMPUTER PROGRAMS IN AN ERROR-FREE MANNER

The ABA/net FT utility permits you to transmit documents and programs without errors. Because FT preserves all embedded word processor formating codes (including those that control underlining and centering), it enables you to send a brief or contract to another office whose word processor is "compatible" with your word processor without you having to strip out the formating codes prior to "uploading." You may also send computer programs, data, and anything else that can be stored as a file on a computer's disk drive. Error-free transmission is assured by the Xmodem protocol which is built into FT, but your communications program must also support the Xmodem protocol. Look under "Xmodem" in the index of the manual for the communications program supplied with your modem.

(a) Connecting to ABA/Net

Start up your communications program and instruct it to dial up the local number of Telenet, Tymnet, or Dialnet.

You will now hear the dial tone, the dialing touch-tones (or dial pulses), and the familiar ringing sound from your modem. If all goes well, a steady tone will indicate that the remote computer has answered, and then silence.

Next, log into ABA/net:

With Telenet, type "<Enter><Enter><Enter>C 201444<Enter>";

With Tymnet, type "adialwh;44<Enter>"; and

With Dialnet, type "<Enter>c 44<Enter>".

ABA/net next asks you to, "Please sign on >". In response, you type "ABA999 PASSWORD<Enter>", substituting your ABA number for "ABA999" and your password for the word "PASSWORD". Next, the ABA/net main menu will appear. If it does not appear, type "ABA<Enter>" to bring it up.

(b) "Uploading" Documents and Programs Into ABA/Net

Assume that you wish to send a word processing document whose file name is "contract.doc" to author Sprowl. Assume the file is on a floppy disk that you have inserted into drive b: of your computer. You have completed the above steps and are looking at ABA/net's main menu.

Select item 2 "Electronic Communication Services" on the main menu by typing "2<Enter>". This will bring up the "ELECTRONIC COMMUNICATIONS SERVICES" menu. Select item 6 "File Transfer (FT)" by typing "6<Enter>".

The FT program now comes to life and asks you a series of questions. Answer as follows: "6<Enter>" (this identifies your program as PC–Talk; if you use some other program, type its number, or type "6<Enter>" to select the general Xmodem protocol for any program); "U<Enter>" (for "uploading" documents into ABA/net); "e<Enter>" (to have your document stored in "hex" notation—essential if it is to be sent by electronic mail); "contract.doc <Enter>" (the name of the file you wish to send); and "<Enter>" (to start the file transfer process). If you are asked the question "Single or batch file protocol (S,B)?" answer by typing "S<Enter>". If you are asked the question, "Are you using CRC (C) or Checksum (K) error detection (C,K)?", if you don't know, type "K<Enter>" to get the most common Xmodem checksum error detection protocol. But if your communications program does support CRC (which means "cyclic redundancy check"), select CRC, since it is a much better error-checking protocol than the Xmodem simple checksum.

FT is now ready to receive your document. You must now follow the instructions that come with your communications program that initiate the sending of a document under the Xmodem error-free protocol.

You have now transferred the document into ABA/net, and it is stored in your account under the file name "contract.doc". Next, you must mail the document to author Sprowl using the electronic mail facility.

The ELECTRONIC COMMUNICATION SERVICES menu will reappear. Now select item 2, "Electronic Mail (MAIL)" by typing "2<Enter>". The mail system asks whether you wish to "Send, Read, or Scan:" You type "send sprowl.j<Enter>" (or type whatever address you wish to send the document to). You are next prompted with "Subject:" At this point, you should type something that will warn the recipient of the fact that this is a document transfer, and not a normal electronic letter. State the name of the file and what type of file it is, and mention that FT must be used to download it. For example, you might type: "Use FT to download WordPerfect file contract.doc<Enter>". In addition, send the recipient a regular electronic letter explaining what you are doing and explaining precisely what is happening.

The system next prompts you to provide "Text:" At this point, instead of typing in a letter as you usually do, type ".Load contract.doc<Enter>" and on the next line type ".SEND<Enter>."

Your document or program is now safely resting in author Sprowl's mailbox, ready to be "downloaded" into his computer.

(c) "Downloading" Documents and Programs From ABA/Net

Now pretend that you are author Sprowl, and you wish to download the above document into your computer. You have logged into ABA/net, and the main ABA/net menu is on your screen.

Select item 2 "Electronic Communication Services" on the menu by typing "2<Enter>". This will bring up the "ELECTRONIC COMMUNICATIONS SERVICES" menu. Now select item 2, "Electronic Mail (MAIL)" by typing "2<Enter>". The mail system asks whether you wish to "Send, Read, or Scan:" You type "READ" as you usually do. Next you come across an e-mail item whose subject line reads as follows: "Use FT to download WordPerfect file CONTRACT.DOC". Hopefully, this item was preceded by one that explained precisely what this item is, so that you are not entirely caught by surprise.

At this point, the prompt "—More—" appears upon your screen. There is no point in viewing this document, since it contains unreadable "hexadecimal digit pairs" and is not intended for human eyes.

At this point, type "save text contract.doc<Enter>". This command saves the document and prepares it for downloading. The word ". . . text . . . " in this command causes only the document text to be saved—the name of the sender and the subject line are discarded. If you mistakenly strike <Enter> and display the document, you can still type the "save text contract.doc <Enter>" command at any "—More—" prompt or at the "Disposition:" prompt. After you have saved the document, type "d<Enter>" at the final "Disposition:" prompt to remove the document from your mailbox (but you may want to leave a copy in your mailbox for a time until you are sure that you have successfully completed the downloading).

When you are through reading your mail, the ELECTRONIC COMMUNICATION SERVICES menu will reappear. Select item 6 "File Transfer (FT)" by typing "6<Enter>".

The FT program now comes to life and asks you a series of questions. Answer as follows: "6<Enter>" to select the general Xmodem protocol for any program; "d<Enter>" (for "downloading" documents from ABA/net); "contract.doc<Enter>" (the name of the document to be downloaded); and "<Enter>" (to start the data transfer process). If you are asked the question "Single or batch file protocol (S,B)?" answer by typing "s<Enter>". FT is now ready to send you the document.

If you plan to store the document on a floppy disk, insert the disk into drive b:. Now start the data transfer, following the Xmodem instructions for your communications program.

You have now transferred the document out of ABA/net and onto your diskette. It is stored under the name contract.doc.

While the Xmodem–FT method of downloading does preserve word processing documents and programs intact, it has one undesirable side effect that may cause you some difficulty: It lengthens your documents so that they each contain an even multiple of 128 keystrokes (or "bytes"). It does this by adding anywhere from zero to 127 NUL characters to the end of every document transmitted. NUL characters are sometimes referred to as ZERO characters or ^@s or <Ctrl—@> characters. So if you see a bunch of ^@ symbols at the very end of your contract or brief, simply delete them and do not mistakenly assume that your document was damaged in transit.

(d) Deleting Temporary ABA/Net Files

A temporary file is created both during the uploading and the downloading process. The name of this file is the same as the name of the file that you are transmitting. In the above example, where the file "contract.doc" was transferred, the sender and the receiver each created a temporary file named "contract.doc" which remains on their accounts after the transfer is completed. This file must be deleted, or ABA/net will charge for its continued storage. So both the sender and the receiver must do the following:

Starting at the main ABA/net menu, select item 11, "Command Level" by typing "11<Enter>". Next type "del contract.doc<Enter>" to delete the temporary file. To reenter the menu system, type "ABA<Enter>".

To see if you have any temporary files on your account, go to the "Command Level" as just explained and type "f<Enter>". To see what is in such a file, type "ty contract.doc<Enter>", for example.

§ C–3. PCMAIL—DRAFTING ELECTRONIC MAIL ON YOUR PC AND "UPLOADING" IT IN BULK

(a) Using PCMAIL

The above "error-free" method of transferring documents is not always needed, and it is more difficult than the method that will be described here. Also, the technique just described, which enables one to send programs and word processing documents without any risk that they may be altered, cannot be used to "upload" batches of ordinary electronic mail that may be viewed by the recipient in the usual manner. To draft electronic mail on your personal computer and "upload" it in bulk into ABA/net, you must use the PCMAIL program described here.

You must draft your documents in such a manner that they are free from all embedded commands, such as word processor italic, bold, and centering commands. Also, every line must be terminated by a carriage return. Most word processing documents are not suited for direct uploading into ABA/net in their usual form, but virtually all word processors include some mechanism for stripping control codes from a document and for adding carriage returns to the end of each line. With some word processors, you instruct the word processor to write out a "pure ASCII" file. With others, you enter the "line" editing mode which does not support "word wrapping." With yet others, you instruct the word processor to prepare the document for printing on a "dumb" or "TTY" or "TELETYPE" printer, but you direct the printer output into a file, rather than sending it to a real printer. You may have to call your word processing vendor to learn how this can be done with your program. Your LawComm program automatically adds carriage returns at the ends of lines and clears out any unacceptable control codes that it detects.

If your word processor has difficulty generating documents that are suitable for electronic mail use, you can use the LawWord program provided with this book. So long as you do not use italics or bold or other fancy fonts, the documents produced by LawWord are suitable for use with ABA/net. And since the attorney you are sending to is likely to have a word processor compatible with LawWord (or WordStar), it is an excellent choice if you know ahead of time that you will have to transmit drafts back and forth by E-mail.

The PCMAIL utility in ABA/net ties directly into the ABA/net mail system. A single document you upload into PCMAIL may therefore contain numerous letters and documents each addressed to a different set of recipients. Each letter or document you send must begin with a line containing: the word "MAIL;" the ABA/net address of the recipient; and the letters "SU" followed by the subject matter of the letter. Each letter or document must end with a line containing ".SEND". Then the entire document must end with a single line containing ".END" and nothing else. For example:

```
MAIL SPROWL.J CC ZOARS.TSU Upldg/Downldg

   Jim and Tony, I really enjoyed the latest
issue of the PC Newsletter—particularly the
explanation of PCMAIL, which I did not know
existed until I read your description of it.  If
this letter reaches you, then you will know that
I have figured out how to use it with Word
Perfect.

   I drafted this letter using WordPerfect, an
excellent word processing program.  Normal
WordPerfect documents are unacceptable to ABA/
net.  I tried uploading one using PCMAIL, and it
drove ABA/net into some kind of a comatose state
from which it never recovered until I put it out
```

```
of its misery by turning off the computer!  I
finally called SSI Software, and they explained
that I needed to type a carriage return at the
end of every line and use their special "Text In/
Out" feature to read and write ABA/net files.  I
now write out ABA/net documents by typing "<Ctrl
F5>" and "1" and a file name.  I read them in by
typing "<Ctrl F5>" and "2" and a file name.
This was not at all obvious from the manual
. . . . [on and on, etc., etc.] . . . .
   Please consider the above for inclusion in
your next issue.  I think others can benefit from
my misfortunes.

                              Cordially,

                              Sam W. Solicitor
(ABA/net address:  SOLICITOR.S or ABA000)
.SEND
.END
```

[Tony Zoars is the ABA/net technical advisor at the American Bar Association. You may contact Tony by e-mail if you have any technical questions about ABA/net.]

Since your computer can send text faster than ABA/net can sometimes receive it, you should adjust your file sending program either to pause (for a second or so) after sending each line or, if your program permits, to stop sending whenever ABA/net sends your computer a "<Ctrl–S>" (or "XOFF" or "DC3") control signal and to start sending again when your computer receives a "<Ctrl–Q>" (or "XON" or "DC1") control signal from ABA/net. Otherwise, some of your text may be lost.

To use the PCMAIL feature, enter ABA/net in the usual way. If the main menu does not appear, type "ABA<Enter>" to bring it up.

Starting at the main menu, select option 2, "Electronic Communication Services," by typing "2<Enter>". On the ELECTRONIC COMMUNICATION SERVICES menu, select option 4, "Mail from a Personal Computer or Word Processor (PCMAIL)" by typing "4<Enter>".

You are now under the control of the PCMAIL program. After displaying some very brief instructions, your computer screen will seem to go dead. From now until the end of the PCMAIL session, NOTHING will appear upon your screen! Don't panic. Your information is going out, but the central computer is not echoing it back to your screen the way it normally does when you strike a key.

It is now time for you to "upload" your mail. You must follow the instructions that come with your "upload/download" program at this point. Be patient! The transfer may take between 15 and 30 seconds for each double-spaced, letter-sized page. The red disk drive light will stop winking when the transfer is finished.

Next, if you still see nothing on the screen, hold down the <Ctrl> key and strike the "Q" key.

(b) Expert Options With PCMAIL

Several optional features of PCMAIL may be actuated by entering the PCMAIL program at ABA/net's "Command Level" (option 11 on the main ABA/net menu), rather than from the menu system. Start the program by typing:

PCMAIL –OPTION1 –OPTION2 . . . <Enter> where "–OPTION1 –OPTION2 . . . " are words selected from the following words (you must type a leading hyphen in front of these words):

"–SYNC" This word causes PCMAIL to transmit a "<Ctrl–Q>" (or "XON" or "DC1") control signal to your computer when ABA/net is ready to receive the next line. If you can adjust your "uploading" program to wait for a "<Ctrl–Q>" before sending each line, this option may be faster than providing a fixed delay at the end of each line. But if your uploading program stops and starts in response to "<Ctrl–S>" (or "XOFF" or "DC3") and "<Ctrl–Q>" ("XON" or "DC1"), as most such programs do, this option and the delay are both unnecessary.

"–NOBREAK" This word inhibits ABA/net from turning off the PCMAIL program when a BREAK command or a "<Ctrl–P>" (or "DLE") control signal is received. I do not see any reason why you would ever want to do this.

"–END $$$$" This word permits "$$$" (or whatever code you choose) to be used instead of ".END" to terminate your document. Useful if ".E" is one of your word processor's formatting commands. Users of the old WordStar may need this option.

If you need more assistance, contact Dialcom at: (301) 588–1572.

Appendix D

THE LawWord WORD PROCESSOR

§ D–1. INTRODUCTION

This Appendix is written on the assumption that you have already read Chapter 3 on Word Processing. The Appendix indicates how the word processor functions described in Chapter 3 are incorporated in LawWord, the word processor distributed with this book.

LawWord offers two entirely different methods for entering user commands. One method is based on menus that appear on the screen. This method is extremely simple for the beginner, but somewhat slow and thus frustrating for persons experienced in word processing. The other requires the memorization of a large number of exotic commands. In return it offers great speed to the experienced user. The discussion that follows is aimed mainly at the beginning user. However for the benefit of the would-be expert user, the short command equivalent of each of the menu commands is indicated.

§ D–2. GETTING STARTED

(a) Making a Working Copy of LawWord

The easiest way to make a working copy of LawWord is to find a fellow student who already has a copy and who knows how to use the DOS Diskcopy command. Give the student a blank diskette and ask the student to help you make a working copy. Alternatively, if your law library or law computer center has a working copy of LawWord on reserve, borrow it. If your computer has two floppy diskette drives, put the working copy in Drive a: (usually on the left) and a blank diskette in Drive b. Then type:

diskcopy a: b: <Enter>

When Drive a: stops whirring and a message appears on the screen, strike <Enter> again. In a few moments you will have your own working copy on Drive b:.

If you cannot get a working copy from a fellow student or the law library, you have to follow a somewhat more complex process. First, place a copy of DOS (which you undoubtedly will be able to obtain from your law library or law computer center) in drive a: and turn on the computer. Answer the date and time questions that will appear on the screen. Next, place the law system disk in drive a: and type:

```
install <Enter>.
```

Follow the instructions that appear on the screen.

You may wish to make several copies of LawWord—one for each project, so that you do not overfill your disk. Each copy of your LawWord disk can hold about 50 double-spaced pages of text (assuming an original plus a "backup" copy of each document—actually 200,000 bytes of storage space).

You should also prepare some separate data diskettes for use in larger projects and for use as extra "backup diskettes". To prepare the data diskettes, start your computer as described above. Leaving your DOS diskette in drive a: type.

```
format b:<Enter>
```

The computer will then prompt you through the process of inserting your new data and backup diskettes into drive b: so they can be "formated" or prepared to receive data. WARNING: This formating process erases everything from the disk. It also marks any "bad" places on the disk. You might consider discarding any disks that contains "bad" sectors, since they can only get worse.

In the discussion that follows, the term "file" means a text file stored on your diskette that contains a "document." The term "document" is also used when discussing document text stored within the computer's RAM memory that you are creating and/or revising, and not at that moment stored on your diskette. The context will indicate which meaning is intended.

(b) Running LawWord

To run LawWord, you will need your working copy and a second formated diskette for backup purposes. Periodically, save a copy of your work on the backup disk in drive b: so that your work will survive if someone drops a magnetic screwdriver on your working copy of LawWord.

To start LawWord, put the working copy of LawWord in Drive a: and your backup diskette in Drive b:. Turn on the computer. If all goes well, you will, see the following display on the screen:

```
LawWord
                                              Release 1.00
                               For IBM PC & 100% Compatibles

Software by Peter B. Maggs, Copyright © 1986 West Publishing Co.
Incorporates, with permission, software Copyright © 1984, 85 BOR-
LAND, Inc.

Open File:
```

Type:

a:myfile <Enter>

Here, you type the disk drive letter (plus a colon) of the drive where you wish to have the document stored plus a name (8 letters and/or digits maximum) for the document. Normally, you type "a:name," where "name" is the name of the file you want to edit, to select drive a: which contains your working copy of LawWord. Typing "b:name" selects your backup diskette.

As soon as you strike <Enter>, you will see the following screen display:

```
File:  A:MYFILE
                                                  IN  Line:    1 Col:    1
Block Search Go to Text format Window File            F10 for pulldown menu
```

(c) Editing a Document

Now you are ready to edit the document in RAM memory. Type a few sentences. Experiment with using the arrow keys to move the cursor, and with <Backspace> and <Del> to erase mistakes.

Note that you cannot move the "cursor" below the bottom line of your document. To extend your document, position the cursor at the very end of the last line, and type in some more text.

(d) Saving a Document

Now you should leave LawWord, but first save your document as a file on your diskette. Strike F10, strike <Right Arrow> five times so that "File" is highlighted, and strike <Enter>. The top of the screen will then look like this:

```
File:  A:MYFILE                                          IN   Line:     1  Col:     1
Block Search Go to Text format Window File                      ESC to exit menu
                                         Open
                                         Close
                                         Save
                                         save As
                                         Directory
                                         Logged dir
                                         Print
                                         copY
                                         Rename
                                         Erase
                                         Quit
```

To save your document as a file and quit LawWord, strike the down arrow ten times and strike <Enter> to select the "Quit" option. The computer will ask:

```
Save Changes (Y/N)?
```

Strike <Y>.

WARNING: If you simply "turn off" your computer without formally saving your document as a file, the RAM memory copy of your document will be lost forever.

§ D-3. CURSOR MOVEMENT COMMANDS

The cursor is a small, flashing light on the screen. When text is typed, it goes into the document at the point indicated by the cursor. LawWord automatically adjusts the text window so that the cursor is always visible on the screen. The great advantage of a word processor over an ordinary typewriter is that text can be entered anywhere in a document. In order to do so, it must be possible to move the cursor easily to any point in the document. There are a number of commands to assist in moving the cursor.

The most elementary cursor movement is up or down by a single row or left or right by a single column. To move the cursor up, just strike the up arrow at the right of the keyboard; to move the cursor down, just strike the down arrow; to move left, strike the left arrow; to move right strike the right arrow. There is also an alternative set of commands for the same movement: <Control-S> for left, <Control-D> for right, <Control-E> for up, and <Control-X> for down. This set of commands is intuitively easy to remember because the position of these keys on the typewriter corresponds to their effect in LawWord, in that "S" is to the left, "D" is to the right, "W" is on a higher row, and "X" is on a lower row. In addition, these keys can be reached without moving the hands from the home position on the typewriter, an advantage for touch typists. These reasons are why they were chosen for these functions in the highly popular word processor named WORDSTAR (Trademark of MicroPro International Corporation) and why they have been incorporated in many other word processors.

Other cursor movement commands include: <Control-Left-Arrow> (or <Control-A>) to move left one word; <Control-Right-Arrow> (or <Control-F>) to move right one word; and <Home> to move to the left end of a line; <End> to move to the right end of a line.

§ D–4. TEXT INSERTION AND DELETION

LawWord operates in two modes, insert mode and overwrite mode. In insert mode, whatever you type will be inserted in the text on the screen, which will be moved along to accommodate it. In overwrite mode, whatever is on the screen will be overwritten when you type. When LawWord is started, it is in insert mode. (This is indicated by the letters "IN" near the top right of the screen.) To switch back and forth between insert and overwrite modes, strike <Ins> (or <Control-V>).

Insertion may leave a paragraph looking ragged, with some lines very long. To reformat the paragraph, position the cursor on or before the first long line and strike <Control-B>.

To insert a blank line, strike <Control-N>.

You can delete a character, a word, a line, a whole block of text, or even a whole document. To delete the character to the left of the cursor, strike <Backspace>. To delete the character at the cursor, strike <Del> (or, for WORDSTAR afficianados, <Control-G>). To delete the word to the right of the cursor, strike <Control-T>. To delete a whole line, strike <Control-Y>. If you delete a line by mistake, you can restore it by striking <Esc>. Block deletion is explained in § D–6(d) below; file deletion is explained in § D–11(j) below.

Deletion may leave a paragraph looking ragged, with some lines very short. To reformat the paragraph, position the cursor on or before the first short line and strike <Control-B>.

§ D–5. WINDOW MOVEMENT COMMANDS

Only a portion of the document is visible on the screen at any one time. You may scroll this portion down a line at a time by striking <Control-Z> or up a line at a time by striking <Control-W>. To move up a whole screenful of text, strike <PgUp> (or <Control-R>). To move down a whole screenful of text, strike <PgDn> (or <Control-C>). More options for window movement will be explained in § D–10 below.

§ D-6. BLOCK COMMANDS

The block commands allow the marking of a block of one or more full lines of text so that the block may then be moved, copied, written to disk, or deleted. In addition, they allow reading in a block of text from a disk file. They may be reached from the block menu, which can be accessed by striking <F10> and then <Enter> (or <F10> and <B> for Block). When these keys are struck, the block menu will unfold down the screen, covering up temporarily any text below it. The block commands can also be made more quickly by using a series of hard-to-remember short commands.

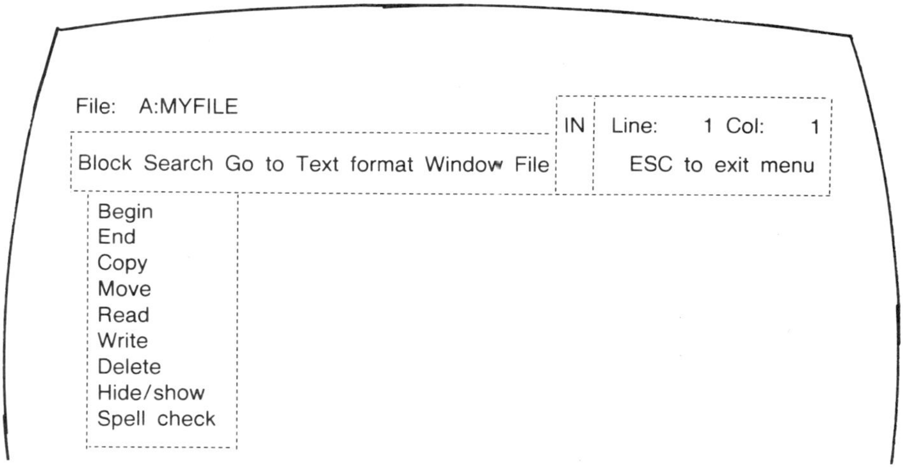

(a) Begin and End

Before a block of text can be moved, copied, written out, or deleted, LawWord must know where the block starts and stops. To indicate the start of the block, position the cursor to the line where you want the block to start, select the Block Menu, and then strike <B> for Begin or strike <Enter>. To indicate the end of the block, position the cursor to the line where you want the block to end, select the Block Menu and strike <E> for End (or strike the down arrow once, and then strike <Enter>). The block will immediately be highlighted on the screen. (Note that a block can be larger than a screenful of text. In this case when you scroll backward and forward, you will see that the whole block is highlighted. One limitation of the current release of LawWord is that a block cannot start or end in the middle of a line.

[Short commands: Begin = <F7> or <Control-K> <Control-B> (B for Begin)
End = <F8> or <Control-K> <Control-K>]

(b) Copy and Move

The Copy Block command makes another copy of a block of text elsewhere in the file. The Move Block command also makes a copy of a block of text, but in addition, it deletes the original block once the copy has been made. Before using these commands you must have designated a block in your file using the Begin and End commands as explained above. To copy a block, move the cursor to where you want the block to go, select the Block Menu and strike <C> for copy (or strike the down arrow twice to select the Copy command, and then strike <Enter>). To move a block, move the cursor to where you want the block to go, select the BLOCK Menu and strike <M> for Move (or strike the down arrow three times to select the Move command and then strike <Enter>.

[Short commands: Copy = <Control-K> <Control-C> (C for Copy)
Move = <Control-K> <Control-V> (V for moVe)]

(c) Read and Write

The Read and Write commands allow you to copy a block of text from a document file on the disk to the document in RAM that you are editing or vice versa. By writing a block of text to a file on the disk, closing (and thereby saving) the document you are editing, opening a new document, and reading the block back in, you can copy text from document to document. To read the text contained in a document file on a disk, move the cursor to where you want the text to go, select the Block Menu and strike <R> for Read (or strike the down arrow 4 times to select Read and then strike <Enter>). LawWord will ask you:

```
Filename:
```

You respond by typing the name of the document you want, with disk drive letter and path names if it is on a different path or disk, for instance:

```
Filename:MYFILE
Filename:B:MYFILE
Filename: \NOTES\ MYFILE
```

After selecting the document name, strike <Enter>, and the total contents of the file will be read in from the disk, into the place in the text where the cursor is located. NOTE: unlike the Copy and Move commands, which highlight the new copy or moved copy of the file so that further block operations may be performed with it, the Read command does not highlight the material read in, and LawWord does not consider this material to be a block. If you want the material to be considered to be a block, create an "empty" block by entering a Begin Block and an End Block command in adjacent places on the screen and Read the file in between them.

To write a block of text to a document file on the disk, create a block containing the text you want to write, select the Block Menu, strike <W> for Write (or strike the down arrow 5 times to select Write and then strike <Enter>). LawWord will ask you:

```
File name:
```

You respond by typing the name of the file into which you wish to write the block of text, with disk drive letter, and path names if it is a different path or disk. After typing your response, strike <Enter>. LawWord will warn you if the document already exists and check to see if you want to go ahead anyway. WARNING: Writing to a document that already exists totally and permanently destroys all the previous contents of that document.

[Short commands: Read = <Control-K> <Control-R> (R for Read)
Write = <Control-K> <Control-W> (W for Write)]

(d) Delete

The Delete Block command is a convenient but dangerous command on many word processors. It provides a quick way to destroy a whole block of text instantly. Luckily, LawWord provides a panic button for use when you realize that you have deleted something by mistake—if you realize your mistake soon enough. If you have a block designated anywhere in your text, you can delete it by selecting the Block Menu and then striking <D> for Delete (or by then striking the down arrow six times to select Delete, and then striking <Enter>). If you immediately realize that you have made a mistake, repeatedly striking <Esc> will "undelete" the block line by line up to the maximum number of lines set as the Undo Limit (see § D–9(f)).

[Short command: Delete = <Control-K> <Control-Y> (Y for Yank out)]

(e) Hide/show

Selecting the Hide/show option on the block menu allows you to turn on or off the highlighting of a block that has been selected. Even if the highlighting is turned off, the block remains a block, and can, for instance, be deleted with the Delete block command. To select Hide/show from the Block Menu, use the down arrow or strike <H>;

[Short command: Hide/show = <Control-K> <Control-H> (H for Hide)]

(f) Spell Check

LawWord is not supplied with a spelling checker. However it is fully compatible with the Turbo Lightning spelling checker and thesaurus sold by Borland International. If you have Turbo Lightning, selecting Spell check from the Block Menu using the down arrow or by striking <S> will automatically activate the spelling checker. For further details, see the instruction manual that comes with Turbo Lightning.

[Short command: Hide/show = <Control-K> <Control-L> (L for Lightning)]

§ D–7. SEARCH COMMANDS

The search commands allow you to find or to find and replace any combination of characters in the text of your word-processing document. They are extremely powerful commands. The find-and-replace command should be used with caution, because it may have unintended results.

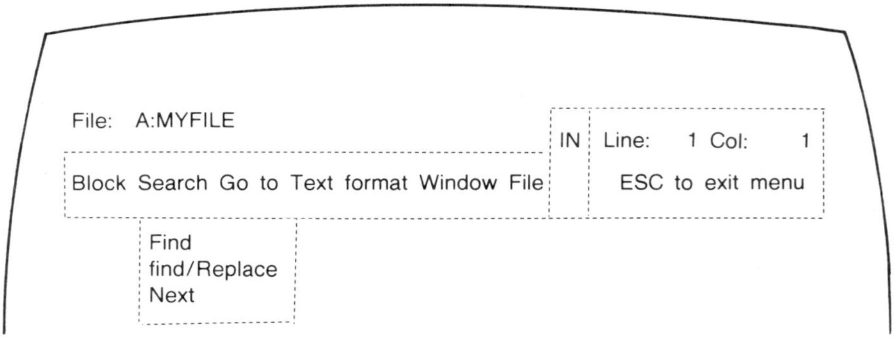

(a) "Find"

To select Find, strike <F10> and then strike <S> for Search (or strike the right arrow, and <Enter>) to get the Search menu. Then strike <Enter> or <F> to select Find. When you do so, the following will appear in a "window" on the screen:

```
Find:
Options:
```

Your first step is to type the string of characters you want to find. For ordinary use, just type a word or phrase and strike <Enter> twice. LawWord will take you forward to the next appearance of this word or phrase in the document. Typing errors can be corrected by moving the cursor with the left and right arrow key and by using <Backspace> and <Del>. A user may select one or more options from the following list:

b Backward search to the beginning of the text;

g Global search—forward search from the beginning to the end of the text;

u Upper and lower case treated as equivalent;

w Whole word search, ignore matches in parts of words. For instance, "man" will match "man", but not "woman".

[a number, n] Start at position of the cursor and find the n'th string corresponding to the search string.

These search commands can be combined. For instance the options "wu" will search for whole words and ignore upper/lower case distinctions.

Finally, you may stop the finding process at any time by striking <Control-U>.

[Short command: Find = <Control-Q> <Control-F> (F for Find)]

(b) "find/Replace"

To select find/Replace, select the Search menu. Then strike <R> for Replace (or strike the down arrow and then <Enter>) to select find/Replace. When you do so, the following will appear in a "window" on the screen:

```
Find:
Replace:
Options:
```

You first type the string of characters you want to find, and strike <Enter>. Then you type the string of characters you want to replace and strike <Enter>. Finally, you select any options you want and strike <Enter>. Everything said above with respect to the "Find" command applies to the "find/Replace" command. The difference is that "find/Replace" replaces the string found with the string you designate as the replace string. Also, the "find/Replace" command has one additional option, the "n" option. The "n" option causes the replacement process to be fully automatic. A very powerful use of the "find/Replace" command is with the "ng" options. These options will cause the command to find and replace all matching strings in the document, for instance, it will replace all occurrences of "Smith" with "Jones". Be careful when using this "global find and replace option"—you may get unintended results if you have not thought through the effects of the command on your document. A slower, but safer method is to omit the "n" option. Then the computer will pause each time a matching string is found and will ask:

```
Replace (Y/N)
```

By striking "Y" or "N" you can indicate whether or not you want the particular string replaced.

[Short command: find/Replace = <Control-Q> <Control-A> (A for find And replace)]

(c) "Next"

To select Next strike <F10>, the right arrow, and <Enter> to get the Search menu. Then strike the down arrow twice and then <Enter> to select Next. The computer will immediately reexecute the most recently executed "Find" or "find/Replace" command.

[Short command: Next = <Control-L> (L for Look for next)]

§ D–8. "GO TO" COMMANDS

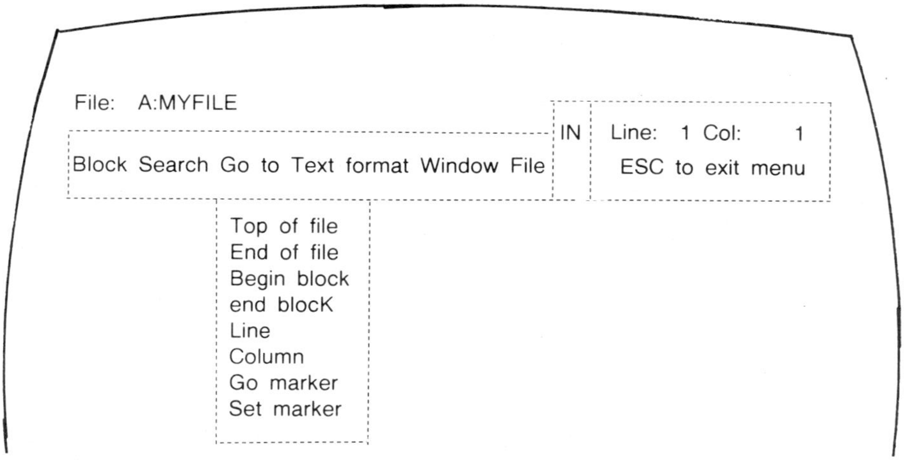

(a) Top of File

To go directly to the top of a document, i.e., to the first character in the document, strike <F10>, and then strike G for Go to (or strike the right arrow twice, and strike <Enter> to select the "Go to" menu. Then strike <T> for Top (or strike <Enter> again) to go to the top of the file.

[Short command: Top of file = <Control-Q> <Control-R> (R for Return to top of file)]

(b) End of File

To go directly to the end of the document, i.e., to the last character in the document, select the "Go to" menu. Then strike <E> for End (or strike the down arrow and then <Enter>) to go to the top of the file.

[Short command: End of file = <Control-Q> <Control-C> (C for Continue to end of file)]

(c) Begin Block

To go directly to the beginning of a marked block, select the "Go to" menu. Then strike <B> for Begin (or strike the down arrow twice and then <Enter>) to go to the beginning of the block.

[Short command: Begin block = <Control-Q> <Control-B> (B being the "first" letter in Block)]

(d) End Block

To go directly to the end of a marked block, select the "Go to" menu. Then strike <K> (or strike the down arrow three times and then <Enter>) to go to the end of the block.

[Short command: end block = <Control-Q> <Control-K>] (K being the "end" letter in "BlocK")

(e) Line

To go directly to a particular line in the document, select the "Go to" menu. Then strike <L> for Line (or strike the down arrow four times and then <Enter>) to select the "go to line" option. The computer will then ask you:

```
Which line:
```

You should type the number of the line to which you want to go and then strike <Enter>. The computer will immediately take you to the line you designate.

[Short command: Line = <Control-O> <N>]

(f) Column

The "go to column" option works the same way as the "go to line" option (except that you strike <C> for Column). However it is probably quicker to just move the cursor key until you get the number of the column you want in the upper right corner of the screen.

[Short command: Column = <Control-O> <I>]

(g) Go Marker

You can mark up to 9 positions in the document, using the "Set marker" command explained below. To go to a previously set marker, select the "Go to" menu. Then strike <G> (or strike the down arrow six times and strike <Enter>). The computer will then ask:

```
Which marker:
```

Type the number of the marker you want to go to and then strike <Enter>. You will immediately be taken to the point designated by this marker.

[Short command: set marker = <Control-Q> <1> . . . <Control-Q> <9>]

(h) Set Marker

You can mark up to 9 positions in the document, using the "Set marker" command. To set a marker, select the "Go to" menu. Then strike <S> for set (or strike the down arrow seven times and strike <Enter>). The computer will then ask:

```
Select marker:
```

Type the number of the marker you want to set and then strike <Enter>. You may go to this marked place at any time using the "go marker" command.

[Short command: Set Marker = <Control-K> <1> . . . <Control-K> <9>]

§ D–9. TEXT FORMAT COMMANDS

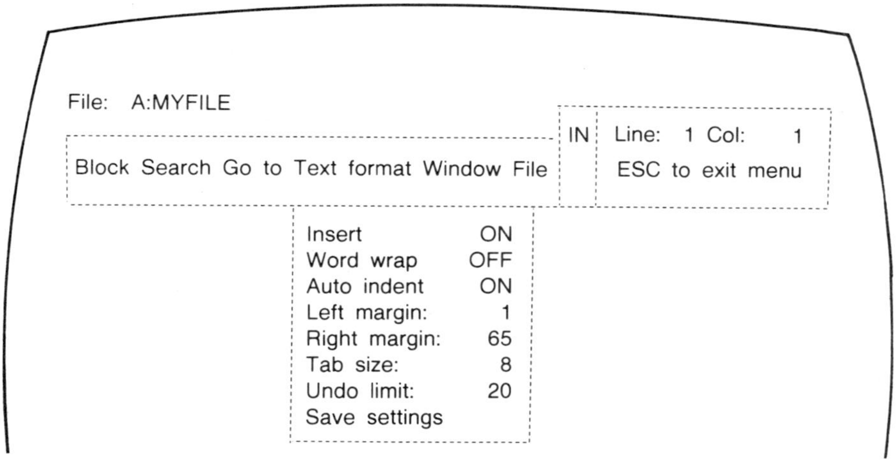

(a) Insert

LawWord has two modes for entering text, the Insert mode and the Overwrite mode. In the Insert mode, everything you type is inserted in the existing text, which is moved along to make room for it. In the Overwrite mode, anything you type replaces the text at the cursor. For most purposes you will probably want to use the insert mode. The Overwrite mode is convenient for making changes in tables and other text with special formats. If you are in insert mode, the letters "IN" will appear in a box toward the upper right of the top of the screen. To switch between the modes, strike <F10> and strike <T> for Text (or strike the right arrow three times, and strike <Enter>) to select the "Text format" menu. Then strike <I> for Insert (or strike <Enter> again).

[Short command: Insert On/Off = <Ins> or <Control-V>]

(b) Word Wrap

Unless you are editing a computer program or some other text where exact placement of line endings is important, you will want to have Word Wrap ON. In word wrap mode, the computer takes responsibility for breaking text between words at the end of lines. You do not have to check how close you are getting to the end of a line; if you type a word that will not fit on a line, the computer moves it to the next line. With Word Wrap OFF, you have full control over and full responsibility for deciding where lines should end. If Word Wrap is on, the letters "WW" will appear in a box toward the upper right of the top of the screen. To switch between Word Wrap ON and Word Wrap OFF, select the "Text format" menu. Then strike <W> for Word Wrap (or strike the down arrow once and strike <Enter> again).

[Short command: Word Wrap On/Off = <Control-O> <W> (W for Word Wrap)]

(c) Auto Indent

If Auto indent is on, each new line will start with the same indentation as the previous line, instead of starting at the left margin. To switch between Auto indent ON and Auto indent OFF, to select the "Text format" menu. Then strike <A> for Auto (or strike the down arrow twice and strike <Enter> again).

[Short Command: Auto Indent On/Off = <Control-Q> <I> (I for Indent)]

(d) Left and Right Margins

These settings are similar to the margin settings on a typewriter. To set the left margin, select the "Text format" menu. Then strike <L> for Left (or strike the down arrow three times and strike <Enter>) again.

The computer will ask:

```
New left margin:   1
```

The number displayed is the present margin. To keep the same margin, just strike <Enter>. To set a new margin, type a number and strike <Enter>. Right margin works analogously.

[Short command: Left Margin = <Control-O> <L> (L for Left)]

[Short Command: Right Margin = <Control-O> <R> (R for Right)]

(e) Tab Size

The tab size setting corresponds to the tab setting on a typewriter. However the present release of LawWord does not allow the setting of individual tab stops. Instead you can only set a fixed number of spaces between tabs. To set the tab size, select the "Text format" menu. Then strike <T> for Tab (or strike the down arrow five times and strike <Enter> again). The computer will ask:

```
New tab size:     8
```

The number displayed is the present tab size. To keep the same size, just strike <Enter>. To set a new size, type a number and strike <Enter>.

[Short Command: Set Tab Size = <Control-K> <T>]

(f) Undo Limit

This command sets the maximum number of text lines that can be saved to be restored with the Undo command (<Esc>). To set the undo limit, select the "Text format" menu. Then strike <U> for Undo (or strike the down arrow six times and strike <Enter> again). The computer will ask:

```
New undo limit:        20
```

The number displayed is the present undo limit. To keep the same limit, just strike <Enter>. To set a new limit, type a number and strike <Enter>.

[Short Command: Set Undo Limit = <Control-O> <S>]

(g) Save Settings

This command saves the text format settings on the disk so that next time you use the editor you will automatically get the settings you have saved. To save the settings, select the "Text format" menu. Then strike <S> for Save (or strike the down arrow seven times and strike <Enter> again).

§ D–10. WINDOW COMMANDS

The window commands allow you to edit two parts of your document simultaneously. This capability can be very useful, for instance, for editing text and associated footnotes. When two windows are active on the screen, you can move from one to the other by typing <Control-O> <Control-G>.

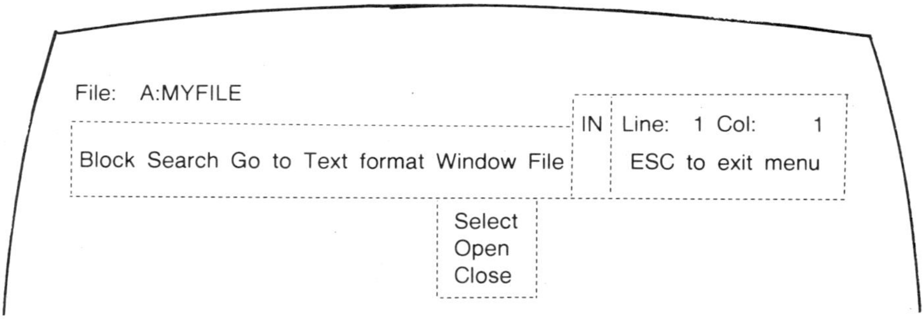

(a) Select

This command allows you to select the window you want to edit. To switch between windows, strike <F10> and strike <W> for Window (or strike the right arrow four times, and then strike <Enter> to select the "Window" menu. Then strike <S> for Select (or strike <Enter> again).

(b) Open

This command activates a second window on the screen. To activate the window, select the "Window" menu. Then strike the letter <O> for Open (or strike the down arrow once and strike <Enter> again).

The computer will ask:

```
How may lines (3 - 7):        10
```

The number displayed is the present window size. To keep the same size, just strike <Enter>. To set a new size, type a number and strike <Enter>.

[Short Command: Open Window = <Control-O> <O> (the letter O for Open)]

(c) Close

This command deactivates the second window on the screen. To deactivate the window, select the "Window" menu. Then strike <C> for Close (or strike the down arrow twice and strike <Enter> again).

[Short Command: Close Window = <Control-O> <Y>]

§ D-11. FILE COMMANDS

The file commands provide convenient ways to deal with whole files or documents on the disk.

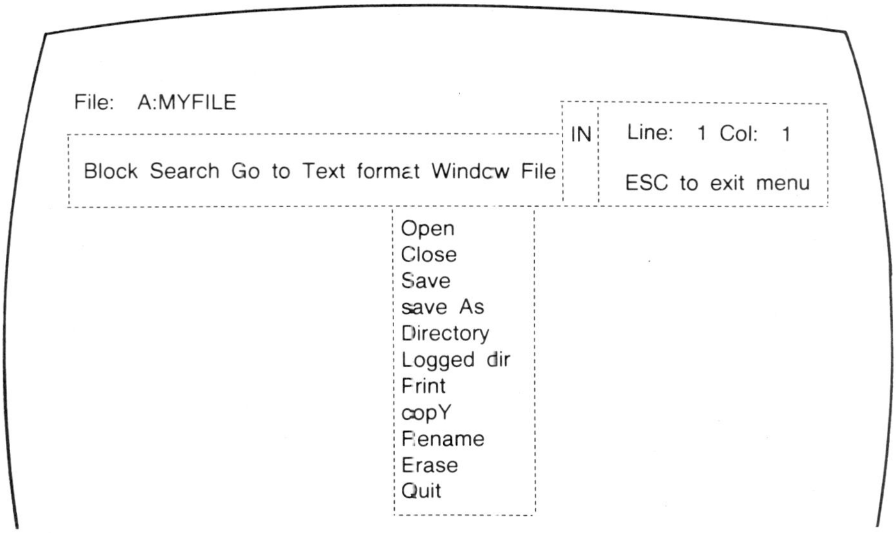

(a) Open

Selecting a file or document for editing and reading a copy of it into RAM memory is called "Opening" the file. To edit a particular document, strike <F10> and strike <F> for File (or strike the right arrow five times, and then strike <Enter> to select the "File" menu). Then strike the letter <O> for Open (or strike <Enter> again) to select the "Open" option. If you are currently editing a document and have changed it, but have not written the changes out to a disk file, the computer will ask:

```
Abandon Changes (Y/N)?
```

If you answer "N," the computer will cancel the "Open" command. If you answer "Y," the computer will ask:

```
Filename:
```

Type in the file name of the document you wish to edit. You may include a disk drive letter (plus a colon) and a path (see the discussion in § D–6(c) above on DOS file names). The file you select will be loaded for editing. The loading process may take a few seconds if the file is long.

[Short Command: Open File = <Control-K> <D> (D for Done—to save present file and open a new file)]

[Short Command: Open File = <Control-K> <Q> (Q for Quit—to abandon present file and open a new file)]

(b) Close

When you are done with the document on which you are working and want to prepare to edit another document, you should select "Close". To select "Close," select the "File" menu. Then strike <C> for Close (or strike the down arrow once and strike <Enter> to select "Close"). The computer will ask:

```
Save changes (Y/N)?
```

If you answer "Y," the document will be saved to disk. If you answer "N," you will lose all changes since you last saved the document to disk.

[Short Command: Open File = <Control-K> <D> (D for Done—to save present document to a file and open a new file)]

[Short Command: Open File = <Control-K> <Q> (Q for Quit—to abandon present document and open a new file)]

(c) Save

It is good practice to frequently save the document you are editing back to the diskette. If there is a loss of electric power or a hardware problem with the computer, you will lose all editing changes you have made since the last time the document was saved. By saving the document often, you minimize these potential losses. To save the document you are editing, strike <F10> and strike <F> to select the "File" menu. Then strike <S> for Save (or strike the down arrow twice and strike <Enter>) to select the "Save" option.

[Short Command: Save = <Control-K> <S> (S for Save)]

(d) Save As

You may want to save a copy of the document with a different name or save a copy on your "backup" diskette. For instance, you may want to keep a copy of an unaltered version of a document, and then make some alterations. The "Save As" command allows you to do so. To save the document you are editing with a different file name, strike <F10> and strike <F> to select the "File" menu. Then strike <A> for As (or strike the down arrow three times and strike <Enter>) to select the "Save As" option. The computer will ask:

```
Filename:
```

Type the file name (including optionally a disk drive letter and path) under which you want the document saved and strike <Enter>.

(e) Directory

You may want to see a directory of files on the disk to refresh your memory. To do so, select the File menu. Then strike <D> for Directory (or strike the down arrow four times and strike <Enter>) to select the "Directory" option. The following display will appear on the screen.

```
Directory mask:    *.*
```

You may now strike <Enter> to view the entire directory. If you understand the DOS directory command, you may want to change the directory mask. This mask is the same as what you type after the "dir" command in DOS, e.g.:

A> dir *.*

If you have files lw.com, brief.law, resume.law, letter.law, and letter.bak on the diskette, after you strike <Enter>, the display would look like this:

```
Directory mask:    *.*
LW.COM   BRIEF.LAW   RESUME.LAW   LETTER.LAW   LETTER.BAK
```

If, before striking <Enter>, you altered the directory mask to read " *.LAW", the display would look like this:

```
Directory mask:    *.LAW
BRIEF.LAW     RESUME.LAW     LETTER.LAW
```

If, before striking <Enter>, you altered the directory mask to read "LETTER.* ", the display would look like this:

```
Directory mask:   LETTER.*
LETTER.LAW        LETTER.BAK
```

(f) Logged Directory

The "Logged Directory" is the directory from which LawWord reads and writes unless you specify some other directory. To change the logged directory, select the "File" menu. Then strike <L> for Logged (or strike the down arrow five times and strike <Enter>) to select the "Logged dir" option. The computer will ask:

```
New Drive/Directory:
```

Answer the question and strike <Enter> to select a new drive and/or directory. For example, type "b:<return>" to select the diskette in Drive b:.

(g) Print

LawWord can print out one document in background mode while you are editing another. (It cannot, however, print out the document you are currently editing.) To print a file, select the "File" menu. Then strike <P> for Print (or strike the down arrow six times and strike <Enter>) to select the "Print" option. The computer will ask:

```
Enter filename to print:
```

Be sure the printer is ready, type in the document file name, and strike <Enter>. Note: before printing, you will probably want to insert some commands to control the format of the printed output. See § D-12. Print Format Commands.

(h) copY

To make a copy of a document stored as a file, select the "File" menu. Then strike (Y) for copY (or strike the down arrow seven times and strike <Enter>) to select the "copY" option. The computer will ask:

```
Source file:
Target file:
```

Answer the questions and the document will be copied from the Source file to the Target file. The Source file will remain undisturbed. If the Target file already exists, the computer will save you from accidentally destroying it by asking:

```
Source file:
Target file:
Target file exists. Delete (Y/N):
```

(i) Rename

To change the name of a file on the disk, strike (F10), select the "File" menu. Then strike <R> for rename (or strike the down arrow eight times and strike <Enter>) to select the "rename" option. The computer will ask:

```
Old file name:
New file name:
```

Answer the questions, striking <Enter> after each answer and the file with "Old file name" will be renamed as "New file name."

(j) Erase

To erase a file, strike <F10>, to select the "File" menu. Then strike <E> for Erase (or strike the down arrow nine times and strike <Enter>) to select the "Erase" option. The computer will ask:

```
File to delete:
```

Type the name of the file you want to delete and then strike <Enter>. To protect you against accidentally deleting a file you really want to save, the computer will ask:

```
File to delete:  MYNOTES.LAW
Are you sure (Y/N):
```

(k) Quit

To quit LawWord, strike <F10>, select the "File" menu. Then strike <Q> for Quit (or strike the down arrow ten times and strike <Enter>) to select the "Quit" option. The computer will ask:

```
Save Changes (Y/N)?
```

If you answer "Y," the computer will save the document you are currently editing as a file and then leave the program. If you answer "N," the computer will immediately leave the program, and you will lose any changes you made since the document you are currently editing was last saved as a diskette file.

[Short Command: Exit = <Control-K> <X> (X for eXit)]

§ D–12. PRINT FORMAT COMMANDS

The print format commands allow the user to control spacing (single or double), where pages end, and page numbering. Print format commands are typed into an appropriate point in the document in the form of a line beginning with a period. The commands appear on the screen, but they do not appear on the printed copy.

WARNING: These commands must begin in column 1 of a new line and must be the only thing on that line.

(a) Spacing

When a document is printed, it will be single spaced, unless a double spacing command is used. To start double spacing text, insert the following line:

```
.DS
```

(DS is an abbreviation for Double Spacing.) To start single spacing text, insert the following line:

```
.SS
```

(SS is an abbreviation for Single Spacing.) You can change back and forth between double and single spacing as often as you want in a single document.

(b) Page Breaks

The user is responsible for designating page breaks. There are two types of page breaks that can be entered, "hard" page breaks and "soft" page breaks.

A hard page break is entered by inserting the following line:

```
.PA
```

(PA is an abbreviation for PAge.) This hard page break will survive the semiautomatic repaging process described below. A hard page break would be suitable, for instance, before the start of a new chapter that must begin on a new page.

A soft page break is entered by inserting the following line:

```
.PS
```

(P for Page, S for Soft) This soft page break will be removed during the semiautomatic repaging process described below.

(c) Semiautomatic Repaging

Semiautomatic repaging provides computer assistance to a user in setting page breaks in a document that has no page breaks or has been edited to the point that some pages are too long and others are too short. To repage the document, first position the cursor at the very start of the document—in the first column of the first line. Now strike <Control-PgDn>. The cursor will advance 55 lines, removing any soft page break commands in the intervening lines. In counting lines it will automatically take account of double and single spacing. If the cursor lands at a good place to insert a page break, strike <Control-End> to end the page. The following line will automatically be inserted:

```
.PS
```

If the cursor does not land at a good place to break the page, move it up as far as necessary or down (not more than two lines) until it is at a good place for a page break, and then strike <Control-End>. Repeat this process of striking <Control-PgDn> and <Control-End> through the whole document.

(d) Automatic Page Numbering

You can number pages by hand, by typing a page number at the top or bottom of each page. However, adding or deleting material will immediately throw the page number system out of line.

Therefore an automatic page numbering command is supplied. With automatic numbering, a page number will be inserted at each page break. To turn on automatic page numbering, with the first page numbered "2", type:

```
.PN2
```

(PN is an abbreviation for page numbering). You can start page numbering with any number between 1 and 9999, however page numbers may not exceed 9999. Thus to start on page 18, type:

```
.PN18
```

You can turn off page numbering by inserting the following line:

```
.OP
```

(O for Off, P for Page numbering).

§ D–13. PRINTER COMMANDS

Printer commands are special codes placed in the document to instruct the printer to perform such functions as underlining, boldfacing, superscripting, or subscripting. Unfortunately, not all printers respond to the same set of commands. The closest thing to an industry standard are the commands accepted by Epson brand printers. Probably over 50% of all personal computer printers are Epson-compatible.

LawWord offers a set of commands for use with Epson-compatible printers. It offers an additional generic approach to printer commands applicable to almost any printer. The user can switch between Epson-compatible and generic commands by including the following line in the document for Epson-compatible commands:

```
.EP
```

and the following line for generic commands:

```
.GE
```

If the user does not select a command mode, the document will be printed in Epson-compatible mode.

(a) Commands for Epson-Compatible Printers

The following commands are automatically translated by LawWord into Epson-compatible commands and are sent to the printer when the document is being printed.

Underlining

To indicate where to start underlining text, strike <Control-P> <Control-S>. A strange symbol, such as a double exclamation point will appear on the screen. Now move the cursor to where you want to stop underlining and strike <Control-P> <Control-S> again. If you forget to stop underlining, you may find a large portion of your document underlined to your dismay.

Boldface

To indicate where to start underlining text, strike <Control-P> <Control-B> (B for Boldface). A strange symbol, such as a happy face will appear on the screen. Now move the cursor to where you want to stop boldfacing and strike <Control-P> <Control-B> again.

Doublestrike

To indicate where you want to start doublestriking (a form of printing that gives something nearer to letter quality), strike <Control-P> <Control-D> (D for Doublestrike). A strange symbol, such as a diamond will appear on the screen. Now move the cursor to where you want to stop doublestriking and strike <Control-P> <Control-D> again.

Superscript

To indicate where you want to start a superscript, for instance for a footnote number, strike <Control-P> <Control-T>. A strange symbol, such as a paragraph sign will appear on the screen. Now move the cursor to the end of the superscript and strike <Control-P> <Control-T> again.

Subscript

To indicate where you want to start a subscript, strike <Control-P> <Control-V>. A strange symbol, such as a low fat dash will appear on the screen. Now move the cursor to the end of the subscript and strike <Control-P> <Control-V> again.

Alternate and Standard Pitch

Many printers offer Pica pitch as standard and Elite (smaller) type pitch as an alternate pitch. To select the alternate pitch, strike <Control-P> <Control-A>. A symbol such as a shaded happy face will appear on the screen. To select the standard pitch strike <Control-P> <Control-N>. A symbol such as some musical notes will appear on the screen.

Overprint a character

To overprint a character, type one character, then strike <Control-P> <Control-H> and then strike another character. The second character will be printed at the same spot as the first. This way, for instance, you can make the French character "é" by typing <e> <Control-P> <Control-H> <´>.

(b) Generic Printer Commands

Generic printer commands allow the user to implement the commands for any printer. The first step is to read the manual for the printer to be used and to note what must be sent to the printer to achieve a desired result. Typically a command will be <Esc> or a control character followed by one or more regular characters. To enter <Esc> in the document, type <Control-P> <Esc>. To enter a control character, for instance <Control-A> in the document, type <Control-P> followed by the control character, for instance <Control-P> <Control-A>.

Be sure to enter the line:

```
.GE
```

before using generic printer commands.

§ D–14. THE BACKUP FILE

A final word of encouragement. Whenever you change a document with LawWord, a backup file with the file name suffix ".BAK" is automatically created. If you make some disastrous error in editing the file, you can exit without saving your changes, and the original file will be restored. If you have already exited and saved the changes, the previous version of the file is still safe in a file with the same name, but with the name ending ".BAK".

Appendix E

THE LAWSPREAD SPREADSHEET

§ E–1. INTRODUCTION

LawSpread, a minimal spreadsheet program, is supplied on the diskette that accompanies this book. LawSpread is far more limited in its powers than commercial spreadsheets such as Lotus 1–2–3 or Multiplan. However it does have the basic capabilities needed for the spreadsheet problems presented in this book.

§ E–2. GETTING STARTED

(a) Making a Working Copy of LawSpread

The easiest way to make a working copy of LawSpread is to find a fellow student who already has a copy and who knows how to use the Diskcopy command. Give the student a blank diskette and ask the student to help you make a working copy. Alternatively, if your law library or law computer center has a working copy of LawSpread on reserve, borrow it. If your computer has two floppy diskette drives, put the working copy in Drive A (usually on the left) and a blank diskette in Drive B. Then type:

```
diskcopy a: b: <Enter>
```

When Drive A stops whirring and a message appears on the screen, press <Enter> again. In a few moments you will have your own working copy.

If you cannot get a working copy from a fellow student or the law library, you have to follow a somewhat more complex process. First, place a copy of DOS (which you undoubtedly will be able to obtain from your law library or law computer center) in Drive A and turn on the computer. Answer the date and time questions, that will appear on the screen. Next, place the law system diskette in drive A and type: install <Enter>. Follow the instructions that appear on the screen.

You will also need some backup data diskettes (see Appendix D).

(b) Running LawSpread

To run LawSpread, you will need your working copy and a second diskette for backup purposes. To start LawSpread, put the working copy of LawSpread in Drive A and your backup data diskette in Drive B. Turn on the computer. If all goes well you will see the following display on the screen:

```
LawSpread                                              Release 1.00
                                    For IBM PC & 100% Compatibles

Software by Peter B. Maggs and Bruce M. Maggs
Copyright © 1986 West Publishing Co.

                  — Press Any Key to Begin —
```

Now press <Enter> (or any other key) and you will see the following screen display:

```
A1:                                                  READY
            A        B        C        D        E
1    __
2
3
4
5
6
7
8
9
10
11
12
13
14
15
16
17
18
19
20
```

Unlike commercial spreadsheets, which have hundreds of cells in every direction, only a few dozen of which can be displayed on the screen at a time, LawSpread has only the cells you see on the screen. To go to a particular cell, just use the up, down, right, and left arrow keys on the computer keyboard. You will see a short flashing line (called a cursor) move from cell to cell. You have only two choices of type of entry to make for a cell: a "LABEL" or a "VALUE".

§ E-3. LABELS

To insert a label move the cursor to the cell where you want the label, press <Enter> and then type something starting with a letter, such as INCOME. Labels must start with a letter (or a space) and cannot be over 11 characters long. You will see the label you are typing on the second line of the screen.

```
A1: INCOME_                                 READY
        A          B        C        D        E
1
2
3
```

If you make a mistake, use <Backspace> to erase the mistake. If you decide you do not want a label for this cell after all, press the <Esc> and <Enter> keys. When you are satisfied with the label, press <Enter>, and the label will appear in the appropriate place on the screen, replacing whatever was there. It will also appear to the right of the cell name at the top left of the screen. The top right of the screen will say "LABEL" to indicate that a label is present.

```
A1: INCOME                                  LABEL
        A          B        C        D        E
1   INCOME
2
3
```

§ E-4. VALUES

To insert a value (a number or a formula), move the cursor to the cell where you want the value, press <Enter>, and then type something starting with a number, left parenthesis, plus sign, minus sign, or decimal point)—for instance: 27.84, (A2+B3), or +B4+B5. All operators and functions described in Chapter 5 of this book are legal. The maximum length for a value is 30 characters. You will see the value you are typing on the second line of the screen like this:

```
B3: (B1-B2)_                                   READY
        A          B          C        D        E
1   INCOME        800
2   EXPENSES      500
3   PROFIT
```

If you make a mistake, use the <Backspace> to erase the mistake. If you decide you do not want a value for this cell after all, press the <Esc> and <Enter> keys. When you are satisfied with the value, press <Enter> and a number corresponding to the number you typed or the result of the calculation implied by the formula you typed will appear in the appropriate place on the screen, replacing whatever was there. In addition, the formula will appear after the cell name at the top left of the screen and the word "VALUE" will appear at the top right of the screen.

```
B3:  (B1-B2)                                    VALUE
          A              B          C       D       E
1   INCOME            800
2   EXPENSES          500
3   PROFIT           _300
```

§ E–5. COMMANDS

(a) Introduction

There are a number of commands that affect the whole worksheet and one that affects the format of individual items on the worksheet. To select one of these options press </> or <Flo>. A list of options will appear at the top of the screen.

```
A1:  INCOME                                         LABEL
    Decimals Save Retrieve Print Erase Quit  _
        A          B          C          D        E
1   INCOME     800
2   EXPENSES   500
3   PROFIT     300
```

To return to your spreadsheet after completing your command, type <Esc>.

(b) Decimals

When you enter the spreadsheet program, all numbers are displayed to three decimal places. The Decimals option lets you select the number of decimal places you want displayed for the whole spreadsheet or individual cells. To choose Decimals, press <D> (the first letter of Decimals).

The following will then appear on the screen:

```
"Cell or Whole Spreadsheet (C/W)?"_
```

Press <C> or <W> (C for Cell, W for Whole spreadsheet), depending upon whether you want to set the number of decimal places for a single cell or for the whole spreadsheet.

Now the following will appear:

```
Number of Decimal Places (0, 1, 2, or 3)? _
```

Press <0>, <1>, <2>, or <3>, depending upon how many places you want after the decimal point. (If you select "0" no decimal point will be printed).

If you have indicated that you want the change to affect the whole spreadsheet, the change will be made immediately. However, if you indicated that you wanted to change only the number of decimal places for a single cell, the following will appear:

```
Which Cell? _
```

Type the designator of the cell you want to affect, for instance:

```
Which Cell? B12 _
```

The number of decimal places for this cell will be changed; that for the other cells will remain the same. Type <Esc> to return to your spreadsheet.

(c) Save

This command saves the worksheet to disk. To select Save from the Command Menu, press <S>. The following will then appear on the second line of the screen.

```
Save as file named? _
```

You should type in the name of the file, which may be prefixed with a disk drive letter (plus a colon) and a path name if you wish, for instance:

```
Save as file named? b: \mypath\myfile _
```

Then type <Enter> and <Esc>.

(d) Retrieve

This command retrieves a saved worksheet from the diskette. To select Retrieve from the Command Menu, press <R>. The following will then appear on the second line of the screen.

```
Retrieve what file?
```

You should type in the name of the file, which may be prefixed with a disk drive letter (plus a colon) and a path name if you wish, for instance:

```
Retrieve what file? b: \mypath\ myfile _
```

Then type <Enter> and <Esc>.

(e) Print

This command prints the worksheet (without the letters above and without the numbers at the left side). To select Print from the

Command Menu, press <P>. The following will then appear on the second line of the screen:

```
Print to Printer or Disk? (P/D)? _
```

Press <P> to print to the printer. Make sure your printer is ready before pressing <P>; otherwise the computer will "hang up" waiting for the printer to be readied. Alternatively, you may press <D> to "print" to disk. If you do so, the following will appear on the second line of the screen:

```
Print to disk file named what? _
```

Type in the disk file name you want, for instance:

```
Print to disk file named what? pfile _
```

Then type <Enter>and<Esc>. The worksheet (without the letters above and without the numbers at the left side) will be printed to the disk file you specify. After leaving LawSpread, you can load the disk file into a word processor with the commands the word processor uses to read a text file, or you can print the file with a command such as:

```
copy pfile prn:<Enter>
```

Warning: do not try to read a file "printed" to disk back into LawSpread with the Retrieve command. The print file does not contain all the worksheet information (for instance it lacks the formulas), so Retrieve will not work with the print file.

(f) Erase

This is a dangerous command. It causes the whole worksheet to be erased. Any information that has not been saved to disk will be lost. To select Erase from the Command Menu, press <E>. The following will then appear on the third line of the screen to prevent inadvertent erasure:

```
You will lose everything not saved. Proceed (Y/
N)? _
```

If you really want to erase the worksheet, press <Y>.

Then type <Esc> to return to your spreadsheet.

(g) Quit

This is also a dangerous command. It causes you to leave LawSpread. Any information in the worksheet that has not been saved to disk will be lost. To select Quit from the Command Menu, press <Q>. The following will appear:

```
Do you really want to quit and lose everything
not saved (Y/N)?
```

If you press <Y> you will immediately leave LawSpread.

Appendix F

THE LAWCOMM COMMUNICATION PROGRAM

§ F–1. INTRODUCTION

LawComm, a "Junior" version of the American Bar Association's "LawLink" menuing and communications program, is supplied on the diskette that accompanies this book. LawComm provides you with up to five menus and submenus that you may set up to organize your programs and communication destinations (the ABA's "LawLink" program provides up to 50 menus and submenus). LawComm occupies about 90,000 bytes of high-speed memory and can run your programs in the remaining high-speed memory on your machine (LawLink occupies only 18,000 bytes of memory when large programs are run). LawComm can be set up to auto-dial and auto-handshake its way to any remote communications destination, and it provides special terminal emulations and help menus for WESTLAW, LEXIS, and ABA/net, the American Bar Association's electronic mail service (LawLink includes, in addition, facilities for automatic "error-free" transmission of word processing documents and programs by electronic mail).

§ F–2. GETTING STARTED

(a) Making a Working Copy of LawComm

The easiest way to make a working copy of LawComm is to find a fellow student who already has a copy and who knows how to use the Diskcopy command. Give the student a blank diskette and ask the student to help you make a working copy. Alternatively, if your law library or law computer center has a working copy of LawComm on reserve, borrow it. If your computer has two floppy diskette drives, put the working copy in Drive A: (usually on the left) and a blank diskette in Drive B:. Then type

```
diskcopy a: b: <Enter>
```

When Drive A stops whirring and a message appears on the screen, press <Enter> again. In a few moments you will have your own working copy.

If you cannot get a working copy from a fellow student or the law library, you will have to follow a somewhat more complex process. First, place a copy of DOS (which you undoubtedly will be able to obtain from your law library or law computer center) in Drive A and turn on the computer. Answer the date and time questions that will appear on the screen. Next, place the law system diskette in Drive A and type:

```
install<Enter>
```

Follow the instructions that appear on the screen.

You will also need some backup diskettes (see Appendix D).

(b) Running LawComm

To run LawComm, you will need only your working copy. To start LawComm, put the working copy of LawComm in Drive A. Turn on the computer. If all goes well, you will see a menu on the screen. This menu may vary from school to school. It may simply list the communication destinations that you will have occasion to access. It may list programs, such as LawWord, LawSpread, and LawProcess, that you will use during this course (and all of those programs may be present on the LawComm diskette at some schools). It may list "Communications" as a single item. If you select this item, a second "submenu" will appear listing WESTLAW, LEXIS, VERALEX, Dialog, PHINET, ABA/net, and any other communications destinations that you may have occasion to access.

Your main menu may list "Utilities" as a separate item. If you select this item, another "submenu" will appear listing a variety of useful tasks that the LawComm program can help you to perform such as formatting new floppy disks (see the glossary under "format"), copying files, and displaying directories of the files that are present on a disk.

To select a menu item, simply type its number and then strike <Enter>. The program, communications task, or utility that you select will then run automatically. Or the submenu that you select will appear.

To escape from a submenu, or to escape from the LawComm program when viewing the main menu, simply strike the <Esc> key. The A> prompt will appear. To return to LawComm, type:

```
lc<Enter>
```

When viewing any menu, you may type any command that you would normally type at the A> or C> prompt. For example, type

```
dir<Enter>
```

at the main menu prompt, and you will be presented with a directory of all the files on your diskette. After displaying this directory, the program will pause so that you may view the directory. To return to the menu, simply strike any key. The usual prompt A> or C> will appear in the lower-left corner of the menu to let you know what disk is the "current" disk and what subdirectory (if any) you are in.

If you ever need help, simply strike the F1 function key, and a help screen will be written on the screen. To make it disappear again, strike the F1 key again. You will find that the help menus associated with LEXIS, WESTLAW, and ABA/net actually list all of the commands that you are likely to want to use with these services. And with LEXIS and WESTLAW, many of the commands are permanently associated with the various special function keys on the computer's keyboard. To the maximum degree possible, the command performed by a given key when accessing WESTLAW will perform that same function when accessing LEXIS, so it should be easy for you to move from one to the other and compare how they operate.

The disk as distributed is set up to access WESTLAW, LEXIS, and ABA/net but may not have your local telephone number for those services. And in the case of WESTLAW, the disk needs to be modified so that it contains your "line group letter" and "terminal ID code." You may modify the existing communication setups by simply typing the menu number of the entry you wish to modify followed by an asterisk, as is explained below.

Note also that LawComm emulates an "IBM 3101" block mode terminal for both WESTLAW and LEXIS. LawComm automatically informs LEXIS of this fact. With WESTLAW, you must be sure to obtain from WESTLAW a line group letter, terminal ID code, and account number/password that connects you to WESTLAW's "IBM 3101" terminal service. (This is different from the service normally associated with WALT terminals and WESTMATE software—contact your WESTLAW representative for assistance.)

(c) Uploading and Downloading

When communicating, you may "capture" material to your floppy disk by simply inserting a diskette into Drive A:. Then type <Ctrl-PrtSc>. The text on the screen will be written into a file "save" on the diskette in Drive A:.

To "capture" continuously, or to "transmit" a file to a remote computer, strike <PrtSc> (unshifted) while communicating. The "Communications Control Panel" will appear. It will give you the option of either transmitting a file of text or of capturing all incoming information into a disk file. You may turn on the "word wrap" option which will strip hard carriage returns out of incoming text, thereby causing the material to "word wrap" and automatically adjust to the left and right margins of your word processor. Turn on "word wrap" if the incoming text is headed for your word processor; leave "word wrap" off if not. You may change the name of the "capture" file and also the name of the "capture" disk. If you select either "capture" or "transmit," you will be given an opportunity to change the name of the "capture" or "transmit" disk letter and file name before the process of transferring text to or from the disk begins. Simply "backspace" when the cursor pauses by the file name to change the name of the file and/

or the disk drive letter. Strike <Esc> to cancel the request to capture or transmit text.

§ F–3. REVISING THE MENUS

The reason why your school may have an entirely different arrangement of menus than some other school is because the menu system is actually very simple to modify. To modify any entry on a menu, simply type its number followed by an asterisk and <Enter>, and follow the instructions that will appear, striking the F1 function key whenever you need additional help.

Try, for example, creating a new "submenu" menu entry as number 10 on the main menu of your LawComm program. Type:

```
10*<Enter>
```

at the main menu prompt. The menu will disappear, and you will be asked to type a letter (plus <Enter>) to indicate what type of new entry you wish to create. You may create any of the following:

`m<Enter>` This creates a new, blank "submenu."

`p<Enter>` This creates a menu entry that runs a "program."

`t<Enter>` This creates a menu entry that "telephones."

Let us create a new, blank "submenu" by typing:

```
m<Enter>
```

The computer next prompts you to type in a title for the menu entry. Type:

```
My Personal Menu<Enter>
```

(or perhaps you can think up a better name). The system now has all the information it needs to create the new submenu. It asks:

```
OK to make changes permanent?
```

Up to this point, your changes have been recorded, but they have not yet been stored in the file "menu.aba" on your diskette. If you answer "yes<Enter>" or "y<Enter>", the new submenu will be created and added to your personal menu system.

Note that your main menu is now redrawn to leave room for ten menu entries. You may shift your new entry number 10 to any other open position by simply typing its number with an asterisk again:

```
10*<Enter>
```

This time you are presented with a longer list of options, including options to:

`s<Enter>` "Shift" the menu entry to another position

`c<Enter>` "Copy" (or duplicate) the menu entry

`e<Enter>` "Erase" the menu entry

If you select the "s" option, you may move the menu entry to any open position on the main menu or on any other existing menus (note that all the menus are numbered).

Now select the new menu entry that you have created by typing its number (without an asterisk) and <Enter>. The new menu will appear, but it will be "blank," since you have not yet installed any programs or communication tasks on the new menu. Strike <Esc> to return to the main menu.

§ F-4. INSTALLING A PROGRAM TO RUN UNDER LAWCOMM

As a very simple example of how one installs a program under the menu system, let us arrange for item 1 on the menu to produce a directory listing of the files on the LawComm diskette. While looking at your blank, new menu, type

```
1*<Enter>
```

You will be asked what type of menu entry you wish to create. Type

```
p<Enter>
```

to signal that you wish to install a program. When prompted for a name, type

```
Directory<Enter>
```

Carefully read the instructions that appear next; then type any key. The screen will go completely blank. (Don't be afraid! As always, striking the F1 function key will bring up a "help" display which will disappear when you strike any key).

You are now in a "full screen text editor." The cursor is in the upper left-hand corner of the screen Type

```
dir
```

Then examine your work. If you made an error, use the arrow keys to move the cursor about; use the <Del> and <Backspace> keys to delete any incorrect material; and type in any corrections that are needed. The <Ins> key will toggle you between "insert" and "overstrike" mode. F3 will insert a blank line, and F4 will delete a blank line. F5 will erase a line, and F6 will erase to the end of a line. The END key will erase from the cursor to the end of the screen. The HOME key will move the cursor to the HOME position in the upper-left corner of the screen. "Play" with this little text editor for a moment before we proceed. Note that you may type up to 24 lines of commands on the screen.

When you are finished, strike the <Esc> key to signal that you are done. We have only typed one command on the screen (the "dir" command that caused a directory to be displayed), but in general you might have to type many commands on the screen to run some programs. You simply type on the screen all the commands that the program instruction book says must be typed to run a given program. LawComm thus "memorizes" all of the commands needed to run a program so they may be executed automatically in response to your typing a single menu number plus <Enter>.

Once again, you are asked if you wish to make this change permanent. Answer "yes<Enter>" or "y<Enter>". Now the new submenu appears again, but this time it has a new entry

```
1. Directory
```

on its face. If you type

```
1<Enter>
```

you will see a directory listing of all the programs on your diskette.

To modify this new menu entry in any way, simply type its number with an asterisk, and then strike <Enter>. You will be given an opportunity to erase it, move it, copy it, change it to some other type of entry (in which case it is erased first), or to change its name or edit the screenfull of commands that are associated with it.

§ F–5. INSTALLING A COMMUNICATIONS MENU ENTRY

Now suppose we wish to set up LawComm to communicate with ABA/net, the ABA's electronic mail service. Again when viewing the new menu that you just created, type

```
2*<Enter>
```

to create a new menu item number two. When prompted to type a letter, type

```
t<Enter>
```

to signify that this is a "telephone call" menu entry. You will next be asked to supply a name for the new entry. Type:

```
ABA/net<Enter>
```

Now once again, carefully read the instructions that will appear next. When you strike any key, the screen will once again go blank, and you will again be confronted with a full-screen text editor (see the preceding section). Once again, if you need assistance, strike the F1 help key, and two screens full of helpful information will be displayed, one after the other. The first screen simply explains how the full-screen editor works. The second screen contains a list of special "communications script" commands that you may use to instruct the computer how to place your call and handshake its way into ABA/net. To the far left on the second help screen are three examples illustrating how to reach ABA/net, WESTLAW, and LEXIS.

Begin by typing the DIAL command followed by the local telephone number of Telenet in your city or region. In Cook County, Illinois, one would type:

```
DIAL 938 0600<Enter>
```

Next, type the TELENET command followed by "C 201 444", the address of ABA/net on Telenet:

```
TELENET C 201 444<Enter>
```

Finally, type the ABANET command:

```
ABANET<Enter>
```

Optionally, you may include an account number following the ABA/net command and, on a separate line, the ABANETPW command followed by the password for that account:

```
ABANET ABA506

ABANETPW mypswd
```

When you are finished, type <Esc> and then, when asked whether to make this change permanent, type "y<Enter>" or "yes<Enter>". Now type

```
2<Enter>
```

and watch the computer call up ABA/net in a completely automated fashion. Instead of using the TELENET command, you could substitute type the TYMNET or DATAPAC commands if you use those networks.

When accessing WESTLAW or LEXIS instead of ABA/net, simply proceed as above but substitute the LEXIS or WESTLAW command for the ABANET command in the above example. The WESTLAW command should be followed by your "terminal ID" code, and optionally an additional WESTLAWPW command may be added (on a separate line) with your WESTLAW account number and password. With LEXIS, the LEXIS command may optionally be followed by your LEXIS user ID for a fully automatic logon.

With WESTLAW, you may access the service via WESTNET, using the WESTNET command to submit your WESTNET address "WLAWJJ" (where "JJ" is two copies of your line group letter code), and on the line following you add the WESTNETPW command to submit the WESTNET password (which is always "PVT"). With LEXIS, there is no need for a special MEADNET command when accessing LEXIS using MEADNET.

Many other commands are listed in the HELP menu which is displayed when you strike F1. Most of these you will not have occasion to use, but those of you who become "communication gurus" will find LawComm to be comparable in power to the best communications programs that you can buy today. For example, it can "prompt" you to supply information that it may then incorporate into a command which it can issue to your computer. Those wishing to learn more about these commands are invited to explore the menu system, particularly the utility menu entries, by typing menu numbers with asterisks and observing how the various entries are configured. (To learn more, you are invited to purchase a copy of the American Bar Association's "LawLink" program which comes with complete documentation and many additional features.)

§ F–6. ADDITIONAL TECHNICAL DETAILS

The file "Menu.lc" contains all of your menus, submenus, program command sequences, and communication script command sequences. It should be stored with the program "command.com" on the disk drive that you use to "boot" your computer. If your system uses the file "autoexec.bat", you can include in that file a PATH command telling the system where the LawComm program is stored so that it may be run from any diskette (see your DOS manual under "PATH"). If the last line of your "autoexec.bat" file is "LC", the menu program will start automatically every time you turn on your computer.

The LawComm program is very forgiving of how your computer's hardware is configured. You must attach a "Hayes compatible" modem (one that responds to commands beginning with the letters "AT" and that hangs up or returns to its "command" state in response to "<1 sec delay> + + + <1 sec delay>"). Either a "card" modem or an "external" modem is acceptable. Preferably, set the modem card to select the "COM1" serial port of your computer; but the LawComm program will still work on "COM2". If you must use "COM2," the program will dial faster if the command "PORT 2" or "PORT COM2" is inserted at the start of every communications command script. You should also designate a specific port if your computer is equipped with a "mouse" or other device that also uses a communications port (this will prevent LawComm from accidently "clobbering" your mouse while hunting for the port with the modem attached).

Set your modem to the "factory default" settings, and it should work fine. To improve its performance somewhat, adjust it so that it returns to "command" state or hangs up the telephone in response to the computer's "Data Terminal Ready" signal going low, rather than ignoring this signal. This adjustment will speed up the "hangup" sequence. Also adjust it so that it generates the "Carrier Detect" signal only when another computer's carrier is present, and the LawComm program will be able to signal you when the remote computer hangs up or you become disconnected.

The LawComm program normally operates at "1200 baud, no parity, eight data bits, one stop bit, full duplex (or no echo)." This setting should work with almost all services and should not be changed without a good reason. You may change most of these settings by inserting the appropriate script commands ahead of the DIAL command in your script command sequences.

The LawComm program can also operate at 300 or 2400 baud. Simply insert the SPEED command ahead of the DIAL command:

```
SPEED 2400
```

The program has not been tested at speeds above 2400 baud, but it can be set to 4800 or 9600 baud. If you have an "in-house" minicomputer, you may test out the program at these higher speeds. When not accessing LEXIS or WESTLAW, the LawComm program emulates an

ANSI standard terminal. This emulation is a partial emulation of a Digital Equipment Corporation VT-100 terminal, so LawComm may be used in place of such a terminal. When accessing DEC minicomputers, you may have to use <Ctrl-Backspace> for backspacing (this generates a DEL control character).

GLOSSARY

ANSI. American National Standards Institute, a private not-for-profit organization that develops technical standards. Working in cooperation with the Consultative Committee on International Telephone and Telegraph (CCITT-part of the United Nation's International Telecommunications Union or ITU), International Organization for Standardization (ISO), the Electronic Industry Association (EIA), the Association for Computational Machinery (ACM), and the Institute of Electrical and Electronic Engineers' Computer Society (IEEE–CS), ANSI has developed numerous technical standards for computers that have been widely adopted and that facilitate data interchange and the interconnection of devices manufactured by different companies. IBM also develops many of the technical standards that are adopted by the computer industry. ANSI developed the ASCII code (below).

ASCII. American Standard Code for Information Interchange. This standard coding scheme assigns a standardized numeric value to all the letters, numbers, and commands that are associated with keystrokes on a computer's keyboard (see § 5–2(b) for further details) as well as to various commands that are used in telecommunications. All personal and minicomputers comply with this standard, but IBM mainframe equipment and Displaywriter word processors comply with IBM's very different EBCDIC standard instead.

Arrow keys. Keys on the keyboard of a computer or terminal that are clustered together and that bear arrows pointing up, down, left, and right. Depression of one of these keys normally causes the bright spot on the screen (called the "cursor") to move in the direction indicated by the arrow key depressed. On IBM-type personal computers, a key labelled <Num Lock> can cause the arrow keys to become number keys, and the <Shift> key also converts the arrow keys to number keys or vice-versa, depending upon the state of the <Num Lock> key. The upward-pointing arrow on the "6" key in the top row of most keyboards and the left and right pointing arrows on the comma and period keys are not arrow keys that position the cursor. They are simply keys that cause arrows to be printed upon the screen when they are struck. Although the <Enter> key and the <Backspace> key above it have arrows on them, these are not considered to be "arrow keys."

Asynchronous. When information flows from a computer over a single wire, each character transmitted is represented by a Morse-code-like fluctuation of the voltage on the wire. If a character (such as a letter or a number) can be sent out at any time starting with a positive voltage swing and ending with a negative voltage swing which are the same for all characters, the transmission is said to be "asynchronous." Virtually all personal computer communication from an "RS–232c serial port" out to a printer or telephone "modem" is "asynchronous" (meaning *not* synchronized). But many mainframe computers require characters to be sent to them one after another in rapid succession at exact times with no starting and ending voltage swings. This "mainframe" mode of communication is called "synchronous" communication. Accordingly, your computer may need different hardware and modems to reach a mainframe than it uses to reach WESTLAW and LEXIS.

AT protocol. See "Hayes compatible" infra.

BASIC. A high-level computer programming language. The name stands for "Beginner's All-purpose Symbolic Instruction Code." Originally developed as a language for instructing college students in how to program on mainframe computers, BASIC was established as a standard language for programming microcomputers by the Microsoft corporation. Microsoft BASIC is built into all Apple II computers ("Applesoft BASIC") and into all IBM Personal Computers. Most non-IBM copies of the IBM Personal Computer come without BASIC built in but with it sold separately under the name "GW–BASIC." One must be careful when using IBM's "PC–DOS" operating system on non-IBM-manufactured computers not to use IBM's "basica.com" program, supplied with PC–DOS, since it will not work on computers manufactured by Zenith, Compaq, or other "clone" manufacturers. The much larger GW–BASIC program called "basica.exe" must be purchased separately and used with these machines, since they do not contain BASIC ROMs built into their hardware structure. Those wishing to learn programming should consider purchasing "True BASIC" from Addison Wesley Educational Media Systems, Reading, Massachusetts.

Baud. The "Baud" rate indicates the maximum speed at which information can be transmitted over a single wire to or from a computer. The term "Baud" is derived from the name of Jean M. E. Baudot, the inventor of the five-signal-fluctuations-per-keystroke printing telegraph system that is still widely used for international transmissions (now largely displaced by the seven-signal-fluctuations-per-keystroke ASCII code). The "Baud" rate is the maximum number of signal line fluctuations per second that can be sent if characters are transmitted continuously without any pauses. Since each modern ASCII-encoded keystroke is represented by seven signal fluctuations plus an eighth "parity bit" fluctuation and "character start" and "character end" fluctuations for each keystroke, it takes ten signal line fluctuations to transmit a keystroke between two computers. So the "Baud" rate is exactly ten times the maximum "keystrokes per second" rate at which data can be transmitted. "1200 Baud" thus means "120 keystrokes per second." Assuming each page of double-spaced text contains 2000 keystrokes, "1200 Baud" is equivalent to slightly under four pages per minute. "300 Baud" is slightly under one page per minute. "9600 Baud" is slightly under 32 pages per minute.

Bit. Claude Shannon, the father of information theory, coined the term "BIT" as an acronym for "Binary Information Digit." A "bit" is the amount of information that may be stored in any information storage device that is "binary"—that is, that has two states. For example, a light switch has two states: ON and OFF. Viewed as an information storage device, a light switch can store "one bit" of information. Two light switches can store "two bits" of information, three light switches can store "three bits" of information, and so on. A set of eight light switches can store "eight BITS" or "one BYTE" of information. Since eight light switches can be set into any one of 256 unique "ON"–"OFF" patterns, these 256 states may be arbitrarily assigned to represent every possible letter, number, punctuation symbol, and command ("Enter," "Tab," etc.) that can be typed upon the keyboard of a computer. Accordingly, eight bits or one byte of information is enough to "store" a "keystroke." In modern computers, each addressable memory cell contains eight bits, or one byte, or one keystroke, of information.

Block mode. Computer terminals come in two flavors: "character mode" and "block mode." Most computer terminals are "character mode" terminals. A "character mode" terminal transmits a character to the central computer every time you strike a key. The fanciest WESTLAW and LEXIS terminals, and many mainframe computer terminals, are "block mode" terminals. A "block mode" terminal writes each character you type to the screen, but does not transmit any characters to the central computer until after you hit a special <Transmit> or <Enter> key. When using a "block mode" terminal, you may use the terminal's arrow keys to move the bright spot or "cursor" around upon the screen and edit or revise the information on the screen before you "Transmit" it back to the central computer as a single "block." You may send multiple lines of information from a "block mode" terminal to the central computer with a single keystroke. When used to communicate with a computer in your office or in your city, a "character mode" terminal may sometimes behave in an even more friendly manner than a "block mode" terminal, since the central computer can respond intelligently to every keystroke. When used to communicate with a computer in another city, typically the central computer receives nothing until you strike the <Enter> key, so character mode terminals then send one line at a time, and the central computer does not respond intelligently until a complete line has been sent.

Byte. See "bit" above.

C. A "high level" programming language developed at Bell Laboratories, C is rapidly becoming the most widely used language for writing programs for microcomputers and minicomputers. Professional programmers like C because it has a well-defined language standard that makes it easy to move programs from one machine to another without rewriting the programs. C also contains some features that give professional programmers the ability to optimize the speed and size of a program in ways that other "high level" languages do not permit. Because of its complexity, C is not used widely as a language for students, but anyone who knows the language Pascal will have little difficulty in mastering C. The "classic" book that defines the C language is "The C Programming Language" by Brian W. Kernighan and Dennis M. Ritchie (Prentice-Hall Software Series 1978). Microsoft, Lattice, Mark Williams Company, and many others market C language systems for the IBM PC and its clones.

Centrex. A form of "PBX system" (see definition below) that can interconnect the telephones within a law firm, university, or business and permit 4-digit dialing "in-house" and "dial-9" access to the outside world. But instead of installing a local "private branch exchange" switching system within the law firm, university, or business, Centrex connects all of the telephones to a telephone-company-owned central switch in the same way that telephones in homes are connected to the same switch. The central office switch (which is controlled by a programmable digital computer) is then simply programmed to implement all of the PBX features desired. Centrex lines are much more likely to be "clean" for data communication purposes than PBX lines. But sometimes the telephone company routes the lines to a distant switch, and then the Centrex lines may be too noisy for reliable use in data communications.

Character mode. See "block mode" above.

Check digit. A check digit is a digit that is added to information transmitted in an "error-free" manner from one computer to another. The check digit is computed from the remaining transmitted information. The receiving computer recomputes the check digit from the received information and then compares the computed check digit to the check digit received from the transmitter. If they match, then there is a high probability that the transmission was error-free, so the transmission is accepted, and the receiving computer signals the transmitting computer that all is well. If they do not match, then the transmission contains errors and is rejected. The receiving computer then signals for a retransmission of the information. See Xmodem.

Checksum. A checksum is simply the sum of the numbers that are used to represent the keystrokes in a message transmitted between two computers. It can be used as a "check digit." See "check digit" supra for more information on the "error free" transmission of information.

COBOL. The "high level" programming language COBOL is widely used by businesses for the production of financial computational programs, particularly on mainframe computers. Developed by the Department of Defense's CODASYL committee, it is extremely well standardized, so programs written in COBOL may be easily moved between machines without rewriting. On microcomputers, many programs that might have been written in COBOL some years ago are now developed using special data base programs and spreadsheet programs.

Compiler. Computer programmers write out instructions for their computers in "high level" English-like languages such as FORTRAN, COBOL, Pascal, C, PL/1, and BASIC. These programs are unintelligible to the computers. They must be machine-translated into the native numeric "machine language" of the target computer before they can actually take over control of the computer. The translation process is performed by a "compiler" program. So a "compiler" is a program which can translate the quasi-English that computer programmers write into the numeric machine gibberish that the computer actually "understands."

Commands. In the standardized ASCII code for information interchange between computers, the numbers 0 to 31 and 127 are assigned to "commands" while the numbers 32 to 126 are assigned to the printable characters (letters, digits, punctuation, and the space). Just as the printable characters in the ASCII code may be thought of as keystrokes on the computer's keyboard, most of the commands of interest to attorneys also correspond to command keystrokes such as <Enter> (ASCII "carriage return"), <Tab>, <Backspace>, and <Esc>. Other commands of interest to attorneys may be generated by holding down the <Ctrl> shift key on a computer or terminal and typing a letter: <Ctrl–C> (end of transmission—sometimes works as a "halt" command), <Ctrl–G> (ring the bell), <Ctrl–J> (move to next line or "line feed"), <Ctrl–L> (move to next page or "form feed"), <Ctrl–P> (data link escape—sometimes works as a "halt" command), <Ctrl–S> (stop sending), <Ctrl–Q> (start sending again), and <Ctrl–Z> (on personal computers, "end of file"). See chapter 5 for more information.

Communications program. A program that transforms your personal computer into a terminal that can communicate with remote services such as WESTLAW and LEXIS and that can also supervise the transmission of information between your computer and another computer. See "emulate," "upload," "download," "XON– XOFF," and "Xmodem" below.

Computer program. See "program" and "software," infra. See also "text editor," "spreadsheet," and "communications program."

Conferencing. A central computer may be programmed to host an electronic conference between individuals located in towns all over the world. Typically the conference continues for a number of weeks or months. The participants typically call up the conference computer several times each week from their office or home computers. The conference is organized into "agenda items," and each participant "registers" for all agenda items of interest. Over the course of the conference, all comments contributed by the participants that relate to an agenda item are recorded in order by date and time of receipt in a single long document that anyone having access to the conference may read through. The computer keeps careful track of which information each participant in the conference has read. Accordingly, each time a participant calls up the conference computer, the computer immediately displays to that participant only the new contributions to the agenda items of interest to that participant and invites the participant to add an additional comment following each such new entry. The computer thus coordinates and facilitates an ongoing dialog between the participants in the conference. Typically, the conference is "public," and separate provision is made for "private" electronic mail transmission between the conference participants that other participants cannot see. Conferencing is a powerful tool that will be widely used by the legal profession in future years. The American Bar Association just released its first study of the ethical problems of interstate conferencing involving attorney and non-attorney participants.

Control. The <Ctrl> key on virtually all computer and terminal keyboards is a "shift key" that changes the meaning of the letter keys. When <Ctrl> is depressed, letter keystrokes become "command" keystrokes. For example, when the G key is struck while depressing the <Ctrl> key, the "ring the bell" command is produced by the keyboard instead of the printable letter "G" or "g". See "Commands" supra for more information. In addition to the letter keys (all of which produce commands when struck while the <Ctrl> shift key is depressed), certain other keys may also produce commands. For example, the @ key, the square bracket keys, the "up arrow" key, the "backwards slash" key, the backspace key, and the underscore key may produce commands, although there is no standard except for the letter keys. In the ASCII code, there are 33 possible commands, and typically every keyboard can generate all 33 in one way or another.

Cursor. A bright, flashing marker on the screen. Sometimes it appears as an "underscore," sometimes as a bright rectangle, and sometimes it takes on other forms. The cursor marks the point on the screen that will be affected by your next keystroke. Normally, you can move the cursor about by striking the arrow keys. When using a word processor, the cursor key indicates where the next keystroke will be inserted or which character on the screen will be "over-struck" by the next keystroke.

Custom terminal. A computer terminal provided by the vendor of a remote service that is not a "standard" terminal and that may not be usable for other purposes. The WESTLAW WALT custom terminal and the latest LEXIS UBIQ II custom terminal may be used to access other services. The main advantage of such terminals are the labelled special function keys and the other "ergonomics" that they provide. Most vendors, including WESTLAW and LEXIS, now provide software for personal computers that provide all the functionality of their custom terminals but without the permanently-labeled function keys.

Data base. A collection of information stored on a computer-readable medium. "Data base" is a generic term that can refer to any type of data collection—textual, numeric, financial, or whatever. A data base has a "structure"—the data is not just stored randomly, it is organized in some manner to facilitate its retrieval. Many data bases include one or more indices of the data.

Disk. A "disk" is a device upon which information is stored. Disk storage is "permanent," in the sense that it is safe even when the computer has been turned off. See "floppy disk" and "hard disk." See also "file" and "extension."

Directory. Information stored on computer disks is organized into separate files. A "directory listing" is a listing of the names of all the files stored on a given disk. To produce a directory listing using DOS when the "A>" or "C>" prompt appears on your screen, type "dir<Enter>". When using a "hard disk," the disk can hold so many files that the directory listing becomes too long and unmanageable. In that case, you should create multiple directories, storing no more than 100 files in each directory. On many computers, the name of one directory, called a "subdirectory," may appear in the file name list of some other directory. Multiple directories may thus be arranged in a hierarchal manner—in an outline structure. The main directory lists some file names plus the names of a first set of "subdirectories." You enter a subdirectory, and by listing its files, you discover that it contains files plus other lower-level subdirectories that you may enter.

Document. In this book, the term "document" refers to a collection of keystrokes and commands stored together either in a file or in the computer's high-speed memory. These keystrokes and commands define the content, margins, and layout of a textual document. A "model" document is one prepared for automated assembly. When stored in a file, the name of a model document has the extension ".mdl". A "new question" document is a model document that can be assembled into a question to be displayed during an automated client interview. When stored in a file, the name of a new question document has the extension ".qn". A "draft" document is a "client-customized" version of a model document. A "client" document is one containing client data that is generated by the LawProcess program following an automated client interview. When stored in a file, the name of a client document has the extension ".cit".

DOS. Abbreviation for "disk operating system." See "Operating system."

Download. The process of transferring a document, program, or data file "down" from a central or remote computer to your computer. "Pure ASCII" documents (documents containing only printable characters and line ending commands) can be downloaded simply by having the remote computer send them to you and commanding your own computer to write the incoming text into a disk file. Programs, complex data sets, and word processing documents may not survive the transmission process. For them, you should use an "error free" transmission protocol such as the Xmodem protocol.

Dumb terminal. All terminals are at least "dumb terminals." A dumb terminal is one that behaves exactly like the venerable Teletype machines of old—text scrolls up from the bottom of the screen like a piece of paper. The cursor cannot be positioned, and the screen cannot be selectively erased. For maximum compatibility with all terminals and personal computer "terminal emulators," a central service must provide only "dumb terminal" commands—nothing fancy. Both WESTLAW and LEXIS offer such a service that can be accessed from almost any type of terminal or personal computer, but when using such a service, one loses the ability to edit and transmit back to WESTLAW or LEXIS a multiple-line search request.

EBCDIC. A code developed by IBM for representing letters, digits, punctuation, and commands by numbers within a computer. Used on IBM mini and mainframe computers and on IBM's Displaywriter dedicated word processors. The ASCII code is used on virtually all other computers, including IBM micro-computers. An EBCDIC to ASCII conversion must be performed when data is transferred from the IBM mainframe world to the rest of the world, and this complicates the process of transferring data back and forth.

Electronic mail. A method of transmitting documents, programs, and data from one office to another without the use of paper. Most electronic mail systems utilize a central computer as an intermediary between the sender and the receiver, and most systems cannot handle anything but "pure ASCII" documents (see "document" supra). To view incoming mail, one contacts the central computer and commands the incoming mail to be displayed upon one's personal computer or terminal. After reading each note, one may type in a "reply" and then optionally either delete or save the note for future reference. To send a short note, one accesses the central computer from a terminal or personal computer, types out the note, and orders the central computer to place it in the addressee's "mailbox." Some services such as MCI Mail can deliver a "real" letter (in an envelope) to destinations that are not equipped for electronic mail. See Appendix C for an explanation of how to send word processing documents, programs, and data files in an "error free" manner using ABA/net, the American Bar Association's electronic mail service.

Emulate. When communicating with remote data bases and services, frequently a special kind of computer terminal is required.

WESTLAW access requires a WALT custom terminal and LEXIS access requires a UBIQ custom terminal, for example. Both of these services may also be accessed from an IBM Model 3101 terminal. LEXIS and Prentice-Hall's PHINET tax service may be accessed from a Digital Equipment Model VT–100 terminal—a terminal sometimes called an "ANSI Standard" terminal because it implements a substantial subset of a new ANSI standard for terminal design. Personal computers may be programmed to "emulate" any of these terminals. Accordingly, a single personal computer can serve as a WESTLAW terminal at one time, as a LEXIS terminal at another time, and as a PHINET terminal at yet another time. A "terminal emulator" is a communications program for a personal computer that is able to "emulate" one or more terminals. (Watch out: many "IBM Model 3101" emulators do not implement the "block mode" capability essential for WESTLAW or LEXIS access or the "transmit message" capability essential for the LEXIS 3101 service.)

Enter. The <Enter> key on a computer or terminal is the enlarged key that occupies the position where the "carriage return" key is to be found on a standard electric typewriter—just to the right of the main keypad. On the IBM Personal Computer, it bears an arrow pointing down and to the left. On the IBM PC AT, it is labeled "Enter." On many other computers and terminals, it is labeled "Return." Regardless of how it is labeled, this key always generates a "carriage return" command. With word processors, this command usually produces a paragraph ending in the document that is being drafted. When you are typing a command, striking this key "enters" the command and causes it to be executed. When you are formulating a WESTLAW or LEXIS search request, striking this key "transmits" the search request to the central computer and causes the search to be carried out. When communicating with other remote services, striking this key sends the line just typed to the central computer and causes that computer to respond.

Esc. See "Escape" below.

Escape. A key labelled <Esc> on the keyboard of virtually all personal computers and terminals is a command key that generates an "escape" command. When running programs, striking this key typically permits you to "escape" from whatever it is that you are doing or terminate the current task and move back out to some higher "command" level. When communicating with a central computer (and assuming that some program has not "reassigned" this key to some other use), striking the <Esc> key causes an escape command to be transmitted to the central computer. Typically, you then type a special "escape sequence" immediately afterwards that is interpreted as a special command by the central computer. Escape commands embedded in documents and followed by "escape sequences" can cause a printer to produce different type fonts, superscripts, subscripts, and other operations—but your word processor may not let you type one directly into your document. To do so when using LawWord, you must type <Control-P> <Esc>.

Ethernet. One of several "local area networks" that can be used to interconnect multiple personal computers so that they may share files, programs, and printers. Ethernet "daisy-chains" the computers together using a single long, coaxial cable that extends from a first computer to each computer in the network and terminates at the last computer. Ethernet can handle 70 or 80 computers for printer and file sharing so long as the network traffic is not too heavy, but its "overload" characteristics are not as good as the "token passing" networks.

Expert system. A computer programmed in such a way that it can give "specialist advice" to an attorney who requires such advice. The LawProcess program provided with this book is a simple expert system that can ask questions and assemble legal documents for clients. Such "automated law practice systems" are not presently widely used—your generation of attorneys will be the first to use them in everyday practice. Much more sophisticated expert systems that will take advantage of ongoing research in artificial intelligence and parallel processing that will emerge over the next two decades.

Extension. Documents, programs, and data are stored on computer disks as "files" having names. File names may have two parts separated by a period—a "name" part, which may contain up to eight letters or digits, and an optional "extension" part, which may contain up to three letters or digits. For example, a model will document prepared for automated assembly by the LawProcess program could be stored as a file having the name "will.mdl" where "will" is the name and ".mdl" is the extension that identifies this as a "model" designed for automated assembly. The final will prepared for a specific client would be assigned the file name "will" with no extension. Programs must be stored as files having one of three extensions: small programs have the extension ".com", large programs the extension ".exe", and "batch file" programs (written by you using your word processor) the extension ".bat".

Field. See "record" below.

File. By analogy to a file cabinet, the information stored on computer disks is said to be stored within individual "files" on the surface of the diskette. A "file" may contain any kind of information. Sets of related files may be stored together in "directories" or "subdirectories" on the disk, where the directories and subdirectories are analogous to file drawers. A file may be a program, a document, or a data set containing numbers. All files have names formed from up to eight letters and numbers. Some file names also have "extensions" (see "Extension" above).

File name. See "file" above.

Floppy disk. A flexible, circular piece of plastic coated with a magnetic oxide so that information may be recorded on its surface in circular tracks. A typical floppy disk for the IBM Personal Computer can hold roughly 360,000 bytes of data, or about 180 pages of double-spaced text. Disks for the newer PC–AT hold considerably more, and diskette capacities will continue to increase. Floppy disks can only be read slowly, so they presently limit the performance of your computer. Preferably, you should obtain a "hard disk" that operates much faster and use floppy disks for backing up the hard disk and for data transfer. Floppy disks are permanently mounted in cardboard, plastic or metal cases.

Format. Before a "floppy disk" or "hard disk" can be used, magnetic marks must be written upon its surface to mark the regions where data can be written. These marks define the fixed-sized "sectors" within which information can be written. The process of writing these timing marks upon the surface of a disk, testing the disk to see if information can be written onto its surface and read accurately from its surface, and marking as "bad sectors" all of those areas that are unusable is called "formating" the disk. The DOS command "format b:<Enter>" is usually used to format floppy disks (the DOS diskette must be in disk drive A: if this command is to work). WARNING: Formating destroys any information written on the disk. Hard disks are formatted by the factory. The DOS "format c:<Enter>" command does not actually reformat a hard disk, but it does erase the disk and check it for bad sectors. Adding a "/s" to the DOS format command ("format b:/s<Enter>") causes the DOS operating system to be copied onto the disk and makes it possible for you to start the computer using the newly-formated diskette.

Formula. In a "spreadsheet," every cell may contain a text string (which serves as a label for the cell), a number, or a formula. The formula tells how the numeric value to be displayed in a cell is to be computed from the numeric values stored in other cells. See the spreadsheet section of the programming chapter, § 4–4, and Appendix E for more information on formulas.

FORTRAN. A high level programming language widely used by engineers and scientists to perform "number crunching" types of tasks. FORTRAN is an acronym for "FORmula TRANslator." Developed in the late 1950s and early 1960s, it is the oldest of the widely-used programming languages. Considered an "obsolete" language by many computer scientists, it was extensively revised in the 1970s to conform more closely to the syntax of Pascal and other languages developed in the 1960s and 1970s. The syntax of FORTRAN and BASIC are quite similar, so learning BASIC is a good way to prepare oneself to learn FORTRAN.

Function. A function is a portion of a computer program that stands by itself and that can be called upon to compute a single value. Typically, the function is supplied one or more numbers or other values, and it returns a single value computed from the values supplied. A typical function might be one that computes the square root of any number. Rather than insert programming instructions on how to compute a square root at ten different points, one simply writes a single "square root" function and calls upon that function to compute a square root from ten different locations in the main program. A function is a "subroutine," but a "subroutine" is not necessarily a function, since it may also be a "procedure." A function is also a "computer program," although typically it cannot run by itself but must be embedded into some larger computer program.

Gate. In the mind of a circuit design engineer, a "signal" flowing through a computer is analogous to water flowing through a channel. A water channel could be equipped with a gate that blocks or permits its flow under the control of water flowing in a side channel. In a completely analogous manner, a simple "computer signal" gate can be constructed from a single transistor. Accordingly, the transistor switches that form the "atoms" of all computers are called "logic gates." See Chapter 1 for an explanation of how such gates may be used to construct a digital computer.

Gigabyte. "Giga-" means "1000 million." Accordingly, a "gigabyte" memory contains 1000 million bytes of information, or 1000 million keystrokes, or 500,000 double-spaced pages of text. Optical disks have been introduced this year that can hold this information on a single diskette that can be mass-produced. Such disks as this one will enable an entire law library to be stored in a single bookshelf.

Handshake. In ancient days, so the story goes, two enemies would go through an elaborate "handshake" ritual involving laying down their weapons and then gripping hands in such a manner that neither could stab the other in the back. Computer "handshakes" are similar rituals that two computers, or a computer and a printer, or a computer and a modem, or a computer and a packet switching network, go through as they pass information back and forth. When communicating with a printer, for example, the computer presents a keystroke (one "byte" of information) on eight data wires leading to the printer and applies a brief signal pulse to a "come and get it" signal wire called the "strobe" wire. The printer responds by sending the computer an "I'm busy" signal on a "busy" wire. When the printer has either printed the character or saved it internally for later printing, it sends an "acknowledge" signal pulse back to the computer over yet another wire and terminates the "busy" signal. The computer is thus informed that it may now send another character to the printer. If the printer's internal storage is full, the printer simply keeps its "busy" signal high until there is room in storage for another character. Additional wires carry the signals "select," "auto feed," and "initialize printer" from the computer to the printer and "select input," "error," and "out of paper" signals back from the printer to the computer. Add eight wires that simply connect the chassis of the computer and printer together and shield some of the other wires from each other, and you have 25 wires! An amazingly complicated "handshake" just to run the printer. Clearly, standards are essential when equipment from different vendors is interconnected in this manner. The printer handshake is called the "Centronics convention" after the company whose printer port wiring has been adopted as the "de facto" industry-wide standard.

Hard disk. "Floppy disks" hold only a limited amount of information—about 360,000 bytes in the case of those currently supplied with the IBM Personal Computer, for example. Floppy disks also cannot be spun very rapidly, so they greatly slow down your computer whenever it attempts to transfer information to or from the disk. A "hard disk" is a rigid disk constructed from aluminum that is coated with a metallic oxide. Because of its rigidity, it can rotate many times faster than can a floppy disk, so it can transfer information to and from the computer much more rapidly. It also can store many times more information, and its information storage capacity can be further increased by stacking multiple platters within a single drive unit. "Twenty megabyte" hard disks that can store the same amount of information as 55 floppy disks now sell for under $500. Hard disks having capacities up to 200 megabytes are available for personal computers. WARNING: Most hard disks must be "parked" before they are moved about. Failure to park your hard disk can result in the loss of data.

Hardware. That part of any computer that is constructed from transistors and wires and logic gates. The RAM and ROM memories of a computer are part of "hardware," but the information and programs that they contain is part of "software."

Hayes Compatible. There are many "de facto" standards in the computer industry. These arise when ten different vendors bring out ten different products that require the same program to behave in ten different ways. Such was the case with "auto-dial" modems. These devices connect a microcomputer to the telephone line, dial the telephone automatically under computer control, and then transmit and receive data to and from such remote destinations as WESTLAW and LEXIS. Every modem manufacturer came up with its own way of informing the modem of how rapidly the information was to be transmitted, of whether to use "touch tone" or "pulse" dialing, and of what number to dial. Faced with this "tower of babel," the companies developing and marketing telecommunications programs chose to implement only the protocol of the Hayes Microcomputer Products Company modems. All the other modem manufacturers, including IBM, have since been forced to adopt the Hayes' protocol. The Hayes protocol is sometimes called the "AT" protocol, since all commands sent to the modem by the computer must begin with the capitalized letters "AT." (See Appendix A–3(h).)

Hexadecimal. Imagine for a moment that each of us has sixteen fingers and toes, instead of ten. Then our system of counting would work like this: 1, 2, 3, 4, 5, 6, 7, 8, 9, A, B, C, D, E, F, 10, 11, 12, 13, 14, 15, 16, 17, 18, 19, 1A, 1B, 1C, 1D, 1E, 1F, 20. Instead of a "decimal" system of counting, we would then have a "hexadecimal" system of counting. Hexadecimal numbers are frequently used by computer scientists to represent computer data. For an example, insert your second DOS diskette into your computer and type "debug filename<Enter>" where "filename" is the name of a document prepared using your word processor. Then type "d<Enter>" repeatedly, and you will see the hexadecimal numbers that are assigned to all the printable characters and non-printable commands that the document contains. Your DOS manual will teach you how you may use the "debug" program to alter a document using the "e<Enter>" command.

IBM 3101 Terminal. A terminal sold by IBM that may be used to access both WESTLAW and LEXIS. Programs emulating this terminal can access both WESTLAW and LEXIS in a uniform manner. Both WESTLAW and LEXIS require the "block mode" feature of this terminal, a feature that many programs claiming to "emulate" this terminal do not implement. LEXIS, in addition, requires the "transmit message" feature of this terminal to be usable—a feature that IBM's own "3101 Terminal Emulator Program" (Version 1.00) did not implement.

Interpreter. Computer programs written out in a "high level," English-like language normally must be translated by programs called "compilers" into the native numeric language of a given computer before they may control the operation of a computer. Once "compiled," such programs run very fast. But the compilation process is difficult and time-consuming. If there is no need to have a program run at maximum speed, and if one does not wish to take the time to "compile" the program, then one can use an "interpreter" program to read and interpret the English-like language directly and then instruct the computer what to do without compiling the program. Microsoft's BASIC language is normally interpreted in this manner, but Microsoft also markets a compiler for its BASIC that speeds up programs written in BASIC by a factor of ten.

Kermit. A communications program developed at Columbia University that permits the "error-free" transmission of documents, programs, and data files between personal computers and also to and from mini- and mainframe computers. It is widely used on university campuses. We have used it to transfer book manuscripts, recorded on mainframe computer tapes by the publisher, onto microcomputers for revision without retyping.

LAN. Local area network. See "Ethernet" and "token ring." A local area network is normally a computer-to-computer cabling system that "daisy-chains" computers together into linear or circular networks so that they may share data storage devices and printers.

Machine language. The native language of all computers is a numeric language that is unintelligible to humans. Programmers normally write out their programs in a "high level," English-like language that is then translated (or "compiled") into the machine language of the target computer. Machine language instructions specify such steps as fetching a number, placing it in one of sixteen registers, adding that number to some other number in another register, and storing the result.

Mainframe. A very large computer that can perform a very large number of instructions per second, servicing large number of users so fast that all appear to be receiving service simultaneously. "Mainframes" and "IBM" are synonymous, since IBM dominates the market for these machines. Too large for most law firm applications, these computers are used by large corporations and governmental agencies having very heavy data processing requirements. Corporate law departments frequently have access to these behemoths. They may be used very effectively for the maintenance of litigation support databases using programs such as IBM's STAIRS. Both WESTLAW and LEXIS are based upon mainframe computers.

Megabytes. Millions of bytes. A ten megabyte "hard disk" (see definition supra) can hold about 5,000 double-spaced pages of text or its equivalent.

Microcode. Many computer programmers erroneously think that the lowest level programming language on most computers is the "machine language" that only they know how to write. But the electrical engineers who design microcomputers know that the "machine language" instructions of most modern computers are not implemented directly in "hardware." There is an even lower level of programming. Sequences of "microinstructions" are used to implement each of the "machine language" instructions. Each microinstruction defines one data transfer operation within the computer's hardware. A whole sequence of such instructions is required, for example, to implement the simple "add" machine language instruction.

Microcomputer. A computer whose central processing unit is contained on a single chip of silicon. Formerly microcomputers were less powerful than "minicomputers," but the distinctions are blurring with each passing year as the manufacturers of these chips are able to cram more and more transistors onto a single chip with each passing year. The Intel line of microcomputers, the 8080, 8086/8088, 80186/80188, 80286, and the forthcoming 80386 are probably the most successful due to the adoption of the 8088 in the IBM PC and the 80286 in the IBM PC AT. The 80386, recently released by Intel for a few hundred dollars, has minicomputer power and promises to give us another microcomputer revolution over the next two years. The Motorola line, including the 6800, 6809, 68000, 68010, and 68020 is more advanced than the Intel line but not as "upwardly" compatible. The 68000 is used in the Apple Macintosh, Atari 1040ST, and Commodore Amiga 1000. The 68020, like the Intel 80386, has minicomputer power. National Semiconductor also has a very powerful microcomputer line that has yet to appear in retail products. The venerable 6502 chip used in the Apple II, looking very weak next to the newer chips, has just been replaced with a much more powerful upgrade. In the operating system field, look for Microsoft's "Windows" product to emerge as an operating system environment that crosses the IBM PC/Macintosh boundary and enables future programs to run on both sides, and look for UNIX to emerge slowly as an operating system that merges the microcomputer/minicomputer gap.

Minicomputer. A "multi-user" computer that connects to anywhere from three to fifty terminals and that may be used by several people simultaneously. An AT&T operating system called UNIX is coming into widespread use as a standard minicomputer operating system. IBM's 4300 series minicomputers are sometimes used in larger firms with IBM's VM/CMS operating system or UM and UNIX. Digital Equipment Corporation's VAX minicomputer, either with DEC's VMS operating system or with UNIX, is coming into widespread use and is now available in a "desk top" version. A number of law schools have VAXs. Hewlett Packard and Data General also have lines of minicomputers that are seen in law firms. Look for UNIX to become the standard in future years as more and more programs are written for UNIX to gain hardware independence.

Modem. The term modem is an acronym for "MODulator and DEModulator." In the field of radio, a "modulator" is the device that shifts the transmitting frequency of an FM radio station up and down at precisely the same rate at which the phonograph needle vibrates in the groove of a record whose music is being transmitted over FM radio. A "demodulator" in the radio receiver then causes its speaker to move in and out in synchronism with the up and down shifts in the frequency of the incoming FM radio signal. When computers send information over telephone lines, they present a fluctuating voltage to a modulator that varies the frequency of an audio tone up and down to match the fluctuations of the computer signal. The tone flows over the telephone circuits to a demodulator at the other end that generates a voltage for the receiving computer that fluctuates up and down in synchronism with the pitch fluctuations of the incoming tone. Since typically the computers at both ends must both send and receive information, each computer must be connected to the telephone line by both a modulator and a demodulator. The combination is called a "modem." The tones generated by the modems at opposite ends of the telephone linkage must be set to different frequencies so that they do not mask each other. On old fashioned modems, an "originate/answer" switch selects the tone frequency, and the modems at opposite ends of the communication channel must have their switches set in opposite positions. Newer modems normally do this switching automatically, but if you have trouble communicating, this is something that you may have to check out.

Modula–2. See "Pascal" below.

Monitor. A monitor is simply a television display device. A "television set" is a monitor that is permanently connected to a "tuner" or television radio signal receiver. Modern component televisions separate these two components and permit one to switch a high-quality monitor to a tuner, a VCR, or to a personal computer. A monitor must be supplied with one or more "video signals." Television tuners generate a standard NTSC composite video signal, which includes both black and white and color components, and which flows over a single wire to the monitor. Apple II computers also generate this same NTSC composite video signal, and the "color graphics" adapter card supplied with IBM personal computers can also generate this signal. Unfortunately, the resolution of standard television signals is quite low, and the way in which the color components are integrated into this signal makes it impossible for such a signal to convey both a sharp 80 column computer text display and also color at the same time. When color is present, 80-column text becomes unreadable. So any monitor that connects to a computer by means of a single wire connector can only display 40 columns of text in color or 80 columns of text in black and white. To display 80 columns of text in color, the computer must generate three video signals—a red signal, a blue signal, and a green signal—or one for each of the electron guns in the monitor. These must be fed over separate wires to the monitor. Additional wires convey timing signals and a brightness signal. The three signals are called an "RGB" signal, and such a signal is generated by IBM's "color graphics adapter" card. In all other respects, the signals are standard NTSC signals that may be fed into a standard television monitor having an RGB signal input. But many computer monitors are not in accord with the NTSC standard—they utilize different horizontal and vertical scanning frequencies. IBM's "monochrome" adapter card and monitor and the compatible Hercules graphics card provide far more vertical detail than does IBM's "color graphics" card, and the monitors used by these two types of cards cannot be interchanged without possible serious damage. IBM's new "enhanced graphics adapter" card employs yet another set of scanning frequencies, as does Atari's new ST line of computers. Another potential problem: Some new monitors require continuously variable "analog RGB" input signals instead of the more traditional "TTL RGB" signals that are always either high or low and never at intermediate levels. So be very careful when you match up a monitor to a computer to make sure they do not give each other indigestion.

MS–DOS. Microsoft's disk operating system for "clones" of the IBM personal computer. See "Operating system."

Network. A large number of computers connected together. They may all be connected to a central "minicomputer" or "mainframe" computer, or they may be interconnected by a "local area network," or they may be interconnected through your "PBX System." Always consider the "no network" alternative, and don't network any more than you have to, since it limits your flexibility.

Operand. A "function" is a computer program that accepts one or more values and computes something from them. The values accepted are the "operands" of the function. When using WESTLAW and LEXIS, you type out search requests that contain "operators" such as AND and OR along with words and phrases. The words and phrases are the "operands" for the "operators" AND and OR. Within the WESTLAW and LEXIS computers programs called "functions" actually exist to which the words are passed and which return the results of the ANDing and ORing operations.

Operating system. A layer of computer programs that effectively separates the computer programs from the "hardware" elements of the computer and provides a standardized way in which the programs can access the keyboard, monitor, disk drives, and the modem without the programmers needing to understand how the hardware works. Another portion of the operating system, called the "shell," communicates with the "user" and carries out the user's instructions concerning which program is to be run. An operating system also typically includes numerous utilities for performing such tasks as "formating" disks, copying disks, and displaying the directories of what is stored on the disks. See "UNIX" below for more on operating systems.

Operator. See "operand" above.

Optical disk. A disk drive that is written on and read by means of a very tiny laser beam, using the same technology that is used in compact audio disks. Optical disks can be mass-produced very inexpensively, and they can hold up to a gigabyte of information. These optical disks will make it possible to provide "in house" WESTLAW and LEXIS types of services, eliminating the need for telephone linkages. "In house" brief banks containing many years worth of your firm's work product in a form that may be readily searched for words and phrases will also be facilitated by this new technology.

Packet switching. An economical way of connecting many scattered individuals to centralized computers such as those of WESTLAW and LEXIS. The packet switching network provides data lines linking key cities into a national network. Everyone using the network shares these same data lines. Transmissions are broken up into "packets" of information which contain the address of their destination. These packets are routed about the network until they reach the destination computer. Telenet, Tymnet, and Datapac are the principal packet switching networks at the present time. When using such a network, do not expect a response from the central computer until you strike the

<Enter> key or <Ctrl–C> or <Ctrl–P>, since only those characters are likely to cause a packet to be closed up and sent to your central computer.

Parallel port. A multi-wire socket on the back of many computers designed to be connected to a printer. It is called a "parallel port" because the eight data bytes that comprise each letter, number, punctuation symbol or command are each transmitted to the printer over a separate wire. The eight data bytes are thus all sent to the printer in parallel, as opposed to being sent "serially," one-at-a-time, over a single wire as is customary when sending data to a "modem" for telephone transmission. See "handshake" above for a description of how the parallel port functions.

Pascal. A "high level" programming language developed in Switzerland at the ETH (Federal Institute of Technology) by Niklaus Wirth, one of the pioneers of modern programming techniques. Developed originally to be used as a teaching language, Pascal is now the standard language used to train beginning computer science students in programming. Wirth's newer language, Modula–2, is beginning to displace Pascal. The best Pascal compiler for new users is Turbo Pascal sold by Borland, International. Microsoft provides a Pascal that can be used to design larger systems but that is harder to use. For Modula–2, contact Logitech, Incorporated in Redwood City, California.

Path. Large capacity "hard disks" may be broken up into numerous "subdirectories" each containing a number of "files." When you are in one subdirectory and wish to access a file in some other subdirectory, you must append a "path" as a prefix to the file's name to assist the computer in locating the file. For example, if a file is in a subdirectory "tax" which subdirectory is itself in another subdirectory "spdshts" on drive "c:", then when referring to a file named "1040form" while you are working in some other subdirectory, you must type the name of the file as: "c:\spdshts\tax\1040form" rather than as "1040form." The expression "c:\spdshts\tax" is called the "path" that leads to the file. The DOS "path" command instructs the DOS operating system where your programs are stored.

PBX system. A "private branch exchange" telephone system is a telephone system designed to be used within a law firm, school, or business to provide four-digit access to individuals within the firm, school, or business and "dial–9" access to outsiders. PBX systems frequently are not designed to support computer telephone access to remote computers. Many law firms have found that they must install separate telephone lines that do not pass through their PBX system to access WESTLAW and LEXIS, for example.

PC–DOS. IBM's disk operating system for the IBM personal computer. See "Operating systems."

PL/1. A programming language widely used on IBM mainframe computers. It attempts to combine the features of Cobol, Fortran, and Algol into a single, rather complex language.

Port. See "Parallel port" (printer port) or "Serial port" (modem port).

Printable characters. All the characters that you can type on a computer's keyboard and that appear upon its screen as visible characters, including letters, numbers, and punctuation symbols. Also, graphical characters that you may be able to generate by holding down the <Alt> key on your IBM PC or compatible keyboard and typing a number below 32 or above 126 on the numeric keypad before releasing the <Alt> key.

Procedure. A procedure is a self-contained portion of a program which any other portion of a program may call upon to perform some computation or other action. Some procedures simply take the same action every time they are called upon, such as a procedure that makes a computer go "beep" whenever it is called. Other procedures are passed values which alter the way they function, as when a "set color of the screen" procedure is called upon to color the screen red. Still other procedures are passed values and return other values. For example, an encryption procedure might be passed a document and might return an encrypted version of the document. Procedures are "subroutines." Procedures differ from functions in their ability to return multiple values and in sometimes returning no values, as when the procedure simply makes the computer go "beep." When a procedure returns a single computed value, it differs from a function only in its form (the way it is written out by a programmer). For more information, see any good textbook on Pascal.

Program. A set of instructions that determine precisely what actions a computer is to take and in what order. See "software," infra.

RAM. The high speed memory of a computer. Most modern microcomputers contain between 250,000 and 1 million "bytes" of RAM memory. The computer's microprocessor can retrieve information from RAM and store information in RAM extremely rapidly—much more rapidly than it can access even the fastest of "hard disks." Each location in RAM can store one "byte," or eight "bits" or information. Each location has a unique numeric address. The name RAM, which is derived from "random access memory," indicates that the microprocessor may address and access any location in RAM memory at any time. This name distinguishes RAM from earlier forms of memory which did not give random access to the stored data, but it does not distinguish RAM from ROM—"read only memory"—which also can be accessed in a random manner. Think of RAM memory as "writable and readable" memory so that you can distinguish it from ROM memory which is "read only memory." Also note that RAM forgets its contents as soon as electric power is removed. If your computer has extra RAM memory not otherwise used by your programs, you should put it to good use. Set up a "RAM disk drive"—a "pretend" additional disk drive that behaves as if it were another disk but that simply stores data in your extra RAM memory. Since this "disk" has no mechanical parts, it is super fast—far faster than even a "hard disk." You may also set up a "print spooler" in your extra RAM—a storage reservoir between your programs and your slow printer into which your programs can write data rapidly and out of which your printer may draw the data slowly without your programs having to halt and wait for the printer.

Record. A file full of data is broken into records, and each record is further broken into fields. In a litigation support data base, for example, each record might relate to one piece of evidence—a letter, for example; and the fields within the record would contain the date, the name of the addressor, the name of the addressee, codes indicating the issue to which the letter relates, and a brief abstract of its contents.

Return. Another name for the <Enter> key. See "enter" above.

ROM. ROM memory can be read, but it cannot be altered. Programs stored in ROM are always present and do not need to be loaded into the computer from disk storage when the computer is first turned on. Examples of ROM are the cartridge programs that come with children's computers. Portable, battery-powered computers frequently come with all of their programs stored in ROM memory chips. See "RAM" supra for an explanation of the difference between RAM and ROM memory.

RS–232c. An internationally standardized connector for connecting "terminals" to "modems." The precise shape of this 25-pin connector, and the precise meaning of each signal wire, is standardized. This connector is also sometimes used to connect a computer to a printer having a "serial" data input rather than the more common "parallel" data input. This connector is designed for "serial" communication, where data is fed over a single wire to the modem or printer. Generally, only nine of the 25 pins are used (pins 1 through 8 and 20), so you need not purchase 25-wire cables. But do not use cables with less than nine leads. If you wish to send data from one computer to another directly, interconnect their RS–232c connectors with a special cable called a "null modem" which you may purchase from your computer store. Unfortunately, the usage of the various "handshake" wires is not fully standardized, and you may have to study the manuals that accompany the two pieces of equipment you wish to interconnect and then do some rewiring of the connectors before you can get them to communicate properly. You may need some expert help. Experts usually use "breakout boxes" that help analyze and try various wiring combinations.

Serial port. A port on a computer, terminal, or modem out of which and/or into which the information flows over a single wire. Almost always the port is an "RS–232c" industry standard port, although sometimes a connector is used that has less than 25 pins. See chapter 5 and Appendix § A–3 for a detailed explanation of how information is transmitted serially.

Shell. See "operating system" above.

Software. Computer programs. Those portions of a computer's structure that are stored on disks or in ROMs (read only memories) constitute the "software" that gives a computer its personality and determines whether the computer is a word processor, a timekeeping, accounting, and billing system, a spreadsheet, a WESTLAW or LEXIS terminal, or an electronic mail system. Different software can transform the same computer "hardware" into an entirely different machine at different times.

Spreadsheet. A computer program that creates a financial statement on the screen and permits you to change some numbers in the statement and have the remaining numbers automatically recomputed. Each cell in the financial statement contains either a number that you may alter, a label or comment, or an expression that instructs the computer of how the value displayed in that particular cell is to be computed from the values in other cells. See § 4–4 and Appendix E.

Subdirectory. See "directory" above.

Subroutine. A portion of a computer program that is self-contained and that may be called upon by other portions to perform some specific task. See "function" and "procedure" supra.

Synchronous. See "asynchronous" above.

Systems programmer. A programmer who is intimately familiar with the hardware details of a computer and who knows how to write "machine language" programs. Systems programmers write the "operating system" and "compiler" programs for a computer. They are the gurus of the programming profession.

Telenet. A commercial "packet switching" network that can connect you to computers all over the United States. Telenet can be used to access WESTLAW, LEXIS, DIALOG, and ABA/net, the American Bar Association's electronic mail service and many other services as well.

Teletype. The communications protocol that was used by the old Teletype machines which used to be seen in every newspaper wire room. Since virtually all computers, terminals, and printers are in complete accord with this protocol, it represents a "lowest common denominator"—a communication protocol that always works even when all else fails. If your word processor has trouble communicating with your printer, simply set up your word processor to communicate with a Teletype or TTY device. You will lose italics and superscripts, but the text will flow smoothly to your printer. Likewise, when attempting to reach WESTLAW or LEXIS from an incompatible piece of equipment, use the WESTLAW or LEXIS "dumb terminal" or Teletype or TTY service. You will not be able to edit and submit multi-line search requests, but you will get your work done.

Terminal. A terminal is a microcomputer that contains only one program—a program that permits it to communicate with a remote computer. This program is stored permanently in read only memory, so it is always present. The only difference between a terminal and a personal computer is the computer's disk drives and increased amounts of RAM memory that can be used to store interchangeable programs. Ask yourself: when a computer actually costs no more than a terminal, why buy a terminal that can be used for only one function when you can buy a personal computer and then program it to emulate any terminal or function in any one of a hundred other useful ways?

Terminal emulator. See "emulate" above.

Text editor. A text editor is a computer program that converts your personal computer into a "word processor"—a special purpose machine that assists you in creating, viewing, revising, and printing documents such as letters, briefs, contracts, pleadings, and the like. The LawWord program provided with this book is a text editor. See chapter 2 for more information. Sometimes "text editor" is used to describe word-processor software with limited or no printer control facilities. LawWord is described in Appendix D.

Token ring. A form of "local area network" that can be used to interconnect a large number of personal computers together so they may share storage and printing resources and also share the same cables when accessing shared minicomputers or mainframe computers. A "token ring" network, as the name implies, is a loop of cable that closes to form a circle. Attachments to this loop have cables that extend outward to individual personal computers, data storage devices, printers, and mini- and mainframe computers. The token ring, which is an architecture strongly advocated by IBM as being superior to "Ethernet," has better "overload" characteristics than does an Ethernet network. When the network traffic is heavy, a token ring network insures that each device attached to the network gets a chance to communicate over the network no matter how heavy the traffic may become. Under overload conditions, the simpler Ethernet network can block up and pass very little information. IBM's present token ring network, newly introduced, transfers data at the rate of 4,000,000 "bits" of information each second—half the rate at which most Ethernet networks function. Apparently, this slower network speed was adopted so that ordinary telephone wire could be used for some of the network connections, rather than the coaxial cable that Ethernet requires. As of this writing, the decision is still out as to which networking philosophy is the best.

Transistor. A device developed at Bell Telephone Laboratories, Incorporated to replace the vacuum tube. Initially each transistor was mounted in its own tiny case, but then researchers at Texas Instruments, Westinghouse, and Fairchild figured out how to produce numerous transistors on the surface of a wafer of pure silicon by a series of photographic masking and impurity diffusing steps. Transistors may be thought of as tiny electrical switches in which the flow of a relatively large current through the transistor can be controlled by the presence or absence of a relatively small current flow into a control lead called a "gate" or "base." A transistor can enable a weak electrical current to turn on and off the flow of an electrical current 100 to 200 times stronger. High speed transistors used in building computers must be capable of turning on and off more than 10,000,000 times each second. See Chapter 1 for an explanation of how a computer can be constructed from transistors.

TTY. See "Teletype" above.

Tymnet. A "packet switching" network. See "packet switching" and "Telenet" supra. Tymnet may be used to access WESTLAW, ABA/net, and DIALOG.

UNIX. An "operating system" developed by Bell Telephone Laboratories, Incorporated. See "operating system" supra. UNIX was developed originally to be a "portable" program development environment that could be ported to many different computers and that would enable Bell engineers designing telephone switching systems to move from IBM equipment to Digital equipment to Hewlett Packard equipment without having to be retrained. UNIX is written almost entirely in the C language, so the first step to installing UNIX on a new computer is writing a "C" language "compiler" for the new computer. Once that step has been completed, the bulk of the UNIX system can be brought up on the new computer quite easily. During the AT&T telephone monopoly years when AT&T was prohibited from entering the computer business by an antitrust decision, AT&T used UNIX "in house" and practically gave it away to universities. Accordingly, many university sites use UNIX, and most computer science graduates are trained to use UNIX. Now that AT&T is free to compete in the computer business, it is promoting "UNIX System V" as the industry standard operating system for use on multi-user microcomputers and minicomputers. Even IBM has made UNIX available on the PC–AT and the brand new RT–PC, on which UNIX is the standard operating system. The PC–DOS and MS–DOS operating systems used on the IBM PC and its many clones is heavily modelled after UNIX, and Microsoft's version of UNIX (called "XENIX") is coming into widespread use on small computers. Look for Microsoft to try and merge XENIX and MS–DOS into a single operating system in the future, if they can. Already, some programs compiled using Microsoft's latest compilers can be ported directly between an MS–DOS system and a UNIX system without even the need for recompiling.

Upload. The process of sending a "program," "document," or data set from your computer to some other computer or to a central computer. "Uploading" is simple: you simply command your communications program or "terminal emulator" program to send a "file" to the remote destination. If both computers understand and utilize the "XON–XOFF" protocol, then the file should flow across without difficulty. If you cannot use "XON–XOFF" to control the speed at which the information is sent, then you must be careful not to send too rapidly—instruct your program to pause for a second or two at the end of each line, or to wait for the "line prompt" character to be received from the destination before sending the next line, or to wait for each character to be echoed before sending the next. You should have no difficulty sending files that contain only printable characters and line and paragraph breaks. But sending word processing documents, programs, and some data sets can be tricky. Use the Xmodem or Kermit or Microcom error-free transmission protocols for such documents to insure that they are not damaged in transit.

VT–100 Terminal. A "terminal" manufactured by the Digital Equipment Corporation that has come into widespread use as a "de facto" industry standard terminal for "character mode," "asynchronous" communication to minicomputers. The VT–100 was the first commercial terminal to implement the new "ANSI" standard codes for controlling terminals and printers. The new ANSI standard has also been supported more recently by AT&T and by IBM. VT–100 emulation programs are available for most microcomputers, although they are rarely complete emulations of this sophisticated terminal. Access to Prentice Hall's PHINET service must be carried out using a VT–100 terminal or emulator. LEXIS may also be accessed using a VT–100, and while the LEXIS VT–100 service is a "character mode" service, it is as high in quality as the "block mode" LEXIS services (such as that provided for the IBM Model 3101 terminal).

Window. Until recently, it was customary for the computer program that is running on a microcomputer to take over the entire screen from corner to corner. "Windowing" is the concept of opening up a rectangular "window" on the screen within which a program's information can be viewed. By using a "window manager" such as that in Apple's Macintosh and those provided for the IBM PC such as IBM's TopView, Microsoft's Windows, and Quarterdeck Office System's DESQview, one can have several programs up and running simultaneously, each assigned to its own window on the screen. The windows may overlap (TopView and DESQview) or they may fit together like tiles (Windows). Extra memory may be required to permit several large programs to run in windows. Additionally, many programs are not "well-behaved" enough to run within a window and need to take over the entire screen when they are operating. Some programs, such as Ashton Tate's Framework, Microsoft's Word, and the LawWord word processor, permit you to open up two or more windows so that you may view parts of several documents simultaneously or view two parts of the same document simultaneously.

Workstation. The super-powerful personal computer that will sit beside your desk five years from now, giving you instant access to WESTLAW or LEXIS, to the firm's brief bank, to your "timekeeping, accounting, and billing" computer, to other attorneys through electronic mail, to your own personal note card data bases, and to the briefs and other documents that you are drafting with the help of your assistants and secretaries.

Xmodem. A widely-used, error-free technique for transmitting "documents," "programs," and data sets over telephone lines. Developed by Ward Christenson and placed in the public domain, it has become the "de facto" industry standard way to transmit documents to and from personal computers. ABA/net, the American Bar Association's electronic mail service, supports the Xmodem protocol, and you may use it to transmit briefs, contracts, and other documents across the country. WARNING: Xmodem appends NULL characters to the end of a word processing document, and these may have to be edited out by the recipient. The document is otherwise unharmed, so this should cause you no great concern.

XON–XOFF. These two ASCII commands are used to start and stop the flow of information between two computers. For example, to halt the scrolling of incoming information on your screen, type "<Ctrl–S>" to generate an XOFF command (the ANSI standard calls this "DC3" or "device code three"). To restart the scrolling, type "<Ctrl–Q>" to generate an XON command (the ANSI standard calls this "DC1" or "device code one"). When you send or receive information, if both the sending and receiving computer understand and use the XON–XOFF protocol, then the receiver can use the XOFF command to halt the sender whenever the receiver's storage is about to overflow and can use the XON command to restart the sender when there is room for more incoming information.

Ymodem. An improved version of Xmodem. See Xmodem above.

*

Index

References are to pages

†